French National Cinema

This examination of France's national cinema takes its primary artefact, the feature film, and discusses both popular cinema and the 'avant-garde' cinema that contests it, and the ways in which each cross-fertilises the other.

Susan Hayward argues that writing on French national cinema has tended to focus on either 'great' film-makers (following the auteurist approach) or on specific movements, addressing moments of exception rather than the global picture of cinematic history. Her work offers a thorough and much-needed historical textualisation of such moments and relocates them in their wider political and cultural context, and discusses the social and political concerns reflected by the different movements.

Filling in the gaps between the auteurs and the movements, Hayward begins with an 'ecohistory' of the French film industry, charting its beginnings in the 1890s and the rise to power of the three major studios: Pathé, Gaumont and Eclair. She traces key movements in French cinema and the directors associated with them, including the avant-garde: Germaine Dulac, Marie and Jean Epstein; Poetic-Realist: Jean Renoir and Marcel Carné; New Wave: Jean-Luc Godard and François Truffaut, and today's postmodern cinema of Jean-Jacques Beineix, Luc Besson and Colinne Serreau.

French National Cinema breaks new ground in the writing on French cinema, and its fresh approach will also further our understanding of how France's cinema interfaces with France's concept of itself as a nation.

Susan Hayward is Professor of French at the University of Exeter. She is co-editor with Ginette Vincendeau of *French Film: Texts and Contexts* (Routledge 1990) and the author of numerous related articles.

National Cinemas series

General Editor: Susan Hayward

Reflecting growing interest in cinema as a national cultural institution, the new Routledge *National Cinemas* series brings together the most recent developments in cultural studies and film history. Its purpose is to deepen our understanding of film directors and movements by placing them within the context of national cinematic production and global culture and exploring the traditions and cultural values expressed within each. Each book provides students with a thorough and accessible introduction to a different national cinema.

Australian National Cinema
Tom O'Regan

Italian National Cinema 1896–1996
Pierre Sorlin

British National Cinema
Sarah Street

Nordic National Cinema
Tytti Soila, Astrid Soderbergh Widding and Gunnar Iverson

French National Cinema

Susan Hayward

First published 1993
by Routledge
11 New Fetter Lane, London EC4P 4EE

Simultaneously published in the USA and Canada
by Routledge
29 West 35th Street, New York, NY 10001

Routledge is an imprint of the Taylor & Francis Group

Reprinted 1996, 1999

Typeset in Times by Florencetype Ltd, Stoodleigh, Devon
Printed in Great Britain by Butler & Tanner, Frome and London

British Library Cataloguing in Publication Data
Hayward, Susan
  French National Cinema – (National Cinemas Series)
  I. Title II. Series
  791.430944

Library of Congress Cataloguing in Publication Data
Hayward, Susan
  French National Cinema / Susan Hayward.
    p. cm. – (National cinemas)
  Includes bibliographical references and index.
  1. Motion pictures – France – History. I. Title. II. Series.
PN1993.5.F7H39 1993
791.43′0944–dc20   92–39603

ISBN 0–415–05728–0 (hbk)
ISBN 0–415–05729–9 (pbk)

For my dearest parents,
Kathleen Elizabeth Hayward and
William Andrew Hayward

Contents

Plates

Preface

Writing about the 'national' of a cinema is undoubtedly either a *brave* or a foolish undertaking because of the dangerous pitfalls into which an author can tumble. It is often difficult to distinguish, for example, when one is addressing society or political culture but not necessarily (or even to the exclusion of) 'nation-ness'. In this study, the two former elements are implicitly inscribed into the discussions of the 'national' of France's cinema, but these issues are kept in check or at least in line with the central address of this book. In the chapters that follow, it is questions of nation-ness that are addressed primarily.

Readers will not be surprised to find that describing a nation presents no few problems in itself and the Introduction will endeavour to set out some useful parameters. With this in mind, some markers will now be posited that will serve either as guides to the narrative of this text or as mnemonic devices upon which this book and the reader can draw as the text unfolds.

Throughout history there has been a constant interaction between social organisation and culture. By definition culture is a term which refers both to material production (artefacts) and to symbolic production (the aesthetic). In both instances, culture functions as the record and reflection of social history and the social process. Concepts of nation and national identity are also bound up in this socio-cultural functioning. For example, the standardisation of the French language over the whole of France was both a national and a socio-cultural hegemonising process. The use of conscription, still in practice today, is equally a political cultural mode of asserting a sense of national identity. It is the synergy between socio-political organisation and culture that is at the basis of political culture whereby in Marxist terms, the productive base (material production) will find its reflection in the non-productive superstructure (the aesthetic). In other words, political culture – which Raymond Williams usefully delimits on a five-point map as industry, democracy, class, art and culture – is a signifying process which unceasingly reflects socio-political change. Political culture, in this respect, becomes the process whereby myths are created about a nation's various and particular institutions. Once again the notion of cultural reflexiveness is in evidence here because those same institutions must sustain and perpetuate those myths which have been created to explain them. In this respect, political culture affirms what it reflects, and is affirmed by what it reflects.

To date, Marxist theory on culture has predominantly stressed this odd unidirectional relationship between base and superstructure and it is not difficult to point to the problematics in this limited definition. Viewed in this light, culture becomes a series of discourses which have become solidified into truth (culture affirms the social and, therefore, the political and economic relations). However, certain neo-Marxists (Gramsci, Althusser and Marcuse in particular) have argued that the superstructure can react back on to its determining base and that culture can function to subvert these discourses by opposing the affirmative character of culture. By refusing the Marxist notion of transparence, culture displays its radical potential effectiveness to innovate. This negative culture can react back through the subversion of codes (including aesthetic conventions), thus creating a two-directional relationship between base and superstructure. According to this view, when subverting political cultural convention, culture brings into question the ideological nature of cultural signs and renders institutional mythologies unstable. Conversely, when it upholds the affirmative function of political culture, culture serves to reinforce and even naturalise (through its transparence on the dominant ideology) those same institutional mythologies.

In the light of the description of this synergy, I shall now focus on just one of a nation's cultural arenas/aesthetic artefacts, cinema, and explore how it functions in relation to the social and the 'national'. Concepts of nation and national identity, when they are perceived in terms of socio-political processes and the cultural/cinematic articulations of these pro-cesses, inevitably mean that cinema speaks the national and the national speaks the cinema. In other words, within the specific context addressed here, film functions as a cultural articulation of a nation (even if it subverts it, it still addresses/reflects it, albeit negatively or oppositionally). In so doing, film textualises the nation and subsequently constructs a series of relations around the concepts, first, of state and citizen, then of state, citizen and other (and so on). In this way, cinema – a 'national' cinema – is ineluctably 'reduced' to a series of enunciations that reverberate around two fundamental concepts: identity and difference.

Culture is made up of art, among other things. That art, however, is almost unexceptionally class-inflected within Western societies and is pre-dominantly middle class. Therefore, issues of identity in discourses will be primarily framed and focused within that particular notion of a 'national' identity. National identity and, thereby, unity will tend to mean middle-class consensus; the rest will be difference/otherness. Art reflects this double perception. Within every art movement and every art form there are (at least) two apparently codifiable trends. These two trends are usually codified as mainstream and avant-garde. For the greater part both are produced by the dominant class, the main difference being, of course, that the latter art form's intentionality is to refuse consensuality. As a cultural production, cinema represents no exception. However, this study will also introduce, where necessary, the concept of non-mainstream or opposi-tional cinemas, for the simple reason that this binary divide does not always function sufficiently well for the way in which it is proposed to talk about France's national cinema.

The purpose of this book is to examine France's national cinema through its major artefact, the feature film. There is insufficient space in a book of this length to include documentaries, shorts, and cartoons (and specifically children's films). It has been necessary to limit the analysis to popular and mainstream cinema on the one hand and, on the other, to cinemas that 'contest' it (avant-garde, oppositional, peripheral, etc.). This will not lead to a simplistic duopolism, however, for the very reason that cinemas tend to cross-fertilise and recuperate cinematic practices the one from the other. The purpose of this book is also to posit historical approaches and concep-tual frameworks that should facilitate a reading of France's 'national' cinema and provide a text that is more encompassing than any existing one (at least those written in English). Other studies whose intention is not to give a full study of France's national cinema, but to focus on certain epochs, or specialise their analyses around specific film-makers, are all texts that are vital in their endeavour and serve, through their excellence, to enhance the subject. There are other texts where the representation of the national cinema of France has been the intention, but which have suffered from a somewhat narrow focus and inconsistencies in terms of the approaches adopted by the writers, because they have tended to concen-trate either on 'great' film-makers (following the auteurist approach) or on specific movements. Almost invariably this representation has been the province of high art rather than popular culture. In a sense, the writing of a national cinema has predominantly addressed moments of exception and not the 'global' picture. What is lacking in these texts is a proper historical contexualisation of those moments and their location in wider political cultural considerations. There is a need, therefore, to posit a different historical approach and a different conceptual framework in the writing of France's national cinema. This approach, a synchronic and diachronic filling of the gaps between the auteurs and movements, is the one proposed here and one, it is hoped, that will further our understanding of the nation's cinema.

In the present analysis, many films and film-makers get passed over in silence, because the purpose of this book is not to give an encyclopaedic summary of 'all that is there'. Rather, its intention is to endeavour to see what the different cinemas of this nation have been saying about themselves and their nation over the last hundred years – how they differed, how they reiterated themselves, and how, too, the nation impacted upon their discourses. The intention, therefore, is to give you, the reader, an all-round sense of France's cinema and cinematic industry since their beginnings. If this is achieved, then it will have been worth the effort that has gone into the book, and far more importantly I trust, worth the read!

Acknowledgements

I would like to extend my thanks to friends for their advice and support: to Michèle Lagny for her help in reading some of the chapters, to Ginette Vincendeau for locating and providing film materials, to Mike Townson and Fee Wellhofer for saving me from the consequences of the irretrievability of lost text on the word processor, and to Anne Witz for her incisive editing comments. My thanks go to my editor Rebecca Barden for her enthusiasm for the project. I would like to thank the librarians at the BFI for their attentiveness to my archival needs, in particular Lira Fernandes for helping me to locate some fairly unfindable figures. My thanks also go to my Head of Department, Jennifer Birkett, for her support and making time available for writing up the manuscript. Finally and especially my thanks go to Valerie Swales for her unwavering confidence in my ability to write this book, for her advice and feedback and, last but not least, her moral support when I thought the end would never be in sight.

Introduction:
Defining the 'national' of a country's cinematographic production

A glance at the holdings of any cinema library or bookshelf of texts on a specific country's cinema will reveal a predominant tendency to address the national cinema almost exclusively as those films which have been canonised by critics and historians of film. A perusal of these texts will also reveal that the term national will have been taken for granted, taken as read. However, this term cannot be assumed as unproblematic and does require examination. How does one enunciate the 'national' of a country's cinema? When is a cinema 'national'? What does possessing a national identity imply? Equally important, what constitutes a nation's cinema? To be more specific still, what is meant by a nation? Is it defined by its geography, its history, its politics? These seemingly innocent questions raise the whole problematic of addressing the issue of a national cinema, an issue which this chapter will attempt to unravel in an endeavour to chart possible ways of writing the 'national' of national cinema.

CONCEPTS OF A NATION

It seems necessary to try to position current debates around what a nation is, before going on to discuss ways of writing the 'national'. Most political scientists are agreed on two fundamental issues. First, that of all the political doctrines, it is the one which lacks a founding father (*sic*) and, second, that it is notoriously difficult to define despite the fact that as a term it has such common currency.[1] It has almost tautological proportions: 'it's there because it's there'. As Hugh Seton-Watson says, 'no "scientific definition" of the nation can be devised; yet the phenomenon has existed and exists' (quoted in Anderson: 1990, 13). Furthermore, it appears teleological in purpose: the idea of nation promotes the notion of nationhood (that is, the notion of belonging to a community or a collectivity) and this national solidarity, in turn, plays a vital role in maintaining social order.[2] Already it is not difficult to perceive that the concepts of nation bring it very close to myth. Indeed, Benedict Anderson puts it quite aptly when, in offering his definition of nation, he says 'it is an imagined political community – and imagined as both inherently limited and sovereign' (1990, 15).

To understand why it is there (even though, if it is myth, there is no 'there'), we need to understand how it got there. Both Anderson and Fredric Jameson talk of cultural artefacts as part of this process. Anderson sees 'nation-ness, as well as nationalism [as] cultural artefacts of a particular kind' (1990, 13). Jameson talks of 'cultural artefacts as socially symbolic acts' (1986, 20). The political and social cultures produce a meaning to be put where there was a lack of one. This begs the question, what caused an earlier meaning to be emptied of its signification in the first place? The way in which Anderson and Anthony Birch address this question helps us to provide an answer. The concept of nation-ness and the emergence of nationalism as an ideology, in a global sense, emerged as a consequence of the French Enlightenment and the French Revolution (there were antecedents in the thirteenth and fourteenth centuries, but those faded away; by the nineteenth century no such fading occurred). There are three major reasons why this was so. If they are viewed as icons of change, the Enlightenment and Revolution generate the following causal chain or (to keep with the metaphor) triptych of meanings: arrogance, morosity, security. This triptych makes nation-ness inevitable and makes the creation of the concept of the nation-state constitute a form of counter-iconoclasm.

Early theories of the nation-state emerged, in part, in response to how France was perceived from outside. At the forefront of these onlookers were the German theoreticians who, at the beginning of the nineteenth century, felt strong resentment towards the French for both cultural and military reasons. Birch (1989, 17), in speaking about Herder (the coiner of the term *Nationalismus*), makes the point that the

> Germans were governed by a multitude of petty principalities and the German educated classes were profoundly conscious of the fact that France was the dominant power in Europe, not only in the sense that it was the most populous and powerful state but also in the sense that French intellectuals were the leaders of the Enlightenment and the French upper classes were the leaders of fashion. As a German, Herder resented the French assumption that they were the leaders and bearers of a civilization that had universal validity. In opposition to this he developed the view that humanity had its roots in and derived its values from a number of national cultures, each of which had its own virtues and no one of which could rightly lay claims to universality.

The crucial term here is universal validity, which ties into the first order of the meaning of the triptych – arrogance or optimism. The principle of universalism as espoused at this time by the French was based on the assumption of equality (but of course equality in their terms). To quote Birch (1989, 13) again:

The two great political events that embodied Enlightenment ideas were the American Declaration of Independence and the French Revolution, and it is no accident that the French and the Americans have been the two peoples most optimistic about the power of reason to fashion human progress and most confident that their forms of civilization and their concepts of good government were suitable for export.

Universalism, although based in equality, has inherent within it political cultural empire-building. The concept of nation and nationalism becomes, therefore, a concept mobilised in relation to, and as a counteraction against universalism. As an oppositional concept, nation is based *in* an assumption of difference (because its different-ness is its starting point) and based *upon* the assumption of difference.

The legacy of the Enlightenment and Revolution was not just one of optimism. These two moments in history also brought in their wake a feeling of profound malaise and morosity (the second part of the triptych); malaise because the Enlightenment marked the 'dusk of religious modes of thought', and morosity because the Enlightenment and Revolution destroyed the 'legitimacy of the divinely-ordained . . . dynastic realm' (Anderson: 1990, 16). Religious modes of thought were symbolically put to death in the act of executing the Monarch – 'he who is chosen by God'. This left a breach that had to be filled. As Anderson (1990, 19) says:

> With the ebbing of religious belief, the suffering which belief in part composed did not disappear. Disintegration of paradise: nothing makes fatality more arbitrary. Absurdity of salvation: nothing makes another style of continuity more necessary. What then was required was a secular transformation of fatality into continuity, contingency into meaning . . . few things were (are) better suited to this end than an idea of nation.

Viewed in this light, the concept of nation-ness becomes rooted in that of continuity and not, as was the case in the first instance, in difference (difference as a motivated concept against universal validity). Nation, in this second instance, becomes a secular transformation of religion and divine monarchy into a sovereign state, hence Anderson's definition of nation as limited (because it has finite boundaries) and sovereign (because the state has replaced the former artefacts).

This brings us to the third part of the triptych – security. In Anderson's definition of nation he uses the word 'imagined'. At the beginning of this Introduction, it was argued that the concepts of nation bring it very close to myth. The point here is that nation had to be imagined to give people a secure sense of identity. It had to be imagined as the 'other' in relation to 'rule by empire-building' cultures (many nation-states subsequently showed a pronounced proclivity to become such empire-builders themselves, but this is another aspect which I do not intend to address here). In this respect, the nation becomes an imagined collectivity whose whole *raison d'être* lies in its imagined otherness.

If problems arise in defining nation, therefore, it is surely because of its imagined status. It is that which makes 'nation' such a slippery concept. As we have seen, it is alternately based on the assumption of difference, continuity and, finally, imagined otherness.

By way of drawing this section to a close, let us return to the question of the function and value of nation-ness – a consideration of which will bring into the forum of debate a term not yet addressed, ideology. In order to understand why ideology is part, but only part, of the issue of the function and value of nation-ness, it is necessary to go back to the theoreticians of the nineteenth century. Both Herder and Fichte saw language as the basis for nationhood. Fichte was quite categorical: to each separate language a separate nation (we should not forget that this was early in the nineteenth century and Germans had no nation-state at this stage). Herder was not as limited in his conceptualisation of nationhood as was Fichte. He 'believed that languages had intrinsic value as the expression of *Volk* cultures', but he also 'emphasized the emotional importance to human beings of their membership of a distinct cultural group and the desirability of basing political authority upon such groups' (Birch: 1989, 18). In the second part of his thinking he gets close to Hegel whose 'emphasis was on the virtues of the national state as a form of political organization rather than on the importance of culture' (ibid., 21). Ideology inserts itself at the interface of these two concepts (language and political organisation). Language (culture) is mobilised to signify the new political organisations which have emerged following the breakdown of traditional societies (starting with the French Revolution but culminating in the Industrial Revolution). Ideology, then, is the discourse that invests a nation with meaning and is, therefore, no less problematic than the concept of nation-ness. Since it reflects the way in which a nation is signified, ideology is as closely aligned to myth as is nation-ness.

Louis Althusser (1984, 37) makes the point that ideology is not just a case of a controlling few imposing an interpretation of the nation upon the subjects of the state but that, in ideology, the subjects also represent to themselves 'their relation to those conditions of existence which is represented to them there'. In other words, they make ideology have meaning by colluding with and acting according to it. Why this consensuality? Because of the reassuring nature of national identity. As Birch (1989, 221) says, the nation-state gives 'people a secure sense of identity, status and (usually) pride'. The state is *their* state, the governing body is *their* indigenous governing body, not some foreign ruler's (and so on). They look at it and see themselves in it, and it is precisely this narcissism which keeps them within it. But, as the myth of Narcissus reminds us, this mirror effect has a double edge for it implies both the individuation of the subject (within the state) and the sacrifice of the self (to the state).

It seems appropriate to end our discussion, in broad terms, of the concepts of nation here. It will be useful to retain, from this section, the essential notions of nation as myth and nation as difference and continuity as well as the notion of the enunciative role of ideology. They will serve as a useful framework and reference points in what follows.

CONCEPTS OF A NATIONAL CINEMA

The nineteenth century was the age of nationalism. Since then, first European states and subsequently other countries have 'ideologised themselves into nations'.[3] It seems more than appropriate that cinema was born in that age of nationalism, but it must be added that it was also born at a time which was the age of the *fin-de-sièclisme* (because the birth was towards the end of the century) – two very distinct modalities and mentalities, the first reflecting the rapid ascendancy in national individualism, the second the decadence and ruin mobilised by the implicit narcissism of such a nationalism. A product born at the interface of these two moments, cinema becomes inscribed (metaphorically at least) with the juxtapositional traces of ascendancy and decline on the one hand, and on the other, of nationalism and narcissism both associated with that time. This was also an age that saw the 'birth' of psychoanalysis – of concern for the psyche (with all the resonances in that word of the mirror image and individual identity which, as has already been stated, are resonances of nation-ness as well). It is significant too that in France, almost as soon as cinema was born, books were being written entitled *L'Histoire du cinéma*. By the early 1900s, film theory was already an arena of debate (as the sixth art and then the seventh) and, by the 1920s, calls were being made for a truly national cinema as a defence against the American hegemony, all of which (in the implicit concern for the well-being of cinema) points to a historicism and narcissism of sorts. In the 1990s, we are once more in an age of *fin-de-sièclisme* and in an age where a whole series of questions in relation to national identity are being raised, especially in Europe and in post-colonialist countries – countries which are seeking a nationalism, something other than that which prevailed before.

In the writing of a national cinema there are two fundamental yet crucial axes of reflection to be considered. First, how is the national enunciated? In other words, what are the texts and what meanings do they mobilise? And, second, how to enunciate the national? That is, what typologies must be traced into a cartography of the national? Or, expressed more simply, what is there, what does it mean and how do we write its meaning?

Let us start with the first axis of reflection. Essentially, with regard to the cinema as a 'national' institution, there are three modes of enunciation: the films themselves, the written discourses which surround them and, finally, the archival institutes in which they are housed (cinémathèques and distributors' vaults) and displayed (cinémathèques, ciné-clubs and cinema theatres). This triad in turn generates the question of which cinema we are addressing, for there is not just one cinema, but several. Here the concern is not simply with art and popular cinemas' cultural production, but with mainstream and peripheral cinemas, with *the* cinema and the cinemas – that is, with regard to *the* cinema, that which is at the centre of the nation. This shifts according to which particular nation is being referred to because the concept of a nation's cinema will change according to a nation's ideology. Thus, it could be capital culture or official culture that is at the centre of the hegemony (for example, in America it is capital/Hollywood culture that is at the centre; in the former Communist countries it was the official culture). Furthermore this cinema of the centre changes in its identity depending on who is canonising it as central. Mainstream, popular cinema is one that is canonised in distribution catalogues, fanzines, the press, on television, etc. Non-mainstream and avant-garde is canonised in the annals of film institutes or in critical writings. There are, of course, other cinemas still (be they censured, proscribed or cult cinemas) and also the cinema of others (the voices from the margins).

Thus, in relation to the films themselves, the first line of enquiry becomes which films should constitute the corpus of a 'national' cinema? French cinema, with an average official production of 100-plus feature films per year since the advent of sound (prior to that time there were very many more), could seem a daunting prospect for examination. However, co-productions have had an impact on this figure, a factor that will be explored more fully in Chapter 1. Clearly, popular cinema production – in its true proportion to the other cinemas – will inform the corpus to be researched as will consumption practices. This assertion already raises an initial problematic. Since much of the early popular cinema is inaccessible (it has disappeared either literally through nitrate dissolution or figuratively into impenetrable archives) and no detailed statistics were kept in France until the mid-1930s, other sources (such as contemporaneous accounts, scholarly researched texts on audience venues and exhibition practices, etc.) will have to serve as partial guidelines for establishing what constituted France's national cinema in the first third of its history. Already we are at one remove from the text itself and into a secondary, at times tertiary enunciation of the original document. It is at this juncture that imprecision risks slipping in.

This point brings us to the second mode of enunciation, that of the written discourses. Many discourses surround a nation's cinema. But which cinemas do they mobilise and which do they leave unspoken? Where France is concerned, and in very general terms, there are three discursive modalities which re-present the cinema as institution – a triumvirate composed of historical, critical and state discourses. Historical documentation would include histories of the indigenous cinema, pamphlets published by unions and other sectors representing the industry and memoirs of industrialists (such as Pathé). The critical discourses would range from film criticism to film theory. Finally, state discourses would include such texts as ministerial decrees, documentation on state intervention, publications emanating from the *Centre national de la cinématographie* (CNC), and official statistics on all aspects of cinematic praxis. Although state discourses might appear to be a closed text and of little interpretative value, in that they record legislative measures and provide figures, their impact on cinematic production and style has been and still is quite considerable.

All three written discourse modalities, therefore, have served to shape the nation's cinema history and to cause things to happen to films (e.g. critical discourses can elevate the popular to the high art or, alternatively, to cult status). It would seem likely that the first two categories of discourses would be most instrumental in identifying the nature of the national cinema, but in privileging a certain type of cinema, these discourses have not been spared the problematics of historicism. Thus, in its concentration either on directors (following the auteurist approach) or on specific movements (e.g., the New Wave), so far the representation of France's national cinema has suffered from too narrow a focus and inconsistencies in terms of the approaches adopted. Invariably, too, this representation has overwhelmingly been the province of high art rather than popular culture.[4] Yet, France has produced a substantial body of films of both social and aesthetic value and high audience appeal which has been largely overlooked and inadequately represented by existing works. Whereas the emphasis on auteurs or movements is often justified in terms of the excellence of the works concerned, what is lacking is their proper historical contextualisation within wider cultural considerations.

The third mode of enunciation of a national cinema, archival institutions (in the form of national archival institutes) create, albeit differently, similar problems since in their role as conservators of the culture, they also act as monuments to cinema. More crucially still, unlike the more mainstream distribution companies for whom films can have a critically and cynically short shelf-life, they serve to inform and preserve the perception of the nation's cinema. Although it is clear that they perform a vital function in keeping the cultural heritage 'alive' (i.e., it is there, preserved), none the less they simultaneously act as agents of petrification of that heritage (i.e., this is it, this *is* the heritage). This then generates a further set of problems because the question now becomes, which films are in a fit state to be screened? Which ones have been privileged over others that are 'waiting to be restored'? Preservation of the culture means, therefore, that a mausoleumification takes place which mobilises a specified construction of the cultural. As Sean Cubitt (1989, 3) points out, when discussing the function of museums in general, they 'ossify history into tradition' and 'mobilise the myth of the fixity of cultural capital'.

Already, with this first axis of reflection on how the national is enunciated, it is clear that the three modes of representation, as outlined above, articulate at the denotative (i.e., this is it) and connotative (i.e., these are the various readings/cultural reflections 'it' gives of the nation) levels of the sign to the point where national cinema becomes myth. Turning now to the second axis of reflection, how to enunciate the national, I shall consider how cinema itself contributes to the construction of the concept of the nation and, thereby, to the myth of the 'national' in national cinema.

Traditionally the 'national' of a cinema is defined in terms of its difference from other cinemas of other nations, primarily in terms of its difference from the cinema of the United States (i.e., Hollywood). This juxtapositional way of establishing the 'national' of a cinema runs the risk of being too reductionist, but that does not mean that it is a definition that should be rejected, for it must be recognised that every national cinema, especially in the West, will be defined in relation to that very specific other, the American cinema, given the latter's dominance in the field from 1914 onwards. However, there are other forces that push a country towards a definition of its cinema as different and distinct. It is often the case that appeals for a 'real national cinema' are launched in reaction to international pressures (political and economic), as will be illustrated in later chapters.

Difference, then, is a first way of enunciating the national but, because of its limitations, it has to be seen in the light of other equally important considerations. One way of resolving how to enunciate the 'national' would be to talk about national cinema in terms of typologies or in terms of what Dick Hebdige might call a cartography of the national.[5]

Notionally, but without being exhaustive, there are seven discernible typologies that will assist in the enunciation of the 'national' of a cinema. Although the way in which the 'national' can be enunciated (i.e., through using these typologies) may remain constant, clearly what the term national signifies will change according to social, economic and political mutations and pressures. Since they will thread their way through the overall text and thereby receive further elucidation, these typologies will be elaborated upon here only briefly by way of explanation and definition. The seven typologies are as follows:

1 narratives;
2 genres;
3 codes and conventions;
4 gesturality and morphology;
5 the star as sign;
6 cinema of the centre and cinema of the periphery;

7 cinema as the mobiliser of the nation's myths and of the myth of the nation.

Narratives

In a very useful study on national fictions, Graeme Turner, basing his approach in part on the work of Propp and Lévi-Strauss, makes the point that a country's narratives are produced by the indigenous culture and that these narratives serve a reflexive role in that a culture uses them in order to understand its own signification – in other words, 'narrative [is] a culture's way of making sense of itself' (1986, 18).[6] Summarising Lévi-Strauss's line of argument, he goes on to state that the narrative form probably serves the same function in all cultures, but that the specificity of its articulation is determined by the particular culture.

It is in its specificity, therefore, that a filmic narrative can be perceived as a reflection of the nation. This reflexivity can occur in two ways (at least), neither one of which excludes the other. First, the filmic narrative can be based on a literary adaptation of an indigenous text. In this respect, reflexivity operates by virtue of a reinscription of one existing cultural artefact into a filmic text. In this mode, the film, in transposing an indigenous text, offers up a double nation-narration, the text it refers to and its own filmic text. Literature (narration one) is on screen (narration two) confirming the natural heritage (the nation). This would explain why some literary adaptations simply do not work when removed from their indigenous culture – the narrative's specificity is too strong. The filmic text, therefore, offers (albeit in a different medium) a reflection of that nation. In France's case, this is a particularly crucial point since, in the history of its cinema, literary adaptation has been its mainstay to the degree that it is perceived as the major tradition of its classical-narrative cinema (one thinks immediately of the numerous adaptations of Zola's novels, but there are countless others).

In the second instance, the film can confront the spectator with an explicit or implicit textual construction of the nation.[7] Explicit films are those which set out to signify the nation, however problematic that notion is (because they appear to reinforce dominant myths). For example, Gance's *Napoléon* is less about the military campaigner than it is Gance's own vision of Napoleon, *Napoléon, vu par Abel Gance*. Similarly, D.W. Griffith's *Birth of a Nation* seems to address the birth of America yet, in fact, it is more about the stretching of studio and cinematic practices than it is about a 'truthful' rendition of how America was born. None the less, these films construct moments in a nation's history and become (intentionally or not) propagandist in their narratives. Implicit films are closer to a myth-construction of a nation (as opposed to myth-reinforcement) since their narratives function on a more connotative level. The nation is implicitly present and in this respect this category of films can be either propagandist in their narrative or subversive (two films made during the Occupation period, Stelli's *Le Voile bleu* and Grémillon's *Le Ciel est à vous* are good illustrations of the former and Godard's films of the 1960s, *Weekend* or *La Chinoise*, of the latter). I shall return to this question of narrative and the construction of a nation in the last section of this Introduction, but it is clear that the two types of reflexivity described above will mobilise, within a national cinema, certain genres and formalistic tendencies and privilege certain codes and conventions and modes of production over others.

Genres

Grand epics, with one or two big exceptions (e.g., Gance's *Napoléon*), are not France's style. There are filmic modalities which are specific to a particular nation and in France's case the first dominant generic mode in the history of its cinema (with the exception of the World War I period and the Occupation) is the comedy film which goes back to its earliest cinema and often makes up half of the industry's output. After that certainty, genres are less reliable in their popularity and staying power. Thus the very popular melodrama – also known as the psychological drama film – of the silent cinema and the 1930s has dropped from its second place and equally dropped its more melodramatic connotations. Now its form is a psychological/intimist film which is less perceivable as a genre because it slips over so many (i.e., thrillers, adventure, historical reconstruction, etc.). At present the second most popular genre is the *polar* (the cop and/or thriller genre), which has many antecedents (French and American). What is least evident, apart from epics, is the adventure film, to say nothing of the western. These three genres having been relinquished to the Americans. It is also true that there are universal genres which become specified, amplified, even subverted, within a particular culture. A prime example for France is the *polar* film which, in the 1950s, quite radically changed its look and more readily referred to (but not necessarily imitated) the American genre. What mobilises this specificity is, of course, indigenous praxis, that is to say the codes and conventions of cinematic production in its widest sense and the gesturality and morphology of the nation's acting class.

Codes and conventions

It is important here to think in terms of both the mode of production and the iconography of the image. A product, emanating from the French film industry, will remain 'intrinsically' French from the point of view of labour and production practices. Legislation and union practices will affect the

product just as much as the traditions of production. On this last point, what springs immediately to mind are the French production traditions of artisanal films, films made by working as a team (on the theatre principle), and small- and medium-budget films. However, these are not the only traditions. There are periods when big-budget films are in favour, usually to counter American dominance, as was the case in the mid-1920s with the modern studio spectacular. At present, this tendency is again in vogue, albeit on a more moderate scale, but only in terms of actual output, not in terms of cost. Production practices here have tended to favour one or two 'blockbuster' films per year to draw in not just the regular consumers but also the once- or twice-a-year cinema-goers (top French films of the mid-1980s onwards make instructive reading, starting in 1986 with *Jean de Florette*, *L'Ours*, in 1988, *Le Grand bleu*, in 1989 – only one medium-budget production made it during this period, *Le Grand chemin*, in 1987, and ended up in third place). Then there is the thorny problem of co-productions which raises, more fulsomely than any other type of production, questions of ownership (if it is more than 50 per cent financed by the French, if the film-maker is French, if the cast is mostly French, etc., is it a French product?). This difficult issue will be addressed in Chapter 1. However, because co-productions have figured heavily at times in France's output (the 1920s, late 1950s and early 1970s especially) and because nowadays co-productions are not just limited to the international field but can receive direct investment from television channels (French and otherwise), it is unlikely that the issue of how to address them will be resolved. For the moment bear in mind, first, that a nation does have several production practices and, second, that modes of production do raise questions of ownership.

With regard to the iconography of the image, there are two questions to be addressed. How does the representation of the nation (through the image) carve up and/or construct the nation? And what problematics does this representation engender? In other words, what is represented and what is left out? Who or what remains un-visible? As can be seen, the iconography of the image generates a series of binary paradigms of which the very first is absence/presence. The effect of this precise duopoly is to make possible a homogenised and conciliatory myth of the national context. Thus, for example, in the 1930s French cinema, the working class is represented in specific locations, many of which, however, by this time would no longer have existed (or would have been very peripheral). The music-hall, the café concert and even the *guinguette* were all part of the working-class's topos that had their heyday at the turn of the century but which, ironically, by the 1930s were dying out thanks to the new attractions of silent cinema and, later, of sound cinema (Ory: 1989, 22). But the conciliatory myth is in place: 'that is where the working class goes for entertainment [play]'. All national cinemas, therefore, are affected by this same problematic of hegemonic transparence, but in each instance the iconographic codes and conventions remain specific to the cultural patrimony.

Gesturality and morphology

Maurice Chevalier, Fernandel and Jean Gabin have more in common than Jean Gabin and John Wayne. Such a statement could affront. A rephrasing might make the point less brutally. What separates Arletty, Simone Signoret and Brigitte Bardot on the one hand from Bette Davis, Joan Crawford or Susan Hayward on the other? The answer? The gesturality and the morphology of the body. Gestures, words, intonations, attitudes, postures – all of these separate them, thus affirming the plurality of the cultures. Indeed, it could be argued that the gestural codes, even more so than the narrative codes, are deeply rooted in a nation's culture.[8] Thus, when analysing the nation's cinema, traditions of performance must also be brought into consideration as a further marker of this differentiation and specificity.[9]

The star as sign

Sign of the indigenous cultural codes, institutional metonymy and site of the class war in its national specificity, the signification of the star 'naturally' changes according to the social, economic and political environment. Thus the Gabin of the 1930s will become, first, the Belmondo of the 1960s and, then, the Depardieu of the 1980s – three very different types of 'proletarian' heroes. In addition, the spectators impose on the stars their own expectations: the stars are the mediators between the real and the imaginary. If one just considers the area of female sexuality over the last fifty years, one can perceive how there is transference and mutation. Thus the femino-masculine eroticism of the 1930s (e.g., Arletty) is replaced by the female-in-her-own right eroticism of the 1950s (e.g., Simone Signoret) which, in turn, is at first complemented (in the mid-1950s) and later supplanted by the infantilo-innocent eroticism of the late 1950s and early 1960s (e.g., Brigitte Bardot), and this becomes the cool, reserved, almost inopportune eroticism of the 1980s (e.g., Sandrine Bonnaire). These four moments correspond, first, to the different stages in the representation/reification of the French woman's sexuality and, second, to the social, political and economic conditions that prevailed in each of those epochs (it is noteworthy that the so-called sexual liberty of the French youth in the 1960s and 1970s – in evidence in the cinema of that time – no longer has the same resonances of joy and innocence today).

1 THE STAR AS A NATIONAL SIGNIFIER

Jean Gabin

Fernandel

John Wayne

Arletty

Simone Signoret

Brigitte Bardot

Joan Crawford

Susan Hayward

Cinema of the centre and cinema of the periphery

Guy Gauthier has written very helpfully about this issue which is the sixth typology on this cartography of the 'national'.[10] In his analysis he sets up a hierarchy of these two cinemas which are not always necessarily antagonistic but between which there is considerable slippage. There are three main antagons within this hierarchy which cannot be fixed entirely in a decreasing order. These antagons are as follows:

– the centre Hollywood/US and the indigenous cinema which is peripheral in relation to the epicentre *par excellence* that Hollywood/US represents;
– the homogeneity of equipment and, conversely, the heterodoxy of the production which is peripheral by virtue of its gestural and narrational specificities;
– the central indigenous cinema and the artisanal cinema and auteur cinema which is peripheral.

These antagons require further explanation. The first is an evident one. America/Hollywood is the epicentre because it is the leading exporter of films and because all other cinemas define their difference in relation to this dominant cinematic culture against which they cannot compete either on the economic or on the production level. The curious thing is that as one progresses 'down' the ladder, that which was on the periphery eventually becomes central. On the first rung, Hollywood is the centre, and all other national cinemas are peripheral. On the second, standardised equipment and its homogenising effect on cinema represent the centre – the global effect of uniformalised technology causing cinema to normalise its production. This first happened in the late 1920s with the advent of sound and then again, more specifically, in the 1950s with a greater standardisation of the cinematic technology. However, cinema does not just standardise. Cinema also particularises. The technology may be uniform, but national specificities will emerge, through editing style for example, or in the way a narrative is narrated. The peripheral production practices, therefore, operate outside of technology. On the third rung, what was originally peripheral (indigenous cinema) now becomes central for the following reasons. Since the indigenous industry, in this instance the French cinema industry, cannot compete with that in the United States, it tends (with the exception of periods when it participated heavily in co-productions, i.e., the 1920s and the late 1950s to the early 1970s) to invest in what constitutes, in relation to Hollywood, the periphery. The peripheral (i.e., the home product) becomes central thanks to this investment. However, because the industry knows how difficult it is to export (especially to the United States), it produces films for the indigenous market only. This immobilism in production practices (producing for a safe home market), which the Hollywood ascendancy imposes, leads to an unwitting complicity on the part of the industry in the construction of a national cinema. This cinema is made by those who are at the centre of the culture starting with the major production and distribution companies.

These are not the only bodies that currently control the 'look' of France's cinema. This centre now includes television channels which, although they invest in films, none the less perceive these films' ultimate destination as the television screen. This particular cinema of the centre has a textual formation that is inevitably homogeneous (e.g., safety in repeating the same formula, using the same director, etc.). In this respect, cinema normalises and functions very similarly to the centre on the second rung (i.e., the homogenisation of the product through standardised equipment). Nor, by this logic, does the peripheral cinema on this third rung escape the centre. This cinema, which is financed by independent producers or by the film-makers themselves, is made by those who are outside the culture of the centre. However, this cinema's praxis, be it avant-garde, artisanal or auteur, can be co-opted, normalised by the cinema of the centre, as recent films by Beineix, Besson and Carax demonstrate. Indeed, were we to continue with this hierarchy, the next antagon would probably place this cinema of the periphery in the centre and at the periphery would lie regional cinema. This antagon would in turn generate a further one where regional cinema would become the centre and Beur cinema the periphery, and so on.

This typology helps to make the point that there is no single cinema that is *the* national cinema, but several. It thereby puts an end to the dangers of historicism which identify a national cinema with specific movements or directors and suggests, rather, that there is flux, slippage even, between the various cinemas which constitute the nation's cinema. This typology also suggests that discourses around a national cinema no longer need address cinema in an exclusive way such as, for example, defining it as the work of pioneers alone or as an ideological institution. These are some of the discourses, but they are just some among others.

Cinema as the mobiliser of the nation's myths and the myth of the nation

It was stated at the beginning of this Introduction that the nineteenth century was the age of nationalism and that as a product born at the interface of these two moments, cinema was inscribed with the juxtapositional traces of ascendancy and decline, nationalism and narcissism associated with that time. Similarities were identified between the moment of its birth and the present moment of *fin-de-sièclisme* and the forging of new national identities.

Since the history of cinema coincides with this hundred-year span (1895–1995), it invites the following question: to what extent and how does cinema reflect the texture of society on a national level? It follows from the previous section that the cinemas that make up a national cinema will reflect both from within and from without (centre and periphery). Reflecting from within the centre of the culture, cinema becomes auto-reflexive, revealing the narcissistic trace of its heritage. Reflecting from without, cinema becomes individuated – an individuated reflection of, and even upon, the nation. In the first instance, cinema normalises, in the latter it particularises. In its normalising process it shows its state of decline, in its particularising it reveals its ascendant role. Filmic narration, calls upon the available discourses and myths of its own culture. It is evident that these cultural, nationalistic myths are not pure and simple reflections of history, but a transformation of history. Thus, they work to construct a specific way of perceiving the nation. Cinema, whether it is of the centre or the periphery, is no exception to this nation-construction (both address the nation, however distinctly) and the question becomes, what myths does a national cinema put in place and what are the consequences?

Without being too reductionist, the first point to be made is that the cinemas of the centre and the periphery will re-present the myths in radically opposite ways. The former in its reconstruction will provide, in the main, hegemonic transparence. The latter will challenge, even deconstruct, that transparence and hegemony. In any event, given that cinema is an industry and therefore an affair of capital, it is obvious that the cinema of the centre will dominate the other in its myth-making practices (if only from the point of view of the pure volume of production) and there is little to suggest that this dynamic will change. However, although there will always be a preponderance of the centre over the periphery, none the less, there is within that dynamic a degree of unfixity. Take, for example, moments in a nation's history when the nationalistic character of a society is valorised and, as a result, the more nationalistic discourses become areas occupied by motivated interests that are seeking to centre themselves within the culture. In these periods it is evident that the peripheral will be forced out beyond the peripheral margins themselves (if not censored completely). In this respect, the prime, though not unique, example for France would be the cinema during the Vichy period. Film scenarios that were consonant with the new triumvirate of the National Revolution of '*famille, patrie, travail*' which Pétain, as leader of the *Etat Français* (as Vichy France was then known), insisted upon to create national unity in a new moral order – or at least scenarios that appeared not to challenge these values – were easily allowed through censorship and were produced and distributed.

A national cinema, then, is historically fluctuating.[11] But it is simultaneously constructing a historicity of the nation in that it is reconstructing myths already mobilised by the nation as they are inscribed in the indigenous culture. Thus, although this textualisation of the nation reinforces the popular myth of cultural specificity (and, thereby, of difference), that specificity will necessarily change over the course of history. It will change because the signification of the term 'national' changes according to political, social and economic pressures and mutations, just as the state of the nation changes in time according to its position in the world.

The intention behind this outline of the seven typologies was to chart possible ways of enunciating the national of a cinema. Before embarking on the actual journey of writing it, the relationship between the French state and culture must be addressed. Ever since the Revolution, the French state has had a cultural policy which has evolved along three essential lines: the state as protector of the national heritage (e.g., putting it in museums), the state as its patron (e.g., providing aid and passing laws to protect the indigenous culture) and the state as facilitator of equal access to that heritage (through education and dissemination of the cultural product). Protector and patron of its culture, the French state perceives the role of culture as a unifying one, as being the buttress of the nation's moral unity. For the state, the products of its culture are both a sign of the health of the nation and an exportable commodity that serves the renown of the nation. Within the French nation, therefore, there is a mutuality between state and culture of long standing.[12] It is for this reason that cinema, when in crisis, turns to the state and demands support. After all, President de Gaulle consecrated cinema when he created the Ministry of Culture (with André Malraux as its first minister) and placed cinema alongside the fine arts. The advantages of this support notwithstanding, this reliance upon the state is not without its drawbacks, as will be demonstrated in the next chapter.

NOTES

1 See Benedict Anderson's (1990) very useful Introduction.
2 See Birch (1989), especially Part One: Theory and Principles.
3 This term is borrowed from a text which I would like to draw to the reader's attention. *The Concept of National Cinema*, by Marcia Butzel, Marvin D'Lugo and Philip Rosen, is to be the first full-length study of its sort on the concept of 'national' in national cinema, and is to be published by Routledge. At the time of writing, I have only seen the book proposal. However, it is clear that it will be dealing far more substantively with the issues raised here and I wish to acknowledge the usefulness of the proposal in refining some of the remarks made in this Introduction.
4 But see Vincendeau (1985), Lagny (1989) and Abel (1984 and 1988).
5 I am borrowing the nomenclature from Hebdige (1988, 45) in his chapter entitled 'Towards a cartography of taste 1935–1962'.
6 See Lévi-Strauss, C. (1972) 'The structural study of myth', in Richard and Ferdinande de George (eds) *The Structuralists from Marx to Lévi-Strauss*, New York, Doubleday; and Propp, V. (1975) *The Morphology of the Folk Tale*, Austin, Austin University Press.

7 This distinction is made by Marcia Butzel and Marvin D'Lugo in their book proposal (see n. 3).
8 Guy Gauthier in a thought-provoking series of articles (entitled 'Cent fleurs pour l'audiovisuel' in *Revue du cinéma*, nos. 389–401, October 1984 to January 1985) presents just such a case. See his second article 'Technique et normalisation, in *Revue du cinéma*, no. 399, November 1984.
9 Ginette Vincendeau (1985) has explored this question in considerable depth in relation to traditions of performance in the films of the 1930s.
10 'Centre et Périphérie', *Revue du cinéma*, no. 400, December 1984.
11 I quote Philip Rosen's expression here which occurs in the book proposal mentioned in n. 3.
12 For further details on the relationship between state and culture, I refer the reader to Rémi Caron (1989) *L'Etat et la culture*, Paris, Economica.

BIBLIOGRAPHY

Abel, R. (1984) *French Cinema: The First New Wave, 1915–1929*, New Jersey, Princeton University Press.
—— (1988) *French Film Theory and Criticism: A History/Anthology Volume II, 1920–1939*, New Jersey, Princeton University Press.
Althusser, L. (1984) 'Ideology and the State', in *Essays on Ideology*, London, Verso.
Anderson, B. (1990) *Imagined Communities: Reflections on the Origin and Spread of Nationalism*, London, Verso.
Bhabha H.K. (ed.) (1990) *Nation and Narration*, London, Routledge.
Birch, A.H. (1989) *Nationalism and National Integration*, London, Unwin Hyman.
Cubitt, S. (1989) Introduction to 'Over The Borderlines', *Screen*, vol. 30, no. 4 (issue on questioning national identities).
Heath, S. (1978) 'Questions of property: film and nationhood', *Cinetracts*, vol. 1, no. 4.
Hebdige, D. (1988) *Hiding in the Light*, London, Comedia/Routledge.
Jameson, F. (1986) *The Political Unconsciousness: Narrative as a Socially Symbolic Act*, London, Routledge.
Lagny, M. (1989) 'Epistémologie de l'histoire', in *Histoire du cinéma: nouvelles approches*, Paris, Publications de la Sorbonne.
Ory, P. (1989) *L'Aventure culturelle française*, Paris, Flammarion.
Rosen, P. (1984) 'History, textuality, nation: Kracauer, Burch, and some problems in the study of national cinemas', *Iris*, vol. 2, no. 2.
Turner, G. (1986) *National Fictions*, Sydney, Allen and Unwin.
Vincendeau, G. (1985) 'French Cinema in the 1930s: Social Texts and Contexts of a Popular Entertainment Medium', unpublished Ph.D. dissertation, University of East Anglia.

Chapter 1

A brief ecohistory of France's cinema industry 1895–1992

MAPPING THE TERRAIN

By all accounts, the French cinema industry has been in crisis almost since its inception. Georges Sadoul (1962, 10) puts the date as early as 1908; Richard Abel (1984, 10) points to 1914 as the moment of France's decline as film leader and 1918 (i.e., post-World War I) as the year when the industry first experienced a crisis. Mapping the ecohistory (ecological history) of the French cinema reveals an intriguing pattern of repetition and stagnation from which the industry has rarely managed to disengage itself.

Until World War I, France had the monopoly of the cinematic market world-wide. Thus, until then there was indeed a national cinema in France, at least in economic terms. However, the French cinema industry entered into a state of crisis shortly after its meteoric emergence (within about ten years of its birth) because the industry failed to modernise and to rethink its product through a lack of vision and a sense of complacency. This is not to say that France could have sustained effectively her monopoly over the challenge from the United States, which had monopolised 90 per cent of the British programmes by 1914, thereby taking an important, accessible market away from the French. None the less, had the major French distribution companies seen the need for a different product, then at least the decline would have been less rapid and remarkable.

A first mapping reveals three contributory causes to the crisis and two consequences which in turn have contributed to its perpetuation. If the US colonisation was a major factor, then so too was the effect on the industry of state intervention and taxation and, moreover, the industry's own navel-gazing production practices. As far as this third factor is concerned, France has been in a self-perpetuating chicken and egg situation in which economic difficulties – lack of investment generally and poor investment practices at crucial moments in the evolution of the industry – have produced an immobilism which in turn has fostered an unwillingness to invest. The concomitant consequences of this lack of change have been a repetition of previous patterns and, quite naturally, a decline in audience.

A second mapping of France's cinema industry provides five main axes from which to examine this case for a crisis. First, there has been the celluloid war, principally with the United States (as will be revealed, Germany has had its part to play as well); second, the whole question of production and distribution practices; third, state aid and taxation and the issue of censorship; fourth, audiences, venues and exhibition practices; and last, but not least, the impact of television.

Until the arrival/a-rival of television as an ascendant competitor, the blocks of time that can be carved out as meaningful units of history are fairly regular. Thus, the first and second cycles (1895–1914 and 1914–39 respectively) last some twenty to twenty-five years and both are pulled short or brought to an end by World Wars. The third cycle (1940–58), stretching from the Occupation to the return to power of General de Gaulle and the installation of the Fifth Republic, is a little shorter. The justification for this block of time lies with the fact that the impact of policies concerning the film industry – put in place by the Germans during the Occupation – were still to be felt during the 1950s. The year 1957–8 also marks the last time that the cinema-going audience peaked (411 million), since when the decline has been constant. The fourth and final cycle (1959–92) represents a natural time block marked out at either end by contrastive (some might say radical) changes in production practices – those of the so-called New Wave (1959) and the Post-New Wave of the mid- to late 1980s.

A final way of mapping this industry's history would be to centre it around the two World Wars, for it is in this respect that patterns of repetition emerge. Prior to the two wars, the industry was quite prestigiously placed. By 1939, French cinema had regained its prestige, albeit this time in terms of the reputation of its product rather than its economic monopoly (as was the case before World War I). In this respect, it had virtually won back its 1908 reputation. After the two wars, the uncertainty of the nation showed up in the meteoric rise in co-productions and the dearth of French cinema production (the most radical drop being from 90 per cent to 20 per cent after World War I). This uncertainty also revealed itself in the defeatist mood in the industry, as with the nation as a whole, at the crucial moment of its reconstruction. Furthermore, given the poor state of its own technology and the difficulty of rebuilding the industry in the face of mounting costs, in both post-war periods France was incapable of producing films as cheaply as the United States, which meant that the flood-gates were opened to American products. This situation was compounded by the inability of the small home market to pay off the costs of French-made films. These characteristics in turn led the industry into a plethora of co-productions, predominantly with Germany after World War I and with Italy after World War II). Thus, in those two periods, the majority of films screened in France were first and foremost American, and subsequently co-productions, all of which begs the question: what price

France's national cinema? In fact, by a curious irony, this state of affairs allowed for the emergence in the 1920s and again in the late 1950s of the artisanal film which, through its experimental film-making practices in response to economic exigencies, did establish one distinctive aspect of French national cinema – the artisanal mode or what Abel (1984, 37) calls a concern for Frenchness.

Since it offers a more global approach to the question of France's cinema ecohistory, taking into account as it does social, political and economic determinants, the second mapping rather than the first will be adopted – that of the five axes – as the major structure through which to examine this story of a crisis and the other will be used as a substructural underpinning to this approach.

THE CELLULOID WAR

Although French cinema distribution practices in the United States were not properly in place until first, 1904 with the Pathé brothers and second, Gaumont in 1907, it is interesting to note that from the very beginning America showed signs of resistance towards any infiltration of French cinematographic products. As early as 1896, after initial successes in major American cities, representatives of the pioneering Lumière brothers – inventors of the *cinématographe* (the dual-purpose camera-projector) – met with attempts to thwart their plans to demonstrate their projection equipment. Screening séances were inexplicably cancelled, the equipment was boycotted by the Americans and was even confiscated by customs under the pretext that it contravened customs' regulations. In their desperation to be the sole patent holders, the Americans (primarily at this juncture in the form of Edison) made it impossible for the representatives to stay.[1] Having lost this first round of the patents' war, the French returned home after only six weeks.

Although on the equipment front France was and continued to be unsuccessful against her main competitors, this was not the case with regard to its distribution practices, at least not until World War I. For example, by 1908 Pathé (the first of the major French distribution companies) was selling twice as many films to the United States as all the American production companies put together. Pathé had a factory in New York, studios in New Jersey and outlets all over the world from Berlin to Calcutta. Gaumont was quick to imitate and established an office in New York and studios in Fort Lee, New Jersey (D'Hugues and Marmin: 1986, 32). By 1910, the hegemony of the French cinema was perhaps more total than that of Hollywood would ever be, even in the 1950s, in that up to 70 per cent of the films exported world-wide were from Parisian studios, principally from the three big companies: Pathé, Gaumont and Eclair (Sadoul: 1962, 12). On this issue of hegemony it is worth noting that where production style and content are concerned, Pathé was well in advance of its American rivals. In terms of style, anonymity was the rule at Pathé. From scriptwriters right through to the actors, names remained unknown to the public (this changed for actors, especially after 1908 and the *Film d'Art* series, then after 1919 for scriptwriters when the *droits d'auteur* extended to include original film scripts). Later on, in Hollywood, it was mostly the names of scriptwriters which were passed over in silence.[2] In terms of content, Pathé was the first company (as early as 1901) to make crime and erotic films, realising the potential of the pistol and sex-appeal long before Hollywood.

Although the years 1908–10 marked the acme of cinema exports for France, they also marked the beginning of its decline as an industry. The French cinema industry failed to renew its equipment and continued to follow its old, established practices, believing that it could maintain its international monopoly with cheaply produced films. However, by 1914 competition, industrially-speaking, was growing apace especially from the United States, but also from Germany and Sweden. As far as America was concerned, her film industry was both booming and producing the kind of films which the American public wanted, thus eliminating the need for the 'immoral' (i.e., adulterous) French films (Sadoul: 1962, 19). Moreover, the war years witnessed a dramatic shift in the French cinema-goers' taste away from their own national product towards that of the United States. Two factors fed into this apparent 'fickleness' on the part of the French audience. First, most of the genres 'invented' and 'developed by the French prior to the war . . . had been taken over by the Americans' (Abel: 1984, 10). Second, during the war France (mostly Pathé) produced heroic nationalistic films deliberately geared to the war effort. Compounding this effort, the four major companies (Pathé, Gaumont, Eclipse and Eclair) joined with the *Service photographique et cinématographique* in producing weekly newsreels (ibid., 11). Amongst an audience saturated by images of fighting, demand quickly grew for the popular entertainment-packed pre-war genres (now being produced primarily by the Americans). With France's production levels at an all-time low, it was clear that American products would be in a prime position to invade the debilitated market.

That a rejection of nationalistic and patriotic representation should lead to a cultural colonisation is not without its irony. It also indicates, however, that cinematic production is led by supply and demand and this has always been so, at least since World War I. Throughout its subsequent history, this particular 'truth', seemingly overlooked by the industry, will be a crucial factor to France's crises with the cinema-going audience. Conversely, during World War II, almost by way of a reverse irony, a similar revulsion for propagandistic films – this time in the form of German products – culminated in a boycott of cinemas and a demand for French-made products which in turn led to an up-turn for the French film industry

(Sadoul: 1962, 89). All in all, some 220 French feature films were made during the four years of the Occupation (Léglise: 1977, 207). This picture of French cinema's supremacy must be qualified, however, in two ways. In the first instance, by 1942 all Anglo-Saxon films were banned over the whole of the territory. In the second, the German production companies Tobis, UFA and Continental set up a cartel within the occupied zone. This controlled all aspects of the industry so that, effectively, one-third of the French cinema industry became German property (of that cartel, Continental was the biggest producer with thirty films to its name).

This infiltration by others into a nation's industry is a particularly poignant issue when considering cinematic production and points to a contradiction that is a specificity of cinema and to the contradiction that the term 'national cinema' connotes. In other words, cinema is both an industry and an art (in the largest sense of the term). Being an industry, it has to comply with commercial exigencies. If, as a national cinema, it cannot respond to the market forces of supply and demand, then distributors must import to keep exhibitors and audiences satisfied. Thus, the concept of a national cinema becomes quite subsumed within the more important order of capital. France has not escaped this paradoxical positioning: infiltration into her industry first occurred as early as the second decade of its existence.

By the end of the 1920s, France's cinema industry was virtually non-existent. Some reasons have already been pointed to – lack of renewal before World War I and the effect of the War itself – but partial responsibility must lie with the two big majors, Pathé and Gaumont. The first to be hit was Pathé in 1918. Charles Pathé's confidence in the profitability of cinema production had become eroded and, refusing all further financial risk, he sold off (bit by bit) his entire industrial complex, limiting his investment to distribution. Most significantly, he sold off his film stock factory to the American company Eastman-Kodak. Through these measures, he effectively ransomed the future of France's cinematic industrial development and left it victim to the incursions of foreign technology – notably that of the Germans and Americans. Further still, these two industries infiltrated the production and distribution lines as well, setting up their own companies within the country or signing contracts with established French companies. In this respect Gaumont, which was teetering on the brink of financial ruin in 1924, dealt an equally mortuaristic blow to the cinema industry when it merged with MGM. As Richard Abel (1984, 44) puts it, 'the once French giant was now MGM's branch office in Paris'. This relationship lasted for four years. In 1928, Gaumont severed its alliance with MGM and set off on its own to develop its own sound-on-film system. However, being weaker in resources than the American and German magnates, Gaumont found that refining the system was very costly. This in turn rendered it difficult to market the system cheaply enough against its big competitors.

Thus although the first sound film projected in France was actually on Gaumont equipment, sales for its system never took off. Clearly the most immediately dire consequence of this dismantling of the industry was the phenomenal rise in production costs for the French. Equipment and film stock now had to be purchased from the few foreign magnates who, because of their virtual monopoly, could dictate the price.

By 1929, fifteen years after being the leader, France's production had dropped to an all-time low of fifty-two feature films (Abel: 1984, 30). Out of a market of 437 feature films, America contributed 211 and Germany 130 (Léglise: 1977, 207). Throughout the 1920s, then, it was America that dominated and, to a lesser degree, Germany, and not just through imports which, by 1928, were subject to a quota system (an import–export ratio of seven foreign films to one French film was instituted in that year by the Herriot decree). Both countries set up their own production companies in France. Paramount (headed by the charismatic and forceful Robert Kane), which had set up in Paris, made multi-language films with an eye to making a European Hollywood and to maximising on profitability. Tobis, with a studio in Epinay, pursued a more prudent practice and invested in individual French directors with a view to producing quality films rather than the simple rehashes made by Paramount. In the 1930s, Tobis produced some twenty films, including one or two quite prestigious ones – René Clair's *Sous les toits de Paris* and *A nous la liberté* (Sadoul: 1962, 53).

Lack of capital for 'home' products led the industry to depend on outside investment. In the 1920s, this came primarily from Germany and Russian *émigré* money, with some funding coming from America. This, in turn, led to two types of production. Either money was invested in independent producers which allowed them to finance individual film-makers, or capital investment meant signing international agreements to finance co-productions. In the first case, this proved to be beneficial to the cinema in so far as experimentation within (a national) cinema was concerned – because the money mostly funded quality or art cinema, such as Abel Gance's *Napoléon* or Epstein's avant garde films (Abel: 1984, 37) – but disastrous for the industry since no capital was invested in modernising it. In the second case, that of co-productions, the results were equally dire. This time, all pretences to a national cinema were dropped and no strengthening of the industry took place since the foreign co-producers held the purse and equipment strings.

If the 1920s marked the nadir of France's cinematic industry in terms of both economy and production, then the advent of sound in 1929 did little to rescue it from its dire straits. Sound machinery was the province of two foreign magnates – Western (US) and Tobis (Germany) – and cost a fortune. Paradoxically, this initial blow to the industry provided a partial but short-lived reprieve. The industry briefly emerged from its state of crisis because audience taste did not take to sound films in a foreign language or to Paramount's multi-language rehashes or tin-canned medi-ocrity, to rephrase Sadoul (1962, 54).[3] For a few years, French production went up, peaking in 1932 with 157 feature films. But, as Ginette Vincendeau (1985, 52) points out, by the middle of the decade it was clear that, as before, the industry was in serious financial difficulty. This was mostly because of the collapse of the big French companies Gaumont-Franco-Films-Aubert (GFFA) and Pathé-Natan (which had had to consolidate), the withdrawal of Paramount (recalled to America be-cause of financial difficulties resulting from the Depression) and the rapid turnover of small production companies which abounded but which, in many instances, had dubious financial standing and easily went bankrupt.[4] In the early 1930s more than half of the films came out of small production companies (ibid., 48) and during the period 1935–9 there were 102 inde-pendent production companies (ibid., 50).

The fact that dubbing for sound films was not initially in existence constituted another factor accounting for the brief respite from crisis for French cinema. Its introduction in 1932, though not directly linked to production practices in the French film industry, certainly affected exhi-bition practices. In that same year, the double bill was instituted in order to sustain audience numbers and to assuage the effects of the Depression on people's purchasing power (i.e., it represented a response to a demand for better value for money). However, because by law exhibitors could not raise the price of the tickets in line with real costs, the principle of the double bill meant that, effectively, the spectator was paying for only one of the two feature films. Ever the pragmatists, it was evident to distributors that now that American imports were dubbed, these cheaper products – cheaper because they had already paid their way in the States – would regain their former popularity and help fill the bill at little extra cost.[5]

France, it would appear, has been incapable of instituting an effective control to curb what some term the 'cocacolonisation' practice of the United States. If quota systems are imposed, then the Americans find other ways to infiltrate with their products. The problem dates back to the early 1920s: in 1921, 85 per cent of the films screened were imports, but by 1924 that same percentage represented the American share of the market alone (Flitterman-Lewis: 1990, 79). By the time the first quota decree was imposed in 1928 (the Herriot decree), it was already too late as a defensive measure against a country that had obtained such a strong foothold. The advent of sound, with France in no position to respond, merely consoli-dated America's domination. This first example of state intervention, attempted protectionism and limited failure, served as a metonymy for any future legislation aimed at protecting France's industry against America's monopolising tendencies. In 1936, the government fixed the number of American dubbed imports at 150 films; by 1952, the quota was reduced to 110 (Léglise: 1977, 169). A further quota system to protect France's ailing industry was introduced in 1946 and had to do with exhibition practices. In an accord signed between Washington and Paris, the Blum–Byrnes agreements, it was decreed that French exhibitors must screen French-produced films for four weeks out of every thirteen; in 1948, this number was subsequently changed to five weeks out of thirteen. Whilst on paper these two protectionist procedures may appear to have bite, when what happened in practice is considered, a quite different picture emerges.

For a start, there was the first quota strategy – the limits on imports first established in 1928. In this respect, it is relevant to recall that immediately after World War I, there was a boom in cinema-building. The exhibitors knew that they could make money as a result of the huge escalation in American imports and thanks to access to a larger audience due to increased leisure time, as working hours were reduced to an eight-hour day over five and a half days (Abel: 1984, 55). Thus, with a potential growth in cinema audience and a plethora of films with which to entertain them, a three-year cinema construction programme was undertaken which doubled the number of cinemas. Once the quota system was in place (1928), however, it was clear that distributors were going to experience difficulties catering for the number of cinemas because insufficient French films were produced to fill the shortfall. Some figures (albeit not complete) will help to illustrate their dilemma.[6]

Year	Number of cinemas	Number of films	
		French	Imports
1918	1,444	53	530
1920	2,400	101	no figures found
1925	no figures found	73	573
1929	4,200	52	385
1937	3,700	134	290

The quota system led to a situation where there were less products and yet, conversely, more screens. Showing the same products for longer periods of time in multiple places would necessarily lead to cinemas running out of potential audiences. (There are no statistics on audience attendance over this period, since this practice only began during the 1930s. However, if the period after World War II – when a very similar pattern was in place – is used as a guide, it can be assumed that there was a loss of audience and thus of revenue.) In the end, therefore, this particular form of protectionism did not profit the industry.

With regard to the second form of protectionism, exhibition quotas, it could be argued (as does Sadoul: 1962, 101) that although the status of the celluloid war was far from felicitous during the inter-war years, at least it was more advantageous through its protectionism than in 1946. France's industry after 1945 was in a poor state and there was a dearth of producers which led to studios closing. It was in these circumstances that the Blum–Byrnes accord was signed, lifting the quota system and replacing it with the screen quota system. But, as with the 1920s, France was incapable of producing enough films. She had to build up her industry again in the face of mounting prices, and above all, she was incapable of producing films as cheaply as the United States because her home market was (and still is) not big enough to pay off the costs. Furthermore, after five years of deprivation, audience preference was for American films which came as a great relief after the gloom of the Occupation (1947 was the peak year for audience attendance, at 424 million). The craze was such that the American distributors threw all that they had on the market 'including turkeys'.[7] In a few months, American competition threatened the extinction of French film production. In 1946, the United States brought in 400 films for 4,000 cinemas, thus in a way returning to figures of the late 1920s (see p. 25) with the one big difference that the double bill was no longer in existence, having been banned for exigency's sake in 1940. In the period 1946–7, 70 per cent of the films shown in France were American which led, according to Sadoul (1948, 94–5), to the following threat to the indigenous industry:

> Between 1936 and 1946, the French film was protected by the so-called quota system . . . Here we come to the chief cause of the present crisis, the agreement signed at Washington [Blum–Byrnes accord] . . . which did away with the old system and replaced it by a screen quota . . . Whereas for over 10 years, French screens had shown French films in a proportion exceeding 50 per cent, about 75 per cent of the takings benefitting the national industry in 1938, the Washington agreements fixed a legal quota of 31 per cent . . .
>
> After a lapse of two years, the results of the agreement became apparent. The proportion of French films shown in French picture theatres has dropped to 38 per cent, while American films received over half the takings falling to the producer's share.

While Sadoul may be overextolling the merits of the pre-war quota system – in 1936 and the subsequent two years, for example, France produced one-third of the total number of films released for general exhibition – he is right in stating categorically that the new quota system did little to enable a struggling industry to get back on to its feet. It is worth noting that in the peak year of audience attendance, 1947, only seventy-four French films were produced. Thanks to pressure from lobbying groups (*Comités de la défense du cinéma français*) and demonstrations by actors in the big Paris boulevards, in 1948 the government repealed the existing accord. They reinstituted the film import quota (120 dubbed films from America) and increased the screen quota for French films from four to five weeks out of every thirteen. Last, but not least, they introduced a special fund for the French cinema industry, the *Fonds spécial d'aide temporaire*. By 1950, French receipts were once again above 50 per cent (France had produced 107 films and imported 100 dubbed films from the United States), proving that these measures were effective. In addition, audience taste had once again swung back in favour of its nation's own products (Sadoul: 1962, 103).

Although ever since the celluloid war began some seventy years ago viewers' predilection for French or American cinema has varied over the years, none the less figures show that in the main France's film industry has managed to sustain a 50 per cent return on its production (Bonnell: 1989, 104). It would seem, therefore, that the issue of quantity may not be the key question to address, but rather the issue of economies of scale. For France's industry to be viable, it needs an audience of around 450 million, a figure not even nearly attained since 1957 and unlikely, given the demographic decline and ageing population, to be achieved again. What does emerge from an overview of the swings in fortune of France's industry is that about every twenty years it is grossly disadvantaged when compared against American products. Thus, after the two World Wars and again since 1986, the imbalance in favour of the United States has been in the order of 60 per cent of the market to France's 40 per cent (ibid., 106). As has already been pointed out, in the case of the first two periods, supply and demand were key factors. With regard to this latest period (post-1986), the same story holds true with a slight qualification where demand is concerned. The present tendency is for audience frequentation to concentrate around a smaller number of films (often American blockbusters). Demand, then, is more precise. In terms of distribution, as in 1920, it is the same old story of pocket-book management, with distributors and exhibitors having an eye to profit. Thus, since 1986 there has been a marked increase in the buying of foreign films – especially American films (going from 115 in 1975 to 150 in 1988) – because they are thought to be more competitive than the national product (ibid., 105).

This quixotic battle with the United States, therefore, has not changed much in character since its beginning. On the one hand, America has its official quota and, on the other, all exhibitors in France have to obey (in principle) the screening quota. However, throughout the seventy-year war, with the exception of a ten-year gap (1935–45), the United States has managed to get round both these forms of protectionism by infiltrating through their 'nationally' based companies – a practice that is still ongoing and unlikely to cease even with the advent of the single European market. Thus films which appear French in fact have American distributors (in 1976, for example, up to 40 per cent of the films distributed in France were by American companies).[8] There is, however, a paradox. France has a vested interest in maintaining at least a parity with the United States for the very good reason that the latter, like all film companies exhibiting in France, has to pay a tax to assist the French film industry. In force since 1948 when the first *Loi d'aide au cinéma* was instituted, this tax (*soutien automatique*) is automatically levied on all cinema ticket receipts at the box-office and goes into the *Fonds de soutien* or *Compte de soutien* (as this state subvention to cinema production is currently called). The more successful French cinema is, therefore, the less the United States pays and, the greater that success, the more demands are placed on the *Fonds de soutien* by French production companies, which in turn further weakens the financing of production.

France's uneasy relationship with the United States has been even further aggravated by the advent of the Common Market (EEC) and nowhere more evidently than in the area of co-production. According to EEC law, where multinationals are concerned, the subsidiary companies that they have established in an EEC country are considered to be of that particular country. In other words, previously films that were produced in France for French consumption but made by American companies counted as an American product but were not subject to the import quota. Now, however, an American subsidiary in France and its product will be seen as French. Thus a subsidiary film production company can lay claim to the same advantages from the *Fonds de soutien* as a French production company. An example cited by Claude Degan (1974, 12) will serve to explain how this works. It concerns *Last Tango in Paris* (Bertolucci, 1972). This film was co-produced by an Italian firm (60 per cent) and a French subsidiary of the American company United Artists (40 per cent); it was then distributed by United Artists in France and on the company's world-wide circuit. This firm then received its share of the receipts made in France (both as producer and distributor), its share of the *Fonds de soutien*, plus 40 per cent of receipts made in the other world markets.[9]

It is ironic that the first to benefit from EEC legislation are the multi-nationals and not the national industries proper, who are stuck within the structures of their respective countries. But, apart from the depletion of resources away from 'truly French' products, there are other more cultural consequences, which also touch upon this concept of a truly national cinema. The free-market policy advocated by the EEC is quite capable of causing the disappearance of smaller independent production companies, enabling the stronger, major French and American companies to take over. Such a cartel could eliminate the artisanal cinema so identified as a specificity of French national cinema. Equally, large, vertically integrated companies in a dominant position could mark a return to the more consolidated system that existed in the French film industry before World War I, the very collapse of which led to the never-ending state of crisis within which the industry incessantly finds itself. Financially unempowered against the majors, small production companies will have to go for low-budget productions (not always a bad thing), leaving the top pickings of renowned actors and directors to the big guys. American majors are even more formidable competitors for talent than the French ones because they have the means to finance ambitious projects and thus to tempt directors and actors over to America to make their films (Louis Malle and Jean-Jacques Annaud being two current prime examples within the field of directors). Naturally, this 'cultural and economic vassalisation' (Bonnell: 1989, 269) is not just a problem for France, but for the whole of the EEC. However, it is worth pointing out how yet again we are confronted with a familiar pattern: a repetition of the self-same silver-screen drain to the United States which occurred after both World Wars (and during the Occupation, albeit at that time for very different reasons).

American co-productions are also possibly a larger threat to the specificity of a national cinema than any European co-production. The success of American cinema is due to the fact that its stories are based on universal themes or narratives – adventure, action and grand passions – a practice followed in an effort to erase cultural differences within the American public (which remains its main audience after all). This melting-pot approach is hardly consonant with Europe's sense of cultural pluralism, let alone France's fierce pride in her own culture. For example, is *Adèle H.*, directed by Truffaut but produced by United Artists, a story about a specifically French woman's passionate, but doomed love for a man who spurns her? Is it the sad tale of the daughter of France's 'most famous writer'? Or is it the story of a fatal attraction the like of which resurfaces just as easily in a 100 per cent American production (*Fatal Attraction*, Adrian Lyne, 1987)?

American film products, be they imports or co-productions, will never cease to be viewed ambivalently from both a cultural and an economic point of view by the French. As early as the 1920s, there was concern expressed that French co-productions were imitating the 'American way of life' (Abel: 1984, 38). Again, in the 1930s there was 'talk of the Western peril', of the American influence on France's youth who seemed to 'desire life to be more or less as in the films'.[10] For the American companies, the European market is and always has been perceived as a fruitful one to exploit for profit. Fears of a cultural takeover, of the establishment of American hegemony which then becomes naturalised (who doesn't drink Coca-Cola?) may well need to be expressed. In the seventy years to date, however, such a takeover has never occurred. What can be said is that in countries with a national cinema, there tend to be two poles of distribution and frequentation – the national cinema and the American one. If the American one is as successful as it is abroad, it is because its narratives appeal to large audiences, and because of the efficiency of its distribution network which has been strongly in place in France and elsewhere in Europe since the 1920s.

In return, since that same period France's distribution practices have been the weakest component of her film industry. Poor investment has always been the dominant factor quoted for its failure to export well, especially to the American market. But the alternating face of the French distribution network must also be pointed to as a factor. Over the past seventy years, this aspect of the industry has been seesawed between two extremes. At times, it has been made up of an overabundance of small companies – all independent of one another – which has led, on the one hand, to lack of co-ordination and, on the other, to poor financing of the distribution project. Conversely, at other times it has been very centralised in the hands of a few who, because they know the foreign market is a very small one, will in the main content themselves with nationwide distribution (which they control through their cinema chains) and invest little into overseas exploitation. Having said this, it must be noted that France is, and has been since World War II, the second exporter of films after the United States. Furthermore, America is the second market for French films (Germany is her first). Finally, France is the first producer of films in Europe. Even if all the advice of the pundits were followed (greater investment, better distribution practices through an understanding of the American modalities, dubbing all exports, etc.), there is no evidence to suggest that matters would be improved.

What history does tell us is that the greatest export successes always come as a surprise and that, with regard to exports to the United States, the tendency is for just one film per year really to take off – and not necessarily the one expected to do so. *La Cage aux folles* (Edouard Molinaro, 1978 and two sequels) is an excellent case in point (although there is a slight sting to the tale/tail in that it was produced by the French branch of United Artists). Usually the French cinema that does really well at the box-office in France – her comedy films for instance – is unsellable in the United States. *La Cage aux folles*, which is a comedy-vaudeville film about drag queens, is one such film that, to all intents and purposes, should have bombed. It didn't. In New York alone it was on for a nineteen-month exclusive run. What this says about the universality of camp I leave the reader to ponder.

France's distribution practices for films cannot be held up as the sole perpetrator of her poor export record. Ever since the 1920s, American distributors have been unkeen to facilitate their promotion (Abel: 1984, 42). Possessing a plethora of their own products, they have no need for or interest in foreign ones. Accordingly, in the period 1920–5, no more than a dozen foreign films were screened annually (ibid., 42). Ironically, after World War II and in the 1950s, when French films were growing in popularity once more with American audiences, exhibition resources did not permit their full exploitation (Meadow: 1947, 24). Due to a lack of 'suitable' theatres (i.e., intimate theatres with 300–400 seats of which, in 1947, there were only twelve in America nationwide), French films could not be screened at the rate of their importation (about fifty annually).

To return to economies of scale, it is clear why France cannot really hope to improve on her takings from America (which have stood for a long time between 10 and 12 per cent of her total earnings). Insufficient outlets (there are still only a handful of cities – New York, Boston, Los Angeles, Washington DC, Chicago and San Francisco – and the university circuit 'suited' for foreign films) and the other prohibitive expense of bringing out a film in the United States (so that an American distributor would think twice about investing in a film whose potential for economic return is very limited) are the two major stumbling blocks that look unlikely to disappear. If one takes into account that the 1950s were considered by American distributors to be the heyday for foreign film imports in the United States, with some mere twelve films per year doing well, then the fact that now only two or three succeed annually should confirm, if needs be, that America is a no-growth market area.[11]

PRODUCTION PRACTICES AND DISTRIBUTION

For the most part, economic exigencies and not aesthetic considerations have dictated production practices. However, cinema, paradoxically poised as it is between industry and art, quite naturally generates its own paradoxes. In this respect, economic exigencies (in the form of downswings) do entail, at brief intervals, a 'supremacy' of the aesthetic over the economic, when artisanal and auteur cinemas flourish in the face of constraint.

The dominant pattern to emerge, not surprisingly, is one of duopolistic alternation. Production is alternately centralised and decentralised; studios are in and out of utilisation; co-productions are alternately on the increase or decrease. This mercurial, not to say heterodoxical reality also affects what is produced. Thus, there will be quite large fluctuations in the number of films produced either from year to year or between longer time-spans. Given that the golden mean for production numbers is around 113 films per annum (a quota self-imposed by the industry in the 1930s) it is worth pointing out that, over the period 1930–90, that figure has been achieved or surpassed only 38 per cent of the time.

The acknowledged pioneering spirits where production and distribution practices are concerned are, first, Charles Pathé and second, Léon Gaumont. By the early 1900s, both had created and developed their companies into the major representatives of the cinema industry, in 1902 and 1905 respectively. The ranks of these two majors were joined in 1907 by a third company, Eclair and in 1908 a fourth, Eclipse. In these early years, each company contributed significantly to the development of the industry in terms of equipment, studios, cinema theatres and of course the film product itself. Pathé and Gaumont were the biggest investors covering all four developments. Eclair and Eclipse, because they were smaller and had less resources, concerned themselves primarily with the areas of studios (Eclair set up studios in France and the United States) and production. Pathé and Gaumont showed no inclination to monopolise the market but chose rather to co-exist alongside the smaller companies (Abel: 1984, 8). In terms of a national cinema culture, this synergy was a healthy sign, allowing as it did for full exploitation of the market in France and abroad. Few would dispute that this magnanimity was in direct correlation to a booming market. For, as it turned out some sixty years later on, in the face of a diminishing market these two greats were not incapable of consolidating into a virtual cartel to protect their interests.

The Pathé Frères company was first established in 1896. Prior to this time, Charles Pathé had already created a profitable business in the production of phonographic cylinders, eventually setting up a retail shop in Vincennes (1894). Fascinated by emerging technology, he subsequently turned his attention to the Edison Kinetoscope which he reproduced and adapted both to shoot and screen film (D'Hugues and Marmin: 1986, 31). By 1895, he was ready to launch into the cinema business in a big way and by 1897, he had extended his premises in Vincennes to include film laboratories and studios. This period coincides with Léon Gaumont's entry into the same arena. With a background in photographic equipment, he was quick to move into camera manufacturing and launched his first prototype – Bioscope Demenÿ – in 1895. Shortly afterwards, he set up (albeit on a smaller scale) his own studios in Belleville under the direction of Alice Guy.

It was Pathé, around 1902, who first saw the profitability of renting rather than selling films outright and so revolutionised distribution practices whilst simultaneously increasing his business figures tenfold (Bonnell: 1989, 89 and Abel: 1984, 8).[12] In a very brief period (1902–8), he established outlets all over the world (including India) and opened up a factory and a studio in the United States. Similarly, Gaumont – close on the heels of his precursor – set up branches far and wide abroad. By 1907, both Pathé and Gaumont were the leading production and distribution companies with, as their only rival, the *Agence générale cinématographique* (AGC), which chiefly distributed the films of Eclair, Eclipse and the smaller production company *Film d'Art*. The latter was launched in 1908 and, as its name connotes, it made exclusively 'cultural' films (Abel: 1984, 9). A measure of the scope of Pathé and Gaumont's success at this time can be seen in their confident investment in the construction of studios in Paris and elsewhere (in Nice and Marseilles) and in the building of large cinema theatres on the *grands boulevards* of Paris (and subsequently in the provinces).[13] The first of these was Omnia-Pathé (1906) with 1,000 seats, but the prime example of this manifestation of confidence on a truly grand scale was Gaumont Palace, built in 1910, with 5,000 seats.

Ten years later, everything had changed. What had been a homogeneous national cinema culture was now dissolute. The majors had lost all confidence in the production side of the industry: they retrenched, sold off or merged. It was now the turn of the American products to push, encourage even, French distributors (including the majors) to build the large, luxury cinemas that had formerly housed their own products. Mostly, these theatres were built on the *grands boulevards* alongside the great department stores and there is perhaps a certain irony attached to this practice (both before and after World War I) in that it may well have set the precedent for that practice still in effect today of placing cinema theatres in the commercial areas of towns and cities. This practice may have been suited to the earlier times of film exhibition, but over the last thirty years, it has proved to be a contributory factor to declining audiences.

Measured against nearly a century of French cinema's history, the halcyon days of synergistic harmony between the majors and the smaller companies were short-lived. What followed was a series of troughs and peaks for the majors which had seemingly direct consequences for the small independent companies. Each low profited the latter and each high the former. Thus, periods of retrenchment or dissolution enabled the emergence of even more independents. For example, in the 1930s, before the demise of Pathé and Gaumont (GFFA), 'half the French films . . . came out of small independent production companies' (Vincendeau: 1985, 47). After this demise, during the period 1935–9, on average 90 per cent of the French films were produced by small French companies, with the rest by German production companies either acknowledged (Tobis) or camou-flaged (ACE, the French subsidiary for the German company UFA).[14] Another example, more contemporaneous this time: during the 1980s, independent production companies doubled in size over the number in existence in the 1950s, from an average of 500 in the 1950s to one of 900 in the 1980s (Bonnell: 1989, 55).

The 1950s saw the majors back on top, but by the 1980s the Pathé-Gaumont cartel (established in 1969 in the light of another period of decentralisation and fragmentation of the industry during the 1960s) had been dissolved. This was done in 1982 by an act of government deliberately intended to give greater access to the market for independents (producers and exhibitors alike). At that time, three large production companies monopolised distribution and exhibition: UGC-France (originally state-owned but subsequently privatised in 1971) with about 20 per cent of the market, Parafrance (linked with Paramount) with 5 per cent, and Pathé-Gaumont with 30 per cent. The rest was shared by independent exhibitor-distributors struggling to survive on the smaller circuits. The government, conscious that concentration of distribution in the hands of a few represents a danger to production, passed the decree in the belief that the French film industry is at its healthiest when an equitable balance permits the coexistence between majors and small to medium-sized distributors. This time, therefore, state intervention brought about what happened more 'organically' in the 1930s. It may well be that this action was enlightened in its thinking; however, if more independents were enabled by this policy, there is very little evidence, in the cinema of the 1980s, of the 'quality' product which Jack Lang (the then Minister of Culture) was seeking.

It is relatively easy to see why there are so many independents in France, even at a time when the majors are in a dominant position. Major producers are unlikely to back unknowns or risky projects because of the uncertainty of the outlays and the returns. Studio costs are high and have been so at least since World War II. Location shooting, though once quite cheap, is currently as expensive as using the studio (because of all the hidden costs, the difficulty in renting suitable apartments and traffic congestion). In general, the cost of making a film has risen tenfold since the late 1960s. Considering that the return on receipts has only risen fivefold over the same period, it is hardly surprising that caution is exercised by the producers and that they tend to opt for established names (Bonnell: 1989, 62). The more a film costs, the greater the tendency to go for those with the best reputations. In response to this vicious circle, which has been in place since at least the 1950s (and been in evidence since the 1930s), film-makers and independent producers have set up their own production companies with varying success as already noted.

Restrictive and regressive practices on the part of the majors, therefore, affect both the economics and the aesthetics of the industry. A no-risk policy leads to stagnation, making it difficult for new talent to emerge. An overabundance of production companies means first, that there is not enough money to go round – in 1988, of the 900 production companies in existence, only 163 either produced or co-produced a film (ibid., 56) – and second, that consequently the quality of the product can suffer due to lack of finance.

If the only certainty of France's cinema industry is its very uncertainty, its precariousness has, paradoxically, produced some remarkable moments in its history – moments which have occurred primarily during periods of decentralisation (when the majors have been neither vertically integrated nor in a quasi-monopoly situation). Ever since the first wave of decentralisation in the 1920s, the pattern pursued has been one of 'entrepreneurial independence and artisan- or atelier-based praxis' (Abel: 1984, 37). Without taking a voluntarist approach, it is not difficult to observe that the first wave of decentralisation of the mid- to late 1920s coincides with the experimental and avant-garde films of the likes of Germaine Dulac, Marie

Epstein and Jean Epstein (among others); the second wave, in the second half of the 1930s, with the Poetic Realist films exemplified by the directors Jean Renoir and Marcel Carné (again, among others); the third wave, in the late 1950s, with the films of the New Wave auteur directors; and the fourth wave, in the 1980s, with the postmodern anti-elitist and anti-intellectual works of such film-makers as Luc Besson, Jean-Jacques Beineix and Colinne Serreau. Naturally, this vitality of experimentation and risk-taking is not without its Oedipal consequences. Each wave has 'aggressed' the prevailing cinema of the period, the *cinéma de papa* (as the New Wave termed it), either by deconstructing and subverting existing codes and conventions or, quite literally, by removing the older generation (making it impossible for them to continue to make films because of their *passéisme*).

Uncertainty for the industry also means uncertainty for the studios, whose history has been just as peripatetic as that of the rest of the industry. Their fluctuating fortunes have been dictated not just by the vagaries of economics but also by advances in technology and, of course, by the reality of two World Wars. In the early years, France's industry could boast nine studios of which two were based in Nice, the rest in the Paris region. By the mid-1940s there were thirteen studios with forty sets. This number of sets rose to forty-nine by the mid-1950s but declined to nineteen by the beginning of the 1970s. Today there are only seven studios remaining (six in the Paris region and one in Nice), but investment in the mid-1980s has brought the number of sets back up to around thirty.

Decentralising practices have not necessarily been the cause of the decline in studio use, however. With the exception of the New Wave, the after-effects of which were effectively responsible for the closing down of numerous studios, periods of decentralisation have brought about a greater accessibility to studios rather than the reverse.[15] For example, in the mid-1930s, the liquidation of the two great film trusts, Pathé and Gaumont, 'stimulated the independent producers to greater achievements. Instead of hampering such producers, these two ex-producing organisations now help[ed] them by putting studio, technical services and cinema circuits at their disposal' (Rose: 1937, 71). Thus the collapse of the major commercial studios at that time in point of fact facilitated France's art cinema. Independent producer-directors could make their films, loosely banded under the label of the Poetic Realism school, and, despite their small number, they none the less re-established France's cinematic reputation, lost since the advent of World War I.

This happy state of affairs contrasts quite starkly, thanks to a shift in union practices, with what occurred after World War II when the majors were back in ascendancy but studios, once again, were in decline (by 1952, studios were under utilised by 60 per cent). Pre-World War II and during the Poetic Realist period, unions for the most part refused to adopt the five-day week introduced by the government of the *Front populaire*. Their objections to this socially positive legislation were that it would impose too many limitations on their film-making practices. In the 1950s, however, attitudes reversed. Although new technology in the form of faster film stock did have its role to play, it was primarily the restrictive practices of the unions that were responsible for the decline in studio use, the cost of which was rendered prohibitive on two counts: first, because studios required specialised technicians, and second, because union laws stipulated a five-day week for studio work (as opposed to a six-day week for location shooting).[16] As a result, the look of French cinema changed. Out on location, surrounded by natural decor and lighting, the camera provided a documentary look to the film. In the early 1950s, the Côte d'Azur, the Arrière Pays and the Mediterranean, for evident reasons of lighting consistency, became popular locations with film-makers and around one-third of France's annual production was shot in these areas.[17] These production practices were in place in the early 1930s (one thinks immediately of Renoir's *Toni*, 1934), although it must be stressed that at that time, they were very much in the minority. Given the increased scale of these practices in the 1950s and, because of the widespread nature of the change in style, it is clear that they would have an impact on film narrative. Indeed, eventually this look culminated in the work of the New Wave directors where almost inevitably films became style- rather than scenario-led.

Repeatedly, we have seen how production practices affect the concept of national cinema. Changes in its specificities have been as much for socioeconomic reasons as for aesthetic ones, a factor which in turn raises the complex issue of what is national. As has already been pointed out, nowhere is this more clear than in the case of co-productions, the last area that needs to be discussed in relation to production practices.

Ever since their inception, co-productions have been a necessity due to the non-viability of the industry's economy. Thus, in both post-World War periods, numerous co-production agreements were signed. But, and here comes the first of several paradoxes, they have always been very costly affairs both in themselves and to the nation's industry. In the first instance co-produced films cost on average twice as much as films that are entirely French. In the second, because investment in the promotion of co-productions is far greater than that for French films (more money is fronted by virtue of the films' very expensiveness), the tendency is for them to take more of the receipts than purely French-made film (up to three times as much). It will be recalled that the *Fonds de soutien* depends for a large part of its resources on a percentage levy on the box-office receipts and that, based on this initial round of receipts, a producer is entitled to an automatic loan for his or her new production or co-production. In other words, money levied on a co-production gets ploughed back into yet another co-production. For some twenty-nine years, up until 1967, any co-production company, as long as it included a 'French' company and the film's original version was French, was entitled to this state subsidy. As we have seen, the Americans took full advantage of this production incentive. In 1967, a new decree legislated that for a film to receive this aid it must be at least 50 per cent French-produced. However, the decree can easily be circumvented. So to this first, financial paradox we must add another, this time created by protectionist practices. By trying to preserve (through subsidies) France's national cinema against the onslaught of the Americans, the state effectively perpetuated the former's vulnerability to the latter. More recently the situation has changed again, this time with co-productions in tandem with television companies representing the greatest problem for France's national cinema.

It is in this murky area of co-productions, especially when they are the predominant production practice, that the identity of a national cinema becomes confused – as was the case in the 1920s and in the 1960s. In the 1920s, international co-productions (mainly with Germany) became necessary in an attempt to rival Hollywood. However, because they were costly, these 'prestige' productions 'threatened to monopolise the production capital and energy of the French film industry' (Abel: 1984, 35). In effect, this style of protectionism is one that backfires, eroding as it does both the economic and, equally important, the national in France's national cinema. It is not just the loss of the specificity of a national identity that such practices can entail. As can be deduced from the other peak period of co-productions from the late 1950s to the early 1970s – when, at times, co-productions outnumbered films of French origin[18] – the pursuance of these practices also caused a loss of small- to medium-budget films which are the mainstay and hallmark of the French national cinema. This erosion of style, which such a drop in national output represents, is further compounded by the fact that, given the high costs involved, the tendency is not to engage new talent in the form of film-makers or actors, which results in a lack of renovation and innovation.

The decline in co-productions, coming as it did in the mid-1970s, had little to do with deliberate strategy. France's major co-producing partner was Italy. The two countries had a reciprocal arrangement (for every co-production made in France, one was made in Italy). This marriage of convenience lasted almost thirty years (1948–75) and its ending, or rather decline, came as the result of a third party's intrusion on the scene. By the mid-1970s both France and Italy, but particularly Italy, were feeling the full impact of a declining audience seduced away from the large screen by its smaller rival, the television.

Irrespective of the fact that the state's protectionist measures (be they with regard to co-productions or quota systems) produced mixed results, it remains the case that, all its faults notwithstanding, state aid has enabled France to protect her cinema more successfully than any of her European counterparts of similar demographic size, and it is to matters of state aid and intervention that I shall now turn.

STATE INTERVENTION: ISSUES OF AID, TAXATION AND CENSORSHIP

Let us take a maxim – 'what the state gives with one hand it takes away with the other' – and see if it applies to the story of state intervention in the French cinema industry. Before doing so, let us also insert a couple of paradoxical realities that aptly sum up the present status and organisation of the industry. The first paradox is a straightforward one: ever since World War II, France's cinema, more than that of any other Western country, has been at the receiving end of state aid and legislation intended to facilitate its growth. Yet the more it receives, the less productive it becomes, both in terms of film output and in terms of generating income by increasing audience numbers. The second paradox is slightly more complex because of its originating point. During the Occupation and Vichy period, a considerable amount of legislation was introduced to advance the position of cinema as a state-protected institution and to establish the foundations of the cinematographic industry. The legacy of these measures remains with the industry today. That a repressive regime should put in place a framework which in many respects enhanced the industry is not without its irony. This irony becomes compounded when one considers that most of these measures had been conceived of but never implemented during the Third Republic and, most especially, during the period when the *Front populaire* was in power. It is a sad testimony to immobilism that it took the death of the Republic, which is what the installation of the Vichy government meant, to make possible a rationalisation of the industry which effectively improved its production practices (through better and more systematised working practices) and for the first time in its history placed it more securely under state protection.

It is convenient to consider the history of state intervention in terms of two epochs and styles: the lighter touch of the pre-1940 epoch and the more systematised control of the post-1940 one. In the pre-1940 epoch the lightest aspect of state intervention was in the area of aid, that is to say it was all but non-existent until the mid-1930s. Censorship, with one or two exceptions, was quite liberal and light-handed. The heaviest touch came, not unpredictably, with taxation on the industry.

I shall deal with the question of censorship first and then examine the lengthier issues of tax and aid. Officially, in the pre-1940 epoch, there was no censorship. Before World War I, the control of exhibition and theatrical performances was vested in local authorities by virtue of an 1864 decree. A further law, of 1888, vested in police and local authorities the right to proscribe films with scenes that were prejudicial to public order and that might offend. In 1919, a visa system was introduced with a central *Commission de contrôle* (set up by the Ministry of the Interior), but local authorities still maintained their right to ban films and did so – Griffith's *Birth of a Nation* and, more pertinently, *Intolerance* being but two examples (Léglise: 1970, 65). The Herriot decree of 1928 replaced the 1919 decree with a view to strengthening the power of the commission and limiting that of the local authorities. It met with mixed success since authorities, especially in the south-east region of France, still persisted in exacting their 1864 proscription rights. The primary targets for control were as always foreign imports, but not primarily American products, as one might at first expect. The 'real brunt of censorship was borne by the Soviet films . . . [and] after the Rightist victory in the 1928 elections, the ban on Soviet films became total' (Abel: 1984, 40) – a foretaste of the Cold War of the 1950s, if there ever was one (although the Soviet films were screened in private venues).[19] During this period, then, the two major exceptions to the light-touch approach were local authority censorship and film censorship operating indirectly as a means of limiting imports.

In this inter-war period, official control over the film industry fluctuated between different ministerial bodies. At first the Ministry of the Interior had sole control, then the Ministry of Fine Arts had the upper hand, and later still the Ministry of Education (Léglise: 1970, 65). During the Occupation, this control passed into the hands of the military and was placed under the jurisdiction of the General Secretary for Information and Propaganda. As one would anticipate, during this period of war, censorship was at its tightest. Two censoring bodies were established – one, Vichyite, for the 'Free Zone', the other, German, for the Occupied Zone (*Propagandastaffel*). Their remit was to censor not just films but scripts as well. The films of that period reflect the effect of censorship in that, with a few exceptions, most of them are far removed from reality, dealing mostly with melodramas (including historical melodramas) (Léglise: 1977, 18).[20] For the first time in French cinema history, cinema critics also contributed to this repression (the most notorious of whom was François Vinneuil, the *nom-de-plume* for Lucien Rebatet, of the Fascist *Je suis partout*).

As might be expected, the aftermath of the war inherited some of the censorial measures put in place during that period. The military relinquished its control of the censoring of films (although during the Algerian crisis, the military once again acted as a censoring agent – albeit indirectly), but censorship remained an affair of state. A censorship board, the *Commission de contrôle des films*, was established in July 1945 with the main objective of preventing 'publications contrary to good morals, or liable to disturb public order' (ibid., 151). Composed of various ministerial representatives, it was dependent, at first directly and subsequently indirectly – after its re-creation through the *Centre national de la cinématographie* established in 1946 – on the Minister of Industry and Commerce, who had the power of veto over the Commission. Overall tutelage and control of the visa remained with the Minister of Information. Pre-censorship was maintained, and film scripts were still submitted to a commission, the *Commission d'autorisation de tournage*. The policy for the protection of minors, first introduced in 1941, was also retained, but the age limit concerned was reduced from 18 to 15 years of age. Subsequently, in 1961, two visas were introduced for the protection of minors, with age limits of 13 and 18 years. Post-censorship, in the form of local authority bans, still prevailed. Some local authorities even extended their powers to imposing their own age limits for the protection of minors and in some areas, although boys of 16 were admitted, girls under 21 were forbidden access to cinema theatres screening 'unsuitable' films (ibid., 33).

The 1950s and 1960s were periods of tight censorship equal to that of the Occupation. The explanation lies, again, with the issues of war and political instability. These years were initially marked by France's impotence in dealing with the problems of her declining empire, first in Indo-China, then in Algeria. They were subsequently tainted by her inability to come to terms with the aftermath of losing that empire. The two peak years for proscribing films were 1952 (with fourteen films) and 1960 (ten films) – years that coincide with moments of tremendous political turmoil. The instability of the early 1950s was manifest in the typically short-lived governments (as was the case for the lifetime of the Fourth Republic). The year 1952 coincided with the return of the Radicals and the conservatives to power under the prime ministership of the former Vichyite, Antoine Pinay. The Pinay cabinet marked a swing to the Right and an important stage in the rehabilitation of ex-Vichyites.

The other date, 1960, is also quite crucial, but for different political reasons. By then, the Algerian war had reached a critical stage and the outcome was far from clear. De Gaulle wanted to find a political solution. Meanwhile, the French army in Algeria was on the one hand, up in arms in an attempted revolt against his proposals, and on the other, fighting the 'rebel' Algerians. Small surprise, therefore, that 1952 and 1960 were the tightest years censorship-wise, the first because of the radical swing to the Right, the second because of its critical positioning within the history of the Franco-Algerian conflict. However, this does not mean that censorship was not heavily in place at all other times over this two-decade period – quite the opposite. During the eight-year war with Algeria (1954–62), not a single film on the Algerian question was granted a visa (Vautier's *Afrique 50* of 1955 was banned and his *L'Algérie en flammes*, though made in 1958, was not screened officially until 1972). In the 1960s, films which tried to address this conflict, or the role of the army in any context, were again effectively blocked. To quote the two most famous examples, Pontecorvo's *La Bataille d'Alger*, made in 1966 and winner of the *Lion d'Or* at the Venice Film Festival, was not screened until 1970 and Godard's *Le Petit soldat*, made in 1960 about army torture, was not screened until 1963 after the Algerian conflict was over.

Not until 1969 was censorship transferred from the Ministry of Information (abolished in that year) to the Ministry for Cultural Affairs (this ministry was created in 1959 and André Malraux was its first minister), and some of the other draconian measures were not removed until the mid-1970s (censorship was 'officially' abolished in 1974 by Giscard d'Estaing). Since then, the visa has been granted by the Minister for Culture, who makes a decision based on the advice of the *Commission de contrôle des films*, whose function is purely consultative. There are four categories of visa: one for the general public, one forbidding under-13s, another under-18s and last but not least the 'X' certificate, which again applies to under-18s. The pre-censorship of scripts has been abrogated. Conversely, the laws of 1864 and 1888 are still in effect today and local authorities and police continue to be empowered to ban films thought liable to disrupt public order. After a thirty-year period (1940–70), during which time censorship was on an ascending curve, this particular aspect of state intervention has returned to the lighter touch of pre-war years with one exception – the introduction of the protection of minors. The other aspects of state inter-vention – taxation and aid – have had very different trajectories.

Taxation on receipts was first instituted in 1916 in the form of a gradu-ated tax on receipts to aid the war effort. After the war ended, the state saw little reason to drop it, so it was retained as a national tax on entertainment (ranging from 17 to 40 per cent depending on the product) with the revenue going directly into the Treasury's coffers. Not until 1935 did the government change its policy and rechannel this tax (which by this time ranged from 20 to 25 per cent) to assist the ailing industry.

It was at this juncture (1935) that the state perceived the need for a consolidation of the industry's operations. Doubtless this imperative for coherence was directly related to the fact that the state was investing in the industry. A threat made by the *Conseil national économique* (in 1935) to place the industry under state control had its desired effect. By 1936, the French cinema industry had gathered into a single organisation, the *Confédération générale du cinéma* (CGC), which grouped together all the employers' branches (production, distribution, exhibition and technicians) and represented the industry in its dealings with the government. Apart from constituting a first real endeavour at corporate control – the two previous bodies, the *Office national du cinématographe* (1927) and the *Conseil supérieur du cinéma* (1931) had had little effect in centralising/rationalising the industry – one of its objectives was to establish general statistics concerning the industry. This meant collating figures on output, costs and audience viewing patterns – a practice still ongoing today, but now under the auspices of a government-appointed body, the *Centre cinématographique français* (instituted in 1946).

In the post-1940 epoch, taxation on receipts became an even greater burden for the industry to bear, evolving as it did from the pre-1940 level of 20–5 per cent to a new level, in the early 1950s, of 35 per cent and then, in the late 1950s, to between 30 and 48 per cent. In addition to this taxation, a special tax on the seat prices, the *taxe spéciale additionnelle* (TSA), of 8 per cent had to be paid by exhibitors whose cinemas received financial aid from the state (about 80 per cent of the theatres). Over the decades, however, the taxation on receipts progressively diminished from its 1950s average of 33 per cent, reaching 23 per cent in the mid-1960s. In 1970, this tax system was replaced by the VAT system and, in line with all other VAT charges, was set at 14.5 per cent. Eventually, in 1979, it was reduced to a special rate of 7 per cent and is presently fixed at 5.5 per cent. In exchange, the TSA has risen to around 12 per cent, so in effect the taxation rate now ranges from 17 to 19 per cent.

An interesting little moral taxation anecdote needs to be related here. The mid-1970s saw a considerable rise in the production of pornographic or X-rated films. This rise is thought to have coincided with the new liberalism of the Giscard d'Estaing presidential style and the abolition of censorship, but another reason concerns the fiscal measures imposed on foreign X-rated films which led to a considerable drop in their importation. This rise in home products could therefore represent a filling of the gap/lack. Whichever the reason, French X-rated films had to pay a special extra tax on top of the existing ones of 4 per cent (Bonnell: 1989, 607).[21]

Because the tax on receipts goes into the industry via the *Fonds de soutien*, any move toward partial detaxation profits the exhibitor only and production suffers because the tax revenue from ticket sales goes into aid for production. Governments prior to those of the Socialist party in the 1980s made little to no provision within their budget for direct contribution to the *Fonds de soutien*. In the mid-1970s, for instance, the state's direct contribution represented a mere 10 per cent in relation to the yield made by the TSA. In contrast, under the first Socialist government, the actual contribution was tripled giving a percentage ratio of 23 per cent in relation to the TSA yield. During the brief return of the Right to power (1986–8), this subsidy was proscribed. However, once back in government, the Socialists reinstituted it, albeit on a more moderate scale. In the period 1988–90 their contribution averaged around 7.7 per cent of the total budget of the *Fonds de soutien* (by this period the measurements for government contribution had changed from being in relation to the TSA, to the total budget of the *Fonds*).

The other, ultimately major source of finance for the industry comes from television. Instituted by the state in the 1960s, television contributed 8 per cent to the *Fonds de soutien*. In a sense, because television at that time was a state monopoly, it could be argued that this was a form of indirect state aid. Whatever the case, until the mid-1980s the contribution was relatively small and hardly in proportion to the important role played by cinema in television programming. However, since privatisation (post-1986), television's contribution to the fund has increased considerably and now stands at 53 per cent. Thus television is the biggest purveyor to the industry. Forty years after the cinema industry had expressed its confidence in a fruitful co-operation with television, it now sees itself dependent for over half of its resources on the very industry that has sapped its audience strength. As if to mark this dramatic turn in fortunes, in 1986 the *Fonds de soutien* was renamed (for the fourth time in its forty years' existence) the *Compte de soutien financier de l'industrie cinématographique et de l'industrie des programmes audiovisuels* (i.e., the fund subsidises both film and television production, both being perceived as equally important).

Although government did little to assist the industry in the inter-war years (at least until 1935), this was certainly not the case after World War II. How it came about, however, is one of the many ironies surrounding this industry's case for survival. That there was a need for a centralised institution was clear from the ailing fortunes of the industry from World War I onwards. In this respect it should be noted that the three critical moments in the industry's inter-war years did in fact coincide with the establishment of three bodies the remit of which was to organise the cinema industry. First came the *Office national du cinématographe* (1927), then the *Conseil supérieur du cinéma* (1931) and finally the *Commission interministérielle du cinéma* (1935). It would seem, however, that their establishment in such a short space of time was more indicative of their inability to consolidate and effect change than it was of heavy-handed state interventionism. Interventionism that worked would come, but not in the lifetime of the Third Republic. Not until the Occupation and the repressive hand of the Vichy government would the institutional framework, so necessary to the industry's survival, be imposed.

By a decree of 2 November 1940, the *Comité d'organisation de l'industrie cinématographique* (COIC) was created as a consolidated organism covering the industry's disparate systems. This committee was in charge of five areas: the technical industry (film laboratories, studios, machinery), the film producers, the film personnel (actors, directors, technicians), the distributors and exporters and the exhibitors. Whilst there is little question that this organisation of the industry under one centralised institution revitalised the French cinema, the paradox remains that it was accomplished by the French but under the aegis of the Germans. This raises again the very problematic question of how one talks of a French national cinema when its very survival was ensured by the consolidation and rationalisation practices put in place by the Germans and when most of the films made during the Occupation were produced by German companies. It could be argued, as does Léglise (1977, 152), that Guy de Carmoy's report of 1936 and Jean Zay's 1939 proposals were quite seminal in the thinking behind the creation of the COIC and that, therefore, the Occupation merely precipitated its occurrence. This could be countered, however, with the argument that, for at least twelve years prior to the war, no such institution had been put in place successfully despite three attempts to do so. Viewed in this light, the COIC could be seen as a Vichyite creation, which is indeed how Jeancolas (1983, 302) perceives it. Thus, although the COIC undoubtedly took on board the ideas of the Carmoy and Zay reports, none the less, the fact remains that it was the COIC that was instrumental in changing the face of France's cinema industry and left a legacy that is still with it today in the form of the *Centre national de la cinématographie* (CNC).

The CNC was created in 1946 and is *the* overseeing body for the French film industry. Before looking at its remit it is worth pausing a brief moment to consider the shift in nomenclature. The key word for the governing body during the Occupation, COIC, was *l'industrie*; for its counterpart after the war, CNC, it was *national*. Indeed, in the former period, the authorities demonstrated, through legislation that was primarily industrial and commercial, that they considered cinema as first and foremost an industry. It is also the case that during that same period, the German Minister for Propaganda, Goebbels, in his ambition to make Germany into the cinematographic power of Europe, had as a major objective the prevention of any other European country developing a national cinema industry. That France did not totally succumb to this ruling says much about its reserves of courage. But what is significant in the context of this debate is the unwitting paradox that emerges from these two positionings (Goebbels' and COIC's). On the one hand, there was the desire to kill off any idea of a national cinema but, on the other, there was the establishment of an institution which, in rationalising the industry, made two things possible first, a revitalisation of French cinema (the list of films produced during the Occupation attests to this) and, second, a renewal after the war of the concept of a national cinema, as was evidenced by the renaming of COIC, in 1946, as the *Centre national de la cinématographie*. Through this resignification, France effectively reinserted her cinema back into the national, with all that that denotes and connotes. On a first level this change of name signifies an eradication of the past (COIC is no more), whilst on a second level it connotes a reclaiming of that which was lost (the national identity of France's cinema). Together these levels produce a third level of signification, the myth of the national cinema. The renaming – the shift in nomenclature – reaffirms then, that such a phenomenon does exist.

In fact, there are many ironic outcomes surrounding the Occupation period in relation to France's cinema history. In the case of the CNC the irony is double. Before the war, the CGC (the *Confédération générale du cinéma*) was a body autonomous from the state. Now the governing body for the cinema industry is under state tutelage. A shift in control, therefore, that is not without its obvious problematics. Repeatedly through the decades, successive governments have commissioned reports which have led to the passing of new laws intended to assist or improve the industry. Repeatedly, the complaint sent back to the government by the film industry is that the reforms pay too much attention to the industry side of things and not enough to the art side. In this respect, the legacy of the Occupation left the industry burdened with the slow-moving interventionist state bureaucracy which it might well have been better off without. Centralising in this instance becomes a mixed blessing. There are other, more felicitous outcomes, however. For example, the period of the Occupation also saw the establishment of a film school. Until then, there was nothing in place to nurture film-makers. There was a training centre for camera technicians on the rue Vaugirard in Paris, but that was all. The idea of establishing a school had been close to the film-maker Marcel L'Herbier's heart (and the minister Jean Zay) since the early 1920s, but it took the rationalising and organisational modalities of the Occupation to put in place a fully fledged school of film studies and the *Institut des hautes études cinématographiques* (IDHEC) was opened on 6 January 1944. One last example of these ironic outcomes, already mentioned in the discussion of censorship, concerns the legal measures adopted for the protection of minors first in 1941 (fixing the age at 18 years), then again in 1942 (reducing it to 16 years). Repression and morality are never far apart it would seem, even when it might be for the better good. Once again, there had been discussions in the late 1930s about the advisability of such measures, but nothing was done. Once again, external forces (i.e., non-national ones) made its implementation a fact.

But what of the CNC's remit? It is charged with maintaining control over the financing of films, the receipts from box-office takings and statistics pertaining to the totality of film practices. The CNC is responsible for the management of the *Compte de soutien* (formerly the *Fonds de soutien*). Money comes into this fund from three directions – tax, banks, and the state – and it goes out in two major directions – production and exhibition. The funnelling of these resources, however, invaluable though they may be, is not without its problematics.

The fund was first put in place in 1948 in response to protests from the industry that because costs of production had risen so much, it was hard for producers to make enough films to stem the tide of American imports. Figures show an increase, post-1948, in the number of films produced, but they are rather deceptive because the actual increase comes mostly as a result of co-productions and not an increase in wholly French products.[22] The 'fault' does not lie exclusively with the production side of the industry because up until 1959, due to the urgent need for the refurbishment and construction of cinema theatres after the war, the tendency had been to prioritise the needs of the exhibitors over the producers. After 1959, production took priority and, more specifically, attention was paid to the artistic, creative projects which otherwise might never have got off the ground.

Essentially, the support from this fund takes two forms: the *soutien automatique* and the *avance sur recettes* (also known as the *aide sélective*).[23] The *soutien automatique* is a system of autofinancing from a compulsory levy on box-office receipts in France. All French films and co-productions benefit from this subsidy which is pro-rated according to their success at the box-office, the intention being that the subsidy serves to finance a subsequent film.[24] It was relatively effective in the 1950s. Then the subsidy ranged from 15 to 25 per cent of production costs and helped stimulate 'national' products to compete against the Americans. At present, with a percentage investment of only 8 per cent, its importance is considerably less. Since its inception in 1948, this subsidy has had one major flaw; more recently, it has developed a second. The basic problem with the system is that, since it will only subsidise a new film project based on the takings of the preceding one, it tends to profit producers who are already established and runs the risk of fostering very little new talent (for reasons already explained above, producers are inclined to be low risk-takers). The more recent problem ties in with the rising costs of film production which has led to a regressive use of the subsidy. The tendency has been to use a fair proportion (around 28 per cent) of the subsidy to pay off outstanding debts from the previous film (Bonnell: 1989, 574).

The second measure, *avance sur recettes*, was instituted in 1960 by the state in the face of the industry's financial crisis caused by declining audiences. This financing, which is still in place, is a selective one (benefiting 20 per cent of the films made and representing 5 per cent of investment in production). It deliberately targets films of quality and is attributed to a producer or film-maker upon the successful acceptance, by a government-appointed commission, of her or his film script. In this respect, the *avance* came at a fortuitous time because it allowed for a certain success in terms of French film production, in that its timing coincided with the emergent New Wave film-makers, many of whose films were aided by this *avance* (after the New Wave's initial success in 1958). This advance is not intended as a subsidy since it is to be repaid. However, of the 1,116 films that benefited from this advance payment system between 1960 and 1988, only 106 have paid off the loan in full (860 have repaid in part). This situation is due mostly to the films' non-viability at the box-office. The reason is that the type of film produced under this system of financing is often experimental or auteur. This cultural production practice (a state and art symbiosis) may well be the result of its coincidence with the advent of the New Wave (many of whose projects were facilitated by this method of funding). However, state intervention is not without its paradox, for it sets in place a causal conflation between art and the purpose of state funding. The state, in the form of the commission, is seen as actively seeking to promote projects that correspond to the French cinema's cultural heritage as the Seventh Art. This confirms the intentionality of the state to have a policy for creativity and innovation (*politique de création*). But this causal conflation is a contradiction in terms. Bureaucracy has little to do with innovation and this contradiction, while less apparent in the 1960s and 1970s, has come fully to the fore in the 1980s.

Nowhere has the intentionality of the state been more in evidence than during the Socialists' two terms in power during the 1980s and early 1990s. It is significant that François Mitterrand's Minister of Culture, Jack Lang, held his portfolio for both terms – a clear indicator of a desire for continuity and effective planning. The Socialist governments, through Jack Lang, have been more proactive than any of their predecessors both in terms of strategy and financing. On the financial front there are two major developments to be singled out over and above the already mentioned tripling of the government subsidy to the industry. First, in 1981, Lang managed to obtain a doubling of the advance fund. Second, in order further to enhance capital availability to producers and film-makers, he set up a tax shelter whereby private investors could set up a financial group (called SOFICA – *Société pour le financement du cinéma et de l'audiovisuel*). This group can invest up to 25 per cent of taxable revenue on an individual basis or 50 per cent as a collective for a minimum period of five years and receive tax benefit. On the strategic front, in addition to the dissolution of the Pathé-Gaumont group mentioned earlier, there are two further essential implementations to note during this period. First, the ranking financially of high art over popular culture films was removed. Direct investment from the fund would no longer discriminate in favour of the former – both were equally entitled. The motivating goal in this instance was less a desire to break down elitist barriers than to get audiences back into the cinemas. Second, in the belief that a separating out would foster new talent, the allocating commission was split into two colleges, one to deal with first- or second-time submissions, the other with projects submitted by those with greater film-making experience.[25]

These, then, are some of the major changes. What of their implementation? As might be expected, the troubles of the cinema industry can not easily be resolved by imposing upon it a facilitating framework, however well-intentioned. The industry is not an institution in the traditional sense of the social, economic or political institutions that serve to construct and represent France as a nation. It is an art and an industry and, therefore, no normal institution. The paradox remains that the state has tried to normalise it, but it is not a state institution, it is not nationalised. Herein lies the root of the problem. The industry is a heterodox community composed of individuals which an outside body has attempted, since the Occupation at least and with differing degrees of volition, to normalise. Thus, as Bonnell (1989, 579) points out, the ability of the *avance sur recettes* to promote new talent will always be compromised because it is a constituent collegiate body (the allocation commission) that makes the decisions on the submitted projects. Collegiality, he maintains, implies the law of the majority, the median choice. At best the majority sanctions safe innovation, eclecticism going mostly by the board. A uniformity or normalisation ensues, potentially bringing in its wake the mediocrity of stagnation.

A second, but equally important shortcoming of the advance system is its lack of realistically sufficient resources. Each year, between thirty and fifty projects are financed by this system to the tune of 1–2.5 million francs (ibid., 577). Since 1983, however, because of the move towards super-productions, the cost of film-making has become artificially standardised and very few films get made for under 5 million francs. This trend towards big-budget films was and still is consonant with yet another attempt to compete with the Americans (because of the audiences' predilection for blockbusters). But it also marks a move away from the traditional French cinema production practices (of artisanal and low-budget films) for the first time since the heyday of the co-productions in the 1960s. At that time, the *avance* was implemented to counter the effect of co-productions on national cinema and to ensure its survival. These practices, then, have now become virtually inoperable given the standardisation of costs. For example, of the ninety-three films made in 1988, only fourteen cost under 5 million francs. The artisanal, experimental, low-budget or auteur film, though not in danger of extinction, none the less becomes (relatively speaking) marginalised.

There is some truth to the maxim, therefore, with which this section began. The state gives, but not sufficiently. The state is interventionist, but not effectively. Thus, there is a diminution in the production practices that are the specificity of French national cinema, the very cinema the state seeks to protect. The paradox is very plain to see. Never has the French cinema been so well taken care of by the state as in the 1980s (and early 1990s), and yet its critical condition still cannot be stabilised. But stability, to say nothing of an upturn in fortune, depends by and large on getting the audiences back into the cinemas. This has proved to be an impossible task. I shall now consider this apparently feckless phenomenon of the lapsed cinema-goer and the reasons for its 'infidelity'.

AUDIENCES, VENUES AND EXHIBITION PRACTICES

When looking at statistics for cinema-going audiences, the first factor to note is that the cultural myth of the cinephilic French is just that – a myth. The French are not and, with the exception of one period in history, have never been avid film-goers. During the inter-war years, the average audience ranged from 7 to 12 per cent of the population. In the peak period between the late 1940s and the late 1950s, the audience doubled in size (from around 200 million to 400 million), only to decline very rapidly until 1969, when it reached an all-time low of around 6 per cent – a percentage that has been sustained ever since. It is interesting that this almost bell-shaped curve (the various dips make it look more like a trilby hat) is consistent, albeit on a much smaller scale, with only one other European country of similar demographic size: Italy. For example, audiences in Germany (even though after 1945 the statistics only relate to West Germany) and Great Britain peaked in either the early 1950s (for Britain) or the mid-1950s (for Germany), after which the decline became a continuous sliding one. However, as late as the early 1960s their audience levels were still much higher than those ever obtained by France. Although the swifter incursion into public life of modern technology on a massive scale (in the form of televisions and motor cars) in Germany and Britain serves as an explanation for the divergent modalities of cinema-going audiences, none the less, until the 1970s, France's cinema-going audience had been consistently smaller than that of any of her European counterparts (in 1955, Britain had an audience of 1,200 million, Italy 810, Germany 790 and France a mere 400 million; by 1990 the figures were, respectively, 145 million, 155, 160 and 175 million). Thus, even though for the past two decades France's cinema has been the leading European one, it has an audience half the size of its needs (200 million instead of 400+ million).

Size of audience is still no guarantee of national success, however. For ten years (1947–57), France had an audience size that should have ensured her cinematic industry's viability (around 400 million spectators). Since audience taste does not necessarily favour the home product, however, secure cushioning for the indigenous industry is far from assured. Thus money raised from actual 'bums on seats', even in the best years for French films in terms of attendance, will at most only benefit home production by around 50 per cent, the rest going predominantly into American coffers.

Audience-going practices, therefore, contribute not only to the crisis of France's national cinema, but also to that of the venues themselves. Ever since the 1960s, exhibition practices have attempted to stem the tide of dwindling audiences. However, they have been mainly ineffectual, primarily because they have adopted the wrong strategy. Thus, for the meantime, exhibitors have to content themselves with the average yearly audience of 180–200 million that has been their lot since the late 1960s. Failure to attract wider audiences is the result of numerous factors, most of which are economic or social, a point to which I shall return after I have considered the more pressing question, who are the cinema-goers?

There are, of course, several audiences, and here issues of class, age and 'taste' are relevant. At its inception, before cinema moved from the tents of local fairs, vaudeville theatre and music-halls (*café-concerts* or *caf'conc'*) into cinema theatres of bricks and mortar, film-viewing was predominantly a working- (or popular-) class activity.[26] By 1906, however, the venue had changed and so had the audiences. During the period 1906–14, Charles Pathé set up a chain of cinema palaces, first in Paris and subsequently in other cities, which brought cinema into the rich and the middle-class quarters, thus changing, through a widening of the class bands, the predominantly populist nature of cinema-going audiences. The working-class areas were not neglected, however. They too had their theatres and the earlier genres of film (crime serials and sentimental melodramas) were still produced (or imported, as increasingly became the case) and exhibited for the entertainment of this important group of film viewers (Abel: 1984, 52).

None the less, the extensive theatre building programme – first by Pathé, then by Gaumont – on the *grands boulevards* brought about a gentrification of cinema-going practices which in turn engendered a similar gentrification of the product. Cinema, Pathé believed, had to respond to middle-class taste. It is true too that, out of economic necessity, Pathé was obliged to turn his attention to a different type of product because America had garnered the popular cinema market. It was in answer to this double exigency that a special form of cinema, the *Cinéma d'Art*, was launched, its prototype being *L'Assassinat du duc de Guise* (1908), produced by *Film d'Art*. What distinguished this form of cinema from the popular genres was first, that it was filmed theatre and second, that it was accompanied by music composed by renowned composers – in this instance Saint-Saëns. It therefore had the bourgeois trappings of acceptability – legitimate art (theatre and music) worthy of attendance. That this derivative practice (borrowing from other art forms), rather than any preceding cinematic production practice, became the leverage whereby cinema obtained its cachet as the Seventh Art, is surely not without its irony.

On the issue of age and class and the mutating nature of cinema audiences, three further points need to be made before examining the reasons for the post-1960s decline in attendance. First, France has always been and still is by and large a rural country. Even today, around 48 per cent of the population live in rural communities that are without cinema theatres. Until the mid-1950s, such rural communities were served by roving cinemas. The abandonment of this practice could only contribute to the decline in audience numbers. Second, by the 1930s a new dimension of the clientele emerged in the form of a cinema-going youth class of significant proportions. Finally, by the 1960s cinema-going had become less a popular-class activity and more one which attracted a type of person more closely associated with the theatre-going public. As distinct from America and most other European countries, the level of education has progressively become a favourable factor for cinema attendance in France.[27]

With regard to the rural communities and their dearth of cinema theatres, it is now easy to see why France's cinema audience – even in its heyday – never obtained the same dizzy heights as Italy (the country with which France can most readily be compared), whose small communities did have their theatres until the mid-1970s. Attempts in recent history to tap this resource have met with mixed results. In 1982, Jack Lang set up an *Agence pour le développement régional du cinéma* to implement plans to build or refurbish cinema theatres in these rural areas. According to the *Agence*, these efforts have produced some 2.3 million new spectators (*Film français*: 1983, 13). However, as global figures show, this addition has not served to increase the audience numbers overall. In 1982 there were 200 million spectators, in 1983, 197 million, in 1984, 188 million and, by 1988, 183 million. It is quite possible that the low age of the audience (15–24 years) may be a contributory factor to this shortfall, despite the audience increase in rural areas. Demographic decline in the birth rate since the mid-1960s has meant that by the 1980s the youth age group, which represents the largest percentage subset of the cinema-going audience in France, has diminished enough in size to outweigh the gains made by Lang's regionalisation policies. As Bonnell (1989, 27) rightly points out, a deficit of 50,000–100,000 births for an age group can cause a decrease in audience entries by several millions.

If, as has been the case since the 1930s, youth is the preponderant audience, then it stands to reason that to quite a large extent it will dictate what is on offer. Of course, ever since the 1930s, governments, intellectuals, conservatives and radicals alike have voiced their concern and their desire to protect the youth of France. In the 1930s, 60 per cent of the films shown to the French public were American productions. Visas for the protection of minors were not in existence at that time. Perturbed by the easy-going attitude of the young generation, blame was quickly attributed by the various morally concerned groups to these foreign imports and also to the venues themselves, whose decor and programming, according to these same groups, did little to deter youth from enjoying what they had to offer. To quote Vincendeau (1985, 77):

> These increasingly long and mixed programmes, together with continuous performances (unknown in the 1920s) did not fail to attract criticism from both morally conservative quarters and from left-wing intellectuals, such as the Communist critic Moussinac, who protested against the public's 'intoxication' with the luxuriously decorated cinema 'palaces' and what they offered. Moussinac concludes his indictment of cinemas like the Paramount with a suggestion that cinema appealed to the spectator's mysticism: 'Organ music, with illuminations and projectors, acts as a reminder of the golden decoration of churches and the reflection of the stained-glass windows in the memory of the religious ceremonies of their childhood.'

Public *engouement* for luxurious cinemas has never diminished, a fact overlooked by exhibitors in the 1960s when they were trying to secure their diminishing markets by offering more (films) in less space (multiscreen theatres). Public survey after public survey repeats the message that small, uncomfortable theatres are a deterrent. If only the moralists had had the knowledge of cinema sociologists of today! Even so, present-day history still echoes these same concerns for the moral well-being of France's youth. In the 1960s, for example, under de Gaulle, films that promoted youth *and* the family, and cinemas that screened them, benefited from lower taxes (the Pétainist resonances should not escape the reader). A further example of moralising occurred in the 1980s, when the Catholic church lobbied successfully with local mayors in many districts in France to ban the screening of Scorcese's *The Last Temptation of Christ* (1988).

Whereas once French cinema, as all cinemas, was a popular urban form of entertainment that attracted all classes, since 1962 there has been a shift in terms of audiences to the effect that cinema has gained the selective socio-cultural status of the other arts (i.e., the audiences who now attend are the same socio-professionally as those who attend other forms of aesthetic production). In terms of percentages of yearly entries, working-class audiences with primary education have declined from 50 per cent in 1962 to 4.6 per cent in 1988. Middle-class audiences with further education have risen from 5 per cent to 44 per cent over that same period. Although these figures do not need to be glossed in the case of working-class audiences where there has been a real decline in actual numbers, greater precision is required where the more socio-economically privileged classes are concerned to prevent misinterpretation. In terms of actual percentages of the number of spectators, the 1988 figures for this class of audience are virtually the same as those for 1962 (79.5 per cent and 79.7 per cent respectively). Simply stated, as the total audience has dwindled, the 'edu-cated' classes have remained more constant in their cinema-going practices and thus represent a higher percentage of the total number of cinema-goers even though the actual numbers for the privileged classes have not changed drastically (Bonnell: 1989, 29).

In the meantime, the working-class audiences have all but abandoned the silver screen and for two major reasons – one economic, the other social. Over the past two decades alone, the price of cinema tickets has gone up more than threefold. Over that same period, the concentration of cinema theatres in town and city centres, to the detriment of the working-class suburbs and the provinces, has meant a loss of accessibility to that means of entertainment for this class. It should escape no one that this chicken and egg situation (concentration of cinemas away from the popular audiences puts up the price of the tickets, and the price of tickets deters such audiences) will take a great deal of ingenious planning to resolve and there is no guarantee that the 'lost' audiences will return, given that they have turned to other sources of entertainment (such as television) which, at least in terms of 'value for money', they find quite satisfactory.

If urban centralisation of cinemas (started in the mid-1960s and still very much the practice today) in the face of a contrary socio-demographic movement of the working class and young couples out into the suburbs and new townships was a primary strategic error in trying to limit audience decline, then so too was (and to a large extent still is) the lack of comfortable cinemas. The discomfitures felt by the cinema audiences were several. In the mid-1960s, the formerly large and spacious theatres were transformed into complexes with several screens. Since that period, no sustained attempt has been made to redress this practice (briefly, in the mid-1970s, exhibitors did benefit, as they had done previously in the 1950s, from refurbishing monies out of the *Fonds de soutien*) and cinemas have progressively diminished in size – from an average of 477 seats in 1964 to 227 in 1988 – without diminishing substantially in number – in 1988 cinema screens represented 87 per cent of the 1964 figures (ibid., 112). Added to the inhospitality of these small cinemas inside (then as now) were the equally inhospitable queuing conditions outside. Audiences, finding cinema-going conditions inadequate, turned elsewhere for their leisure culture and so the decline in attendance continued until it stabilised around the 180–200 million figure that has been maintained since the end of the 1960s.

It would be unjust to single out poor strategy on the exhibitors' part as the sole reason for audience decline. To the socio-ergonomic reasons just outlined, it must be added that economic reasons also played their part. Here there are two stories to relate, both connected to purchasing power. The first concerns periods of negative purchasing potential. In 1952 and again in 1983, a drop in purchasing power (due, respectively, to inflation and recession) was an important contributing factor to audience decline. However, the 1950s decline warrants further attention because, by 1957, audience numbers had risen once again to above the 400 million mark. Two reasons account for this resurgence, one economic, the other technological. On the one hand, by 1957 inflation was curbed and purchasing power improved; on the other, the second half of the decade witnessed a technical revolution in the cinema industry with the advent of cinemascope and technicolor. The combination made cinema an irresistible attraction once more. Sadly, this story would have no reruns, the decline in the 1980s having done no more than come to a halt.

This brings me to the second story. Paradoxically, a similar upswing in economic conditions to that of the late 1950s occurred from the mid-1960s to the early 1970s. It improved purchasing power, but did not bring in its wake a reversal in the fortunes of cinema attendance. Again there were two apparent reasons for this failure of audiences to grow. The first one, poor exhibition strategy through the expansion of multiscreen theatres, did little to entice. The second, greater ease financially, did the rest. Money, at that time, was spread more evenly over leisure, and cinema no longer had the monopoly over entertainment. A more affluent society, therefore, was a contributing factor, along with impoverishment of the venues, to the 58 per cent drop in audience attendance during the 1960s. Television, cars and weekends now replaced the former attraction of the cinema palace so feared by the moralists of the 1930s. In this light, Godard's *Weekend* (1967) is not just a satire on consumerism but also a virulent attack against its effect on cinema.

Returning to exhibition practices, their impact on audience attendance is not without its knock-on effect: production will be affected by exhibition strategies. Perhaps the most significant outcome of the 1960s strategy of cinema multicomplexes is that, although the initial intention behind these multiscreen cinemas was to provide more choice, the end result has been to create less. The introduction of multiscreens has effectively shortened the distribution life of films in the following way. One film in Paris could be on in as many as fifty film theatres at the same time. Obviously, because more people can see it at the same time, it will come off the circuit more quickly. Thus the financial success and appeal is short-lived, ranging as it does from six to ten weeks (the period during which the main money is made on a film distributed under these conditions). Because films are so expensive to produce, it is clear that this inflationist situation is a major, if not the major reason for the economic crisis in which France's cinema now finds itself. Only American products can survive this swift turnover practice because their product is paid for by the home audience, money made from exports being pure profit.

Multiscreens, therefore, create a situation whereby exhibitors quickly run out of material and whereby good products can get drowned in the choice of films simultaneously on offer. The short life of a film means that home products rarely recoup their costs and this, in turn, means that fewer home products get made. The fewer French films there are, the fewer film-goers there will be for French films, and the fewer patrons there are, the fewer French films there will be.[28] Indeed, figures show a decline in attendance of the assiduous and regular cinema-goer from 50 per cent of the cinema population in 1962 to 34 per cent in 1988, which would indicate a disenchantment with what is on offer. Conversely, figures for this same period show a rise in the attendance of the irregular film-viewer from 50 per cent to 65.5 per cent of the cinema population (Bonnell: 1989, 24) – a rise which is explained by successful niche targeting by distributors aware of this group's predilection for a blockbuster (often American but occasionally French). Needless to say this viewing practice, producing as it does an uneven spread of receipts, only serves to disinherit the indigenous industry. As a result, production strategy tends to centre more on fewer, bigger films, following the example of *Jean de Florette* (Claude Berri, 1986) and *Nom de la Rose* (Jean-Jacques Annaud, 1986). Reminders that this should not be the sole strategy to follow, however, come in the form of certain recent low-budget films that have been resoundingly successful. Films such as *Trois hommes et un couffin* (Colinne Serreau, 1985), *Le Grand chemin* (Jean-Loup Hubert, 1987) and *Au revoir les enfants* (Louis Malle, 1987) immediately spring to mind and serve notice that audience taste is not totally predictable.

If cinema is a lottery, what then of its audiences? In summary, only slightly more men than women go to the cinema (the difference on average is a mere 2 per cent). The largest group of cinema-goers is the 15–24 age range. The choice of which film to see is largely determined, in the first instance, by the genre and the actors (directors do influence choice but on a much smaller scale, as do prizes awarded to films). Posters and word of mouth also influence choice. Where generic preferences are concerned, four genres dominate: comic films (especially liked by the male audience), police films, fantasy films and finally intimist films (those that observe human nature and relationships and which are especially liked by the female audience). Thus, by way of an example, in September 1987 the top five films were as follows: *Crocodile Dundee*, *Platoon*, *Le Grand chemin*, *Les Enfants du silence* and *Beverly Hills Cop II* (the dominance of Anglo-Saxon products will not have escaped the reader's attention). Last, but not least, cinema is now only third on the list of preferred entertainment coming after first, television, and second, music.

I shall now move on to consider the last of the main axes that serve to explain the decline in popularity of cinema – the silver screen's purported arch rival, television.

THE IMPACT OF TELEVISION: RE-WRITING THE MYTH OF CAIN AND ABEL

Will the unravelling of this last part of the story of a crisis reveal that television came and cinema was unable to defend itself against the voracious appetite of its little brother/sister whose greed knew no bounds as it sought to bring the consumer back into the home to idle away her/his time in front of a menu of easily accessible and quite inexpensive goods? Is French cinema truly the victim of this second age of moving-image technology, or does some of the responsibility lie with cinema's tendency at crucial moments in history to be more sclerotic than innovative?

Although it was inevitable that television would usurp cinema's monopoly of the moving image and replace it as the principal source of entertainment or culture via the image, production practices in the 1970s suffered from two major flaws which undoubtedly assisted the disaffection of cinema audiences. The first contributing flaw was what was perceived, somewhat incorrectly, as the extreme bipolarisation of the film product into, on the one hand, weak popular cultural productions and, on the other, impossible and inpenetrable productions of the 'cinema of research' bequeathed by the New Wave and the post-1968 generation of militant cinema. This latter, deconstructive form of cinema automatically excluded general public audiences, for whom these nombrilistic, 'the-approach-is-all' films had nothing to offer by way of entertainment. The former also fell short of expectations. There were exceptions, of course, but much of the cinema produced for the general cinema-going public was considered 'mass-produced, stereotyped, "ready-made" . . . [their] form and content [were] totally lacking in ambition, inspiration and originality, and [their] aims [were] unashamedly commercial'.[29] This was not the whole picture, however, and, ironically perhaps, some of the better films in this category were those made by former New Wave directors (Truffaut and Chabrol, for example), who had turned their hand to making more populist films.

The second contributing cause, by all critical accounts, appears once more to be the legacy of the New Wave.[30] With their freely improvised filmic texts and stress on *mise-en-scène* and, by dint of their vaunting the *cinéma d'auteurs*, they effectively killed off the scriptwriter so that by the 1970s there were very few good scenarios around (as Chapter 4 will make clear, this is rather an oversimplification: there was good, mainstream cinema even if it was not dominant). This patricide of the author by the *auteur* is consonant with the New Wave's ousting of the *cinéma de papa* which they accomplished first, through their writings in the *Cahiers du cinéma* and second, through their own films during the 1960s. However, the blame surely cannot lie entirely with the New Wave. It would seem that critics have looked in one direction only for this lack of a 'good story'. Scenario-led films date back to the 1930s (obviously, in some ways, because of the advent of sound, but also because of the influence of the theatre and literary adaptations – a legacy of the silent era). By the 1960s, most of that generation of scriptwriters were either dead or in retirement. More significantly, however, the 1930s generation of scriptwriters dominated the script scene for some twenty-odd years (approximately 1935–55) which meant that very little new talent could emerge. Although they might have been young turks during the first decade of their dominance, by the second decade they were well-established names. Finally, because the 1950s was a period of considerable conservatism where producers were concerned, there was a tendency to stay with established names. This practice, therefore, seriously affected the potential for new talent to come forward in the 1950s, hampering its advance on two fronts, directing and scriptwriting.

There is one final point, the importance of which should not be neglected in this discussion of cinema's responsibility for its diminishing audience. The mid- to late 1970s witnessed a boom in X-rated pornographic films (in 1977, for example, almost half the films were in this category: 100 out of 222). Thus the choice of films available to the young audience was considerably diminished. Given that this age group is the industry's bread and butter, this diminution of choice seems quite perverse.

In twenty years (from 1960 to 1980), the proportion of households owning a television went from 10 per cent to 90 per cent; that percentage now stands at 97 per cent (Ory: 1989, 16). Since 1962, therefore, television has increasingly become the dominant popular spectacle. Let us not forget that although the popular spectacle has changed its format over the millennia, it has always served to attract large or mass audiences. Predominantly, popular spectacle functions as a carnivalisation of the social sphere.[31] In this respect, television is no exception but is simply its most contemporary form. If television is the second age of moving-image technology, what of the first age – cinema – and its effect on the popular spectacle that preceded it? As Pascal Ory (1989, 22) correctly points out, cinema replaced the boulevard and travelling theatres as well as the café music-hall and *café-concert*. Cinema became the new popular spectacle. Ory goes on to say that this mutational process meant that logically cinema in its turn would be superseded. Thus, currently, in the age of electronic arts, it is the turn of television to 'vampirise' (Ory's term) the preceding popular spectacle. Given this process, no doubt television as a production practice will soon be usurped by other forms of electronic art such as video and interactive television.

Thus, viewed historically, cinema could expect its decline in audiences to continue. However, since the late 1960s the numbers have remained relatively stable with a couple of dips first in the 1970s and then again in the 1980s. The causes are attributable, in the first instance (i.e., the 1970s), to the reasons just cited above and in the second, to the effect of television deregulation in the mid-1980s. Cinema may, therefore, have reached its natural plateau in terms of popularity as an electronic art form. But conversely, this does not mean that it is the poor relation of theatre-going audiences. Cinema outstrips theatre and dance audiences fivefold and tenfold, respectively. It is also worth noting that, perhaps surprisingly, its audience is twice the size of those for sporting venues.[32]

How does the story of television relate to cinema? In very general terms, television in France has known two eras to date – pre- and post-deregulation. The first era of television stretches from the year television became a medium of mass communication (1962) until the passing of the first deregulation bill (1982) which paved the way for a subscription TV channel and eventually for two more privately owned, terrestrial channels. The second era, 1982–92, is quite evidently much shorter, yet its importance with regard to cinema has been substantially greater than were the twenty years of the first era.

The first era was marked, post-1964, by three technological moments which did little to enhance television's relationship with cinema. Until 1964, the rivalry between the two did not actually affect film as film in so far as only one film per week was broadcast on France's single television channel, TF1. Also, the film had to have been on general release for at least five years. Thus, in terms of adverse consumption of the filmic product, during this early period television posed no real threat. However, in 1964 everything changed. A second channel was launched, Antenne 2 (A2). Then in 1967 colour came to the small screen. In 1972, a third channel with a regional and cultural remit, FR3, was launched. Further to these three moments of technological change, the required interval between a film going on public release and it being broadcast on television was relaxed to three years. By 1968, films represented 45 per cent of television time. Ten years later this figure had reached 60 per cent. Given that, by law, 50 per cent of the films had to be French in origin and given that, by the end of this first era, the three channels had the legal right to show 540 films between them annually, it is not difficult to perceive that the indigenous cinema industry (with a maximum of 120 films per year) was seriously at risk. Television's rapacious consumption of films seemed destined to exhaust the cinema market of its stocks, thus rendering the home product an endangered species. It must be added, however, that cinema was not the completely passive bystander it might like to claim to have been. With a clear eye to the potential of the television market, the percentage of films in colour went from 9 per cent in 1960 to 92 per cent by 1968 and, over that same period, there was a considerable drop in the number of films made in cinemascope for the simple reason that cinemascope does not go over well on the small screen. There is also some irony attached to this overdetermination in favour of television. It should not be forgotten that it was cinemascope and technicolor that brought about a reversal in the dwindling cinema audiences in the late 1950s.

Television's consumption practice during this first era was counter-productive not only to the market but also to the image of France's national cinema. Films are sold in relation to their commercial value, thus the more popular a film is with the audience in its initial exhibition period, the more it will cost to purchase the rights for television. In order to fulfil the quota imposition, the tendency inevitably will be to purchase the cheaper product. However, most of the financially feasible films 'lie within a fairly narrow range of quality, running from the tolerable to the plainly stupid' (Donnachie: 1979b, 344). Consumption practices in the 1970s coupled with governmental protectionist policies (the 50 per cent quota), therefore, did little to endorse a positive image of French cinema and instead helped 'to propagate the opinion of overall mediocrity which the French population currently [had] of its national cinema' (ibid., 344).

On a financial level too, television was disserving to the big screen. By the late 1960s, films made up the bedrock of television programming. Yet, during this first era television paid a very low premium for the huge profits it made on films through advertising revenue. In terms of purchasing rights and co-production investment, television's contribution to the nation's outlay on films stood at a very meagre 8–9 per cent. Given television's outgoings for buying films, where the average cost of a film was the equivalent of the cost of just one minute of advertising air time on television, it is easy to understand the cinematographic industry's sense of outrage. In an attempt to redress this inequity, in the late 1960s the state instituted a levy on the TV channels which went straight into the *Fonds de soutien*. Modest in size and based on a system of penalties and forfeits, by the mid-1970s this levy represented a paltry 6 per cent of the fund – a percentage figure which remained virtually unchanged until the mid-1980s when deregulation policies forced an increase.

If governmental policy on television subsidies for the cinema industry was rather inchoate during this first era, then doubtless a primary cause can be attributed to the fact that television was state-owned and subsidised by a licence fee. This fee, collected and processed by the state treasury, made up a certain percentage of the three channels' budgets, the rest of the monies coming to a greater or lesser degree (depending on the original budget allocated from the licence fee) from advertising. To increase the levy paid to the fund, therefore, would have meant a decrease in the money available for programming purposes. The shortfall would have had to be either recouped by the state, or suffered by the telespectator in the form of diminished choice or, alternatively, a higher licence fee. None of these eventualities could possibly attract the government of the day, hence the stagnation of the levy.

Fortunately for cinema production practices, the advent of deregulation meant that the dwindling of resources, which the stagnation of the levy represented, could be stemmed thanks to the introduction of new governmental measures which were made possible, in turn, by the decoupling of the state from television. At last, it would seem that the optimism voiced so long ago (in 1946) by the cinema industry for a fruitful co-operation with television would have some foundation in fact and in cash (Léglise: 1977, 101). First, in 1984 a tax was introduced on any new sources of income for televison. Second, and far more significantly, in 1986 a new tax (*taxe audiovisuelle*), this time on the TV channels' total annual turnover, was imposed. The rise in the scale of television's contribution to the fund (now called the *Compte de soutien*) from 1985 to 1989 was a phenomenal one, going from 8 per cent to 53 per cent. This figure must be qualified however. In 1985, France had three terrestrial channels and a barely nascent subscription TV, Canal Plus. By 1989, she had five terrestrial channels and a very buoyant Canal Plus. Thus there was more money around to be taxed. This 53 per cent becomes less significant when one considers that, although it means that 417 million francs in tax goes from television into the fund, this contribution represents only 5.5 per cent of television's turnover. In real terms, therefore, television is not paying an unduly high price given the number of films it consumes. In 1989, for example, 1,330 films were broadcast on all channels – two and a half times as many as by the end of the first, pre-deregulation era (1962–82).

Paradoxically, however, given that since deregulation the number of films shown on all television channels, has more than doubled and that the 50 per cent quota of French films has by and large been respected, there has been only a modest rise in the finance percentage that goes directly to cinema through purchasing rights and co-production investment (the other source of revenue for the cinema industry). The fact that it has risen at all is thanks mostly to Canal Plus, which is the major purchaser of films. The finance percentage did not reach double figures until 1986 (11 per cent). It currently stands at around the 20 per cent mark. If Canal Plus is taken out of the considerations, the percentage figure for all terrestrial stations stands at around 10 per cent – hardly a significant rise on the first era, therefore. This would indicate that the increase in the number of purchasers of films (i.e., channels) has not led to a truly commensurate increase in the price of the product itself. Rarity of stock has not led to a bullish market for the cinema industry. More channels have effectively meant less both in terms of straight cash going directly into the industry and choice available to the consumer-telespectator.

In terms of finance, television's relationship with cinema has grown in importance in so far as indirect funding is concerned. Television's contribution to the *Compte de soutien* is up almost eightfold on its 1977 figures (20 million francs, representing 7 per cent of the fund in 1977; 417 million francs, representing 53 per cent in 1989). On the surface it would appear that deregulation has served cinema reasonably well. However, whilst television's contribution has increased, the fund's other important source of revenue, the TSA (*taxe spéciale additionnelle*) has decreased gradually over the same period (1977–89) because of falling audience attendance. In the latter part of the first era, the TSA provided as much as 90 per cent of the receipts going into the fund; currently its 360 million francs contribution represents 46 per cent of the fund (Bonnell: 1989, 603–7). Thus, to a significant degree, television has assumed much of the financial responsibility originally shouldered by the TSA. Hence it would be fairer to say that television's enforced contribution has allowed the fund to remain more or less constant, but little else. In fact, comparative figures for the fund's budget totals between 1986 and 1989 show that, although the fund grew by 21 per cent (from 1,016 to 1,301 million francs), none the less the average cost of making films over that same period increased by 33 per cent (from 12 to 18 million francs).[33] If anything, then, these figures reveal that the ratio between film costs and the fund has decreased, leaving cinema slightly less privileged than it was in 1986.

In this post-deregulation era, therefore, cinema has become increasingly financially dependent on television for its survival rather than its enrichment. Increasingly, television has exploited cinema to boost its ratings.

According to the cinema industry, this has kept potential film-goers at home. The industry goes on to claim that 4 billion spectators watch films on terrestrial television, whereas only 200 million go to the cinema. This means that effectively this latter group pays 90 per cent of the film costs, and terrestrial television (excluding Canal Plus, the pay TV) supplies the other 10 per cent.

That so many should be privileged by so few, in the industry's eyes, seems grossly injust, but this is to ignore the general social trend towards individuation through technology (i.e., the fact that there are so many more technological choices accessible to, and therefore controllable by, the individual in her/his own space). As Pascal Ory (1989, 16–24) points out, the post-1945 technological revolution has made it increasingly possible to have the illusion of live sound and pictures in one's own home and for that illusion to be immediately accessible. Ory cites radio as an example of the importance of this personalised access to the 'live'. After all radio, which pre-dates by a long way this post-1960s cinema crisis brought about by television, is still as popular a medium as it was pre-television, if not more so. Currently, it is listened to as much as television is watched (15.8 hours per week). It remains a popular medium because technology has rendered it more flexible and adaptable to modern life (thus the radio goes with the listener: car radio, transistor radio, walkman radio, etc.). Television has not killed off radio, and new technologies such as computer games and video cassette recorders do not seem to be killing off television. However, all these technologies have contributed to the drop in cinema attendance because, as Ory goes on to say, the spectrum of the electronic arts has broadened at the same time as it has been domesticated (brought into the home and made central to the family as a whole) and then domiciled (brought into the home for the individual to interact with on her/his own).

Three further points need to be made about this seemingly less than satisfactory relationship between cinema and television. All concern production practices. First, directly or indirectly television accounts for 40 per cent of the financing of French films.[34] As principal producer and consumer it is hardly surprising, therefore, that many films (some critics say the great majority) are overdetermined in favour of televisual rather than cinematographic practices.[35] Thus considerations of pacing, sound track and narrative are patterned around the exigencies of broadcasting rather than screening. Uppermost in the film-maker's mind will be the suitability of the product for television two or three years after its general release. Obviously, this progressive normalisation of the product for the small screen leads to a hegemonic style that has little to do with cinematic writing. Clearly, in this crucial respect television does have a very influential role in the image of France's national cinema.

The second point concerns co-productions. If they co-produce a film, terrestrial channels gain an advantage of one year over the normal required gap of three years following public release before they can show a film on television (because it is a specialist movie channel, Canal Plus only has to wait one year). As expected and for obvious reasons of prestige, television has certainly taken advantage of this special dispensation. However, just a glance over the past six years provides an interesting insight into some rather unaltruistic, not to say greedy practices on television's part. Whilst the number of films to which the channels' names are attached has risen (for example from 1986 to 1988, the number of co-productions has risen from 58 to 73, or by 25 per cent), capital investment in percentage terms has not. It has remained, except in 1987, fairly firmly around the 4.7 per cent mark. At present, terrestrial channels have their signatures on 63 per cent of all French cinematic production, yet their outlay is quite minimal (an average of 1.3 million francs per film, or 0.07 per cent of the average cost of a film). This is a small price indeed to pay for the cachet of respectability that comes from endorsing a product of the Seventh Art.[36]

The final production practice that needs mentioning also falls into this area of respectability and legitimation. Increasingly since the late 1970s, television has managed to attract film stars and directors to make *téléfilms* and to participate in or take on cameo parts in certain mini-series. On the one hand this innovation, although it helps to temper the danger of drying up the supply of the home film market, could be seen as a cynical response to the consequences of television's own consumption practices. On the other hand, the making and broadcasting of these products does serve to endow television with an aura of respectability. That is to say, these products are not 'popular-class culture' in the sense that game and talk shows are, but carry the hallmarks of legitimate art. In this respect, these productions have the same bourgeois trappings of acceptability that the *Cinéma d'Art* conferred on cinema some eighty years ago. The great advantage for the cinema industry remains visibility for its stars and, provided there is no over-exposure, this could well serve to attract audiences back into the cinemas to see the now more familiar faces, this time on the big screen.[37]

To return to the original questions raised about the relationship between television and cinema, it is clear that, although since 1962 television has been the major cause for cinema's decline (both in terms of audience and product), the relationship is not akin to that between Cain and Abel but rather one of rivalry that has currently reached a consensual truce, perhaps even a healthy symbiosis. Crucially, television supports its electronic art elder which gives much in return (not without protest on either side). The inevitability of the mutationary process of moving-image technology also means that sooner or later television's present dominance will decrease. The video boom has yet to take off in France. Once again state protectionism has stunted this growth market area and at present, with only 6 million video-recorders sold, a mere 28 per cent of all households possess one. The protectionist moves by the government to stem the importation of Japanese goods have meant that for the time being this potentially very lucrative market for the cinema industry has not reached anywhere near its exploitation level.

CONCLUSION

In this chapter I have shown how state intervention in the form of protectionism has simultaneously aided and hindered the cinema industry. Quota systems, be they on foreign imports, primarily American and Japanese products (films and video-recorders respectively) or on the nation's television channels' programming practices (50 per cent French films), have not enhanced French cinema in terms of its productions or economy. The quota system imposed upon the American industry in the 1950s indirectly brought about a loss of audience through a lack of sufficient home products. The television quota has served more to exhaust stock and degrade the image of French cinema than to enrich either. A certain economic chauvinism (the state often bares its protectionist teeth at what it terms the Nippo-American axis) has prevented a viable new market – sale and rental of video-cassettes – from taking off. State intervention in the form of the various taxes imposed on the industry has also suffered from this ambiguous syndrome. The cinema and latterly the television industries consider themselves overburdened by taxation, and yet without the taxation at its maintained level, cinema would lack the necessary funding to be able to struggle on. Since World War II, the state has deemed that cinema, like all other arts, must receive its patronage. Similarly, at all moments of crisis the industry has clamoured for more assistance. However, in this respect, state intervention (in terms of aid and a government-appointed centralising body to administer it as well as other important aspects of the industry), because it is bureaucratic and centralised, is again paradoxically placed to the point where the industry is almost, but not quite, a nationalised institution. Yet, without all these various measures, it is doubtful that France would maintain its position as the European leader in the cinematographic world. All the above reservations notwithstanding, therefore, state intervention has proved overall to be essential to the cinema industry's relative well-being.

Funding has always lagged behind production costs. In that, there is nothing new for the film industry as a whole. More interesting is the fact that, since the 1920s, France has lagged behind other countries on all electronic art fronts. The advent of sound cinema, television and video-recorders has occurred later in France than in other European countries with which she can be compared (Germany, Italy and Britain). This has meant that foreign products, mostly American, have been able to infiltrate successfully into France's home market. Technological immaturity or lack of expediency is not the sole cause for the 'cocacolonisation' and 'Nipponisation' of the electronic art domain. It relates also to France's inability to respond fully and in time to the popular cultural demands of her own electronic art audiences. As Pascal Ory (1989, 33) points out, the first waves of Americanisation were all popular cultural forms (cinema, jazz, strip cartoons and the detective novel) and all these forms predated the American dominance over her allies in the 1950s. The failure of supply to meet demand remains, therefore, a very crucial part of the picture where the story of France's ailing cinema industry is concerned.

Finally, in this chapter questions have been raised concerning the very complex issue of what a national cinema is and problem areas have been identified for the concept of 'national' in the French industry's production practices. I have also shown how the term 'national' shifts in meaning according to the social, political or economic mutations or pressures, and that this shifting also affects questions of cinematic style. This in turn generates other questions. Does state patronage ultimately affect the concept of a national cinema in so far as it may shape its direction? Would the New Wave, for example, have had the impact it did without the introduction by the state of the *avance sur recettes* which helped finance many of its films? Without the *avance*, would auteur cinema have survived to the present day? Without the recent shift in state policy of allocating this *avance*, would the current new talent of the Post-New Wave have emerged? This brings me to another order of questions. Does cinema reflect or construct its nation's social praxis? Is the cultural identity of a nation bound in a set of specifically selected filmic texts or in all texts?

In the chapters that follow, these questions will be uppermost as I unravel the histories of France's cinema. Whilst I feel I have dealt with the industry's ecohistory as amply as is possible in a volume of this size, it has been necessary to leave out some of the detail. However, in the following pages, as the filmic product is focused on within its global environment, many of the issues raised in this chapter, but not yet fully pursued, will be picked up once more and developed.

NOTES

1 *Cinématographie française*, 15 September 1956.
2 Current research is looking into these silent ghosts of the silver screen; interestingly, many of the writers were women (see Ginette Vincendeau's article 'Credit where credit's due' in the *Guardian*, 26 April 1990).
3 Abel (1984, 56) contributes the following remark with regard to the advent of sound. The irony for the United States in promulgating the sound revolution was not just that it divested itself of some of the French market, but that in reaction to that loss it bought rights to French plays and novels and made their films in the target language. However, the result was disastrous because they were produced strictly along American lines.

4 See Vincendeau (1985), Chapter 1.

5 *Cinématographie française*, 25–6 June 1937. It is worth noting that at this time 50 per cent of the American public were cinema-goers compared with 6–7 per cent of the French. Small surprise, therefore, that the American products were paid for by their home audience.

6 Sources include Abel (1984, 50), Léglise (1977, Annexe No. 7) and *Kinematograph Book Directory* (1918, 50–1). I am also indebted to Lira Fernandes of the BFI Library for helping me to complete these figures.

7 *Films in Review*, vol. 1, no. 7, October 1950.

8 *Avant-scène*, no. 178, 15 December 1976.

9 *Adèle H.* and *Cage aux folles* are amongst some of United Artists' 100 per cent productions. When one considers how American distribution companies operate at a high-pitch level to sell their products, small wonder their phenomenal success in France and especially in the United States!

10 *Sight and Sound*, vol. 3, no. 12, 1934, p. 153.

11 Ironically, there is one possible exception – the new televisual markets (cable TV and Home Box Office or HBO – which could create demand. I say ironically because television is seen as the traditional enemy of cinema (having drained it of its audience lifeline) and yet it is that very enemy which is now in a position to aid the ailing film industry (a practice already in place in France).

12 Abel (1984, 9) quotes 1907 as the year Pathé decided on this policy. Bonnell (1989, 89) gives 1902 and D'Hugues and Marmin (1986, 32) quoting Pathé give the year 1904.

13 For more detail on the cinema theatres see Abel (1989, 49–59).

14 See the useful appendix in Guillaume-Grimaud (1986, 198–213), which gives details of producers for 100 films representative of that period. See also Vincendeau (1985, 50–1).

15 For a further analysis see *Film français*, 8 July 1988.

16 See *Ecran*, no. 333, 28 November to 4 December 1951 and *Cinema Papers*, no. 20, March–April 1979.

17 In 1950 31 films and 35 in 1951 out of a total production, including co-productions, of 117 and 112 films respectively. See *Cinématographie française*, 19 January 1952. Interestingly, at the beginning of this century both Pathé and Gaumont set up studios in Nice in order to gain better lighting facilities.

18 The evolution of the relative proportions of predominantly French co-produced films and 100 per cent French films was as follows: in 1949, 7 out of 103 films (7 per cent) were co-produced; by 1953, it was 27 out of 88 (31 per cent); by 1963, 50 out of 86 (58 per cent); and by 1969, 56 out of 91 (62 per cent); *Bulletin d'informations CNC*, February 1970. The archivalist reader will be intrigued to note that no two publications providing statistics concur on numbers, either production or co-production. *Film français*, for instance, gives quite different ones. I have decided to rest my numeric trust in the official state organism for cinema, the *Centre national de la cinématographie* (CNC).

19 Without a visa, no film could be screened publicly. Public screening, however, laid this legislation open to subversion and it was what enabled the French Communist Party in the mid-1930s to screen the proscribed Soviet films privately, for example.

20 Léglise (1977, 17) quotes from Goebbels' diary: 'Nous avons pour but d'empêcher, autant que possible, la création de toute industrie nationale du cinéma.'

21 For further details on X-rated films see *Technicien du film*, no. 266, 15 January to 15 February 1979. For other figures quoted in this paragraph, see Peter Simmons, 'Paris-Hollywood', *Sight and Sound*, February 1950, *Positif*, no. 41,

1962 and Bonnell (1989, 140 and 604).

22 In 1948, 91 films were produced, all of them French. In 1949, 107 films were made, of which 8 were co-productions; in 1950, out of the 117 films 18 were co-productions. Thenceforth the proportion of co-productions rose further, peaking in the 1960s and early 1970s. See Martin (1984, 120).

23 For a detailed analysis of the two parts to the subsidy, see Bonnell (1989, 570–81).

24 The idea of advance financing by the state was first put in place during the Occupation (by Guy de Carmoy, then government representative to COIC). At that time, forward financing was given by the *Crédit National*, the state bank.

25 There are of course other measures – decentralising theatres, rationalising bank pools. The number of decentralised theatres was originally targeted at a further 1,000, then reduced to 600, but by 1986 only 200 were in place, at which point the *alternance* (advent of the right-wing government) put a stop to any further growth. IFCIC (*Institut des financements du cinéma et des industries culturels*) is a system of financing whereby up to 70 per cent of lenders' finance is guaranteed (up to 90 per cent for cultural films). Formerly the CNC controlled this – hence another decentering move by Lang.

26 Occasionally, the bourgeoisie was known to attend film spectacles. Enterprising big department stores screened films as an added attraction for their clientele. This venture was also used in 1897 by the sponsors of the yearly Bazaar de la Charité (a charity drive for the poor) to attract well-wishers to the venue. This promotional bid ended in disaster when fire broke out in the flimsily constructed bazaar. A total of 140 people (including many children) perished.

27 See *Image et son*, no. 184, May 1965, for a special survey on cinema audiences.

28 See E.M. Donnachie's very useful two-part article on 'French cinema in crisis', in *Cinema Papers*, March–April 1979 (a) and May–June 1979 (b).

29 Donnachie (1979b, 345).

30 See, *inter alia*, Donnachie (1979b, 397) and Ory (1989, 186ff).

31 I quote Len Masterman's term here somewhat out of context – he uses it specifically for the function of television (see his excellent study *Teaching about Television*, Macmillan, 1980). However, I perceive earlier forms of popular spectacle as performing this same function.

32 Ory (1989, 21) supplies interesting figures. The actual percentages for 1989 are these: cinema 42 per cent of the population (this percentage is calculated as follows: 180 spectators going on average seven times per year gives a cinema public of 25 million over a total population of approximately 62 million; this in turn yields a percentage of 42 per cent); theatre 7 per cent; dance 4 per cent; sporting venues 20 per cent.

33 Sources for these figures are Bonnell (1989, 604) and *Informations CNC*, no. 223, May–June 1989.

34 Television's contribution to the *Compte de soutien* represents 20 per cent of the total finance budget for French cinema; the other 20 per cent comes from its contribution to co-productions and the purchasing of film rights.

35 See Dominique Païni in *Cahiers du cinéma*, no. 357, March 1984.

36 It is worth recalling that the very first co-production dates back to 1967. The film was *Mouchette* and was made by Robert Bresson. It was hardly a fast-paced film, but one that exemplifies the canons of the Seventh Art.

37 The success of *La Vie devant soi* (Moshe Mizrahi, 1978) may have much to do with the fact that Simone Signoret, the star in this film, had recently completed a very popular television series, *Madame le juge*. Highly visible in films in the 1950s, by the 1970s Signoret was less of a household cinema star name. This TV

series would have brought her back to the forefront of people's memories, reminding them of her great star qualities.

BIBLIOGRAPHY

Abel, R. (1984) *French Cinema: The First Wave, 1915–1929*, New Jersey, Princeton University Press.

Bonnell, R. (1989), *La vingt-cinquième image, une économie de l'audiovisuel*, Paris, Gallimard.

Degan, C. (1974) 'Bilan économique du cinéma français depuis la guerre', *Ecran*, no. 21.

D'Hugues, P. and Marmin, M. (1986) *Le Cinéma français: Le Muet*, Paris, Editions Atlas.

Donnachie, E.M. (1979 a & b) 'French cinema in crisis', *Cinema Papers*, March–April (a), May–June (b).

Flitterman-Lewis, S. (1990) *To Desire Differently: Feminism in the French Cinema*, Urbana and Chicago, University of Illinois Press.

Guillaume-Grimaud, G. (1986) *Le Cinéma du Front Populaire*, Paris, Lherminier.

Léglise, P. (1970) *Histoire de la politique du cinéma français, Tome I: Le Cinéma et la IIIe République*, Paris, Lherminier.

—— (1977) *Histoire de la politique du cinéma français, Tome II: Le Cinéma entre deux Républiques (1940–1946)*, Paris, Lherminier.

Martin, M. (1984) *Le Cinéma français depuis la guerre*, Paris, Edilig.

Meadow, N. (1947) 'Evolution of the French cinema in the US', *Screen Writer*, September.

Ory, P. (1989) *L'Aventure culturelle française: 1945–1989*, Paris, Flammarion.

Rose, F. (1937) 'The cinema in France in 1936', *Sight and Sound*, Summer.

Sadoul, G. (1948), 'Crisis over France', *Sight and Sound*, vol. 17, no. 66.

—— (1962) *Le Cinéma français 1890–1962*, Paris, Flammarion.

Vincendeau, G. (1985) 'French Cinema of the 1930s: Social Texts and Contexts of a Popular Entertainment Medium', unpublished Ph.D. thesis, University of East Anglia.

Chapter 2

Magical moments of musical silence: French cinema's classical age 1895–1929

Carving up cinema into ages is, of course, fraught with problematics, not least of which is the danger of historicism. This first epoch (1895–1929) does, however, have some inherent logic because it marks the period between the cinema's first commercial screening (the Lumière brothers exhibited twelve of their cinematograph productions in the Salon des Indiens, boulevard des Capucines in Paris and charged an entrance fee) and the advent of sound, which at first dramatically disrupted the codes and conventions of narrative film and quite obviously inflected the course of cinema's history. I am tempted to call this first age of French cinema the classical age precisely because it does put in place most of the codes and conventions of this medium that subsequent ages have either reacted against or gone on to develop in different ways. I am well aware that for most critics and historians of French cinema the tendency is for classical French cinema to extend to the late 1950s and it is for this reason that I have termed these epochs 'ages' (so as to avoid confusion). I would then argue for the second age of cinema to span the period 1930–58 and be called French cinema's age of modernism and finally for the period 1958–92 (and onwards until the next age) to be termed French cinema's age of the postmodern. In any event, the chapters in this book will adopt this tri-partite structuring of French cinema and each chapter will argue the case for these categories. Interestingly, the implementation in France of techno-logical developments (first sound and then colour) also permits her cinema's history to be carved up along tripartite lines and yields almost the same division – 1930 marking the first truly sonorised film, the mid-1950s the full implementation of colour. These technologies were first introduced by the Americans into their film industry in an attempt to counter waning audience attendance and were, therefore, in some respects 'forced' upon France (although, as will be argued in Chapter 3, the adoption of colour did not represent a problem for France in the way that sound did). Whatever the case, these technological implementations point once again to the duality of cinema as art and industry, with the labels given to these different ages indicating an aesthetics of cinema subject to change due to artistic and economic exigencies alike.

Cinema was not an immaculate conception. It was born out of curiosity and financial necessity. To take the second point first, for a number of reasons, economic growth had declined since the Franco-Prussian war (1870). In losing the war, France lost the valuable industrially advanced Alsace-Lorraine. In defeat, she had to make retribution to Prussia through indemnity payments. As a result of defeat, which was a tremendous blow to national pride, France stepped up her colonial expansion as a way of proving that she was still a great European power, but this merely compounded her problem. Given the poor state of her economy, a significant number of business people and industrialists refused to invest in the indigenous industry and chose rather to invest abroad, including the colonies. In the manufacturing industries new artefacts were invented to attract if not capital investment then at least attention to their novelty and potential use in many domains which would generate widescale sales of their products, a great majority of which were either entertainment artefacts (the phonograph) or had some scientific application (photographic film). Where the birth of cinema is concerned, on the economic side of the equation, the *Cinématographe* was launched for purely commercial purposes and in an endeavour to revitalise France's ailing industry. By 1896, industrial growth was in the ascendant once more, going from 2.6 per cent per year for the period 1896–1906 to 5 per cent per year for 1906–13 – the very period that witnessed the meteoric emergence and world-wide monopoly of French cinema.

On the other side of the equation concerning the birth of cinema lies curiosity. Science's desire for knowledge – in this instance to know how animals and human beings move – led scientists to experiment with ways of recording movement. At this juncture, 1870–82, recordings were being made on photographic film (celluloid film had been perfected in 1869) by Eadward Muybridge, Jules Janssen and Etienne Marey amongst others. By 1891, the Kinetograph and Kinetoscope (patented by Thomas Edison and W.K. Laurie Dickson) permitted, respectively, the recording and envisioning of movement. By 1895, the Lumière brothers had developed the *Cinématographe*, which could both record and project and, equally uniquely, could produce reversed film motion.[1] Curiously, it was the narrative aesthetic potential of the medium which eventually caused the Lumière brothers to abandon the cinematographic side of their business in 1908. From the very beginning, they had shown no inclination to exploit the entertainment potential of the *Cinématographe* as spectacle (what they saw as filmed theatre and insightfully termed *mise-en-scène*). Instead, they were more interested in its industrial and commercial exploitation. Until 1906, they were perhaps not unwise in their orientation since actuality films were at least as popular with audiences as the narrative films (if not more so). Thus they sent their camera operators all over the world to film and project scenes from the indigenous and local life with the aim of promoting and selling the *Cinématographe*. The second stage of their business enterprise (they stopped production in 1905) consisted of them renting out their equipment to operators in return for half their receipts – hardly the most profitable way of conducting a business. The inability of the Lumière brothers to adapt to consumer demand for narrative films and their failure to see the need for vertical integration left them ill-prepared for the growth in the industry. As has already been mentioned in Chapter 1, this was not the case for the Pathé brothers or indeed Léon Gaumont who, between them, essentially took over the mantle of French cinema production.

The Lumière brothers' withdrawal from the scene coincided, appropriately enough, with the advent of *Film d'Art*'s *L'Assassinat du duc de Guise* (1908). *Film d'Art* productions drew on the famous names in literature and the classical acting tradition of the *Comédie française*, thereby providing cinema with the cachet of legitimacy as an art form. It would be unwise, however, to assume that this was *the* moment when cinema came of age and so caution must be exercised against the tyranny of dates. The fetishisation of 'the first time' should also be avoided whenever possible because it only serves to simplify history, which brings me conveniently back to the beginning of this cinema's history.

Many histories of French cinema have tended to adopt, repeat, accept the 'two trends' approach to its production as exemplified by the now famous Méliès–Lumière duopoly. This canonisation of cinema into two styles (illusion and realism respectively) does not in fact hold true, nor is it necessarily very useful. What is pertinent is first, that from the point of view of narrative and film style, most forms and possibilities had been touched upon in the first decade of the industry's history, and second, that many film-makers, not just one or two, were engaged in constant experimentation. Méliès, after initial success in the 1890s, persisted in making the same sort of fantasy tableaux until 1912 even though, on the one hand, public taste had started to show its disaffection with his films some five years earlier and, on the other, film style and narrative had evolved considerably. The Lumière films were overtaken by these same changes in style and taste. An inability to experiment or to take up new avenues of production are not perhaps the best hallmarks of the French cinematic tradition (even though, as was shown in Chapter 1, the industry has evidenced this disposition on several occasions), so the Méliès–Lumière duopoly is in some regards an unfortunate one. If examples are needed and 1895 is being put forward as the conjunctural date for the birth of cinema and cinematic traditions, then I would propose three: the narrative film tradition as introduced by Alice Guy, the documentary-realist tradition as exemplified by the Lumière brothers, and the cinema of attractions (the illusory power of cinema) as displayed by Méliès.[2] And I would add that these divisions can be traced but only faintly since there is considerable cross-over or cross-fertilisation between the three.

TECHNOLOGIES OF STYLE

In the beginning, films were the length of the roll of film in the camera, around 50 m, so they lasted just under one minute. As early as 1897, however, multi-shot films of long duration were being seen (the Lumières' thirteen-scene version of *La Vie et passion de Jésus Christ*) and, in 1899 Méliès was projecting films of 120 m (e.g., three reels, twenty scenes). Both these examples suggest an early form of continuity-editing in the form of splicing the reels together. Initially, the camera was static with the subjects held in general shot for the most part. Thus movement was created by the subjects' displacements within the frame. Although this proscenium arch effect did tend to dominate in the earliest films, methods were soon found to cut into the shot a medium shot or close-up shot and travelling and panning shots were in evidence as early as 1896–7 (for example, the Lumières mounted a camera on a train in *Quittant Jérusalem par train*, 1896). All editing was done within the camera either through stop-go photography or the use of dissolves. Superimpositions were made by winding the film back and running it forward again. Finally, most cameras at that time were hand-cranked and films were shot at 19–24 frames per second and projected at 22–4 frames per second (fps).[3]

Editing techniques were not terribly sophisticated in these early days and the final effect was more the result of rock of eye than anything else. Mitry (1985, 8) argues that no true editing took place until 1917, after numerous producers and film-makers (Diamant-Berger, Nalpas, Guy) had visited American studios and decided to implement modern editing techniques, which essentially meant using an editing table suite. Until that time, editing was done either by the women laboratory workers who developed the film or by the person directing the film. In this latter case, the film-maker would cut and pin the strips of film together, after which the women in the laboratory would piece it together. It would then be screened and further decisions or cuts would be made. With regard to the former case, it is worth mentioning that this early tradition of women editing films continued on into the 1930s and 1940s, and this practice of women being behind the screen was relatively specific to French cinema.

In the early days, films were projected in vaudeville theatres, music-halls or *café-concerts* and were but a part of the general entertainment, another act amongst other acts. In 1895, the audience affected was fairly small and came predominantly from the popular classes. At first (aside from actuality films), gags and chase sequences were amongst the most popular, much in the tradition of vaudeville theatre itself. Chronologically close on their heels, however, came more sophisticated narratives such as melodrama, thrillers and comedy which, because they were more complex, required the voice-over of a commentator in much the same way as lantern-slide shows had needed it before them. In fact, some show-comperes strung slide shows along with films to make a whole, even more complex narrative. This practice of using the commentator to ascribe a verbal meaning to the images lasted until first, the use of narrative intertitles became widespread in France between 1906 and 1913 (these in turn were replaced progressively by dialogue titles, around 1919) and second, the venue moved to cinema theatres and music was introduced to orchestrate the films. Interestingly the introduction of music has produced a significant problem for the film historian in the form of the necessarily inconclusive analysis of silent cinema not just because so many films have disappeared (out of the 1920s films alone some 75 per cent have been lost), but also because most of the scores for those films have disappeared too (Abel: 1984, 388). This means that films are not so readily readable in terms of rhythm and structure and indeed lose meaning at times (for example, when fast-editing is being used and when music would help to 'explain').

Originally, the Lumière brothers thought that the cinematograph, if it was going to survive, would be used for scientific and documentary news purposes. But for the perspicacity of the likes of Alice Guy at Gaumont who saw its potential for narrative film, that could have been the route it followed. Léon Gaumont held similar views to the Lumières, so the films he produced (during the period 1895–6) were primarily for demonstrating the technology. Guy found the repetitiveness of the films irksome (trains coming into stations and troops marching by had their limitations), and in 1896 she submitted a couple of short comedy scripts to Gaumont. She was given the go-ahead and within a year her film productions were a profitable success.[4] Indubitably, narrative film was not a singular conception for the simple reason that film-making in these earliest days was a truly international affair (at least between France, Britain and the United States) and film-makers were simultaneously working along similar lines. Moreover, there were no rights of authors at this juncture so that what could euphemistically be called cross-fertilisation was inevitable – in other words, all film-makers happily borrowed each others' techniques and narratives.

This early cinema has been described varyingly as primitive (1895–1903), pre-Classical (1895–1908) and the cinema of attractions (1895–1906).[5] I will explain briefly what critics/theorists who have applied these terms mean and then show that they do not necessarily preclude my more general label of Classical for the whole of silent cinema. According to Noël Burch (1984), primitive cinema distinguishes itself from Classical cinema by virtue of having no closure, that is to say the primitive film did not signify in and of itself. Either the referent or the exegesis was external to the film. Early films were either so close to vaudeville, variety or circus practices that their referent was not cinematic but other and outside of cinema or, if more complex in their narrative, they depended for their meaning on an external narrative (the commentator). In what Burch terms Classical cinema, however, there was closure, the first sign of which came with the emblematic shot (first introduced in 1903). This shot is specific to cinema itself and takes the form of a close-up which is present either at the beginning or at the end of the film or both. This close-up functions synecdochically, that is, it sums up the general nature of the film, points to its diegesis, to the narrative to come or to the narrative just concluded.

On another tack, Philip Rosen (1990) argues that pre-Classical film demarcates itself from Classical cinema by virtue of its unseamlessness and its consequent lack of continuity-editing. Two stylistic features in pre-Classical cinema caused this discontinuity, the first being the disjuncture between studio and exterior shooting which occurred as follows: in the studio, the background was flat and there was very little depth of field; outside, the opposite happened. This spatial and textural mismatch was erased in Classical cinema. The second stylistic feature which precluded this early cinema from being Classical was, according to Rosen, the tableau shot or proscenium arch effect, in which the camera takes up a one-shot position for each scene. Classical cinema, by editing into the shot or scene through cuts and thereby permitting the camera to function dynamically (as opposed to statically), provided the other vital ingredient to continuity-editing – a sense of interiority to the action (as opposed to the theatrical exteriority of the tableau shot).

Finally, there is the cinema of attractions which, to paraphrase Tom Gunning (1986), is about the tradition of exhibition and attraction. Early cinema was a fairground experience (itself an attraction) and the films were part of the non-narrative variety inscribed into the tradition of vaudeville and music-hall. Cinema drew attention to itself. For example, characters looked at the camera, the close-up was an attraction in its own right and did not serve to further the narrative, the subject was more a pretext to demonstrate what the camera could do, and so on. In this respect, although the Lumières, early Gaumont and Pathé followed this practice, the master of ceremonialising the magical possibilities of cinema was clearly Méliès. At this stage, then, cinema displayed its practices to the audience, was a cinema of attractions – to be looked at rather than consumed – quite different, therefore, from the voyeuristic nature of narrative cinema.

All three categories have one thing in common in that they point to the notion of exteriority in relation to early cinema as opposed to the interiority that is the inherent signifying practice of Classical cinema. Once again, it is in the dual nature of cinema (as art and industry) that this dialectical tension can be resolved, thus permitting the broader use of the label Classical cinema to refer to the whole silent cinema period. In relation to narrative (i.e., what it could show), the technology of the earliest period – if anything other than actuality films were to be shot – was in many respects ahead of its time. For non-actuality films the only referent, in the first instance, was the theatre which, whether popular, bourgeois or classical, was about spectacle and exteriority of experience (i.e., the spectator was outside the stage looking on). Creating a cinematic diegesis, therefore, is how I would describe the process of these early years – a process marking the movement from exteriority to interiority, from being behind the camera to being both there and on the other side of it. The fact that this earlier part of the process (exteriority) figured in both the avant-garde of the 1920s and the New Wave of the late 1950s indicates further that, rather than being a case of 'either/or', the juxtaposition of interiority/exteriority became a fundamental underlying axis to cinematic *écriture* quite early on.

Other fundamental axes emerge from this early period. In order to make longer films that could be understood easily a strategy of repetition and variation of action was adopted (especially for chase and peeping-Tom films), thus establishing two parts of the triumvirate canon of classical narrative cinema: repetition, variation and opposition. The peeping-Tom films most readily addressed the dialectics of the point of view shot (is the shot subjective or voyeuristic, and whose gaze is it?) and in so doing opened up the question of spectator positioning.

In all the above it must be remembered that technology of style did not belong to one specific country – it was more a case of cross-fertilising experimentation. Two examples, just in terms of editing, will suffice to make the point. The dividing up of the scene into a number of shots, which was first introduced in Britain by George Albert Smith in 1900 (*Grandma's Reading Glass*), reappears in a 1901 Pathé film (*Par le trou de serrure*). A little later, the perfecting of cross-cutting (parallel sequencing) effected by Pathé in 1907 (*Le Cheval emballé*) was seized upon in no time at all by D.W. Griffith and made into his own trademark.[6] This fact points again to the difficulty of enunciating a national cinema and also suggests that a national cinema can get elided as a concept. In this respect, cinematic practice gets confounded with concepts of nation-ness, that is, the adoption of a technique by film-makers (perhaps from another nation) can lead (through its predominance within their production) to its elevation into a sign of national cinematic practice. The example I would point to is the one Barry Salt (1983, 93) mentions, that of low-angle and low-key lighting effects closely associated with the German Expressionist cinema of the 1920s. In point of fact, this type of lighting for emotional effect was already in evidence in Danish films as early as 1910.

As with other countries, France also experimented in colour during these early years. A large number of the films by Méliès and Pathé between 1900 and 1906 were hand-painted – usually the 'fantastic or exotic histori-cal' films (ibid., 79) – and tinting was also used during that period. In 1908, Pathé introduced stencil tinting to speed up the process. This development happily coincided with the launch of its own prestige *Cinéma d'Art* series, thus enhancing what was inherently a rather regressive development in film style – filmed theatre – although, as Salt points out, the acting was far more restrained and untheatrical (ibid., 119). After this period, because of economic exigencies or a refusal to invest, experimentation in colour became the province of the Americans. During the silent period many films were coloured and it was only with the advent of sound that colour disappeared from the screen. At that time colour film could not take sound and, whilst experimentation continued, economic and political events in the form of the effects of the Depression in the early 1930s and World War II in the 1940s dogged its implementation. Not until the 1950s was colour financially viable and desirable (for the American industry in the first instance), initially to counter the adverse effects by monochrome television on audience numbers and, subsequently, to counter those same effects that the advent of colour television brought about. In France, colour was adopted fulsomely in the mid-1950s and again in the late 1960s, but not quite for the same reasons as in the United States (the plethora of co-productions in the 1950s made colour 'affordable' and the market potential of colour television in the 1960s made it an attractive proposition once more).

The year 1908 does appear to mark the beginning of a decline in France's position as the possessor of a pioneering and experimenting film industry even though she was to hold on to her dominant position as leading exporter of films world-wide for a further six years. Lack of investment in these areas in favour of mass production of fiction films was a first reason, but a second equally important one was that compared with other innovative and stylistically flourishing cinemas, primarily those in America and Scandinavia, the French cinematic industry was slow to adopt new techniques – fast-editing, soft focus, iris effect, dialogue intertitles, and reverse angle cutting were only gradually adopted after World War I and into the 1920s. In terms of genre, however, France was still capable of leading the way, particularly with the comedy and crime series which were quickly imitated in Britain, Denmark and the United States. Paradoxically, a further reason for the decline concerns the introduction of the *Film d'Art* series, or rather its coincidence with a number of court decisions made that year 'assuring authors' rights and royalties for film adaptations' (Abel: 1988, 18). As Abel points out, the nett results of these decisions were threefold. First, the *Société des Auteurs* now became a supporter of the *Film d'Art*'s products, thus giving a legitimating cachet to cinema. In so doing it caused an influx of theatre personnel into the industry which in turn provoked a proliferation of 'art films' produced by *Film d'Art* and its emulators as well as adaptations, on a wide scale, of classical and popular dramas (ibid., 18–19). French cinema, more than ever before, was tied to a literary convention that was on the one hand, to seal its legitimacy as an art form and, on the other, to leave it less free as a new art form to explore its aesthetic potential. It was at this point, 1910, that aesthetes and critics, either as individuals or as a collective, began to turn their attention to the meaning of film as an art form and to formulate theories of style. And it is those considerations and their effect on cinematic production that I would now like to address.

THEORIES OF STYLE

The earliest publications concerning cinema were the industry's own publications (Pathé's *Photo-Ciné-Gazette*, 1905–9), film journals that were closely allied to the industry (*Ciné-Journal*, 1908 and *Cinématographie française*, n.d.), the daily Parisian newspapers (from 1908 onwards), books on the cinema (mostly practical guides, but one or two on the history of cinema), literary journals (postwar) and, finally, the more independent and specialised journals (*Le Film*, 1914). It was in this last category that the debate around cinema as an art form mostly took place and it was from this category that writers emerged to forge their own independent journals after World War I, the most influential one being Louis Delluc's *Cinéa* (1921), which became *Cinéa-Ciné-pour-tous* in 1923 (ibid., 5–6, 197). These journals also saw it as their remit to proselytise cinema and act as an educational forum for cinephiles of all classes. This same group of writers, under the initial impetus of Delluc, started up a number of *ciné-clubs*: through giving illustrated talks on film, they hoped to promote cinema to the masses.

The genesis of film theory belongs to France and dates from around 1910. One of the earliest attempts to align cinema with other arts can be found in the film-maker Louis Feuillade's advance publicity sheet for his series *Le Film esthétique*. In his manifesto, he begged the question: since film appeals to our sight and, therefore, has as its natural origins painting and the theatre, surely cinema can provide those same aesthetic sensations? He also perceived cinema as a popular art and, equally significantly, as an economic art (a synergy between technology and the aesthetic) and as an artistic economy (art closely allied with capital).[7] A year later, Ricciotto Canudo published his manifesto 'The Birth of a Sixth Art' (when photography was added later, cinema became the Seventh Art). Abel (1988, 21–2) makes the interesting point that this manifesto established the two main lines of debate that would preoccupy theorists well into the 1920s: the debate around cinema's realism on the one hand and, on the other, around a pure non-representational cinema based on form and rhythm. The two lines of debate ran in parallel and the issues they raised were seen by some as complementary, and by others as juxtapositional. An example of the complementarity position can be found in the writings of one of the leading theorists during the war years, Louis Delluc, who was convinced that film theory should have an impact on film practice. A great advocate of the realist film, he was not lacking in theory for the non-narrative cinema either. In fact, it is in his notion of *Photogénie*, the image as sign – or as Abel puts it 'symbolic as well as indexical, connotative as well as denotative' (ibid., 155) – that a theoretical tendency can be discerned that was partially responsible for bringing Classical cinema to an end and Modernist cinema to the fore.

After World War I, Delluc and his contemporaries, many of whom were or went on to be film-makers, formed a loosely banded collective of film theorists and between them addressed issues of high and popular art, realist versus naturalist film, the spectator–screen relationship, editing styles, simultaneity, subjectivity, the unconscious and the psychoanalytic potential of film, auteur cinema, cinema as rhythm and as a sign. Although a composite of divergent views, all agreed that cinema was not just a reproduction of reality and that to be art it had to transpose nature. Equally importantly, they were united in one goal – rallying French film production to produce a national and cinematic specificity that would stand against the monopolising and hegemonising effects of (primarily) the American film industry. Statistics for the 1920s, however, show that although they were successful in obtaining a French specificity, film production itself after 1923 resisted American dominance very poorly. Economic considerations within and without the cinema industry had their respective effects on production. On average, between 1920 and 1923 France produced 110 films per year. The sharp decline came in 1924 with only 76 films and from 1924 to 1929 the average dropped to 67. Apart from 1923 – the only period of up-turn in France's economy – financial instability troubled the country from the very beginning of the decade. The down-turn in the mid-1920s was very clearly linked to the decline of the two majors Pathé and Gaumont, and as far as the second half of the decade was concerned, the down-turn corresponded to the economic precarity of the time (the franc lost three times its value against the pound sterling between 1924 and 1926).

What strikes a reader of the theoretical writings of that time is their pluralism. Debate was not confined to the idea that there should be film as art and then the rest. In fact, the 1920s was perhaps the first time that the high/low art debate was articulated. It was primarily Delluc, but there were others – Henri Diamant-Berger (a former editor of *Le Film* turned film-maker) and Jacques Feyder to name just two – who perceived cinema as a popular art form. Others, such as Germaine Dulac and Emile Vuillermoz, held the high art position, focusing on the plasticity and musical patterns or rhythms of cinema. This pluralism comprised four branches of theory which covered the thinking on cinema as a whole (i.e., popular and high art). While quite distinct, there is none the less some overlap between them. Bearing in mind that most of these writers were or subsequently became film-makers, it will come as no great surprise, as the diverse and exploratory film practices of that decade attest, that these theories of style crossed over into film.

Stuart Liebman (1983, 1–9) offers the following rubrics for the four branches.[8] The conservative branch, represented by Diamant-Berger and Charles Pathé, advocated a narrative cinema that was script-led. Pathé perceived the scenario as the most important element of a film and felt that prewar scenarii provided by the likes of Henri Bataille and Henri Bernstein would no longer appeal either to the French or, more importantly for his purpose, to the American audience. Diamant-Berger had been to America to observe production practices there. A protégé of Pathé, he too was in favour of script-led (preferably original) cinema. He perceived the role of the film-maker as *metteur-en-scène*, that is, the mediator of the author's aesthetic intentions (Abel: 1988, 103).

The next branch was the naturalist school, represented by André Antoine (a theatre director turned film-maker), which advocated realist cinema on the lines of Emile Zola's socio-realism. Antoine, whose stage-directing career started in 1887, was famous for transposing the aesthetics of naturalism on to the stage. His theory was to get actors to move away from the theatrical gesturality so prevalent at the time. To do this he created the principle of the fourth wall, which meant that the actors would not address or acknowledge the audience. In 1914, Pathé commissioned him to film for his subsidiary art film company SCAGL and Antoine, who made only eight films (six of them after the war), merely extended his naturalist theories to film and insisted on location shooting, the use of a multi-camera point of view (which he believed would parallel the effect of the fourth wall and get film away from the proscenium arch effect) and, finally, an editing style that would involve the spectator in the narrative (through identification with the mediating camera). He also stressed the importance of the scenario, especially for the rebirth of cinema after the war, and the need for professional writers who would transpose the literary classics (preferably those of Hugo and Zola).

The third branch, represented by Delluc, was still in the realist camp but was a realist aesthetic that advocated the auteur principle (that the author of the script and the film-maker should be one and the same). This form of documentary avant-garde, as it was also known, advocated that films should be based on ordinary events and that, in their realism, they should probe the psyche. It is interesting that, even though the realist genre was a popular one during this decade as in the previous one, neither Antoine nor Delluc was particularly successful in his film-making. It could be that the realist school as defined by them was inappropriate for the time. With Antoine there was, on the one hand, a tendency to conflate location shooting with realism and, on the other, to sublimate the picturesque over social analysis, often privileging the non-human as actor (e.g., the city, the river, etc.) – an anthropomorphisation that was more romantic in its ideology than realist. Delluc, it would appear, came unstuck on the issue of the representation of the workings of the psyche which, given his desire for understated directorial style, did not fit in with the mentality and upheavals of postwar France. As Liebman (1983, 5) succinctly puts it, '"Reality" had become too volatile to be captured by a realistic art.'

The final branch was the avant-garde which went through three stages. At the beginning of the decade it was identified as subjective cinema, that is, the filmic representation of the interior life of a character. Towards the middle of the 1920s, the prevalent preoccupation amongst theorists and film-makers (often one and the same) became pure cinema, where film signified in and of itself through its rhythms and plasticity. Lastly came the Surrealist avant-garde stage (in the mid-1920s), which in some respects did not replace the other two modes, but was rather conceived out of a collision of the first two. This avant-garde saw cinema as the perfect mediator for unconscious desire, for combining – because it was itself illogical and logical – the rationality and irrationality of the unconscious and dream state (Abel: 1988, 338).

Looking back over this period, the overall objective of theorists and film-makers, apart from the more conservative branch, was to establish that cinema was a language in its own right. Abel (1988, 206–7), quoting Jean Epstein, explained why this concept seemed so important:

> The aim of French critics and filmmakers, Epstein concluded, was 'to establish the premises for a cinematic grammar or rhetoric . . . a grammar peculiar to itself'. Although the assumption never became explicit, this effort often seemed intent on establishing a uniquely French system of 'film writing' in contrast to the then-dominant American system of spatio-temporal continuity editing.

I want to consider this perceived need for a film language and examine it within another debate that emerges from this decade – the one that pits scenario against auteur-led cinema – first, because it points to a cycle in French film-making practices and second, because it signals one aspect of the specificity of French cinema. Taking the former point first and referring back to Pathé's *crise du scénario*, whilst he may have been over-reacting, none the less, through that statement he was recognising that French cinema was floundering through lack of innovation. Equally revealing in this statement is, of course, Pathé's inability (unwillingness?) to see that an alternative to script-led cinema might exist. There were, after all, enough examples of auteur-led films before World War I. Thus it would be simplistic to say that Classical cinema was script-led and that the demise of this first wave of cinema was caused by the decline of the scenario and the rise of auteur-led cinema (as Pathé would have it). The history of cinema is never as convenient as that! Cinema, as I have already pointed out, changed in the 1920s because of economic and aesthetic exigencies. What does seem to be the case is that when there is a fairly intensive reflective rhetoric *on* cinema, it brings in its wake a perceptible, if evolutive, change in cinematic style. Thus, but by no means exclusively, the discourses of the 1920s ushered in the age of Modernism, the beginnings of which can be seen in the films produced towards the second half of that decade. Much later, but in a similar vein, the discourses of the late 1940s and early 1950s – those of the *Cahiers du cinéma* collective (which, amongst others, focused once again on the scenario/auteur-led cinema debate) – contributed to the advent of the new age of Postmodern cinema. At present in France there are once again rumblings of dissatisfaction about the lack of script-led films being the cause of the latest crisis in the industry, once more opening up the auteur/scenario debate. Perhaps there is another new age on its way.

The second point I want to make concerns the, or rather, a specificity of French cinema. The urge to define cinema has seen it analogised, during this Classical period, with painting, theatre, music and finally language. The predominance of the scenario, often literary adaptations, also grounds French cinema in language, in the word. Theorists such as Delluc, Vuillermoz, Dulac and Epstein were united in their belief that theory – the word – should inflect cinematic praxis. French cinema, therefore, becomes very closely identified with written discourse and therein lies its tension, its specificity, for the following reason: cinema responds to the need we have to see ourselves, to represent the living in much the same way that painting and photography did before. In this need to specularise ourselves, sight has become the dominant sense in our construction of reality (Comolli: 1971, 8).[9] But French cinema does not respond to that need uniquely or predominantly. It is in fact simultaneously a visual and a written discourse and it is this dialectical tension that is a part of French cinema's specificity.

Having identified this first specificity of French cinema, what could be defined as its signifying specificity, it would seem appropriate to move on to a discussion of the various genres present in France's silent (or Classical Age) cinema, and to consider the question of generic specificity – what could be termed its signified specificity.

WHAT THE PUBLIC SAW: A QUESTION OF GENRES

I would like to start with three key points which will form the basis of this section. The first concerns the interrelatedness between genre and socio-economic and political practices, that is, the concept that genre is embedded in its contemporaneous history and that it may or may not have a voice (as illustrated, for example, by the dearth of war films immediately after World War I, versus the plethora of historical reconstruction films). The second point, quite closely aligned to the first, is that genre is the result of the strategies of mimesis, that is, genre is the way in which the transposition of 'reality' is organised/structured or the way in which the construction of our reality is signified (Cawelti: 1985, 55). Third, and last, genre is both synchronic and diachronic, that is, it provides a transparence on the present but in addition it is reflected upon by the past and the future (for example, a genre may be popular at one time, lose favour with the audience and almost disappear only to resurface a decade or so later either in a similar vein or somewhat reconstructed, or it could be subsumed into another genre, etc.).

The rest of this chapter will fall into three sections: first, a brief history of the period; second, a typology of genres; and last, a closer examination of the generic categories.

France 1895–1929: a brief overview

In 1895, the date of the birth of cinema, France's Third Republic (1870–1940) was 25 years old, but it could hardly be described as being at ease with itself. Indeed, the whole of the Third Republic's history is one of financial precarity and more than intermittent social instability, as the frequent calls for national unity and the equally frequent periods of repression of unrest among the working and peasant classes attest. The end of the nineteenth century was marked by political and economic instability. The Commune of 1871 left politicians of the Right with the fear of 'socialist and feminist movements producing "disorder" within the nation' (Birkett: 1986, 11). The stockmarket crash of 1882 'destroyed countless small shareholders, as did the Panama Canal Company scandal in 1888' (Birkett: 1990, 148–9). The Dreyfus affair of 1894 did less to damage army morale than it did to promote integral nationalism and raise the level of anti-semitism endemic to all layers of French society. This year coincided with the assassination of the President of the Republic, Sadi Carnot, by anarchists, a deed which was met with 'draconian repression' (McMillan: 1985, 26). The demographic decline – a growth of only 9.7 per cent during the period 1871–1911 as compared with Germany's 57.8 per cent for the same period – gave cause for considerable alarm for the future safety and prosperity of the country (ibid., 46). Furthermore, although France was still very much a rural society, the spread of mechanisation was having an effect on the industrial working class, which was threatened with less pay and unemployment. Nor did disaster spare rural France. The French wine-growing peasant farmer was hit by the vine-killing disease phylloxera in the 1890s. Urban France was also affected by disease in the form of syphilis. Last, but by no means least, the artistic world was as full of tensions and unrest as the rest of the nation: their *fin-de-sièclisme* mood was most readily exemplified by the works of the symbolists and the decadents (Birkett: 1990, 147).

Not all was doom and gloom. Military service by lottery was replaced by universal conscription in 1899, and the duration was reduced from five to three years (until 1870, it had been eight years). The effect of education was a progressive, if slow urbanisation of France's population. France's educated rural populace left the country in significant numbers to find work in the city. This in turn led to an increase in tension between classes. The bourgeois mentality (which upheld the defence of private property, political hegemony and a code of social behaviour) felt threatened by the increasing size of the urban working-class population from 1900 onwards (McMillan: 1985, 49–50).

The first fourteen years of the twentieth century did not witness a particularly strong wind of change. From 1902 to 1914, the Radical Republicans were in power (a coalition mostly of the Right with a few socialist politicians) and, whilst they promised social reforms, they only succeeded in sustaining social order. Militantly committed to Republicanism and the laicism of the state, their ideology was deeply nationalistic and any threats to social order, such as the serious spate of strikes during 1906–10 (under the respective prime ministerships of Georges Clemenceau and Aristide Briand), were brutally repressed (ibid., 19).

Meanwhile on the other side of the political spectrum, the Left were out of power and remained so until the unfortunate Cartel des gauches came to power in 1924 (lasting just two years). This was so despite the remarkable leadership of Jean Jaurès who brought the Left back from its total fragmentation at the beginning of the century to unification in 1905 and to an unprecedented electoral success in 1914. It was this very success, which would have allowed the Socialists to enter into an alliance in power with the Radicals, that was to result in Jaurès's assassination in that same year.

The year 1914 did, of course, mark a radical change in France's national history. The wastage and the devastation of human lives in World War I has been counted by historians, recounted by poets and authors and recorded from those who were there. But for one film immediately after the war (Gance's *J'accuse*, 1919), it remained unimagined on celluloid until the end of the 1920s – and even then only in a single film. France suffered 1,322,000 dead and 3,000,000 war cripples. The consequences for the demography of the country were disastrous. During the period 1915–19, France's birth-rate was halved. The number of state-registered postwar orphans and widows – 750,000 and 600,000, respectively – also give pause for thought. Before the war, France had a population of 40 million. As a consequence of the war, 12 per cent of her population was immediately affected (either through death, mutilation or loss).

Historians have written amply about the ineptitude of the French military and political leaders to conduct the war on the principle of economising lives, so I will refer only to the battle of Verdun as an example of both the awfulness of that war and the blindness (not to say folly) of those who conducted it. Verdun was a pyrrhic victory which says more about politicians' belief in patriotic or nationalistic myth-making than it does about their concern for the soldiers who had to fight it. Verdun was in reality the moment of crisis for France in the war, not because it had to be won but because in winning it, it soured the soldiers' desire to fight and was a major cause of the mutiny of some 40,000 men in the spring of 1917. I will quote James McMillan's description of this battle – a battle which incidentally (since it does concern myth) would make Pétain into a national hero:

> The slaughter continued throughout 1916, the year of Verdun. From the strategic point of view, the loss of the great fortress would not have been disastrous . . . unbeknown to the French people, who still imagined the fortress to be a key element in the country's defence, it no longer even contained any guns. Thus when the bombardment began in February, Joffre saw no good reason why he should divert resources from the massive Anglo-French offensive he was planning on the Somme. Prime Minister Briand thought otherwise. In his view, the loss of Verdun would be a crushing blow to French morale and would also jeopardize the survival of his own ministry. Joffre was over-ruled and . . . the French committed themselves to the all-out defence of an empty fortress which was made to stand as the symbol of their resolve to see the fight through to the finish. General Pétain . . . promised that 'they shall not pass' . . . but when the fighting finally ended in June 1916, France had lost another 300,000 men, the Germans 280,000.
>
> (McMillan: 1985, 64–5)

Mismanagement of the war, governmental secrecy in parliament, suspicion of treason and political unrest meant that cabinets and their prime ministers were quick to come and go (though this instability should not necessarily be perceived as just a wartime reality in French politics; for the period 1914–29, France had twelve successive governments, almost one a year on average). During 1914–18, France had five successive prime ministers. The legacy of the war-year cabinets, especially the last one under Clemenceau, was a swing to the Right. In the light of the Bolshevik revolution and the possible collapse of France in the war, the military were perceived by Clemenceau as a potential threat to the parliamentary institutions and it was his policies for consolidating 'the legitimacy of the Republican (i.e. civilian) form of government' that were largely responsible for this dominance of the Right in French politics after the war (ibid., 74).

Postwar France was in an economic shambles. During the war, she had abandoned the gold standard, borrowed massively and printed money. Her debt was enormous (175 billion francs, five times that of 1913) and inflation soared (400 per cent since 1914). The shortage of workers meant that she had to bring in immigrant labour (from Spain, Italy, Belgium and Poland). At first a million immigrants were brought in; by 1930 the figure had risen to 3 million. The Bolshevik revolution, too, had consequences for France. First, a significant number of Russian *émigrés*, mostly from the wealthy, educated classes, fled to France. Their cultural and economic significance was not without its resonances. For example, some went into film production (Abel Gance's huge epic *Napoléon, vu par Abel Gance*, 1927, was financed by *émigré* money, as were many of the historical reconstruction films of the 1920s). Other *émigrés* went into film-making, and some continued their acting career. Second, the Soviet Republic's refusal to honour repayment of the Tsars' debts put an end to the Franco-Russian alliance (to which France had been slavishly attached at great expense to herself). Finally, the Bolshevik revolution filled the Right and the bourgeoisie with fears of the red menace and its possible effect on the masses, that is, the working class.

It is worth pausing just briefly on these fears to explain that, since 1870 (if not before), at least where the peasant and working classes were concerned, France had a Left mentality even though the Right was predominantly in power. These popular classes were inflected by the French revolutionary tradition. All political groupings of the Left subscribed to the belief that their task was to complete what was begun in 1789. Thus, social reform would be very much inscribed into their demands. I have already mentioned the repression of strikes before the war – between 1870 and 1890 there were 2,700 strikes (ibid., 55). After the war, despite the legal (but often disregarded) institution of the 48-hour week in 1919, workers' conditions were no better than they had been before the war. In fact, mass-production and the introduction of Taylorism into some factories made them worse in some respects. Mass protests ensued. The great strikes of 1919 and 1920 were again ruthlessly put down. By now, however, disaffection amongst workers did not just target the Right and the bosses. Disillusionment with the unions also set in, with a consequent loss of a million members, leaving the Left fragmented once more. As a direct result, in 1920 a major breakaway group from the Socialist alliance formed, comprising approximately three-quarters of its members. It went on to form the French Communist party (*Parti communiste français* or PCF) which, more significantly still, supported Moscow's terms for the Third International. Ironically, therefore, whilst the bourgeoisie and the Right nurtured the myth of the revolutionary mob, in reality the political and social unrest kept the Left divided and continued to do so until the advent of the Popular Front in 1936 (ibid., 85–6).

This social class was not the only one deemed a threat to national unity. Women were also perceived as potential agents of disorder. During the war years, women constituted 25 per cent of munitions workers. By the end of the war, they represented 40 per cent of the total work-force. After demobilisation, this figure declined, especially in the industrial sector. However, there was a sharp increase in numbers in the tertiary sector (doubling 1906 figures), due to a rapid expansion in female white-collar jobs. As McMillan (1985, 82) points out, 'women were redistributed within the labour force, but without any serious alteration of the sexual division of labour. The "feminine" sector was merely reclassified.' Indeed, where women's rights were concerned, the war brought little if no change. After the war, the pro-natalist discourse that had been voiced in 1906 (when women constituted 36.6 per cent of the working population) was heard once again, but this time the campaign led to legislation. Imprisonment for distributing contraceptives was made law in 1920. The campaign's other demand, imprisonment for abortion, was decreed three years later. Not surprisingly, this pro-natalist discourse was matched by another that was anti-enfranchisement, and in 1922 the bill for female suffrage was defeated – interestingly by the Senators and not the Chamber of Deputies which had voted for it in 1919 (ibid., 83). The motivating reason for its defeat, however, was inspired by a totally different set of mentalities. This time, profound anticlerical republicanism was at work. The separation of state and church did not occur until 1905 (incidentally, a year after the signing of the Entente Cordiale with Britain). The Third Republic had fought long and hard for this separation and it was a commonly held belief that if women got the vote, first, it would be used as a pro-Catholic vote, and second, it would undermine the Church/state separation by voting in *députés* who were vociferous in their opposition to it.

The 1920s, then, saw the containment by the Right of the two movements – socialist and feminist – which they had most feared (since 1871) would cause disorder within the nation. Not surprisingly, the call for national unity was still to be heard, presumably because of the prevailing mood of pacifism. The 1920s was also the age of youth's rebellion (the *années folles* in France) and the 'get rich quick' mentality (times that we more readily associate in our collective memories with the late 1950s, early 1960s and the yuppie decade of the 1980s). In that climate of disgruntlement and unrest, it is small wonder, therefore, that the dominant discourses and icons mobilised by the Right were regressive and retro-nostalgic, harking back as they did to the 'good old days' of the Belle Epoque (when gold was the standard exchange).

By way of conclusion to this history insert it is worth-while noting what other myths these discourses generated, since they form part of the contemporaneous hegemony that must have impacted on film narratives and discourses. They are, in no particular order, motherhood (quite natural in the light of the falling birth-rate, but also to keep woman 'in her rightful place'); earth (the need to return to the land away from the 'evils of the city', but really to combat the bourgeoisie's unease at the process of urbanisation); peasantism (the peasants were still the largest group of voters) either in symbolic form as an ideal society (where the labourer toils the land with his (*sic*) tools), or given the iconic form of Marianne (then the figure of a peasant girl, symbol of labour and fertility – not the Bardot or Deneuve she became in modern iconography); Verdun (a symbol of France's courage and heroism – a double myth that would later be made into ideology by Pétain, the hero of Verdun); Joan of Arc (canonised in 1920 and symbol of France's heroism); and finally, the reification into myth of the one force that threatened to destroy all the preceding ones – the myth of the mob (or the masses) which identified workers with alcoholism, disease, insanity, decadence and anarchy.[10]

Consuming genres: typologies and change

Cinema is and always will be tightly bound up with consumer practice. Because it is tied to capital, it will always be caught between the modernity of its technology – that which is always new and being made new – and the *arrièrisme* of what it enunciates – where, to be consumable, it is obliged to transpose familiar cultural signs. These constraints, however, are not necessarily limitations. Cinema has the power to be at its most imaginative and inventive self in the way it transposes those signs. To illustrate this point, I will take the example of Feuillade's crime series *Fantômas* (1913–14). Although *Fantômas* is inscribed within a well-established genre, none the less, it is in its reformulation of the genre that it transcends repetition. Through a juxtaposition of the real with the unreal, through a tension between the extraordinary feats accomplished by the eponymous but evil hero and the ordinariness of the naturalistic background of Paris and its suburbs, Feuillade creates the thriller anew. Thus each genre, as Neale (1980, 50) puts it, is a repetition in difference.

Spectator taste and economic exigencies will necessarily influence a genre's fate. After all, in the early days of exhibition, departmental stores used to project films to attract customers to come in and browse around their various departments. Client and need, supply and demand are synergies that are ignored at the peril of bankruptcy (be it of ideas or capital). Changes must occur to attract disaffected audiences and new clientele. To that effect, genres will be newly created out of a reaction to another. Older genres will be subverted by new ones, and some will become co-opted or subsumed into others, etc. Other means to attract and secure regular patronage must also be found. In the early days of cinema, one method used was to bring stars on to the screen. Initially, from 1901 onwards, it was the popular entertainment stars from the music-hall, vaudeville or boulevard theatre who were enticed into film acting (although the very first stage star on film was the *Comédie française* suprema Sarah Bernhardt in *Le Duel d'Hamlet*, 1900). Subsequently, after 1908 (the date of the first *Film d'Art* production), the taboo of exchanging the boards for the clapper-board was erased and the film star system proper was born. It was during the 1920s that the star system developed to the massive scale that exists today, with the curious difference that in those days there were as many women stars as men stars.

The other key to building a faithful audience, in these early days, was the introduction of the series system, focusing around a central performer. This first occurred in 1906 with a plethora of comedy series; although initially shorts, by 1908 they were of standard length. Hot on their trail came the crime series *Nick Carter, roi des détectives* starring Pierre Bressol (directed by Victorin Jasset for Eclair) followed shortly thereafter, in 1912, by the western series *Arizona Bill* starring Joë Hamman (for Eclipse) and Jean Durand's series for Gaumont *Scènes de la vie de l'ouest américain*.

Abel (1984) devotes a great deal of his study to the different genres of the period 1915–29 and it has been of invaluable assistance in my endeavour to map the typologies of the whole of the Classical cinema period.[11] Any attempt to establish the typologies of cinema must also bear in mind their permeability and mutability. Thus they will stretch, shrink, fold into one another, and so on. In this first age of cinema, there were seven dominant if not distinct typologies of film, but they were not constant. In the diagram below, I have attempted to give a schematic impression of these typologies (the naming of which is taken from Abel) and their ability to shift.

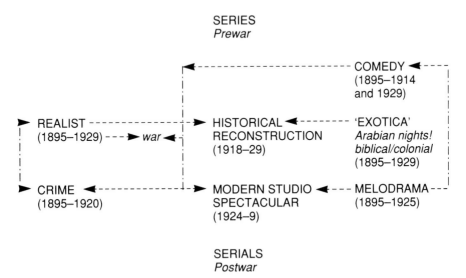

The two chronological modalities (series and serials) above and below serve to denote that, at times, a specific typology will have been produced in one of these ways (e.g., crime, comedy and western *series* prewar, historical reconstruction, melodrama and crime *serials* postwar). Series and serials were very specific to this first age of cinema and they virtually disappeared by 1928 (perhaps because there was not enough difference in repetition). This was not the case, however, for the typologies within the diagram. The arrows within the diagram point to cross-fertilisation between or subsuming of the different typologies. Thus melodrama inflected comedy prewar, and postwar the modern studio spectacular. During the 1920s it also filtered into realist films. After the mid-1920s, it declined in favour against the American imports, only to regain ascendance by the late 1930s. Crime serials, with their popularity on the wane in the early 1920s, were replaced by individual thriller films. Serials, as a format, cast their net elsewhere, picking up colonial and adventurer-brigand/highwayman themes. Serials also picked up with the sentimental film genre (abandoned child, orphan, *ingénue*, etc.) which as a genre belongs, in the first instance, to the melodrama typology but which also has generic traces of the crime serial. Within the 'exotica' typology, the Arabian nights and biblical genres gradually disappeared. It was the colonial film that survived and was reinscribed into the 1930s cinema, albeit with a far more pessimistic message.

As a genre, realist film has had considerably more lasting power than the others in so far as the constancy of its popularity is concerned. However, as a typology it is hardly the most clear cut. Certain realist films run very close to melodramas, others to the crime typology, and when war films enter into consideration, it is easy to see that this particular typology, whilst not a melting pot, is significantly more wide-ranging than the others in what it can encompass. To quote the war film once more, even though it is a subgenre of historical reconstructions, because of its topicality, it comes close to the realist mode. On the issue of historical reconstructions, they were very popular in the 1920s, but declined in the 1930s only to be revived again in the 1950s. The rise and fall of their popularity is clearly dictated by a postwar mentality, that is, the only way the immediate war could be addressed (if at all) was through mediation – thus, the heroics of France's more distant past (Napoleon, the Count of Monte Cristo, the Three Musketeers) mediated, stood in place for, the reality of its most recent past.

Comedy, the most specifically French genre, was almost killed off by the Great War. During the fourteen to fifteen years before its revival in the late 1920s it got integrated into other genres (police thrillers and Arabian nights films at first, and later the modern studio spectacular). As with the rest of French cinema, the advent of sound did much to restore the genre to its former popular status but, unlike the other genres, its popularity has not waned or experienced varied fortunes since that time. The genre which appears to have been the least proactive in terms of cross-fertilisation is, not unexpectedly, the modern studio spectacular. Although it subsumed other genres (the bourgeois melodrama and certain comic styles), it produced little, if any, inscriptions of its own amongst the other typologies. The most obvious reason for this lies with the very internationalism of the genre. Strongly influenced by the American studio spectacular and specifically targeting the American market, these films were more about style than narrative (although there are exceptions, when avant-garde film-makers take on the genre and use it to question capitalism and its effects as well as the genre itself and all that it connotes). Given the literary tradition of French cinema, this lack of a true narrative line represents a second reason for its orthogenetic deficiencies.

Early cinema catered for the popular classes, hence the predominance of slapstick and chase films – two eventual sub-genres of the comic and crime typologies. These films were soon to evolve into genres in their own right (i.e., providing a full narrative rather than a sketch). However, producers were quick to perceive that the public also had a taste for melodrama, including bourgeois melodrama. Theatre and literary adaptations predate the Great Exposition of 1900, where their projection was one of the main attractions (Guy: 1974, 51). But it was Pathé (in 1908), closely followed by Gaumont, who saw the merits of exploiting this particular genre to expand his clientele. In order to attract the bourgeoisie, he gave the label *Cinéma d'Art* to certain of the more prestigious productions within this genre. In so doing, he not only legitimated cinema-going as a middle-class activity but also made it an acceptable venue for theatre actors of repute.

Cinema may well have had as its earliest addressee the popular classes and many of the earliest films may well have seemed quite light in their morals, appealing as they did to the voyeuristic propensity of the spectator, but it would be wrong to assume that audience taste was for a simple diet of vulgarity, sexuality and violence (the myth of sex, drugs and rock 'n' roll in its earliest manifestation?). Indeed, the popular classes were no strangers to theatres and had acquired an exacting taste for a far wider fare of 'pleasurable forms of meaning' (Neale: 1980, 54). In fact, narrative cinema in the form of literary adaptations was a very early phenomenon, as Alice Guy's work for Gaumont exemplifies (1896–1905). Guy was almost certainly the first practitioner of narrative cinema and she was quick to set up a team of assistants including Ferdinand Zecca, Victorin Jasset and Louis Feuillade, all of whom would shortly become directors in their own right (working initially either for Gaumont or Pathé).[12] This cinema not only inscribed theatre into its earliest practices, it also adapted novels or used novelists' narrative style as a source of inspiration and wrote its own scenarios too. Nor were the popular classes without representation, albeit not in an unproblematised way. Early, realist films, as exemplified by Zecca's *L'Histoire d'un crime* (1901), *Victimes de l'alcoolisme* (1902) and *La Grève* (1904), brought the proletariat on to the screen and their subject matter was as much inflected by Zola's realist-naturalism as the acting style was by the naturalist school much in vogue in Paris theatres at the time.

However, these same films also provided a binary reflexivity on the prole-tariat as, in turn, 'without' and criminal, 'without' and alcoholic, 'without' and unruly and, conversely, unhesitatingly privileged the superiority of middle-class values. It might seem too easy to make this last comment with hindsight, but it should not be forgotten that Zola, who predates cinema, was writing precisely from this moralistic point of view (the working-class Lantier family, for example, was doomed not because of poverty, but because of its excesses with drink over so many generations).

Four important factors can be drawn from the above, all of which address the specificity of French cinema. They are first, the literary tradi-tion, second, film-making as team-work (*travail d'équipe*), third, traditions of performance (i.e., that actors traditionally come from the theatre or the music-hall), and finally, the 'true to life' 'anecdotal gaze on the popular and familiar environment' (Sadoul: 1962, 30). In geological terms, these are the primary hallmarks of the French cinema tradition. There will, of course, be secondary and tertiary ones (*cinéma d'auteur* and episodic film are two that come to mind), but it is quite significant that these earliest traditions and signifying practices are still present in much of today's cinema.

A first set of categories: series and serials, comedy and crime

Early film comedies, in the form of chases, gags and skits, soon developed into two major but not necessarily always distinctive strains – the burles-que and situation comedy (or comedy of manners). A second change of emphasis came in 1907 with a change in marketing policy by Pathé closely followed, in 1908, by Gaumont. Realising the capital potential attached to the popularity of the singular comic type (whose stage name was legion with the popular classes), these two companies soon adopted the strategy of the comedy series. Most of the comedians to enter into film were from the circus, the boulevard theatres or the music-hall and they brought their comedy with them. These comedians were predominantly of the first strain of comedy films and played buffoons, comic idiots or simpletons. The most representative of these types were, in order and by their stage name, Onésime (Ernest Bourbon), Boireau (André Deed) and Prince/Rigadin (Charles Petitdemange). More representative of the second strain were the theatre-trained Max Linder and Léonce Perret. A little later a third type of comedy series, occurring almost by accident, was launched by the film-maker Louis Feuillade. Realising the appeal of children in film (based on the success of his 1906 film *Les Deux gosses*), in 1910 he launched a child comic series entitled *Bébé* for Gaumont. He followed this series by *Bout-de-zan* (launched in 1912, again for Gaumont). The *Bébé* series was taken up by Pathé and, in that same year, further competition was brought in by the smaller production company Eclair, with their *Willy* series.

For twenty years French cinema was the 'king' of comedy and 'most historians would agree that it was the French who almost singlehandedly created film comedy' (Abel: 1984, 220). The advent of war put an end to production and the war years themselves saw Chaplin appearing on the French screen and Linder and Perret embarking for the American studios. After the war, the comedy genre all but died. The important point, however, is that this particular specificity of French cinema was openly admired and readily imitated by the United States. Chaplin (whose career in America started in 1916) acknowledged his debt to Max Linder. Mack Sennett's Keystone cops have their forefathers in Jean Durand's comic troupe Les Pouics (the supporting cast to the Onésime series). Finally, the American child comedy series owe more than a little to Feuillade's effective directorial style with children. Of all the genres, then, comedy was the one that had the most visible cross-fertilisation effect, and this time (culturally speaking only) it was to France's advantage. Apart from the predictable 'adorableness' of the naughty little boy or girl, what attracted the Americans was the variety of comic styles which ranged from the zany-surreal of Durand's Onésime films to the more natural, self-mocking and psychologically inflected performance of Max Linder, whose effete dandyism and well-heeled social status none the less did nothing to secure him success in his amorous pursuits.

A similar strategy of running a series around a particular villain or detective/sleuth was adopted equally early for crime films. It also seems appropriate to include westerns as a sub-genre in this category because they too are based on the principle of law and disorder, violence and suspense. Again, but for entirely separate reasons, neither type survived in the series format into the 1920s. The western series fell victim quite early to its own export success and to the war. Although the genre originated in France, it was soon colonised by the Americans – a demise which provides yet another example of cross-fertilisation working against France's film industry. In addition, the crime series lost their appeal because they were either too fantastic or too chauvinistic in their tone for postwar mentality. Public taste was for a greater – although not to the point of graphic – realism. Unlike the western, however, the crime series was not totally effaced, rather it was eclipsed by the sentimental series. Abel (1984, 79) makes the point that the narrative structure of the former inflects that of the latter, that is, there are still victims and rescuers, but now the victims are all either women or orphans (or both) and the rescuers are no longer the force of law but the 'sentimental hero'. But I am jumping the gun: what were the prewar crime series about?

Genres both do things and reveal things. They perpetuate what is there and respond to expectations. For instance, comedy responds to the desire to feel superior as one laughs at the foibles in/of others. In that laughter, a certain recognition takes place (otherwise it would not succeed as comedy) and so one also laughs at one's own weaknesses (albeit indirectly). The comic genre perpetuates the idea that we all have weak points and colludes in our desire to see ourselves as funny, ridiculous even (but not risible). In this respect, it is possible to see how genres institutionalise not just the codes and conventions peculiar to cinema but also the way social codes and conventions are perceived (Neale: 1980, 28). A discussion of the crime genre should make this point clearer. The crime genre is based *par excellence* on the hermeneutic code of enigma and resolution. Amongst its premises are those of good and evil, victims and rescuers (in the form of the judiciary or the hand of retribution), order and disorder, etc. It is the tension between these sets of juxtapositions (rather than the enigma itself, to which we may already have the answer) which creates the suspense that is the vital convention of the genre (e.g., in a western, the suspenseful question is will the good-guy (*sic*) get there in time to rescue the victim (read, female) from the bad-guy?). This tension will also determine the cinematic codes necessary to sustain that state of suspense. Simultaneously, the social codes and conventions, mobilised by the genre, dictate that there must be a solution and retribution (even though it is common knowledge that most crimes go unsolved).

Crime series bring with them the satisfaction of repetition in retribution – satisfaction, that is, for the spectator who knows that Nick Carter (1909–12) or Arizona Bill (1912–14) will solve the enigma and re-establish order. Satisfaction too because that same spectator has been voyeuristically positioned on the tightrope of suspense between good and evil, that is, s/he has been simultaneously the observer/perpetrator, observer/victim and the observer/solver of the crime. What, however, if good does not triumph over evil, or at least not until the very last film in the series (an end that is unknown to the spectator until that last film is projected)? Such was the case for Feuillade's *Fantômas* (1913–14) and it is worth pausing briefly on this series to make the point that early silent cinema was not a primitive 'cinema-in-the-making' but already complex in its representation.

Unlike the *Nick Carter* or *Arizona Bill* series, which were based on American pulp fiction (dime novels), *Fantômas* had as its literary source the very popular French novelettes of the same title written by Marcel Allain and Pierre Souvestre. According to Allain, these texts were very much improvised and the authors' spontaneous fabulations were recorded on to a dictaphone before being written up.[13] Undoubtedly, this *écriture directe* (automatic writing) contributes to the anarchistic tenor of the film series which, intentionally or not, disturbs. Equally disturbing is Fantômas himself (the eponymous hero/protagonist played by René Navarre), not just because he engages in murderous escapades but also because as his name connotes, he is elusive and this renders him virtually invisible. The masked murderer appears from and disappears into the Parisian night. He is unsuccessfuly pursued in the Paris sewers (unlike Harry Lime), eludes arrest in a number of pyrotechnical feats, and becomes the specialist branch detective sent from Scotland Yard to arrest Fantômas (i.e., himself). Still later he becomes the examining magistrate in a provincial town. Needless to say, the two representatives of law and order have succumbed to Fantômas's murdering practices. Even when he is finally arrested and sentenced to the guillotine, he still manages to escape by sending in his place an actor who made a successful career out of mimicking him on the Paris boulevards. What disturbs, therefore, is not just his invisibility but also his mergeability – the fact that he can slip either side of law and order. He threatens both with his evil sadistic practices and with his normalness. Equally, he fascinates through his worldliness and underworldliness. Finally, and perhaps most importantly, he disturbs because of the anarchistic subversiveness of his anti-social and anti-institutional behaviour.

One should remember that the climate of the time was one of increasing international unease. Internally, groups of anarchists were at work. Revolutionary syndicalism (closely aligned with anarchism) in the form of the CGT (*Confédération générale du travail*) was taking a foothold, although it was not then and never did become the threat the bourgeoisie, remembering the strike-riven years 1906–10, believed it to have been. However, those years had left some indelible traces and not just with the bourgeoisie. The popular classes had no great love for the forces of law and order which had been so draconically employed to repress those strikes. The social and political unease of the time, as well as the threat of war, do appear, therefore, to receive reflexivity in this series. As Claude Beylie says, it is difficult not to perceive in *Fantômas* a secretion of revolutionary combativeness – that, and the fear it inspires.[14]

Feuillade's next production, the serial *Vampires* (1915–16), was no less disturbing. As with the *Fantômas* series, the narrative was totally improvised and unpredictable and the disregard for law and order just as poignantly normalised. The fantastic realism of both *Fantômas* and *Vampires* was seized upon later by the Surrealists who, rightly or wrongly, perceived in it the anarchic subversiveness to which Beylie alludes (D'Hugues and Marmin: 1986, 71). Starring Musidora (of music-hall fame, later to become a film-maker) as the notorious Irma Vep (an anagram of vampire), to the glorification of crime and ridiculing of police of *Fantômas* now came the added element of cross-dressing. In her numerous disguises used to escape, Musidora/Vep switches gender with conviction and ease. The hero, a reporter, becomes fascinated by her and, predictably, falls in love with her (to his wife's dismay). However, he is fascinated by all her representations, male and female, and so this infatuation does become problematic as it switches between 'ordinary' fetishism and homoeroticism.

I would not claim that Feuillade is the first to have put on screen the issues of speculation and recognition/misrecognition. What is intriguing is that it occurred at a time when the role and the look of women in society were changing profoundly because of the war. In Renoir's *La Grande illusion* (1937) reference is made to the fact that women have shorter hair and skirts, to which one of the protagonists responds by saying 'it must be like making love to a boy'. Undoubtedly the 'masculinisation' of both their looks and their function (working in traditionally male jobs) did have socio-sexual resonances during that period (and beyond), and who better than Musidora with her 'troubling eroticism' (ibid., 106) to exemplify the ambiguity of female sexuality as sensed by men (and women?) of that time.

During and after the war, series as a modality became transmuted into serials, the difference being that where series were complete units in themselves, serials carried a story over a number of episodes. These serials were known as *ciné-romans* and their texts were published episode by episode. On the crime genre front, Pathé imported its French–American-made products (*Les Mystères de New-York* with Pearl White as its central heroine being its most notorious success) and Gaumont countered with the excellent services of Feuillade who, before turning to sentimental serials in the 1920s, still had four further crime series up his sleeve (*Vampires*, 1915–16, *Judex*, 1916–17, *Tih Minh*, 1919 and *Barrabas*, 1920). However, because serials had become *the* marketing strategy to get the audiences in and to act as a bulwark against the American products, they proceeded to encompass a wider range of genres. Thus, costume and sentimental serials joined ranks briefly with the crime serial – the latter type died out in 1922, but the other two (thanks to the entrepreneurial skills of Jean Sapène and Louis Nalpas) continued well into the 1920s.[15]

Since Richard Abel (1984) has dealt so amply with these two types of serials, rather than separate them out here from the rest of the post-war production, they will be examined in conjunction with other genres not yet discussed (namely realist films, the melodrama and historical reconstruction) and in relation to the socio-political ambiance of the time.

A second set of categories: realism and history

This title might seem a bit bold to cover all the aforementioned genres, but I hope to convince the reader that it is quite a useful category umbrella. Earlier I mentioned the difficulties of defining realist film because, as a typology, it overlaps or slips into other genres and equally can be inflected by others. Thus, melodrama filters into realist films as do war films, a sub-genre of historical reconstructions which in themselves are not without their own paradox for, whilst they are not realist films, none the less their characterisation can be based on real people and this in turn generates the question: are costume dramas a sub-genre of historical reconstructions or melodrama? Evidently crime films can run along this realism/history axis, but as they are less prevalent after the war, they are of less concern here. In any event, this second category of realism and history sets up an axis along which these various genres can slip and slide as they jostle in their impermanence.

After the war, what sort of image did France's cinema project? Comedy came to an end at the outbreak of war and did not reappear again in full force until the late 1920s. Crime series died out in the early 1920s. Evidently, neither genre spoke to the terrible loss of life and the shifts in social structures that were the result of the war. Nor did they sit easily with the corresponding social upheavals that, if not generated by the war, were brought to a critical watershed in its aftermath. As can be perceived, the two major preoccupations for the French mentality after the war were how to deal, on the one hand, with the loss of life (of France's youth) and, on the other, with the conflict of classes. The cinema responded to the former preoccupation with two dominant categories of films: first, the costume drama and historical reconstructions, and second, the sentimental series and realist films. With regard to class conflict, whilst the first category of films did not necessarily bypass it, it was the second category (sentimental and realist films) as well as (later on) the modern studio spectacular which more readily addressed that issue.

Given France's huge losses during the war it is both surprising and unsurprising that there exists such a dearth of films dealing directly with the war. After the war, three films were made which attempted to show its horror – Gance's *J'accuse* (1919), Henri Desfontaines' *Le Film du poilu* (1928) and Léon Poirier's *Verdun, visions d'histoire* (1928). In Desfontaines' film, a youngster who plays at war with his friends and gets seriously hurt is rescued from his fantasies about the glory of war and shown the truth of war when the wounded veteran (*le poilu* in the title) shows him some real images of war. The intention of the film is to show that the horrors of war do not represent a reality that should be glorified. Rather, only labour (*le travail*) will ensure peace and prosperity. In Poirier and Gance's films, veterans of the war actually agreed to return to Verdun to act or re-enact moments (imaginary and real) of the battle that was so costly to human lives, thereby attesting to the mythical importance of that single combat. The intention, however, was not to glorify war, but to condemn it and those responsible for it. Gance's film falls short of the mark because of the melodramatic triangular love story which threads its way through the film but functions metonymically on a much too simplistic level for France's plight during the war. That part of the narrative goes as follows: two Frenchmen are in love with the same French woman; this woman, who is married to one of the two men, gets raped by a third – a

German – by whom she has a child; to avenge this act of violation, the two Frenchmen dissolve their differences and return to the front where one gets killed and the other shell-shocked. 'Seemingly critical of a patriotism that blindly ignores the death it causes, *J'accuse* ends up celebrating the dead's sacrifice as a form of patriotism' (Abel: 1984, 302).

Poirier's film, which he saw as 'a tribute to the collective suffering of the French people' (cited by Abel: 1984, 204), succeeded in depersonalising the message through its blend of documentary and fiction film and through its non-caricatural representation of the German soldiers (who also volunteered to re-enact Verdun). Although it cannot be considered a pacifist film of the same ilk as Renoir's *La Grande illusion*, none the less it does display the common suffering of French and Germans alike and so is considerably less chauvinistic in tone than Gance's film. This is not how Poirier's film was seen some twenty years later when, ironically enough, it was pointed to by the Left as the first in a series of patriotic and colonising films that marked him out as the 'official film-maker of the Third Republic' (i.e., the voice of the Right).[16] It is worth mentioning perhaps that in *Verdun, visions d'histoire* Maréchal Pétain donned his old uniform and played himself. Thus, when Poirier made *Jeannou* (1943) with its clear Vichyite message, his earlier film may have become (s)tarred with the same brush. In any event, *Jeannou* brought Poirier into discredit and four years later he gave up his film-making ambitions. Other than these three films of apparent protest, few others were made in the 1920s (I have come across only nine titles, five of them coming out in 1928, coinciding obviously with the tenth anniversary of the end of the war but perhaps also acting as a bulwark against American products on the same subject).[17] These films either exalted the sacrifice of those French who died to save the nation from the invading German, or reconstructed other arenas of that war, that is, the air or maritime arenas.[18] In both instances, these films were literary adaptations by successful novelists whose version did not counter the official line but served rather to sanitise the unmentionable war.

To this dearth of films, however, corresponded (on the history end of the axis) a plethora of historical reconstruction and costume films, almost as if the experience of the war had been/had to be sublimated into spectacle. In other words, earlier mythologies would have to function as oracles for the present and suggest an interpretation of the present. Marcel Oms (1981), in a truly enlightened piece of writing, demonstrates how these historical reconstructions and literary adaptations should be read as the glorious rendez-vous of the nation with history – a rendez-vous which, without the educational reforms, might not have taken place and which operates as follows. Thanks to education there is a common font of knowledge shared by all – what Oms calls a universality of knowledge or reference points that the spectator has via education. The procedure is to take a precise history episode taught in school and to dramatise it into film. This moment refers back/forward to the 'Great War' (as World War I was then known) and suggests that, by participating in this last war (the war to end all wars), the French had participated in the totality of the History of France. In other words, these films reveal that everything is taking place as if the Great War was the end of an historical process towards national unity. A two-fold process is at work here. What these films are really creating is in the first instance an imaginary history of France as much as a history of an imaginary France, and in the second instance a sense of participation that is totally fictional. Misrecognition passes as recognition. The goal of the Revolution is complete: France is one nation united at last.

In the Introduction to this book, I pointed out how important myth is to the ideology of nationhood and how the concept of nation exists to stop dissent. Earlier in this chapter, I made mention of the civil unrest that categorised the two postwar periods of this epoch (the Franco-Prussian war and the Great War). I also indicated how dear the French revolutionary tradition was to the Left and that France – especially where the peasant class was concerned – had a Left mentality even though, predominantly, she was governed by the Right. Given that the Great War devastated the rural population (54 per cent of those who died were peasants), it was vital to those in power that the deaths were seen to have a purpose because of the huge potential for anarchists and radical revolutionaries to foment unrest. Thus, at least where film was concerned, the myths and icons mobilised by historical reconstructions served the ruling bodies' purpose well. What I am suggesting is not that there was a deliberate propagandist plot afoot, but that dealing with an immediate war (especially the size of World War I) is almost impossible. Any attempt to represent it in an acceptable way will necessarily lead film-makers to go further back in time, and in that they will simultaneously be dealing with the war, they will inevitably sanitise it or make its 'truth' more acceptable.

Oms goes on to remark that the further the fiction is away from the present, the more it appears close to it. He quotes as an example two films that revivify, indirectly in the first intsance and directly in the second, the myth of Joan of Arc. First, there is *Le Miracle des loups* (Bernard, 1924) in which the town under siege is Beauvais and its brave defender who organises victory (just a few years after Jeanne d'Arc's own bravery) is Jeanne Hachette. Second, there is Marc de Gastyne's *La Merveilleuse vie de Jeanne d'Arc* (1929). Since Joan is the symbol of France's heroism she can ask the question: was the battle worth all those dead? It is not a pacifist's question – history books have proved that she was right to fight on in the siege of Orléans. Thus the analogy gets drawn between the mentality of the Great War combatants and that of Joan of Arc and Jeanne Hachette (with the further connotation that Orléans/Beauvais is Verdun). Through their images and narrative, the films eternalise the theme (heroism in adversity, sacrifice, duty, etc.) and bring together the two times.

This same phenomenon is at work in the Napoleonic films, the most exemplary of which are Bernard Duchamps' *L'Agonie des aigles* (1921, with Gaby Morlay in her first important screen role) and Gance's epic *Napoléon vu par Abel Gance* (1927) in which, for the spectator of the 1920s, the *grognard* (Napoleonic footsoldier) was the equivalent of the *poilu* (1914–18 peasant-footsoldier). This time the conflation of the two times points backwards and, in the minds of the French of the 1920s, the 1918 victory avenges Waterloo and represents a duty (at long last) accomplished.[19]

Oms sees the same process at work with literary adaptations/costume films which are again inflected by the notion of a more widespread education. Whereas with historical reconstruction the process is to authenticate the present through the past, here the process becomes one of authenticating fiction through real décor – hence the preoccupation with getting the settings and historical utterances 'right'. Thus, these films – in so far as they respond to what the public will have made of a work of fiction in relation to history (i.e., what has been taught) – quickly become filmed history and therefore indistinguishable in purpose from historical reconstructions. Oms concludes that this totalising intentionality has a political purpose which is to educate, to give history lessons, to make the spectator feel s/he is part of the national community (i.e., France's historic heritage).

It must be remembered that costume films and literary adaptations came to cinema in all seriousness through the *Film d'Art* series (1908) and that their purpose was to elevate cinema to a legitimacy (an aesthetic even) that would attract the bourgeoisie, the point being that Oms' notion of pedagogical credibility is not specific to the 1920s cinema. Indeed, some of the earliest films were adaptations of novels by Zola and Hugo (as the films of Guy and Zecca at the turn of the century attest). In some respects the *Film d'Art* and its imitators (Pathé's SCAGL) made more prestigious and packaged more attractively a practice already in existence (albeit on a smaller scale). In other respects, it did represent a bold new departure and fixed one of the great traditions of performance (stage actor as screen star). In this way, the cultural capital of literary adaptations/costume films was doubled by the advent to the screen of the famous stage actors Le Bargy, Harry Baur, Réjane, Sarah Bernhardt, Albert Dieudonné and Gabrielle Robinne (to name but a few). Just as significantly, the totalising effect quadrupled: '*there* was the nation's author [national cultural heritage, mark one], the author's book [national cultural heritage, mark two], the film of the book [national cultural heritage, mark three] and *there* were the nation's actors [national cultural heritage, mark four]' – a truly national cinema, therefore, that was much liked by its audiences. Given the kudos of the home-grown product over other (foreign literary) texts, which can be measured by the numerous remakes (just within this period) of, for example, *Les Misérables* (1911, 1912, 1925), *L'Assommoir* (under various title guises in 1902, 1909, 1911, 1920), *Les Trois mousquetaires* (1913, 1921–22), *Le Comte de Monte-Cristo* (1914–17, 1929), there can be no doubting the French taste for their own classics, for seeing 'their history' (a tradition that carries on today in a similar reflexive way). All was not pedagogical or historicist zeal, however. There were sound economic reasons, closely allied to the American's taste for this genre, for investing (quite substantially) in these films – national cinema not just as conveyor of myth, but as an exportable commodity.

Less successful as exports, but equally essential to the question of the representation of the war in postwar cinema, were the sentimental melodrama and realist films – films which to differing degrees hooked on to the realist end of the history/realism axis proposed as a paradigm to discuss postwar production. It will come as no surprise that the dominant narratives focused on the orphaned or bereaved child, abandoned mother or vulnerable *ingénue* – all subjects for predatory practices, suffering and exploitation. Apart from the child orphans who were both male and female, the other, displaced victims of loss were women – displaced because what was formerly there in place no longer exists. The extent of the suffering through loss pushed many to attempt suicide. Whilst it may be perceived as a melodramatic convention, none the less the motivating force which pushed the victims to suicide was very different from that which impelled protagonists of the prewar melodrama. Before the war it was marital infidelity that drove one or more of the individuals in the triangular relationship to put, or attempt to put, an end to her/his suffering or guilt. Remorse and forgiveness were the primary moral values which, in the end, would facilitate a restoration of the couple or family unit.

After the war, although not to the exclusion of the love-triangle melodrama, a new discourse was introduced which addressed the victims of loss rather than the transgressors of social codes. Now it was children who almost succeeded in killing themselves (*Visages d'enfants*, Feyder, 1925). Single mothers abandoned their children (where they would be found) and take their lives (as happens at the beginning of Boudrioz's *L'Atre*, 1923); or they were obliged to give up their child and literally die from the loss (*El Dorado*, L'Herbier, 1921); *ingénues* despairing of a safe haven sought an end, through death, to their insecurity (*Nêne*, Baroncelli, 1924); or they were forced away from happiness only to be united with the loved one in death (*Jocelyn*, Fescourt, 1922). In most cases the suicide attempts were unsuccessful. The child or woman was rescued and either came to terms with her/his loss (miraculously) and/or had the good fortune to be recuperated into family or married life. Such endings, of course, glossed over the reality of the pain suffered by the true victims. Equally sanitising, they gave a somewhat unrealistic hope of renewal, set as they were against the very bleak backdrop of loss. However, this very sentimentalism must be perceived as a throwback to the genre of prewar years. This is perhaps best demonstrated by the fact that the child orphans did not always have to come to terms with a lost father (who would have been very absent postwar), but sometimes with a lost mother who has been replaced by a stepmother.

The film-maker Henri Fescourt complained that, with only a few exceptions (including some of his films), postwar cinema did not give a true transparence on France and its huge social problems. Expressing his indignation at cinema's reluctance to reveal the social injustices of the time, he accused this same cinema of not having changed the themes it treated since its prewar days.[20] On the basis of the above paragraphs it would appear that he was neither wrong, but nor was he totally correct. I would like to reinvoke the realism/history axis to make a few more points on this issue of reflexivity before coming to considerations which bear on the other, second preoccupation of the time which Fescourt's comments have brought back on to the agenda, that of social conflict. In answer to Fescourt's claims it could be said that those films positioned toward the history end of the axis tended to reconstruct/reconstrue recent history by making it 'other'. On the one hand, this rewriting sanitises that particular war, and renders it imageless. On the other, it mobilises a myth whereby the war's significance can be historically and mnemonically, but not mentally, understood. Those films positioned toward the realism end (melodrama and realist films) similarly risk trivialising loss because of the recuperation at the end of most, but not all, of them. This sentimental recuperation notwithstanding, these films supplied a psychological *vérisme* based on a demographic fact (and it is worth noting that many of these orphan films are rural-based, thus corresponding to the areas of the greatest loss of life). Similarly, in positioning the bereaved one as subject which many did, they provided a subjectivity on the meaning of loss (albeit not without its problematics because of its bourgeois recuperation, mainly through the narrative).

These films, then, are about personal disruption and historical misrecognition. In that respect they are, respectively, too specific or too general to convey more than individual suffering or collective amnesia. It is not difficult, therefore, to see social injustice – in terms of cinematic representation – as diaspora. But melodrama, as a genre, is the truth of bourgeois, not proletarian, recuperation. It returns a familiar image of deprivation and injustice to the proletariat and a self-satisfying image for the bourgeoisie that its world is best. And for all that this genre, during the narrative, may transgress social, moral or religious codes, none the less these same codes will be firmly reinforced at the end of the film.[21] Thus, when and if social conflict is the subject matter, it is very unlikely that it will escape this canonic representation. Interestingly, this genre, when in the hands of the avant-garde, did not particularly address social conflict, rather it stayed with the dominant discourses of melodrama, albeit with a very different style of representation.

Social conflict, however, did not go unmentioned in the films of the 1920s. Work and capital, education and urbanisation were themes that appeared fairly regularly in three different but not disparate typologies, namely realist films, melodrama and the modern studio spectacular. Realist films and melodrama overlap as do melodrama and the modern studio spectacular. Perhaps the most useful way of expressing their difference as genres (and bearing in mind the realism/history axis) is to see them in relation to the notion of excess. Clearly, realist films will be the lowest in excess whereas the other two will have differing and varied degrees of excess. The modern studio spectacular in terms of set and design alone will already be in excess before its narrative is even in place. Where melodrama is concerned, diegetic space is less likely to be in excess than the narrative line, which will be redolent with possibilities. The most remarkable example of diegetic excess (time- and narrative-wise) is, to my mind, Gance's interminable *La Roue* (1922–3) with its nine hours of a man agonising over his desire for his stepdaughter, during which time he both goes blind and inadvertently drives his son (who also desires the young woman whom he assumes to be his sister) to his death. Although not immediately discernible as a film about social conflict or injustice, it enters into the arena of social matters on the issue of sexuality (because it is about incest, or proto-incest), which is an area of social conflict.

Early efforts to tone down the excesses of melodrama can be found in the prewar series of so-called realist films made by Louis Feuillade for Gaumont (*La Vie telle qu'elle est*, 1912), Ferdinand Zecca and René Leprince for Pathé (*Scènes de la vie cruelle*, *Scènes de la vie bourgeoise*, *Drames de la vie moderne*, 1912) and Victorin Jasset for Eclair (*Les Batailles de la vie*, 1913). The titles are quite revealing in terms of the ingenuousness of their misrepresentation for, as the films themselves reveal, they are anything but the 'slice of life' or 'kitchen sink' realism they purport to be but instead are fairly indistinguishable from the moralising melodramas even though the subject matter is more orientated towards social issues. Thus, for example, the evils of greed and the deleterious effects of strikes and syndicalism make frequent forays on to the screen, only to be swept aside by the recentring forces of right-minded thinking (i.e., the bourgeois morality).

This same right-minded thinking prevailed during the first part of the war, producing patriotic melodramas that either demonised the German enemy (Feuillade's *Herr Doktor*, 1917) or glorified the sacrificial spirit of the ordinary French men and women (Louis Mercanton's *Mères françaises*, 1916). Popular public distaste for these films plus an increased liking for American comedies and serials and, equally importantly, the renown surrounding Cecil B. De Mille's film *The Cheat* (1915), which arrived in France in 1916, meant that styles had to change. The love-triangle melodrama returned to full strength (Perret's *L'Imprévu*, 1916, Gance's *Mater Dolorosa*, 1917), albeit under a slightly different guise, inflected as it was by De Mille's and D.W. Griffith's melodramas and the greater *vérisme* of American acting.

After the war, the prevailing mood of discontentment worried the possessing classes, as did their fear of bolshevism. Many of the realist/melodrama films of that period reflect those areas of concern. In *Dans la tourmente* (Bergerat, 1918) and *La Croisade* (Le Somptier, 1920), anarchy (i.e., bolshevism) is revealed as the danger that could destroy France's plans for reconstruction. In both films it is a beautiful woman who is, respectively, the empassioned bolshevik who will stab her son for her political beliefs or the anarchist temptress who will attempt to seduce a war veteran away from his duty to rebuild his father's factory (in both instances the women are echoes/simulacra of the Mata Hari myth of revolutionary ideology as embodied by feminine beauty). The former film (financed, incidentally, by the official propaganda services) reveals the horrors and tyranny of bolshevism, the latter the invincibility of the patriotic Frenchman who, remembering the sacrifices of the war, returns to the task of reconstruction with a renewed and fraternal enthusiasm.

Le Travail (Pouctal, 1919–20) and *Montée vers l'Acropole* (Le Somptier, 1920) engage in another, but related aspect of this fear of industrial unrest. The importance of the interrelatedness of work and capital is stressed in both films, as are the ways in which it can be achieved or, conversely, undermined. In Pouctal's film, a serial in seven parts adapted from Zola's novel, the threats to the nation's efforts towards reconstruction and economic redress come in the form of strikes which lead to loss of work, hunger and alcoholism (the 'mob's' only recourse, it would appear). On the other hand, in the words of the (middle-class) hero, Luc Froment (an engineer – the nutritional connotations of his name should be noted: 'froment' means wheat), success will come about through collaboration between the classes and through social justice. Both are facilitated by Froment, who acts as the middle-man between his men (from whom he demands much, but whose rights he defends) and the industrial bosses. In Le Somptier's film, the key to success is collaboration not just between the classes, but between generations too. The issue of the conflict of generations and its solution (that the older generation must bow to the younger one for the sake of renovation) are played out almost allegorically with two men (one young, the other older) rivalling each other for the hand of the daughter of a rich industrialist whose name happens to be France. In the end, the older man, who has schemed to destroy his rival's chances (by making him appear responsible for strike-raising in the factory owned by France's father), admits defeat and steps out of the way. Now the aspirations expressed in the title of the film can be achieved. The new Acropolis can be built, youth can go forward with France![22]

The message of moral rearmament in these realist/melodramas is clear, revealing a postwar mentality wishing to believe in a fraternal myth of national unity. In this respect, these films become a moralising agent whose function is to bring the proletariat 'back to its senses'. But it must be remembered that the bourgeoisie did not feel threatened by industrial unrest alone; it also feared the growing urbanisation which resulted from the war and from the effects of more widespread education. The 1920s witnessed numerous realist films set in rural France. Abel (1984, 120) makes the point that the increase in location shooting after the war came about through economic exigencies as much as any other. He also makes the interesting point that the rural areas chosen excluded the devastated north-east of France. Thus an ideal rural France was represented, allowing national sentiment to be exalted through the beauty of the landscape. More than that, this representation legitimated a return to the land as a place better than the city. The myth of the prodigal son abounded, as one would expect, and the dominant narrative of these films addressed the family. Generation and class conflicts, therefore, were 'naturally' inscribed into the narrative. This narrative commonly showed the disintegration and subsequent re-integration of the family structure which came about as the result of differing ambitions between father or parents and (usually) son and their subsequent reconciliation. In Théo Bergerat's film, *La Terre commande* (1920), for example, the son, impelled by his fiancée's fantasies, leaves the country for Paris against his father's express wishes. There, misery and a sick child soon send them scuttling back home, but the father will only accept the child. Not until the couple are truly repentant will they be allowed back into the family fold once more.

Alternative versions reveal the family structure being endangered by the 'over-education' of a daughter (Fescourt's *Blanchette*, 1921). In the somewhat darker *La Bête traquée* (Le Somptier, 1922), the family is assailed by the misguided love of a daughter for a brutal murderer – in choosing the untamed rather than the tempered (her other suitor's) face of nature she brings about the death of her father. Finally, as an apotheosis of pessimism, the family is killed off by the greed of the son or sons (Antoine's *La Terre*, 1921).

It should not escape the reader that family and father are interchangeable signs. Family and patriarchy are one and the same and order can only be sustained if filial duty is maintained. Filial disobedience threatens the continuity of agricultural life, the products of which feed the nation. France's future is as much dependent on rural stability as it is on industrial regeneration. This insistence on filial obedience must be seen as much in respect of the huge war losses for the peasant class as in the light of dominant bourgeois ideology. It is equally evident that the rhetoric of these films is hardly distinguishable from that which was mobilised twenty years later by Pétain's National Revolution, whose motto '*Famille, Patrie, Travail*' summed up the ideology of the Vichy regime. This extolled the virtues of rural life, the labours of the peasant and the importance of motherhood, all in the guise of promoting moral regeneration and national unity. No mention is made in these narratives of the inheritance laws (parcelisation of the land amongst the sibling inheritors) which were effectively crippling the agricultural economy and represented an impelling reason for the younger, educated generation to leave home for the city.

One final point on the rural realist/melodramas concerns an effect of style upon the diegetic functioning of the genre. Abel (1984, 112–17) makes the point that there was a tendency within these films to match the *mise-en-scène* and type of shot to the landscape. Referring to Jean Epstein's *La Belle Nivernaise* (1924), Abel argues that in making cinematic language appropriate to the landscape by using the long shot and the travelling (especially for river and canal landscapes, as in Epstein's film), film-makers refined the conventions of the realist film genre. In one respect, the properties of objective realism associated with the long shot – a shot much advocated by André Bazin in the 1940s for its objectivity – bring the genre close to documentary. However, in another respect, this stylistic practice does something else. This matching of shot with landscape acts metaphorically for the Rousseauian idyll of man (*sic*) and nature – the character is placed in relation to the landscape. Equally, the shot is the eye of the character (and of course that of the spectator) and reflects her/his (usually his) subjectivity in relation to that landscape. In this representation of the landscape as equally vital within the narration, two things occur. First, the inhuman (i.e., landscape) becomes a central character in that it is anthropomorphised by the proto-documentary style of the genre. Second, this reappropriation through matching functions to recuperate and sanitise the 'something and somewhere elseness' of that landscape. The effect of this romantic sentimentalism on the one hand and reductionism on the other is to dilute the narrative and, at the extreme, privilege image-making practices over the narrative function. Thus, issues such as social and generational conflict – though not necessarily glossed over – become simplified, even simplistically evident in their reduction to a one-to-one relationship, as in *La Bête traquée* where the male brutishness is in direct correspondence to the savage landscape. In this respect, the images remain predominantly undisturbing in their ideological resonances that act reflexively for the collective pride in the beauty that is France.

Oms (1981), through a discussion of an exemplary film of this genre – *Le Tour de la France par deux enfants* (Louis de Carbonnat, 1924) – demonstrates how these images contributed to the formation of a collective mentality. Set in 1871 (post-commune and post-Franco-Prussian war), the film tells the story of how two orphans depart from Lorraine (now lost to the Prussians, so also an orphan of France) at the behest of their dead father to find his brother (supposedly in Marseilles) and bring him back to bless his tomb. The two children go all around France, as if in an initiation rite, discovering their mother country (in this respect, this film may well be the prototype of the road movie) and finally stumble upon their uncle in Bordeaux. After fulfilling the father's wishes, they all return to France to live in reasonable comfort (the uncle having come upon a modest fortune). What is important in this film, according to Oms, is that the orphans go through a series of tests (almost as if learning about Mother-France meant submitting to rigorous examination), the first of which is coming to terms with loss, followed by the tests of fire, wind, earth and water. To the concrete tests of the four elements – associated with 'France-as-nature' – corresponds the abstract, more psychological test of absence – the sons without a father and 'Alsace-Lorraine-without-France'. The unificatory message of the film's images, orphans of the orphaned department finding eventual solace in the Mother-Nation, is clear in its ideological resonances. Out of a collective sense of loss comes a sense of national unity.

Even though this is not a war film, it is not difficult to perceive how it spills over into the war/historical reconstruction genre precisely because it is about addressing the effects of war. In going back to 1871 it not only addresses that moment of loss (Franco-Prussian war/Alsace-Lorraine) but also looks forward to another great moment of loss (France's men in World War I) and thus enables the understanding of one moment in history through another. Furthermore, because this film was based on a novel taught in schools, it already had collective cultural capital and so a doubling of collective knowledge enters into effect. This film, along with others already mentioned, bears out the theory that a collectivised notion of nationhood was born out of the war. Whether this theory was based in myth or not does not really matter. What does matter is the belief that absence, be it loss or lack, could forge national unity. For it is in this respect that it is possible to understand how easy it was for Vichy to happen – or rather to 'not happen', having already occurred – because it was a logical end-point to a mentality that was always already in place. National unity and identity is based in the belief of belonging to a community and in an assumption of difference (difference from other nations). Nationalism is also based in pride in that difference and security in that sense of belonging. What confronted France in 1918 was absence. But this sense of loss did not emanate from just that period. In the mind of the possessing classes at least, it went back to 1870 and the loss of the Second Empire, which was equally as important as the loss of the Franco-Prussian war. Calls for national unity were just as strong then as they were after World War I. Loss, therefore, became the galvaniser for national pride. Loss-inflected pride was fertile ground for nostalgia, breeding the desire for a return to an earlier past where there was not absence, that is, at least for the Radical party and the Right (i.e., the ruling classes) – a return to the ideals of the Second Empire. Vichy, then, was the death of the Third Republic (a death devoutly wished for by the Right) and a reaffirmation of a mentality more monarchical than republican, more frankish than gallic.

No doubt it is for these ideological reasons that the theorists of the avant-garde (such as Delluc) tended to disapprove of the commercial, traditional melodrama genre which they saw as oversentimental, cinematically uninventive and, in its moralising tone, as lacking in social vision. However, they made clear that they did not reject the genre in its entirety. The writings in their film journals of the time expressed considerable support for the melodrama as a bulwark against American imports. But they did argue for a different sort of melodrama, one that would be a cinema of emotion, a cinema that would respond both to popular taste and to aesthetic exigencies. Advocating a *juste milieu* between the double peril of popular melodrama and aesthetic research, they pointed to the lessons that could be learned from Griffith's films (use of the close-up) and Swedish cinema (lighting effects). According to them, film-makers who obtained this cinema of emotion did so by creating a convergence of the decor with a psychological state. Nor did they see this cinema as uniquely the province of the avant-garde: indeed the film-makers whom they cited most often in their writings – Boudrioz, Feyder and Poirier – were more readily identifiable as being mainstream and commercially successful.[23]

There were, of course, economic reasons for advocating the merits of the melodrama. Besides being a popular genre, it was cheaper to produce than historical reconstructions/costume films and the modern studio spectacular. This in turn meant that it was a genre where the avant-garde was more likely to be successful in obtaining finance for film-making. Whilst all three genres were part of the cinema industry's strategy to counter the American monopoly, heavy investment went into the historical reconstructions and the studio spectaculars because they were targeted for the export market, and melodrama/realist films were seen first and foremost as potboilers destined for the home market. For economic reasons as much as any other and from the theorists' point of view, therefore, melodrama/realist films became the most 'national' of France's national cinema.

I shall now examine what the avant-garde film-makers produced with regard to their much-advocated cinema of emotion in order to see how it differs from the mainstream cinema, especially melodrama. Then I shall conclude with a few remarks on the least 'national' genre of French cinema, the modern studio spectacular. Since Richard Abel (1984) has dealt so extensively with the cinema of the avant-garde, I will confine my remarks to identifying which film-making practices the avant-garde did in fact pursue before illustrating, through reference to Louis Delluc and Germaine Dulac, how these practices actually manifested themselves.

Essentially, the financing of the avant-garde film-making practices reflected the changing fortunes within the film industry and this, in turn, did much to inform the genre and the length and quality of the product. Thus, film-makers were alternately financed by independent producers or self-financing or working for commercial mainstream production houses. Whichever camp they were working in, experimentation was central to their film-making practices. This experimentation functioned on three imbricated levels: reworking genres, exploring the possibilities of film language and redefining the representation of subjectivity. Thus, whilst they did make (in both production camps) serials and melodramas, they did not allow them to rest safely within their generic modalities or moulds. Genres were mixed, intercalated and juxtaposed. Similarly, the popular was fused with the experimental (mainstream cinema with counter-cinema), socio-realism with the subjective (documentary with melodrama). Working within these popular genres, these film-makers would take the dominant discourses and extend, distort, subvert them even. Avant-garde film-makers took the diegesis and ran. In so doing, they attacked the precept of filmic, narrative and spectator omniscience by disrupting diegetic time and space. This was achieved in a number of ways, the most recurrent of which were shifts from diegetic continuity to discontinuity, fast editing, disruption of conventional transition shots, and disorientating shots either through unmatched shots or a simultaneous representation of disparate images offering a multiplicity of perspectives. The desired effect was to raise questions about subjectivity and its representation. For example, Epstein's film *L'Auberge rouge* (1923) is structured around a double narration in two times and two spaces, and subjectivity and objectivity merge, begging the question of whose subjectivity is it (Abel: 1984, 351–9)? This questioning of subjectivity brought in its wake the issue of gender and sexuality, which I shall now explore through a closer examination of what happened to melodrama in the hands and through the eyes of the avant-garde film-makers.

Melodrama as a sentimental narrative was perceived by the avant-garde as a perfect vehicle for the psychological expression of subjectivity. Subjectivity now became not just a question of point of view, but also included the implicit notion of voyeurism and speculation (of the other) as well as the issue of desire, and the functioning of the conscious and the unconscious mind. Just one melodramatic construct, the love-triangle, will suffice to illustrate the shifts in address in this cinema. Incidentally, this was a construct which the avant-garde frequently used, doubtless because of its potential to address the areas it wished to investigate. Traditionally the narrative was positioned from a single subjectivity (usually the male gaze), but in avant-garde cinema subjectivities shifted and the triangle often had a double.

Louis Delluc's *Fièvre* (1921) – starring Eve Francis, a major silent cinema actress – is exemplary in this respect. Through a series of triangles made up of women and men all desiring someone either in the past, present or future, and by a shifting of subjectivities, Delluc succeeds in bringing into question the traditional representation of the triangle (Abel talks of a circle) of desire (ibid., 322). The scenario is as follows. The return of a sailor, Militis, to his home port (Marseilles) from the Orient sets in motion a series of triangles of desire which will ultimately be deconstructed by his murder. A first triangle is established between three women, in the local port café, who alternate as subjects of desire and whose respective object of desire has a temporal fixation. As the subjectivity shifts, so the women displace each other. With regard to the issue of the temporal fixation of the gaze, the first woman, Patience, is seen gazing to her sailor-lover who will return. The second woman, Sarah, gazes back to a past desire (for Militis, who has not yet appeared). The third woman, Militis's Oriental wife, who has no name, gazes not at Militis (now, by the end of the narrative, dead), but at the artificial flower on the bar. In terms of displacement, each woman in turn is positioned next to the flower at their moment of gazing (the Oriental will remain alone with the flower in the last shot of the film, having displaced Sarah who in turn had displaced Patience as the subject of desire). In each instance, as subjects of desire, their gaze is without an object. In the first two instances, the male is not yet there (Patience's lover and Militis have yet to arrive), in the last instance, the flower – because it is not real – is not there. A first reading of this absence points to the falsity of desire, for both the subject and the object of desire (ibid., 322).

A glance at the second triangle, this time between three men, might yield a different, but conjunctural reading of this absence. The three men – Topinelli (Sarah's husband), Militis and a clerk – all gaze at one woman, Sarah. She rejects the former and the latter's gaze, but accepts Militis's. This rekindling of desire brings about the fatal outcome. Topinelli, with the help of the clerk, kills Militis, but, it is Sarah who is arrested by the police (Topinelli and the clerk having been dragged off by the other sailors in the café). The women as subjects of desire have absence as their object of desire; conversely, the men have presence. Notionally, the woman is 'punished' for being presence (Sarah's arrest), but because her presence caused the death – that is, the absence – of Militis, she is equally 'punished' for making him absence. The female subjects of desire, it will be recalled, gazed at absence – where the male object of desire was not. Since Sarah is 'punished' for making the male absence, a second reading of this absence would suggest either a misfunctioning of female subjectivity, desiring absence, or a misrecognition of the object of desire (the phallus as desired object of absence, not presence). In any event, the ending does not assert women's subjectivity as difference. It is represented either, as with the first reading, as no more or less fetishising than the male gaze, or, as with the second reading, as deviant and therefore a punishable offence.

I have spent some time arguing for this second reading to make the point that whilst the first reading does subvert the canonical love-triangle of mainstream melodrama (by putting desire into question), none the less the second reading suggests that dominant discourses remain that underprivilege female subjectivity and protect the privileging of homo-erotic space. I said above that the women displace each other as they take over the role of subject of desire. Quite the opposite is true for the male. Whilst women, in displacing each other by taking up the same position, are represented as a *mise-en-abyme* of woman as desiring subject, the men are perceived as desiring separately (i.e., not from one position), so no displacement takes effect. What does occur is that once the male (Militis) becomes presence in the desiring space (he arrives after Sarah has gazed at her past desire), that space becomes a space for male display. In other words, once Militis arrives, the gaze shifts into the male domain. All three men gaze at Sarah, but Militis is also the object of Topinelli and the clerk's gaze. In this way he becomes simultaneously subject and object of male desire. As an adjunct to this point, it is worth remarking that in melodramas where escape is the central theme, first, it is mostly the male protagonist who pursues 'freedom', usually from a broken heart, and second, it is the male's characterisation that is represented as 'interesting', not the female's. Men's anguish in desire lets them escape, but women's normally ends in death or at least in 'no escape' – another fixity in representation that immobilises the female.

The avant-garde's attempt at defetishising the male gaze and relocating it showed an awareness of the underprivileging of female subjectivity, but perhaps the film-maker who was most successful in her handling of this problematic was Germaine Dulac, undoubtedly because at the centre of her own filmic discourse lay her feminist preoccupations. Whatever the genre she was using, it became reworked into a psychological and feminine subjective experience. In *La Souriante Mme Beudet* (1923), it is Mme Beudet's inner experience of boredom and her escapes through fantasy to which we, as spectators, are privileged. In *L'Invitation au voyage* (1927), it is the escape fantasy of a young married mother alone in a night-club full of marine officers that we witness.

At the end of *L'Invitation au voyage* there is a hint of how far Dulac will need to go with her 'distinctly feminine voice' to privilege female subjectivity (Flitterman-Lewis: 1990b, 57). This hint becomes the *raison d'être* of her very next film, *La Coquille et le clergyman* (1927), which is considered to be the first Surrealist film and which predates the Spanish exile Buñuel's film *Un Chien andalou* (*the* emblematic Surrealist film to many historians) by two years (Flitterman-Lewis: 1990a, 15). The shift in Dulac's two films is from a representation of the subjectivity of the female protagonist to that of the subjective fetishising gaze of the male and, ultimately, to the exposure of the process of that fetishising gaze through its deconstruction.

In *L'Invitation au voyage*, until the closing shots the subjectivity of the desiring discourse is feminine, that is, it is the young woman who fantasises her escape with the young officer she has just met and danced with in the night-club. The officer, on discovering she is married, withdraws his affections and she returns home. It is in the very representation of fantasy that we get a clue as to Dulac's intentionality in this seemingly banal story. In the woman's fantasising, she conjures up an imaginary porthole which the officer opens on to the sea and a ship where she joins him on board. However, there then occurs a shift in the beholder of the desiring discourse. When she leaves the club, it is now the officer who imagines the two of them on her fantasised ship. In other words, he takes over her subjectivity. Two points need to be made here. First, she conjures up this fantasy after hearing the officer's stories of his sea voyages. Her fantasy, therefore, is based on male discourse, symbolised in the film by his opening the porthole (he lets her in/out of/into his discourse). Her subjectivity becomes immediately ambiguous, problematic even and poses the question: what and who constructs female subjectivity? Second, by shifting the beholder of the fantasy from the female to the male subjectivity, Dulac shows how even that which could be construed as the female subjectivity is, as in most narrations and discourses, a barely disguised male construct. In other words, not only do these end shots, as Abel (1984, 415) points out, 'reaffirm the primacy of the male gaze' and point to the fact that the woman 'is trapped, not only in a social space, but in a way of seeing, a way of imagining', but they also show how the process of co-option of the female subjectivity into the male subjectivity works – through the masculine voice.

In the second film, *La Coquille et le clergyman*, the narrative, the subjective and the sexual subject/object all undergo a process of deconstruction to mobilise, even more clearly than in the preceding film, 'a feminist critique' of the fetishising male gaze.[24] In its unseamlessness and apparent arbitrary collision of scenes and images it not only places before the spectator the actual 'production process of desire' but, because the fantasms of desire are fragmented, it also forces the spectator into the position of 'the producer of the fiction', to be the one producing/ participating in the fantasms, in other words, to become 'the subject of vision and desire' (Flitterman-Lewis: 1990a, 15–16). The spectator is confronted with how the male subject of desire represents the female figure and how, in so doing and in so desiring, the female figure is fetishised. Through the images where conflict and pursuit are repeatedly re-enacted, male desire is represented as obsessive and concomitantly violent. The clergyman as the male subject of desire does not just gaze at the woman, he rips at her clothing, chases her, fantasises strangling her, captures her head in a globe, etc. Conversely, the male object of desire, the woman, is constantly elusive. If he rips at her clothing, it and the body underneath which he wishes to reveal to his gaze become transformed into something else (a carapace!). In other words, the woman is constantly not to be placed where he would have her. In this way, another positioning for the spectator is presented by the film (spectator as non-producer of fiction), which in turn suggests many other possible positionings – non-subject of desire, non-beholder of the fetishising gaze (ibid: 20). Patriarchal power is revealed for what it does to female sexuality. Female subjectivity demonstrates what it will not tolerate.

The modernity of the avant-garde compared with the relative *arrièrisme* of mainstream cinema points to the fact that the 1920s was an age of paradox, as indeed are most ages. What is interesting in relation to each age is the specificity (or not) of those paradoxes (i.e., how each age's paradox differs). In the cinema of the 1920s, on the one hand, there were the 'republican–imperialist' (the Left–Right political) discourses of prewar France, and on the other, the modernising effect of American popular culture. The clash between the Americanisation of the French (read Parisian) culture and the a posteriori glorification of the Belle Epoque created a kind of socio-political schizophrenia amongst the right-thinking classes. The bourgeois mentality was profoundly disturbed by the new consumption practices based on immediacy and debt as opposed to capitalisation. As I mentioned earlier, the general mood of discontent after the war did not confine its expression to a conflict of classes, but also manifested itself in a conflict of generations. In Paris in particular, the youth of the bourgeoisie turned against their elders in their pursuit of pleasure which came in the form of many things American: the jazz club, dancing in night clubs, etc. The 1920s became known as *Les Années folles*, a rubric that does not have quite such positive resonances as the Anglo-Saxon equivalents – the Roaring Twenties (in the UK) and the Gay Twenties (in the US). The reaction of the bourgeoisie, which was the dominating class, was ostrich-like, making it ripe for the satirical films of René Clair (*Paris qui dort* and *Entr'acte*, both 1924). But nowhere was this clash of cultures (old and modern) more in evidence than in the modern studio spectacular film, the most exemplary of which, in the light of the above comments and because it both reflects and subverts the genre's narrative and unmasks the film practices of that period, is L'Herbier's *L'Argent* (1929).[25]

In L'Herbier's film, with the exception of one central character – Saccard the wheeler-dealer financier (whose greed for money knows no limits) – all the protagonists are ambiguously represented. The coldness of the 'good' financier, Gunderman, as well as his environs makes his rescue of the slightly *ingénue* couple, Jacques and Line Hamelin, less than reassuring. The couple themselves are not without their weaknesses. Jacques' desire for success (he is a solo aviator whose vanity and financial impecuniousness Saccard exploits to his own ends) and Line's concupiscence (she is fascinated by Saccard and covets his wealth) make them less than the ideal couple (of traditional melodrama). The film does not rest in its disruptive strategies at just one level – the narrative (of which I have given only one instance of subversion of codes and conventions): the whole film is a *mise-en-abyme* of different narratives, all of which focus around money, *l'argent*, the eponymous protagonist of the film. As Abel (1984, 521) makes clear, in his very comprehensive study of this film, the camera style calls attention to itself (especially in the famous scene where it swings over the financiers' heads in the Bourse, and in the decor, in its larger than life representation). The film shows the fetishising of capital by closely aligning it with the fetishising process in sexuality. Men are not alone in this fetishising process but are represented, as are the women, as both agents and objects of desire which gives as a reading: capitalism and phallus as object of female desire/subjectivity; woman as object of capitalist/male desire. Thus, another series of codes and conventions which the melodrama traditionally mobilises – woman as rapacious deceiver and duper of men, men whom love turns blind – gets firmly stood on its head by these shifts in reflexivity (not for nothing does this film's decor abound with mirrors).[26]

It is perhaps noteworthy that, with this genre, set designers were very much to the fore (with the realist genre, as one might expect, it was the cameraman (*sic*)). Lazare Meerson, André Barsacq, Robert Mallet-Stevens, Ivan Lochakoff, Henri Ménessier, Claude Autant-Lara and Alberto Cavalcanti – all designed lavish settings that echoed the modernity of the *nouveau riche*'s taste in architecture and design. These films were more about visual style than narrative, less still subjectivity. The ideology of consumption found immediate iconic referents in the art deco interiors and the fashionably ultramodern costume designs. To all this excess corresponded a 'lack' in so far as the narrative was concerned in that it tended to limit itself to a reinscription (into modern discourse) of the melodrama's 'love-triangle'. Often, at the centre of the narrative stands the ice-cold modern woman surrounded by a group of admirers out of which two suitors emerge as unafraid of frostbite. One suitor will be as ruthless in his cunning and underhand ways as the mistress he pursues, the other young and courageous. Both will be modern in their outlook. The latter will probably be engaged in perilous work (aviation, the colonies, etc.), the former in finance. Alternatively the narrative will be a rags to riches story (normally for the female protagonist) with a fairy tale ending. In all events, the modern world will be privileged over the old order. Cultural internationalism and the world of finance are strong undercurrents to these films with their international casts and frequent references to good and bad financial practices. Thus, good capitalists outbid bad ones by, for example, speculating to bring down the bad rival whose profiteering risks the ruin of bona fide investors.

Whilst this genre's decor and the costumes gave reflexive nods to the

French cultural artefacts of the time in design and fashion, its casting attested to another rather more xenophobic (or at least ambivalent) than chauvinistic perception of modern times. The modern studio spectacular is peopled not just by the French but also by Germans, Russians and British speculators, princes, princesses (etc.) pointing, on the one hand, to a neutralising of French (Parisian) culture and codes as a result of cultural internationalism, and on the other, to the ambivalence of the French business world towards foreign investors and *émigré* capital. This ambivalence was most strongly felt in relation to Germany and the question of retribution. Some French investors wished to be conciliatory and build up contacts, whilst others wanted full retribution. This ambivalence, transposed into film, revealed another sort of invidious chauvinism. If bad capitalists were not necessarily foreign, they could certainly be Jewish – for instance the especially bad capitalist Nicolas Saccard (played by Pierre Alcover) in L'Herbier's *L'Argent*. Within the film industry's own history, there is a particularly cruel irony attached to the demise of Bernard Natan (both a foreigner – Romanian – and a Jew). He was a speculator and film producer who bought up Pathé in 1929 and who was, at that time, hailed as one of the most important film producers and his company, Pathé-Natan, was also hailed as the witness of a renaissance in the French cinema (Abel: 1984, 34 and 63). Speculation, insider dealing and fraud brought about his arrest in 1935. The company went bankrupt and Natan was sent to prison. During the German Occupation he was sent to a concentration camp, where he perished.

Although the studio spectacular was about surface (the 'look'), none the less it did not totally gloss over the social changes brought about by a change in consumption practices, which in turn were perceived as a consequence of or reaction to World War I. The point that needs to be made here is that all postwar genres addressed, to varying degrees, the prevalent schizophrenic mentality of a nation caught between loss and change on the one hand, and on the other between a need to come to terms with that loss and change and a desire to escape from that confrontation. Symptomatic of that desire for escape in its extreme were the colonial films which must receive a brief mention here if only because of their more vital reinscription in the mid-1930s (i.e., the period that realised the inevitability of a new war). In the 1920s films, the colonies, predominantly North Africa and especially in the form of the desert, were seen as the 'locus of an ideological testing' (ibid., 159). Two types of narrative abound, but both are clearly inscribed into nationalistic sentiment. The first establishes the desert as a site for individual redemption, the second exalts the pioneering spirit of the individual and France's civilising effect on North Africa. Neither, quite obviously, questions France's presence there. This presumption is signified by the fact that, in both narratives, the hero remains in the colony at the end of the film. Either the hero achieves redemption and is subsequently restored into an equivalent of the social hierarchy that rejected him, or the hero exemplifies the bountifulness of France, with whom the indigenous people will happily collaborate (even to the point of marriage). This unquestioning and simplified representation of colonisation continues into the 1930s films but gets challenged by a handful of films made in the middle of the decade. In this latter instance the hero barely achieves redemption and only does so through death (often through his attempt to return to the land, France, which had rejected him or which he had had to leave – most notoriously Duvivier's *Pépé-le-Moko*, 1936). The myth becomes counter-Oedipal (i.e., the son kills himself) and far removed from the sanitised image of France's imperialism. In these few films, the hero is a prisoner in this other culture, fated never to return to his mother country, whom he has wronged.[27]

CONCLUSION

Although, post-1914, France's cinema ceased to dominate because of the war and the hegemonising practices of the American industry, none the less after the war she did not exactly cease to evolve. A major reason for shifts and developments in styles (generic, narrative and cinematic), however slow, was a need to adapt to the changed circumstances of her world status (i.e., economic exigencies), but a further major reason was the effect of cross-fertilisation which occurred in a number of ways. First, France's cinema was enriched by the arrival of other cinemas into her frame of reference either in terms of influence (such as Swedish and German cinematic practices, especially lighting) or actual *émigré* groups (the Russians) who set up studios of their own, financed indigenous projects and significantly impacted upon decor and editing style. The impact of individuals was also felt (such as the Danish film-maker Carl Dreyer or the Russian actor Mosjoukine) and their distinct or revolutionary directorial and actorly styles. A second factor was the cross-fertilisation within France's cinema between mainstream and avant-garde cinema and vice versa. Paradoxically, cross-fertilisation in this latter respect led to the ending of a specificity of France's cinema in terms of editing style. Mainstream cinema co-opted the avant-garde rapid editing style thereby putting to rest the traditionally longer take so identified with French cinema. Pre-1919, the average shot length was 12 seconds. In 1919 it ranged from 6 to 8.5 seconds and by the period 1920–9 the length varied from 5 to 9 seconds and was fairly indistinct from that in America (Salt: 1983, 171–7 and 211–13).

This issue of cross-fertilisation points yet again to the futility of the high/low art debate. What this first age of cinema demonstrated was that mutual borrowings between popular and artistic films should be understood as two aspects of the same process of cultural integration, that popular and artistic cinemas do not lead separate lives but complement one another and that, whilst popular film complies with conventions and artistic film attempts to transcend them, none the less in the dialectical tension between them there is an exchange of meanings, an exchange that is a permanent evolutionary feature. Thus elements that had been artistic now become popular and vice versa.[28] This process, thankfully, is never-ending.

NOTES

1 May I refer the reader to two very different but very useful texts on the emergence of this technology: Salt (1983) and D'Hugues and Marmin (1986). The first reference is an invaluable in-depth study of style and technology from the beginnings of cinema to the 1970s, the second is a less detailed but none the less very well-written overview of French silent cinema.

2 I am using the term cinema of attractions in the way Tom Gunning (1986) intends in his very persuasive essay that argues the case that early cinema was not dominated by the narrative mode but by the fact that cinema was then more about spectacle, exhibiting itself to the audience, displaying its visibility and thus destroying realistic illusion. Gunning then goes on to argue the case that pre-1906 cinema was an inspiration to the avant-garde of the 1920s.

3 See Kevin Brownlow's essay 'Silent films: what was the right speed', *Sight and Sound*, vol. 49, no. 3, 1980.

4 For further discussion of her career see Flitterman-Lewis (1990a & b) and Hayward (1992).

5 In respective order: Noël Burch (1984), Philip Rosen (1990) and Tom Gunning (1986).

6 For more detail see Salt (1983), 60–111.

7 See the special issue on Feuillade in *Avant-scène du cinéma*, no. 270, 15 June 1981, pp. 7–21. For much more information about the debate see Abel (1988) and Abel (1984, 241–51).

8 Abel (1988, 200–6) has four slightly different categories: mainstream narrative (which included Antoine), Impressionism (a Symbolist-inflected discourse which would correspond to the first avant-garde stage), Realism (of the Delluc category) and, finally, plastic non-narrative (which corresponds to the latter two stages of the avant-garde). In Abel (1984, 241) the avant-garde is described as having three factions: narrative avant-garde, pure cinema, documentary avant-garde.

9 May I recommend Comolli's fascinating series of essays on silent cinema in *Cahiers du cinéma*, nos. 229–31, 1971.

10 In this section I have made wide use of James McMillan's (1985) clear exposition of the history of this time. I also referred to Brogan's (1989) study which, while useful, does not take such a detached critical stance as McMillan's.

11 For more detail in these mutations and generic content, see Abel (1984, 69–238). For the earlier cinema of this period see D'Hugues and Marmin (1986), and *Les Cahiers de la cinémathèque*, nos. 28–9, 1979, 30–1, 1980, 33–4, 1981.

12 Although there is some contention about their authorship, all films produced by Gaumont, between 1896 and 1905, are attributed to Alice Guy. For ten years (1897–1907) she was head of film direction and made 406 films. It is true that

most of these films conform to the traditional length of film at that time (between 20 and 90 m) and so by today's standards would be considered shorts, but compared with the contemporaneous output of a single film-maker (Zecca, for example, made around 230), it was a remarkable number for those early years.

13 Quoted in *Avant-scène du cinéma*, nos. 271–2, July 1981. This volume also contains the script of *Fantômas*.

14 Ibid., p. 22.

15 For more detail see Abel (1984, 71–85).

16 Georges Sadoul quoted by D'Hugues and Marmin (1986, 108). Another reason for the dislike of this film-maker was that a film initially shot by André Sauvage was falsely attributed to Poirier (*La Croisière jaune*, 1934). Poirier was employed by Pathé-Natan in the early 1930s to take over from Sauvage and edit this film, commissioned by Citroën, about an expedition in Asia (basically to promote Citroën's new caterpillar car/tractors).

17 The other seven films are: *Les Deux soldats* (Hervé, 1921), *L'Autre aile de Ricciotto Canudo* (Andréani, 1923), *Comment j'ai tué mon enfant* (Ryder, 1925), *La Grande épreuve* (Ryder and Dugès, 1927), *En plongée* (Robert, 1928), *L'Equipage* (Tourneur, 1928), *La Grande envolée de Marcel Nadaud* (Bertin, 1928), *La Menace* (Pelmer, 1928).

18 See Alain Arthouzol's article 'Le Cinéma français des années 20 et la littérature', in *Les Cahiers de la cinémathèque*, nos. 33–4, 1981.

19 Abel (1984, 164) gives an alternative, somewhat more 'pessimistic' reading of Fescourt's *L'Agonie des aigles*, seeing it as representing the French mood of defeatism after the war.

20 Quoted in Prédal (1972, 96–9).

21 See Barthélemy Amengual's article, 'Prépondérants sur le mélodrame d'hier et le faux mélo d'aujourd'hui', in *Les Cahiers de la cinémathèque*, no. 28, 1979, which is a special issue on melodrama in the 1920s.

22 See Oms (1981, 78–9) and D'Hugues and Marmin (1986, 98–9).

23 These views are mostly expressed in the journal *Mon Ciné* (1922–4). For more detail see Maurice Roellens' article '"*Mon Ciné*" et le mélodrame', in *Les Cahiers de la cinémathèque*, no. 28, 1979.

24 This is Wendy Dozoretz's reading of the film, in: 'Dulac versus Artaud', *Wide-Angle*, vol. 3, no. 1, 1979, pp. 51–2.

25 See Abel's (1984, 513–26) very good analysis of this film.

26 On the issue of fetishism, this film becomes a fetish object itself. Jean Dréville made a short documentary of the film as it was being made and subsequently edited it into *Autour de l'Argent* (1928).

27 Films to contrast would be, from the 1920s, *L'Atlantide* (Feyder, 1921), *Le Bled* (Renoir, 1929), Le Somptier's *Les Terres d'or* (1924–5), *Les Fils du soleil* (1924–5) and *La Marche vers le soleil* (1925) and, from the mid-1930s, Feyder's *Le Grand jeu* (1933), Duvivier's *La Bandera* (1935) and *Pépé le Moko* (1936).

28 This interpretation of film culture as a special system of two contradictory tendencies receives an eloquent description in Marek Hendrykowski's unpublished paper, 'Relations between popular and art cinema or is the owl the baker's daughter?', given at the *European Popular Cinema Conference*, Warwick University, 1989.

BIBLIOGRAPHY

Abel, R. (1984) *French Cinema: The First Wave, 1915–1929*, New Jersey, Princeton University Press.

—— (1988) *French Film Theory and Criticism: A History/Anthology Volume I 1907–1929*, New Jersey, Princeton University Press.

Birkett, J. (1986) *The Sins of the Fathers: Decadence in France 1870–1914*, London, Quartet Books.

—— (1990) '*Fin-de-Siècle* painting', in Teich, M. and Porter, R. (eds) *Fin de Siècle and its Legacy*, Cambridge, Cambridge University Press.

Brogan, D.W. (1989) *The French Nation: From Napoleon to Pétain, 1814–1940*, London, Cassell Publishers Ltd (originally published by Hamish Hamilton Ltd, 1957).

Burch, N. (1984) 'Un mode de représentation primitive?' *Iris*, vol. 2, no. 1.

Cawelti, J.G. (1985) 'The question of popular genres', *Journal of Popular Film and TV*, vol. 13, no. 2.

Comolli, J.-L. (1971) 'D'une origine duelle', *Cahiers du cinéma*, no. 229.

D'Hugues, P. and Marmin, M. (1986) *Le Cinéma français: Le Muet*, Paris, Editions Atlas.

Flitterman-Lewis, S. (1990a) '"Poetry of the unconscious": circuits of desire in two films by Germaine Dulac – *La Souriante Mme Beudet* (1923) and *La Coquille et le clergyman* (1927)', in Hayward, S. and Vincendeau, G. (eds) *French Film: Texts and Contexts*, London, Routledge.

—— (1990b) *To Desire Differently: Feminism and the French Cinema*, Urbana and Chicago, University of Illinois Press.

Gunning, T. (1986) 'The cinema of attraction, early film, its spectator and the avant-garde', *Wide-Angle*, vol. 8, no. 3/4.

Guy, A. (1974) 'Alice Guy: La Naissance du cinéma', *Image et Son*, no. 283.

Hayward, S. (1992) 'A history of French cinema: 1895–1991 pioneering film-makers (Guy, Dulac, Varda) and their heritage', *Paragraph*, vol. 15, no. 1.

Liebman, S. (1983) 'French film theory 1910–1921', *Quarterly Review of Film Studies*, vol. 8, no. 1.

McMillan, J.F. (1985) *Dreyfus to De Gaulle: Politics and Society in France 1898–1969*, London, Edward Arnold.

Mitry, J. (1985) 'Au temps du muet', *Cinématographe*, no. 108.

Neale, S. (1980) *Genre*, London, British Film Institute.

Oms, M. (1981) 'Histoire et géographie d'une France imaginaire', *Les Cahiers de la cinémathèque*, no. 33–4 (special series on the 1920s).

Prédal, R. (1972) *La Société française (1914–1945) à travers le cinéma*, Paris, Armand Colin.

Rosen, P. (1990) 'Disjunction and ideology in preclassical film: *A Policeman's Tour of the World*', *Wide-Angle*, vol. 12, no. 3.

Sadoul, G. (1962) *Le Film français*, Paris, Flammarion.

Salt, B. (1983) *Film Style and Technology: History and Analysis*, London, Starword.

2 EMBLEMATIC SHOTS OF THE SILENT ERA

Detective series: *Nick Carter, le roi des détectives*, 1909–12

Crime series: *Fantômas*, Feuillade, 1913–14

Crime series: *Les Vampires*, Feuillade, 1915–16

Literary adaptations: *Les Misérables*,
Fescourt, 1925

Modern studio spectaculars: *L'Argent*,
L'Herbier, 1929

Chapter 3

From clarity to obscurity:
French cinema's age of modernism
1930–58

Since this chapter will attempt to disrupt some of the more widely held preconceived notions about this period in France's cinema history, it seems appropriate to begin by setting a dominant myth on its head – that of 'Great Moments'. Traditional mainstream history (but more particularly those who practise it) has a disquieting way of reifying the past into 'Great Men/Moments/Battles/Wars', etc. Recently, however, historians of French cinema have been unpicking this reification process and dislodging the safely assumed (because canonised) great moments. This is particularly the case for the 1930s cinema and, in this context, the work of Michèle Lagny and Ginette Vincendeau springs most immediately to mind.[1] Conversely and to varying extents, the cinemas of the 1940s and 1950s have been less subjected to this socio-historical contextualisation than the previous decade. The 1940s, for the obvious but complex reason of the Occupation and its aftermath, has been the object of a rigorous analysis that is primarily politically inflected and here mention must be made of the various studies conducted by Jean-Pierre Bertin-Maghit, François Garçon and Jean-Pierre Jeancolas.[2] Of the 1950s, in the belief that the *Cahiers du cinéma* group was right in its dismissal of most of that decade's output and in an acceptance of its *politique des auteurs*, the predominant tendency has been to recognise a new set of canonisable film-makers at the expense of a more sober overview of that period in cinema history which was not so fallow as might be presumed.

Thus this chapter starts with the premise that, whilst there were and still are great films or films that become great or even cultified, none the less there are no 'great' moments in France's national cinema, even though in terms of economics there might be boom years. At the very least, it is unhelpful to conceptualise cinema in this way because of all the other cinemas that get silenced. Similarly, whilst in each age there are great directors, just as with other aesthetic modalities, they are not the dominant tendency and their work must be examined alongside that of their contemporaries. Again, different periods have seen the emergence of film-makers and film actors who have either become totemised by critics and audiences or who have worked towards their own totemisation. Essentially, it can be said that there are moments when discernible styles prevail (and this is perhaps where the confusion with great moments occurs), such as the Poetic Realism of the mid- to late 1930s, the so-called Tradition of Quality of the 1950s, the New Wave of the late 1950s and early 1960s, and finally the Post-New Wave of the 1980s.

The thirty years covered in this chapter represent an epoch of tremendous upheaval for France and witnessed, amongst other events, the rise and decline of her Empire and the death of her Republic during the Occupation. For this reason it is to a brief history of that period that I wish to turn first, before framing and focusing on the cinematographic production of that time.

FRANCE 1930–58

A convenient way to summarise the prevailing spirit of this period is through the triumvirate 'fear, guilt, immobilism' which, over the thirty years, manifested itself in opposing modes. Thus, to the political irrationality and economic immobilism of the 1930s corresponded the economic rationality of the 1950s. Similarly, to the national sense of guilt of the 1940s corresponded the national insecurity of the 1930s and the political immobilism of the 1950s. A closer look at the socio-political arena will help elucidate these synoptic simplifications.

During the last decade of the Third Republic, fear of bolshevism on the one hand and dictatorship (especially military) on the other was as rife amongst the consensual possessing classes of the bourgeoisie and the landowning peasantry as ever before. These possessing classes owed much of their gains to the Revolution and they did not wish to see any change in their *status quo*. But, as was mentioned in Chapter 2, because the French mentality is based in the Revolution, within the bourgeoisie mentality there lurks a fear of non-legitimacy – that what they gained is not rightfully theirs and can therefore be taken away. In the 1930s, this basic insecurity amongst the possessing classes fed into the irrational mode of the time and led them to feel threatened by both the rise of the industrial working class and the discontent of the small peasant farmer caused by the loss of land value. The major reason motivating this new wave of fear was, of course, the Depression, which hit France in 1931–2. The most severely affected was the peasant class whose vigorous protest alongside that of the urban working class did not go unheeded by militants in the Communist and Fascist parties, both of which sought to woo them to their cause (McMillan: 1985, 100). In industry, Taylorisation, which had been introduced on a more widespread basis in the 1920s, had provided brief economic stability, but by 1935 production had dropped massively. Bankruptcies had doubled their 1929 figures, wages were slashed, and unemployment went up from zero in 1929 to half a million in 1935, affecting women and immigrant workers in the first instance (ibid., 99). The state intervened to rescue certain vital companies. Between 1933 and 1937 it became a major shareholder in *Air France* and the *Compagnie générale transatlantique* and (under the Popular Front) nationalised the railway network (the *Société nationale des chemins de fer*) and the Bank of France. It is worth noting here that cinema, albeit in a restricted number of films, gave an immediate reflection of the climate of the time. Clair's *A nous la liberté* (1931) exposes the myth of Taylorisation (i.e., the belief in the fruitful collaboration between capital and labour), Renoir's *Toni* (1934) documents the difficulties of the immigrant working class and Vigo's *L'Atalante* (1934) shows the effects of unemployment on a woman alone in Paris and includes a scene of her walking past an actual unemployment queue.

France's lack of economic growth before the Depression can be attributed to three major causes. The first is economic, the second political and the third demographic. However, all come down to a Malthusianism of spirit. Fear of overproduction meant that France was slow to industrialise. Furthermore, the industry that did exist was concentrated into the hands of a few. In the 1930s, a third of the population still worked the land and provided a quarter of the nation's wealth (Larkin: 1988, 2). This economic stagnation was matched by the political immobilism of the various governments until the Popular Front came to power, by which time it was too late to save France from economic trouble. The Third Republic of the 1930s sought to stabilise (i.e., maintain the bourgeois *status quo*) rather than reform society and this meant that its chief concern was to protect the interests of the individual. Thus, when in the early 1930s the government should have devalued the franc, it chose not to do so, fearing the backlash of the possessing classes who were mindful of the effect on their savings of the fall of the franc in the 1920s. As a result, by the mid-1930s the franc was artificially high and exports fell from 6 per cent to just under 4 per cent (ibid., 10). Curiously, because France had been slow to industrialise, she was in fact less hard hit by the Depression than Germany, Great Britain or the United States. But there was little to be smug about. France's immobilism meant that the effects of the Depression lasted longer than for her Anglo-Saxon or Germanic rivals, whose recovery was well under way by 1935. France's upturn did not occur until the late 1930s and was then due in part, somewhat ironically, to the Popular Front's massive investment in the armaments industry.

Demographic Malthusianism was widely practised as well, so that by 1935 the number of deaths outnumbered births. There were several contributing reasons for this state of affairs. First, until the latter part of the 1930s there was a lack of eligible young men (they were either dead or mutilated in World War I). Women either remained unmarried or had to marry older men. Indeed, as Ginette Vincendeau (1985, 130) points out, many romantic/love-triangle films of this period show the older man winning the hand of the younger woman. Another reason was directly related to the economic climate of uncertainty, which discouraged early marriage. This tendency was compounded by the landed peasantry's inclination to keep their families small in the face of the Napoleonic inheritance laws (division of land equally between heirs – daughters and sons). Furthermore, abortions averaged 400,000 per year and continued at that level into the 1940s despite the increase, in 1939, in the penalty for attempted abortion from six months to ten years (Larkin: 1988, 7). On this last point, abortion became a guillotinable offence under Vichy law (a filmic reference to this draconian punishment came very late in Chabrol's *Une affaire de femmes*, 1988). When the Daladier government took measures to stop the demographic decline through introducing family allowances (*Code de la famille*, 28 July 1939), war was barely more than a month away, and had France (in the form of Pétain) not sued for peace six weeks after hostilities had begun, this measure might have seemed too cruel in its timing to be believed. As it was, the Vichy government pursued this pro-natalist policy and the birth-rate did increase (ibid., 90) – a turn-around that lasted well into the mid-1960s.

In order to talk coherently and succinctly about the political arena of this period, I would like to stretch time to include the Occupation years and to establish a further triumvirate – French Communist Party (PCF), Popular Front, Pétain. As will be seen there exists a strong interconnection between these three 'Ps' and it is appropriate to start with the PCF. Although the party suffered chequered fortunes, its presence in the political arena of the 1930s was of paramount significance. At its peak in popularity in the 1924 elections (the first for which the party ran), the PCF obtained twenty-six seats. By 1928 this dwindled to fourteen. By 1933 it had lost half its 1928 membership. However, by 1934 the party's fortunes were on the rise once more, a rise triggered in that year by the Stavisky affair. Stavisky, wanted for fraud, committed suicide. It transpired he was closely connected with politicians and that, for that very reason, it was more than likely the affair would be swept under the carpet. This brought the right-wing anti-parliamentarian groups out on to the streets, sensing that this was a good moment to hit out at Republicanism and denounce the incompetence of the parliamentary regime. As a result of these riots, Republican politicians gave credence to the notion of a fascist plot aimed at imposing a dictatorship. On the right of the political class there was no move to consolidate against fascism (a position evidenced, for example, by the non-intervention of the government when in November 1935 French administrators of the Tobis Paris branch executed the German film company's orders to dismiss all Jewish personnel). Indeed, the Right as a whole was fragmented and the extreme Right even more so (ranging from intellectuals led by Charles

Maurras of *Action française*, and manufacturers like François Coty and Pierre Taittinger who, respectively, founded *Solidarité française* and *Jeunesse patriotes*, to the military *Croix-de-feu* led by Colonel de la Roque). Even if it was inclined to present a solid front, the Right was unempowered to do so. The reaction on the Left, where fear of fascism within France was compounded by the growing concern at the rise of nazism outside France, was quite different. Significantly, it was the PCF (under the directive of the International, that is, Moscow/Stalin) that proceeded to form a common front against fascism. In 1935, the coalition of the Left – made up of Communists, Socialists and leftist Radicals and launched in 1934 by the Communist leader Maurice Thorez, who coined the term *Front populaire* (Adereth: 1984, 68) – made significant gains in the municipal elections and by the time of the legislatives in 1936, with all parties of the Left willing to make concessions for the sake of unity and ultimate victory at the elections, the coalition was voted into power. Only on two subsequent occasions would a Left victory at the legislative elections be assured by a coalition with the PCF – those of 1946 and 1981 (with the Socialist party gaining the most seats).[3]

Faced with a depressed economy and growing international tension, the Popular Front government, lead by Blum, confronted a momentous task if it was to implement the social reforms that were so high on the Socialists' agenda. Part of these reforms included a cultural dimension that was not without its nationalistic resonances, based as it was on the importance of new building programmes – such as Le Corbusier's social village – which never really saw the light of day (unlike the Socialist governments' building programmes of the 1980s and 1990s). It is a sad testimony to the economic crisis facing the Blum government that, whilst France hosted the World Exhibition in 1937–8, her own particular pavilions (including the cinema pavilion) were not ready on time for the opening – a metonymy for failure indeed (Guillaume-Grimaud: 1986, 42; Brogan: 1989, 288).

Three major events conspired to doom Blum's government: the Matignon agreements, the outbreak of the Spanish Civil War and the huge percentage of the budget devoted to defence (33 per cent). The Matignon agreements came about as a result of a massive factory sit-in strike nationwide (the most extensive one being in the Renault factories). The strike was a euphoric and spontaneous reaction to the Left's victory (McMillan: 1985, 109). In order to get the nation back to work, Blum had to negotiate social legislation much quicker than was healthy for the nation. Thus wage rises of up to 15 per cent were agreed, the forty-hour week and paid holidays were instituted and so was the recognition of trade-union rights and collective bargaining. The second event, the Spanish Civil War, revealed that Blum was prepared to compromise Socialist ideals. When the war broke out in Spain in July 1936, much to the indignation of the Left, Blum, fearing that a pro-interventionist stance might bring about civil war in his own country and under pressure from the British and American allies, opted for a non-interventionist position. The Left, especially the PCF, perceived this decision as a betrayal of the commitment to fight Fascism. As a result, Blum's government lost the support of the PCF and this left him with a far narrower margin over the opposition. Blum did not get to savour, at least as government leader, the PCF's own embarrassment when in 1938 the German–Soviet pact was signed between Stalin and Hitler. At that point the party and its paper (*L'Humanité*) were banned by the then right-wing Daladier government. The third, contributing factor to the Popular Front's demise was the tremendous strains placed upon the state's resources. During the Popular Front era, the franc was under pressure both from within and without the country. French investors took their money out of France, but the franc was also heavily speculated against by foreign currencies and the rise in military spending at home did little to ease the ailing franc. As a result, by early 1937 Blum was obliged to impose a moratorium on social reform. This encouraged employers (such as Renault) to renege on the Matignon agreements despite widespread resistance from the workers (ibid., 111). The PCF, which had refused to join the government all along, could now abrograte any responsibility for the failure of the Blum experiment and in the meantime safeguard its position as the workers' party and the party committed to social reform. All in all the Blum experiment had lasted barely eight months; four months later he resigned. The euphoria of the Left was quickly exposed for what it was – a mirage. The hopes of May 1936 did not go without a cultural record, however, as Renoir's *La Vie est à nous* (1936) attests – indeed they were even foreshadowed in *Le Crime de M. Lange* (Renoir, 1935).

During the troubled 1930s, the hero of Verdun, Maréchal Pétain, was never very far removed from the political arena. We need to go back to the Stavisky affair to see how willing he was to be perceived as the saviour of the regime and how easy it was for the Right to reignite the Pétain myth for political expediency – a myth reinforced by the call for *l'homme providentiel* in Christian-Jaque's *Le Père Lampion* (1934) and by the anti-frondist and eponymous hero of Gance's film *Jérôme Perreau* (1935) who is characterised as *l'homme providentiel*. The aftermath of the Stavisky affair was a massive right-wing demonstration in February 1934 that ended in blood-shed and the collapse of the *Cartel des gauches* government (Brogan: 1989, 282). This event exposed the vulnerability of the regime whose legitimacy could be threatened so easily. The immediate decision was to establish a 'National Government'. In order to give it prestige and credibility, Pétain was brought in as the new Minister of War in the autumn of 1934. Pétain's presence, for the moment, possibly saved the regime or at least made it secure against further extremist assaults. If the Right believed it had put an end to the threat of a right-wing/Fascist plot, this was certainly not a belief shared by the politicians of the Left. As described above, it mobilised them into a coalition and brought them electoral success (however brief). What is interesting in this context of the mentality of the Right is that Pétain's ministership demonstrated that he too believed he had only to be a presence in government. He showed little interest in expanding defence, merely contenting himself with adopting, unchanged, his predecessor's plan (Larkin: 1988, 66–7). With regard to his own defence legacy, the Maginot Line, it goes back further in history to the 1920s, when he advocated it in his capacity as vice-president of the *Conseil supérieur de la guerre* (ibid., 64).

When, in 1940, Pétain was called on again to save the nation, his presence (this time '*un don de ma personne*') was yet again capitalised upon to quell possible unrest. In just six weeks, the Germans had made a mockery of the Maginot Line, taken the north-east of France and advanced as far as Paris. Official organisation of the evacuation of Paris was minimal (the consequences of this abrogation of responsibility can be seen in the devastating opening sequence of Clément's *Jeux interdits*, 1952). Armistice seemed inevitable, not just in the mnemonic light of World War I but also because of the fear, however realistic, of a civil war instigated by the Communists. PCF slogans in early June 1940 – 'Turn the war into an anti-fascist war' and 'Defend Paris by arming the people' (Adereth: 1984, 104) – did little to dissuade Prime Minister Reynaud in his belief that another commune would arise and so Pétain was recalled from the Madrid Embassy. Pétain needed no persuading of the necessity to sue for peace. Indeed he strongly advocated it. What Reynaud and his government realised was that Pétain was crucial to a successful selling of the Armistice to the French people (especially since they had swallowed successive governments' repeated assurances that national security was guaranteed by the Maginot Line and the high priority given to defence). The hero of Verdun had risen a second time to save France and, so the regime's cynical representatives believed, to save the Third Republic (one cannot help but think here of the Verdun soldiers rising from the dead in Gance's *J'Accuse*, 1919). As history has revealed, Pétain had different ideas for the salvation of France.

German victory did indeed mark the death of the Third Republic and the consensual belief of the time was that France had deserved defeat because of its corrupt regime. Pétain did nothing to refute this masochistic interpretation of history. In fact, he was content to nurture it to serve his own objectives. Seven days after signing the armistice, Pétain set up headquarters in Vichy (29 June). Eleven days later the National Assembly voted its own demise. On 10 July 1940 the Third Republic was interred and the *Etat Français* was born. The title of president of the Republic was abolished by Pétain, who had full powers and who named himself *Chef d'Etat*. It is now common knowledge that Pétain was not the frail, senile octogenarian that circumstance drew out of oblivion and, for the sake of

France, pushed into the limelight of power. Indeed, Pétain was not an innocent. He was an incredibly vain person who referred to himself in monarchical terms as '*nous*' (McMillan: 1985, 131). Always a pessimist, by 1940 he had become a defeatist and, even more dangerous, a moralist (Brogan: 1989, 299). The Vichy regime, which he headed, declared war on all elements deemed responsible for the decadence of the 1930s. This included not just the anticlericals, Freemasons, Jews and foreigners, but also primary school teachers, many of whom were members of the Socialist party and whom Pétain accused of having demoralised the nation with socialist pacifism (Larkin: 1988, 46). In its political positioning as anti-republican and anti-parliamentarian, Vichy was a reaction to the Popular Front and a revenge on 1870 (the end of the Second Empire at which time Pétain was 17 years old). Last, but by no means least, Vichy also symbolised security for the bourgeoisie.

A film that exemplifies the mood of this time was one made during the *drôle de guerre* by Duvivier – *Untel père et fils* (1940, but not shown until 1945). To all intents and purposes this is the Vichy spirit before the fact. Duvivier, if not an anti-republican, was certainly of the Right. Nor was he necessarily clear of anti-semitism. In 1930, he had made *David Golder*, the tale of a Jewish financier who goes to the wall. Furthermore, he dedicated *La Bandera* (1935) to Franco, a film based on the Spanish legion in which some of the troops were Franco's soldiers. The bitter ending which he planned for *La Belle équipe* (1936), but was forced to drop, reflects a lack of solidarity that went counter to the *Front populaire* mythology of that time (as evidenced in Renoir's *Le Crime de M. Lange*, 1935 and *La Vie est à nous*, 1936). In any event, late in 1939 Duvivier was commissioned by Jean Giraudoux (then Minister of Propaganda) to make a film exalting national values. What came out of that commission was *Untel père et fils*. The film chronicles the exemplary life of a family called Froment (with all the agricultural connotations that name signifies) over a seventy-year span, 1870–1939. The title has a double resonance since, whilst all generations hold exemplary positions, death strikes one father or son from each generation in their service to their country. The first patriarch gets killed in the 1870 Paris siege during the Franco-Prussian war. One of his sons gets killed in the 1914–18 war. One of the third generation of sons enlists in 1939, and so may well perish. The message is sacrifice and order, all for the good of the nation – a message which clearly corresponds both to Pétain's belief in family, sacrifice and moral constraint and to his key formula '*le plaisir abaisse, la joie élève; le plaisir affaiblit, la joie rend fort*'.[4]

Peculiar to the political culture of France is the fact that, ever since the birth of France as a Republic, it is rather in her moments of anti-republicanism that she appears to facilitate order, Bonapartism being the first example. On a small scale we can see this in the establishing of the COIC during the Occupation. At long last, plans for organising the cinema industry, that had first been put forward in 1936 and 1939 by Guy de Carmoy and Jean Zay respectively, were implemented. Pétainism, though by no means on the same scale as Bonapartism, put in place a new order which was called *La Révolution nationale*. This National Revolution replaced the Republican triumvirate of '*égalité, fraternité, liberté*' with '*patrie, travail, famille*' and, as the words clearly connote, advocated the promotion of the family and development of an agricultural policy – all in the interest of the nation. The National Revolution was perceived as indissoluble from a moral regeneration. To this effect – but more because the anticlericals (including Freemasons) were an object of opprobrium to Vichy France – the Church was allowed back into prominence, especially with regard to the regime's educational policies. Youth was a primary target for this moral regeneration. To pre-existing Catholic movements (e.g., the *Association catholique de la jeunesse française*), Vichy France added the voluntary *Compagnons de France* and, more notoriously, the compulsory civilian service *Chantiers de la jeunesse* (McMillan: 1985, 133) – notorious because they undoubtedly legitimated, at least for the Vichy mentality, the implementation of two labour conscription programmes for work in Germany, the 'voluntary' *Relève* (1942) and subsequently the compulsory *Service de travail obligatoire* (STO, 1943). The STO system of exchange was one prisoner of war in exchange for three people sent to work in Germany. It is estimated that some 650,000 STOs were drafted, including 40,000 women. After the war, 10,000 workers or POWs chose to stay in Germany (Larkin: 1988, 102). It was quite some time before this particular reality found reflection in cinema (*Le Passage du Rhin*, Cayatte, 1960, *La Cuisine au beurre*, Gilles Grangier, 1963 and *Palace*, Edouard Molinaro, 1984).

   The principles of Pétainism have to be interpreted as more of a double-speak smokescreen than anything else if they are to be measured by their success. Here was a regime that decreed the constitutional legality of the logic of persecution, made a virtue out of spying and informing and yet, simultaneously, upheld the principles of moral regeneration and the triumvirate of the National Revolution. How was it possible, given this totally ambiguous message, to know what were the right set of moral values? This could explain the furore, after the war, over Clouzot's *Le Corbeau* (1943), a film which could be read as an allegory on informing (the film depicts how a spate of spiteful, if true, anonymous letters send a small community into turmoil and renders the atmosphere redolent with suspicion and hate). After the Occupation, the film was denounced by some for the negative image it gave of the French but praised by others for its anti-Pétainist stance, this latter group seeing in the film an attack against Vichy's active support of informing (McMillan: 1985, 133) gives a figure of 3–5 million letters sent to the Vichy bureaucracy). However, the film was based on a true story that goes back to 1917, the *Affaire Angèle Laval* at Tulle. Laval sent a spate of anonymous letters, some of which had tragic consequences. In this respect, the film says as much about Clouzot's perception of the unhealthy mean-spiritedness of the bourgeoisie and his desire to unmask its hypocrisy (a fairly constant theme to his work) as it does about the irrationality of the French which, on the one hand, had not come to terms with World War I and, on the other, had refused to come to grips with the approaching one (Oms: 1975, 58).

If there was moral regeneration, then it was of a dubious nature. Furthermore, the official figures for delinquency amongst France's youth doubled between 1940 and 1942 (McMillan: 1985, 133). As for the success of the pro-natalist policies, it is certain that there was a growth in the birth-rate. Historians are reluctant, however, to attribute this growth to Pétain's reforms, which were fairly unsubstantive and merely continued Daladier's 1939 Family Code (Larkin: 1988, 90). The more evident explanation for this growth lies with the increase in the number of potential procreating couples directly emanating from the post-1918 baby-boom (ibid., 90). As far as agricultural policy was concerned, whilst the myth of peasantism and the movement back to the land prevailed on an ideological propagandist level, the truth was in fact quite different. The peasant farmer fell victim to Vichy's larger-scale economic strategy which was to take control directly or indirectly of all aspects of production. The impetus for this state inter-vention was largely a result of the pressures to supply Germany. In any event, the state took over farming corporations and made them more efficient. Thus, despite the Pétainist propaganda that its policies were rescuing the solid, honest, French peasant from the double tyranny of the secular ideologues of the Third Republic and the urban ideologues of the Popular Front, it was more a case of the peasant farmer being sacrificed to the large-scale producers who were in a position to adopt new techniques and equipment (ibid., 94).

By a strange set of circumstances it was in its economic strategy that Vichy was its most forward looking. As a consequence of its strong anti-parliamentarianism, the Vichy government had as few prewar parlia-mentary representatives as possible, preferring instead a government of technocrats (products of the *Grandes écoles*, the *Conseil d'état* and the *Inspecteurs de Finances*, chosen for their expertise). It is also true that this predilection for technocrats was a defensive measure directly linked to the need to plan at top level in order to meet, rather than be taken over by, German economic demands (ibid., 85). In any event, the pressures of supplying Germany were a major factor in accelerating the rationalisation of France's industry and represented a complete break with the economic immobilism of the preceding governments. It is worth making the point that this new style of governing through economic forward planning set a trend that still prevails in the present-day governments of France.

Historians have disclosed how Pétain's positioning in relation to Hitler's

Germany was not ambiguous. Nor was that of his premier – Pierre Laval. In their belief that once the war was over, France would have an important role to play in Germany's New Europe, Pétain and Laval, albeit operating from different ideological motivations, sought active collaboration with the Third Reich (for example, totally unsolicited, they zealously introduced the anti-semitic laws, starting with the *Loi sur le statut des juifs* of 3 October 1940). History was to prove them wrong in their belief, but not before the deportation of around 76,000 Jews (a third of them French citizens and including some 4,000 children) to concentration camps (to say nothing of those killed on site in France by the Milice, Pétain's military police, or of those who died before deportation in the twenty or so detention camps scattered over France's two zones), or before the rounding up and shooting of a very substantial number of PCF members after the collapse of the German–Soviet pact in 1941 when Hitler invaded the Soviet Union (estimates of 75,000 are impossible to substantiate today but do serve as an indication of the toll taken by the party, many of whose members were part of the Resistance). Although the actual death toll of this war was less than the previous one (570,000 versus 1.3 million), the overall effect on the population was about the same as for World War I (the French loss of population for World War II was estimated at 1.4 million; ibid., 118).

The other great Occupation myth that needs to be laid to rest concerns the size of the Resistance. Historians have estimated that approximately 1 per cent of the adult population of France actively served within the Resistance, adding that it was only in 1943, with STO evasion and a general sense that the tide was turning against the Germans, that the ranks swelled to any significant size (from 45,000 to around 170,000 or 270,000, depending on the historian).[5] In any case, the Resistance was made up of numerous groups with divergent, at times rivalling, political tendencies (it is thought that Jean Moulin was a victim of such internal hostilities), so there was probably less coherence in their campaign than postwar discourses might lead one to believe. There is no disputing the heroism of the Resistance, merely the extent of its influence and its numbers.[6] Furthermore, it is easy to perceive why it was necessary, after the war and in the interests of national unity, to keep the myth of *la France Résistante* alive. For fear of a backlash, resulting from the humiliation and shame felt by France, institutional voices, (such as de Gaulle's) seized upon the salutary myth of the Resistance. For similar reasons of national unity, de Gaulle kept the prosecution (*épuration*) of collaborators to a modest level. The myth of widespread resistance made this minimising of reprisals possible. In fact, where the administration of the country was concerned, many ex-collaborators remained in office or were returned as deputies. Indeed, the Prime Minister in 1952, Antoine Pinay, and one of his cabinet ministers, Pierre-Etienne Flandin, were former Vichyites (McMillan: 1985, 153). The Fourth Republic, therefore, was not as clearly separated from

Vichy as myth would have it. Nor, as its subsequent history would demonstrate, was it sufficiently distant from the tattered heritage of the Third Republic.[7]

Of all the institutions hit by the *épuration*, it was the press that was the most severely punished, for the obvious reason that print acted as proof. In the performing arts, reprisals were also imposed on those who had shown too friendly a face to the enemy. In cinema, several careers were brought to an end for those reasons.[8] In industry, the most remarkable case was that of Louis Renault, who had his company confiscated and subsequently nationalised for collaborating with Germany by providing it with armoured and other vehicles (his name was not eradicated, however!). Nor were women who had slept with the enemy spared humiliation. Shunned by their community, who cut their hair off and often sent them naked down the main streets, they were easy scapegoats for a nation's anger at its own humiliation (Hanley et al.: 1989, 1). It is estimated that over 20 per cent of the working population were involved in illicit racketeering of one sort or another (Larkin: 1988, 127). France's mood after the war was more schizoid than irrational (which was how it had been in the 1930s). Her humiliation in defeat was matched by the euphoria of the Liberation. In the light of the shame which the Occupation had generated, the exhilaration and optimism bred by the Liberation smacks more of an hysterical reaction than of the assumption of a collective consciousness of what the recent past meant.

In cinema, paradoxically, there was quite a spate of films after the war – about the Resistance especially – but not surprisingly they served to reinforce the myth of the Resistance rather than to question the nation's behaviour during the war period. Indeed, quite the reverse occurred. Thus, a positive face of resistance could be found in *Boule de suif* (Christian-Jaque, 1945) with its central heroine – a prostitute (played by Micheline Presle) – refusing to sleep with the enemy and accidentally bringing about his death. But since it is set in the Franco-Prussian war, it functions safely on an allegorical level rather than addressing contemporary issues. Not surprisingly very few postwar films attempted to explain why people collaborated. Far more narratives were spent on some kind of revenge. For example, Carné's *Les Portes de la nuit* (1946) was one of the few films about post-Resistance revenge. Others, however, were about individual vendettas not associated with the Resistance. The spurned and vengeful woman of Bresson's *Dames au Bois de Boulogne* (1945), the young suitor avenging the murder (by her lover) of the woman he has loved from a distance in Lacombe's *Martin Roumagnac* (1946), youth's revenge on being cheated by the war in Autant-Lara's *Le Diable au corps* (1946), the harrying of a Jew to his death in Duvivier's *Panique* (1946) and a number of Simenon and Steeman thriller adaptations rife with violence and revenge – all of these films attest to a need to project the immediate past on to a different set of narratives that are removed from the immediate arena of guilt (although *Panique* comes uncomfortably close).

The period 1944–58 saw France endowed with a new Republic and, after months of deliberation, a new constitution (1946). The year 1944 witnessed the enfranchisement of women (married women having been decreed legal majors as late as 1938). It also saw France enter the Cold War (1947), join NATO (1949) and the European Community (1957). Finally, from 1954 onwards, this period saw her forsake or lose her colonial might – often at the risk, if not of civil war, then of civil unrest. Bookending this fourteen-year span was the imposing figure of General de Gaulle. As leader of the Free French during the Occupation, he assumed power upon the liberation of Paris. His 'dictatorship by consent' lasted until January 1946, when party squabbles over the new constitution drove him to resign. When the new constitution was finally endorsed by the electorate in October 1946, there was little (apart from the provision empowering government to dissolve parliament if the government suffered two votes of no-confidence within eighteen months) to differentiate it from that of the Third Republic. At first, thanks to a coalition government of representatives of the three major parties, the Left had a brief moment in power. However, the effects in 1947 of both the Cold War (which meant expelling the Communists) and de Gaulle's newly constituted party (the *Rassemblement du peuple français*, RPF – a right-wing anti-Communist party), forced a shift to the Centre by those remaining in government. In other words, in the face of potential extremism, government was obliged once again to adopt the politics of immobilism.

Thankfully for France, this political stagnation was not reduplicated in the economic arena. Postwar economic reconstruction was aided by the Marshall plan, but the reason for its success must be attributed to two further causes: first, to France's long-standing tradition of *dirigisme* (that is, of the state giving clear, but indicative rather than prescriptive leadership to the private sector) and second, to the more recent Vichy tradition of medium- and long-term planning. To the Malthusianism of the politicians of the Third Republic came the sharp anti-Malthusian retort of the technocrats of the Fourth. Now in the private sector, thanks to the rationality of the governmental five-year plans system which fostered new attitudes, the mood was pro-mergers and international competition. In the public sector the mood was similarly bold and optimistic. Measures introduced to rebuild the economy were twofold. In the first instance, an extension of the nationalisation programme was undertaken, and in the second, the establishment of a welfare state. By 1949, the state employed one-tenth of the working population and, because of its control of banking, directly influenced 47 per cent of all investment. Furthermore, by 1954 generous pro-natality programmes were paying good dividends with a rise of 5.6 per cent in the population (Hanley et al.: 1989, 2).

Obviously the modernisation of France affected the social structure. First, streamlining in the agricultural sector, through the concentration of productive units, caused a rural exodus into the light-industry sector, which had expanded through heavy investment into manufacturing. Second, due to the needs of an expanding industry, immigration was once more on the ascendancy, although not in the proportions of the interwar years (around 700,000 – mostly Maghrébins and Portuguese – growing to 2 million by the early 1970s as opposed to the 3 million of the early 1930s). This meant that by the early 1970s, the overall immigrant class – including pre-Liberation numbers – totalled 3.5 million people and accounted for just over a third of the population increase (Larkin: 1988, 180). These two factors (streamlining and immigration), in the immediate and long term respectively, were made into political issues. They are worth looking at together because of the similarity in the political animal they produced. By the mid-1950s, the effect of streamlining was being felt by certain economic groups rendered obsolete by the new developing economy. Thus, for example, the small shopkeeper was squeezed out by the supermarket or co-operative and the artisan's skills were made redundant in the face of mechanisation (Hanley et al.: 1989, 6).

It was not until the unemployment problems of the 1970s that the immigration factor was raised as a political issue, at which time immigrants were accused of taking jobs away from the French worker. In both instances, however, the extremity of the unfavourable times for the little man produced a leader to represent his cause. In the 1950s, it was Pierre Poujade, and in the 1970s, Jean-Marie Le Pen. Both men were raised in the consciousness of the extreme Right and, together with the parties they personally brought into being, rose politically from small beginnings (Poujade's party obtained fifty-one seats in the 1956 elections; Le Pen's thirty-five in the 1986 elections). The point here is that the political climate after Vichy was not the same as that following World War I, when discontent was more readily (though not exclusively) the fomenting ground for the PCF. Now it was more readily that of the extreme Right. The effects of the Cold War undoubtedly represented a partial reason for this change, but so too did the failure of widespread strikes called in late 1947 by the predominantly Communist union, the CGT (*Confédération générale du travail*) and an unsuccessful miners' strike in late 1948 which caused huge job losses (Larkin: 1988, 161). Even though, by the mid-1950s, the PCF still had a membership equivalent to that of all the other parties put together (ibid., 160), none the less its popularity was on the decline. In the 1930s, the PCF had been at the forefront, leading for change, and its dynamism and modernity had attracted the working class to its cause of unity. Indeed, during the 1930s the PCF, because it was more in touch with its needs, was more widely attractive to the working class than the Fascist spirit which appealed more to the upper classes. By the mid-1950s this attractiveness had waned somewhat. The PCF was out of touch and its toeing of the Moscow line made it look increasingly like a foreign party. This adherence to Moscow meant the party had to support the invasion and repression in Hungary (1956) and denounce the creation of the EEC (1957). By the late 1950s its membership had dropped by 37 per cent, a clear indication that its image was less attractive and stood less for unity and change than it had a quarter of a century earlier (Adereth: 1984, 280).

Standing in the wings, ever watchful over his beloved France, was the man whose claim to understand the French people ('*Français je vous ai compris*') would sweep him to power in 1958. The charismatic declaimer of that memorable and, as it turned out, deeply ambiguous sound bite was General de Gaulle. In the ten years of his self-imposed political exile he had watched France lose the majority of her empire and, equally vitally, her international status. France's political decline in the 1950s was partly the blowing apart of a myth, but mostly the result of the Cold War. The illusory nature of France's international status was crudely exposed by her exclusion from the Yalta and Potsdam talks in 1945 when the vital decisions of 'what to do with Germany' were formulated. In fact, it was more a case of France being returned to her true status of second-rank which had been occluded during the interwar years by the effects of America's isolationist policy and the ostracism of Germany and the Soviet Union. With the three most powerful countries out of the limelight, France was more or less forced centre-stage, as was Britain (Larkin: 1988, 120). Once in power and ever mindful of what he perceived as the cause of France's decline – Britain's perfidy and America's hegemonising practices – de Gaulle's international policies were strongly determined towards a re-enhancing of her image and equally strongly inflected by an anti-American and anti-British stance.

The impact of the Cold War forced France, for reasons of security, to join NATO, thus making her a satellite of the United States. It also obliged her, in the light of the Korean War, to accept the rearmament, within NATO, of her arch-enemy – (West) Germany. Even the loss of her empire was partly a consequence of her relationship with her allies, who refused to see the Indo-China and North African crises confronting her as part of the Cold War and therefore gave no aid to secure a French victory (Hanley et al.: 1989, 213). When the United States did finally intercede in France's fight against the Viet Minh in 1952, it was on a financial basis only and it was already too late. Elected Prime Minister in 1954 on the ticket that he would pull France out of the war, Mendès France effectively fulfilled his promise by passing the problem on to the Americans who proved, disastrously, that they were just as incapable as the French of destroying Ho Chi Minh and the Viet Minh spirit. In the meantime the Algerian crisis, which had reached worrying and violent proportions, was tearing the French nation apart both in the *Hexagone* (mainland France) and in Algeria itself.

By 1958, army chiefs in Algeria were close to mutiny, a sympton of which was their refusal to act against the right-wing extremists and *pieds-noirs* who had seized Algiers. Corsica was already under siege and rumours were rampant of an imminent military coup on the hexagon. In France, censorship was becoming increasingly trenchant (because of allegations of torture in Algeria) and demonstrations in the streets were given short shrift by the police. Colonial nationalism had peaked into hysteria. The Fourth Republic had spiralled out of control and the collapse of the regime, so long predicted by de Gaulle, was now at hand.

The Fourth Republic, just like her older sister, was hounded by political unrest and marked by political immobilism. This unrest manifested itself through the factionalism and deep cleavages which dogged French political life (McMillan: 1985, 152). As has already been pointed out, France's insecurity and political instability stemmed from her deep ambivalence regarding the legitimacy of her republicanism. Uncertainty about the legitimacy (to say nothing of the durability) of the regime finds its roots in the political cultural climate that dates back to the Revolution, when along with the triumivirate of optimistic unity – *'liberté, égalité et fraternité'* – came the rivening triumvirate of preoccupations generated by that same Revolution – 'constitution, clericalism and class' – to which colonialism was added after World War II (Larkin: 1988, 36). I will only focus on the first two 'Cs' because the questions of class (legitimacy of the possessing classes, the myth of the mob, social mobility, etc.) and colonialism have already been addressed, whereas the issues surrounding the constitution and clericalism have been less fully developed.

Concern for the constitution was based primarily upon its mutability. France's republican heritage was one of discontinuity, interrupted as it was by periods of dictatorship (the First and Second Empires and the Occupation). Each new Republic, perceiving in the previous constitution the reason for its downfall, felt it necessary to produce a new constitution. Until the Fifth Republic, however, those drafting the respective constitutions could not bring themselves to invest leadership with enough power to push legislation through, precisely because of the periods of dictatorship. Lacking power meant that only safe short-term policies would be presented to the Assembly. But not even that could guarantee the permanence of a particular government given that there was a multiplicity of parties and that no single party had an out-and-out majority. There have been two major consequences of this hesitancy and instability. First, for fear that delegation and regionalism might heighten the multi-directional split of the electorate, France has been made into a highly centralised state (even its political uprisings are centralised, starting as they do in Paris). Second and very contingent to the first, because of the impermanence of governments, France is a country that is more readily administered than governed. The combination of these two factors means that there is a strong symbiosis between the state and the citizen where the state guarantees the citizen her/his identity and where the citizen, in the name of the state that has assured her/his individual identity (i.e., *voix* which is both the empowerment of speech and the right to vote), can voice either support or rejection of a particular political system.[9]

Anticlericalism is profoundly rooted in the republican spirit of France for the obvious reason that the Church is identified with its monarchistic heritage and perceived as profoundly anti-republican. Its support of Bonaparte, the Second Empire and its dubious relationship with Vichy during the Occupation (i.e., Pétain's exploitation of the Church to wage battle against the anticlericals) confirm that it was more inclined to anti-republican regimes than not. Anticlericalism also explains in part the long delay in the enfranchisement of women which, because females outnumbered male practising Catholics by two to one, was seen as the thin end of the wedge to a conservative majority that would reverse the anticlerical legislation of pre-World War I (i.e., the separation in 1905 of Church and state and ensuing educational reforms; ibid., 21–2). History proved that this fear was partly correct. Women's voting patterns during the 1950s tended to support the conservative parties, including the Christian Democrats (*Mouvement républicain populaire* or MRP) and the Gaullist (RPF) parties, both of which were anti-communist but which suffered an embarrassing influx of ex-Vichyites in 1945 and 1946 respectively (ibid., 157). Furthermore, there was an accentuation of a swing to the Right in the 1951 elections, but it is difficult to discern whether this was due to women's suffrage or to the effect of the Cold War on voting practices.

It is safe to say that, in the first half of the 1950s, clerical issues were on the ascendancy again in education (the overriding issue being: should the state subsidise private Catholic schools?) and that the Catholic vote was significant enough for de Gaulle to exploit the education question to his advantage in order to woo that vote (ibid., 163). By the late 1950s, clericalism (apart from occasional re-emergences of the schools' question) had become significantly less of an issue than before (interestingly, cinema reflects this move away from clericalism as a political issue – by the 1960s anticlerical films, as exemplified by Autant-Lara's 1950s films, had all but disappeared). Indeed, the death of the Fourth Republic was to see the end of a number of long-standing polemical issues and the birth, not surprisingly, of others. However, the questions arising from the advent of the Fifth Republic must wait until the following chapter and it is now to matters cinematographic that I shall turn.

TECHNOLOGIES AND THEORIES OF STYLE

The implementation of three technological developments – sound, colour and cinemascope – were to have a significant impact on France's national cinema. I have already described, (in Chapter 1) how sound exerted a financial strain on film production, but I did also make the point that, initially at least, sound proved to be a boon to the indigenous product from 1929 to 1931 (dubbing was yet to be perfected and the French preferred to hear their own language). Commercial necessity brought sound to the screen and, although France had perfected her own sound system (Gaumont had been working on sound since 1902, and in association with two Danish researchers – Poulsen and Petersen – had completed the process by 1928), it was to be the Germans and the Americans who carved up the international pie. Colour film and cinemascope were introduced in the early 1950s primarily by the Americans in an effort to stem the commercial decline of its own cinema. Whilst colour was as much an American invention as it was Belgian, German and Japanese, this was not the case for the other innovation, cinemascope. The anamorphic lens that made cinemascope possible was devised by the Frenchman Henri Chrétien in 1928 but was not implemented until the Americans revived it in 1953 (Salt: 1983, 316). In two major technological instances (sound and cinemascope) France had the product but not the means, economically, to develop it to her own advantage.

I have already mentioned this lack of investment and its costs to the cinematic industry. What is doubtless of greater and more novel interest is the impact these technological developments had upon film-making practices and subsequently upon theories of style. Film-makers of the 1920s had been striving to perfect a cinematic language based on the expressive qualities of the image (Martin: 1987, 25). Now, however, with the great increase in production costs and the effect of early sound recording on film-making practices, the possibilities for experimenting with film were considerably reduced (Buchsbaum: 1988, 22). In fact, because sound, in its early days, was recorded directly on to the film, the camera, which was a heavy piece of machinery that would be noisy to move around, had to remain more or less static. Hence films reverted back to their earlier prototype of filmed theatre with the static frame creating the proscenium arch effect. This stasis was compounded by the fact that sound scenarios often adapted pre-World War I theatre (the most prolific being Yves Mirande's work) which, by the 1930s, bore little relation to contemporary France.

The very first sound film was André Hugon's *Les Trois masques* (1929), although this was shot in the UK. The first one made in France was Henri Chomette's *Le Requin* (1929), but the first totally sonorised film was L'Herbier's *L'Enfant de l'amour* (1930). There was talk, talk and more talk. Furthermore, in the belief that gesturality must still be allowed the same space as in silent films, there was no real change in tempo. The reasoning was that a slow pace would give time for the characters to have solidity. Whilst this might be true if the performance was good, it also ran the danger of exposing weaknesses and slowing down the film's rhythm. As Jeancolas (1983, 61) points out, these early talkies were made up of a series of long takes and as such put in place codes and conventions that were to prevail in over half of the cinematic production for the first fifteen years of sound cinema. Indeed, where French cinema was concerned and on the down side of its specificity, the emergence of sound brought in its wake much talk and too little action. On the up side, however, economic exigencies created a cinematic code, the filmed song, which became a phenomenon of feature films during the 1930s. In fact, the beginning of sound films was a boom time for shorts, especially songs and short sketches, which were cheaper to make and helped exhibitors to fill their programmes inexpensively. Cinema, long before the radio and phono-graph (which only the middle classes could afford) was the first medium to popularise recorded music and the public liked it so much that it became almost *de rigueur* in a feature-length film.[10] Clair is the most renowned film-maker to have exploited the advantages of song in films. They enabled him to keep dialogue to a minimum, thereby not reproducing filmed theatre (something he abhorred) and to have a freer camera. In fact, the major merit of Clair's early films is that he did not sacrifice visual virtuosity to sound. Sound served only to enhance his images, never to replace them, thus preventing his cinema from going static, as occurred with most of the early sound films (Comes and Marmin: 1984, 13).

The response of film-makers and critics to sound can be summed up as divided. On the one hand, it was warmly welcomed by the likes of Marcel Pagnol and Sacha Guitry – two very popular dramatists of the time who saw in sound the chance to commit their theatre to perpetuity. On the other, it was reviled as the agent of death to the avant-garde and experi-mental cinemas (the critics Moussinac and Vuillermoz were of this opinion and it is significant that their influence on cinema started to wane with the advent of sound). Certain film-makers, especially René Clair, saw in sound the end of cinema as an autonomous art. Clair and Pagnol's polemical debate is the one most often cited today as *the* debate of the 1930s. However, important though their positionings were, it is worth recalling that film theory discourses went further afield than Pagnol's advocacy of filmed theatre and Clair's assertion of the primacy of the image over the word. In fact it would not be unreasonable to state that perhaps the most significant shift was the politicisation of cinema aesthetics.

Abel (1988, 6–12) remarks how film theory reflected the deepening schisms between ideological fronts caused by the rise of fascism. The right-wing press and fascist writers welcomed sound as a possible means for shoring up a coherent national identity. Nationalism also became the concern of film historians even to the point of mythologising the history of France's cinema (ibid., 150). For example, both the right-wing duo Bardèche and Brasillach and the left-wing Sadoul totemised the first avant-garde movement of the 1920s naming it, respectively, the 'school of Delluc' and 'Delluc's impressionist school'. The mythical status of Delluc was reinforced when in 1936 an association of independent film critics instituted the *Prix Louis Delluc* for the year's best French film (the first prize of its kind and one that remains to this day). A further sign of this sense of nationalistic necessity was the creation in that same year, of the *Cinémathèque française* by Georges Franju, Jean Mitry and Henri Langlois. Interestingly, given the now mythic importance of that date in the annals of history, its status as a major cultural institution was not secured until after the Occupation (Jeancolas: 1983, 106n). By 1938, this strain of nationalism had attained cultural propaganda proportions with the institution by Jean Zay (formerly Education Minister in the Popular Front government and now, in the same post, in the Daladier government of the Right) of five *Grands Prix nationaux* for French films and the projected launching in 1939 of an International Film Festival at Cannes. These prizes and the Festival were to counter the nationalistic culture tub-thumping of the Italians and the Germans at the earlier instituted Venice Film Festival. This nationalistic triumphalism was to get short shrift, however. Only one set of prizes would get distributed and the Cannes Festival would have to wait until 1946.

The advent of sound was the death knell for Surrealist cinema of the mid-1920s. A major contributing factor was, of course, the fact that early sound necessitated long takes thus putting an end (for quite some time to come) to the principles of montage editing. This did not mean, however, the loss of a radical or radicalising cinema. Rather, Surrealist cinema's disappearance allowed for the re-emergence of the other two forms of the 1920s avant-garde: the documentarist and the subjective. With regard to the first form, the notion was to link film closely with social praxis (i.e., to reflect society and its interactions with individuals). Advocates of realism as revolutionary included such film-makers as Jean Vigo, Jean Renoir, Marcel Carné, Yves Allégret, Jean Dréville and Jacques Prévert. But many of these film-makers also advocated cinema as revelatory of mental states, that is, they favoured the subjective avant-garde as well. In so doing, they brought about the shift back from the mid-1920s pure cinema as semiotic to cinema's earlier status as revelation (Abel: 1988, 15). It was Jean Epstein who took this second form to its most advanced state in advocating that camera and sound should have equal but independent mobility. He saw, in what he termed *phonogénie* (filmed sound), the complement to Delluc's *photogénie* (filmed image; ibid., 10). Epstein's concept of film as the editing together of these two disparately 'filmed' realities constituted a first theorising of counterpoint (in the Faulknerian sense of the word of running two narratives simultaneously) which, in the 1950s, would become the hallmark of Agnès Varda's and, later, Alain Resnais' film-making practice.

André Bazin, film critic and co-founder of the *Cahiers du cinéma*, was very dismissive of the critic's school of the 1930s (Bazin: 1983, 210), as indeed he was of the Poetic Realist school of that same decade (ibid., 20). Jean-Pierre Jeancolas (1983, 107) echoes the first sentiment by pointing to the lack of discourses on cinema during that decade. However, Abel (1988, xiii) points to the suppressing effect of the *Cahiers du cinéma* group on all that was written prior to the Liberation. It must be added that, thanks to Abel's work on the silent period and his two-volume study on theory in the 1930s as well as other researchers' (Lagny and Vincendeau) work on this period, a much clearer picture of the richness of the debate is now emerging. Thus the *Revue du cinéma* (1929–31 and 1946–9), launched by Jean-Georges Auriol and dismissed by Jeancolas (1983, 106) as full of promise but essentially marginal and without any profound resonance, is now recognised for the precursory role it played to the *Cahiers* (Hillier: 1985, 2). In terms of the politicisation of the debate around cinema in the 1930s, Jeancolas (1983, 107) points only to the press critics Léon Moussinac at *L'Humanité* and François Vinneuil (alias Lucien Rebatet during the Occupation) at *L'Action française* adding that the new magazines born with the advent of sound (e.g., *Pour Vous*, *Cinémonde* and *Cinémagazine*) were by and large promotional in their intent and targeted popular audiences. However, the point needs to be made that regular contributors to these popular magazines included major film-makers. Furthermore, the debate was far more wide-ranging than Jeancolas or Bazin make out, starting in the first instance with the advocacy of literary adaptations (L'Herbier in *Cinémagazine*) and moving on to the polemic surrounding filmed theatre. The major debate there took place between Pagnol, in his own review launched for the purpose and of which there were four issues (*Les Cahiers du film*, 1933) and Clair (writing in *Pour Vous*, 1930 and *Candide*, 1934).

There were numerous other debates ranging from theoretical to polemical aesthetics. The tradition of the theoretical aesthetics of the 1920s was continued by the writings of such critics and film-makers as Jean Epstein (in *Cinéa-Ciné*) or Roger Leenhardt (in Emannuel Mounier's *L'Esprit*, another review considered to predate in spirit the *Cahiers du cinéma* (Comes and Marmin: 1984, 140) and countered by the very prosaic counter-aesthetic (*film-à-thèse*) vision of cinema as exemplified by André Cayatte who founded his own review (along with the poet René Char) *Méridiens* in 1930. Most visibly political was Auriol's nonconformist *Revue du cinéma* as well as Marcel Carné and Valéry Jahier's calls for a socially committed cinema (writing respectively in *Cinémagazine*, in 1933 and *L'Esprit*, during 1934–6). Trenchantly political were, on the Left, the writings of Georges Altman (who, in 1933, replaced Moussinac at *L'Humanité*) and on the Right, those of Vinneuil (in, among several other reviews, *Je suis partout*, which was soon to become infamous). Of the politically engaged, Renoir was one of the most prolific writers from the mid-1930s onwards. Collectives on the Left such as the *Groupe octobre* (1932–6) and *Ciné-Liberté* (1936–7) both polemicised and published about film. The former group, though primarily a theatre collective, had amongst its adherents people directly involved in cinema (Yves Allégret, Roger Blin, Jean-Paul Dreyfus who would become Le Chanois, Paul Grimault, Jacques Prévert and Renoir, for example) and their thinking certainly inflected Renoir's *Le Crime de M. Lange* (1935) and *La Vie est à nous* (1936, sponsored by the PCF) as well as Le Chanois's *Temps des cerises* (1937).

Ciné-Liberté was directly linked to the Popular Front. It absorbed members from the defunct *Groupe octobre* and other radical groupings (such as Germaine Dulac's *Mai '36*) but its roots go back to the *Association des écrivains et artistes révolutionnaires* (AEAR), which launched an independent cinema alliance (ACI) in 1935. The intention of this Collective was to counter the capitalist domination of the industry (Abel: 1988, 153). More politically motivated in an overt way than the 1920s avant-garde, the Collective targeted workers' rights and censorship (surprisingly unsuccessfully in the latter regard given its link with the Popular Front). It also produced films, especially documentary ones (mostly on workers), but there were also educational films (this unit was headed by Jean Painlevé who would become, albeit briefly, head of COIC during the Occupation). *Ciné-Liberté* lasted the lifetime of the Popular Front, its demise coming about as much as a result of factionalism within the Collective as from its overambitious plan to make a full feature historical spectacle film, *La Marseillaise* (Renoir, 1938). In epic terms this film was supposed to counter Gance's right-wing historical epics *Jérôme Perreau* (1935) and the sound version of *Napoléon, vu par Abel Gance* (1934). Funding was to be by public subscription (thus making it a truly Popular Front/Worker's Collective product). However, the funds raised were insufficient to support the grandiose scheme of a five- to twelve-hour film and the final product was a significant compromise, if not failure. The cost of making the film was ten times that of the public subscription. *Ciné-Liberté* was in ruins and all that remained for it to do was to disband.[11]

Before moving on to consider the impact of the other technological developments on cinematic theory and practice, I would like to provide a brief summary of the state of the art in the 1930s. First, whilst the advent of sound did significantly alter the existing boundaries of theoretical discourses and their modes of enunciation, none the less it is important to note that many of the debates during the 1930s prolonged those of the silent era, most particularly the high/low art one and the auteur versus scenario-led film (both of which refuse to go away, even now). Second, in terms of practice, there appear to be four major trends quite naturally corresponding to the dominant theoretical discourses. It is worth pointing out that three out of the four were all advocating a popular, even populist cinema – a difference in balance from the 1920s theories, pointing to the more politicised nature of the 1930s discourses.

These four trends were as follows. First, there was filmed theatre (which was extremely popular). Second, the musical fantasy (visual scenes underscored by songs with a minimum of dialogue and sound effects) which was devised by Clair as the counter-cinema to canned theatre and intended as a popular film form. An alternative form was the operetta or musical comedy, a format much to the liking of public taste in the early 1930s (and which was revived in the 1950s to help the promotion of both the song and film industries). The third trend, realist cinema, was composed of two types, namely, social realism with its stress on the authentic (usually the working class and its environment) and poetic realism where the stress was on an authentic representation of class and milieu but where the narrative was essentially 'not real' but, rather, poetic (both types were, again, intended as a popular, even populist cinema). The final trend, fantasy or subjective narrative films, was – relatively speaking and only in terms of actual production – a fairly minor one. Issued from the legacy of the 1920s Surrealist avant-garde, its film-makers included Clair, Cocteau, the Prévert brothers and Vigo (and the Spanish exile, Buñuel).

The dominance of literary adaptations in cinematic production led to an increased importance being attached to the scriptwriter. The 1930s witnessed a lionising of 'the few and great scriptwriters' who, because of the enormous cultural capital they brought with them, were still giants, in the eyes of producers at least, well into the 1950s. These few – Charles Spaak, Henri Jeanson, Jean Aurenche and Pierre Bost – were the textual progenitors of the so-called 'cinéma de qualité' of the 1950s so much despised by the Cahiers du cinéma critics.

Some twenty years separate the introduction of sound from colour and cinemascope, a virtual quarter of which time (1940–4) France spent in the invidious position of being 'not herself' but 'other' and suppressed, and yet, of having the semblance of being herself – a myth sustained by the illusory power wielded by the Vichy government which continued to administer after 1942 even though the Nazi occupation had spread over the whole of the territory by late 1942. The political and national schizophrenia which this unreal reality created within the French citizen has little to no record in film but does surface in the contemporaneous review L'Ecran français. This review, which was headed by René Blech, was the clandestine organ of the Front national's cinema committee (the Front national was the Communists' Resistance group) and was politically committed to a national cinema. In its first issue, which appeared in December 1943, it clearly revealed the political culture of the times in its revilement of Clouzot's Le Corbeau (France-as-not-herself) and its adulation of Grémillon's Le Ciel est à vous (France as an authentic national truth –

individual heroism manifested in a Frenchwoman's historic transatlantic flight).[12] In all, the review lasted ten years. Its distinctive style, much inflected by the political and intellectual debates of its time (Jean-Paul Sartre and Merleau-Ponty were seminal thinkers for the review), which was so appropriate to the climate and times of the Occupation and the first years of the Liberation, was by 1952 too trenchant, too engaged with ideology to attract a reading public that wanted not to think about its recent past. The impact of the Cold War did the rest. During the Occupation, it was the only voice of opposition to the fascist *Je suis partout* and *Le Film*.[13] In its heyday, it did push forward the debates around cinematic style, most famously through Alexandre Astruc's important essay '*Naissance d'une nouvelle avant-garde*' (no. 144, 1948) in which he launches the concept of the *caméra-stylo* and the notion of cinema as language rather than a sign (which is where it had got to in the late 1920s debate). This review also broadened the product-base to be examined. American, Soviet, Japanese and Chinese cinemas as well as the indigenous cinema were all suitable texts for treatment. In both instances (theory and subject matter), therefore, *L'Ecran français* left an important legacy which first, the *Cahiers du cinéma* in 1951 and a year later, *Positif* were to take on.

The *Cahiers du cinéma* (henceforth referred to as *Cahiers*) marked a return to the auteur theory but, to all intents and purposes, with a difference, because the high/low art debate had been removed. The notion of auteur was now closely bound up with the concept of *mise-en-scène*. These two predicates were seen as essential to a real cinema of quality. The reasoning goes as follows: the auteur was distinctive for his (*sic*) style and not necessarily for the subject matter *per se*. Thus the auteur no longer needed to be the 'totality' of the film (i.e., scriptwriter, editor, etc.). This shift in the meaning of auteur was largely due to the avid attention which the *Cahiers* paid to American cinema where, it must be remembered, a director had little or no say over any of the production. The only space for creativity was with *mise-en-scène*, which became the expressive tool at the film-maker's disposal, and it was through a reading of that *mis-en-scène* – the *Cahiers* critic Pierre Kast was responsible for introducing this important concept of *lecture* – that a critic could both determine the specificity of the cinematographic work and decipher the film's text and subtext (Hillier: 1985, 10 and 222). Hence the focus on *mise-en-scène*.

Small wonder then the enthusiasm expressed by the *Cahiers* group for cinemascope. Not only did it extend the possibilities of *mise-en-scène*, it also represented the death of montage. Montage for the *Cahiers*, but most especially for Bazin, was an anti-realistic film-making practice that manipulated the audience through its juxtapositioning of shots and the carving up of reality. Realism and objectivity could only be assured by the predominance of depth of field/deep focus with its long takes and implicit unimpeded vision – hence the *Cahiers* grand admiration for Renoir, who was supposedly the 'inventor' of depth of field in the 1930s, a belief refuted by Salt (1983, 269)[14] – and the privileging of *mise-en-scène*. Cinemascope was also greeted by the *Cahiers* because of its potential to extend the merits of depth of field. Cinemascope implied a number of things for the *Cahiers* critics. First, it gave breadth (i.e., space) rather than depth and thereby created a frieze effect on the screen. In so doing, claimed Truffaut, it recognised the sculptural nature of cinema's narrative (*Cahiers du cinéma*, no. 25, 1953). Second, according to Rivette, cinema should not try to create depth, but should suggest depth through breadth. Cinema, he argued, is first about lateral movements and space and cinemascope allowed for a freer expression of those two concepts (*Cahiers*, no. 31, 1954). In this respect cinemascope also represented an answer to French film-makers' and critics' long-standing dislike of the prevalence of close-ups (Colette writing in the early days of silent cinema deplored the overabundance of close-ups in American cinema). Now they became the exception and, therefore, remarkable. Rohmer reasoned that cinemascope also implied location shooting and the definitive arrival of colour (*Cahiers*, no. 31, 1954).[15] Finally, Truffaut felt that because cinemascope provided the spectator with almost panoramic vision (i.e., virtually consonant with the way human vision functions), it was the perfect solution to the arbitrary divide between audience and screen.

Bazin, for all his dismissiveness of earlier discourses, did broaden and develop the debates in a number of areas. A first significant debate he opened up was the one on genre, a hitherto fairly (if not completely) neglected question. As Hillier (1985, 223) points out, much of the subsequent writing on genre amongst Anglo-Saxon critics owes a lot to Bazin. Joel Magny (1991, 60) pinpoints two other major contributions made by Bazin, the one addressing the phenomenological dimension of cinema's praxis, the other the question of cinema as language. With regard to the first point, Bazin claims that cinema allows us to see time. Thus, he argues that the theorists of the 1920s misperceived the function of cinema in their attempts to resolve this question of time through space, that is, through a fragmentation of the real (via montage most especially, as per the Soviet school of thought that influenced French film-makers). Nor, according to Bazin, was the solution to be found by analogising film with music and proposing that time could be perceived through the use of rhythm (Germaine Dulac was a major proponent of this school of thought). On this last point, Bazin brought cinema out of the analogising process which it had been subjected to in the 1920s, seeing that as a reductive debate (it must be remembered, however, that the earlier theorists were arguing for the legitimacy of this new art form and so had to argue by analogy). Within this phenomenological dimension of cinema, he argued against the 1920s pure cinema aesthetic, which placed cinematic praxis outside reality, maintaining that its praxis is the revelation of the identity between reproduction and expression, the conjuncture between the ontological and the psychological – thus providing a psychological realism. Incidentally, Truffaut argues for this principle in his essay '*Une certaine tendance du cinéma français*', in this instance singling out for his attack scriptwriters and film-makers of the post-Poetic Realism period (i.e., from the 1940s onwards) and their failure to achieve this psychological realism (*Cahiers*, no. 31, 1954).[16]

Bazin also stressed the importance of an aesthetic realism which he saw as closely bound up in his notion of cinema as language – his other major contribution to film theory. Here Bazin wants film-makers to move away from the ideological nature of montage – resting as it does on the principle of a priori knowledge (i.e., that montage will produce 'x' meaning, a specific reading) – and work towards a naturalism of the image that refuses all a priori analysis of the world. To this effect, he advocates the merits of deep focus, since this style draws least attention to itself and therefore allows for an open reading. He points to the Italian Neo-Realism school as the most advanced state of cinema where cinema seems to be no more than a window on the world (Magny: 1991, 66). This perception is firmly grounded in his belief that cinema's role is to strive towards 'truth' even though it is unattainable and the attaining of it would be the end of truth/cinema. Magny (1991, 67) succinctly formulates his contribution as 'having henceforth placed ontological realism at the centre of an aesthetic conception of cinema'. Since an obvious implication of Bazin's theory is the self-effacement of the film-maker, it is rather curious that the *Cahiers* group, almost in its totality, spawned the *politique des auteurs*. This was in fact a theory which Bazin did not espouse for reasons which I shall address below. However, the other primary *Cahiers* theory, *mise-en-scène*, does seem to emanate more naturally from the phenomenological dimension of Bazin's thinking even though, if taken to extremes (i.e., *mise-en-scène* is all), it too could go counter to Bazin's liberal and humanist vision of cinematic practices (Hillier: 1985, 224).

Although it certainly was a very dominating presence on the theoretical scene, the *Cahiers* group was not the only one of importance. *Positif*, launched in 1952, was similarly a collective of critics writing on cinema. The main difference, however, was that *Positif* was politicised and held overtly Left positions. The *Cahiers* was, with the exception of Pierre Kast, quite culturally conservative and strongly apolitical. This partially explains the *Cahiers* liking for the American cinema, since social problems were addressed socially and not politically (ibid., 7). *Positif*, whilst also addressing American cinema, on the contrary pointed to its lack of political discourses. After the euphoria of Liberation, France became very apolitical and in this respect the *Cahiers* represents a truer reflection of the climate of the times. There were voices of dissent in French intellectual life – Sartre, de Beauvoir and Camus to name the obvious, but also, in the world of cinema, Signoret, Montand and Renoir (the last of whom expressed French cinema's need for a moral renewal) – and to a relative degree *Positif* was a non-conforming voice with its politically motivated writers such as Georges Franju and Alain Resnais.

It might come as some surprise, given the reputation of the *Cahiers* group once it turned to film-making, that very little active opposition to the Algerian war or polemicising against French colonialism was voiced in its writings. The only exception was Pierre Kast, a committed Marxist. I say surprise because Godard (who is thought of as a political film-maker) was part of that group and yet it was not until the mid-1960s that he addressed these two issues that were so central to French political culture in the 1950s. Consonant with this conservatism was the world-view that the group wanted films to reveal – namely, an optimistic image of human potentialities in a corrupt society (which is why it disliked the old guard of scriptwriters who had cut their teeth on the pessimism of Poetic Realism back in the 1930s). Bearing this in mind, the *Cahiers* was not as progressive as it at first appeared and there was something potentially quite reactionary in the group's romantic notion of the artist/auteur providing this impelling world-view.

This obsession with the auteur as artist is exemplified by the prize which the *Cahiers* introduced in 1951 for the best book on film, the *Prix Canudo*. Instituted in memory of Ricciotto Canudo (the film theorist of the 1920s and radical proselytiser of the film-maker as auteur), it says much about the auto-reflexivity of the group's own writerliness/authorial role. As Hillier (1985, 224) points out, there is also a real problematic in 'the enshrinement of *mise-en-scène*' because at its most extreme it threw up 'the distinctly illiberal, anti-humanist "MacMahonist" (so called after the Paris cinema which specialised in showing popular American cinema) tendency'. The danger of this extremism is doubtless what led Bazin (*Cahiers*, no. 70, 1957) to disassociate himself from the *politique des auteurs* because if *mise-en-scène* became all and came to mean auteur, then implicitly the subject matter became reduced to zero – a conflationary and exclusionary process he felt he could not endorse, believing as he did in the merits of literary adaptations (Bazin: 1983, 33–4).

In conclusion to this section, it would seem fair to say that in matters of technology of style, France's cinema was not at the forefront where implementation and experimentation were concerned. How different its fortunes might have been, had it developed cinemascope. How different its product might have looked in the 1950s, had film-makers realised the potential of the French lightweight camera *Eclair Cameflex* (1948) for hand-held work, instead of which, it was the *Nouvelle Vague*, some ten years later, that was to exploit its potential (Salt: 1983, 291). How different the first colour films in the 1950s could have been, had film-makers welcomed this new medium (colour inhibited them, and as a result slowed down their films, which recalls the effect of sound some thirty years earlier). Conversely, how different its cinema of the 1930s might *not* have been without the influx of a new wave of immigrants (most of them Germans this time, many of whom were Jews, some Communists), whose influence was felt despite the fact that a significant number were obliged to move on as war approached. How curious that, as Bazin predicted, the Occupation did not produce much new talent in the 1950s, even though it produced a new group of film-makers. Yet how ironic that, for a brief period, the Occupation made France's industry solvent once more (without the competition from America, for the second time in its life, the national cinema could be paid off by the home market).

As far as theories of style are concerned, there has been far more continuity than the *Cahiers* critics would have us believe. Much of the foregrounding of theoretical enunciation was established in the 1920s. It is more a case of the earliest debates having been carried onward thanks, on the one hand, to the implementation of sound (in the 1930s) and, on the other, to having been developed upon (in the 1950s) in the light of sound and cinemascope. It is also true that, at the same time that there is continuously an advancement upon theories of style, none the less within the framing and focusing of these debates there is always a relative circularity to them. Thus, the movement has been from a 'Politics of Aesthetics Mark I' (1920s), to a 'Politicised Aesthetics Mark I' (1930s), back round to a 'Politics of Aesthetics Mark II' (1950s). The wise reader will be aware that just around the corner, the late 1960s to be precise, there must be a 'Politicised Aesthetics Mark II' (see Chapter 4). I shall now consider what people were looking at first, in general, and second, in more specific terms.

THIRTY YEARS AT THE MOVIES: A PANORAMIC VIEW

In the preceding section, mention was made of the shifting discourses on film from the more political positioning of the theorists/film-makers in the 1930s to the more stylistic one of the late 1940s and the 1950s. Interestingly, the cinemas of those different decades reflect those positionings and by their very reflexivity reveal themselves as signs of those times. This idea can be explained by looking at France's political culture, with special reference to issues of class and political ideology, from both sides of the Occupation. The Vichy government, with its stress on individual effort for the greater good of the nation, represented, for the bourgeoisie at least, the death of the 'mob', or perhaps more precisely the death of the possessing classes' irrational fear of the working class. The cinema of the 1930s, as Ginette Vincendeau (1985 and 1987) convincingly argues, witnessed the emergence on to the screen of the working class in a big way. The proletariat – most especially the Parisian working class and, at times, the underworld, also mainly associated with the working class – became the new iconography denoting 'Frenchness'. This shift in the representation of the proletariat from the silent to the sound eras is, crucially, one of point of view. In the silent films, the working class was present, but always *in relation to* middle-class values and therefore devalorised. Now the proletariat was seen in relation to its own environment and set of values (and if the possessing classes stepped into the proletarian space – mainly the Paris suburbs – it was their turn to be exposed as not belonging). This shift, of course, must be immediately qualified. The subjectivity was still that of the middle class which, after all, wrote the scripts, scored the music and made the films. None the less, social injustice coupled with an exposure of middle-class hypocrisy (whose prurient curiosity towards the 'dangerous classes' was also ridiculed) were firmly represented throughout the 1930s in the films of both the politically engaged directors and others less, if at all, politicised.

During the Occupation and to the relief of the possessing classes, the representation of the proletariat resumed its earlier system of signification. Positive images of the so-called 'mob' disappeared from the screen. Now the proletariat was either a gang of thieves, pimps or prostitutes 'endangering' the security of the possessing classes, or on the other hand, an individual (predominantly a woman) of fallen, or no virtue at all, attempting (unsuccessfully) to seize her/his chance to leave the past behind and enter a new life (most usually through the possibility of marriage into the possessing classes, as in *L'Entraîneuse*, Valentin, 1940). Either way, the security of the possessing classes remained assured by the close of the film and voyeurism was back where it belonged just as it had been in the silent days. This partially explains the predominance of the melodrama as *the* genre of the Occupation – almost half the production (Siclier: 1981, 269–436) – a significant proportion of which is based on the narrative lines outlined above.

After the Occupation and into the 1950s, the working class all but disappeared both as an icon and as a preoccupation (either positive or negative). So too, not surprisingly, did the melodrama. What replaced that icon, the *film policier* (*polar*) or thriller/gangster movie, is revealing both of the mentality of that time and the economic exigencies facing the industry. The *polar* produced a new class. Gone are the *apaches* and hoodlums of the slummy underworld. This new breed of gangster lives in luxurious apartments, wears tailored suits and drives ostentatious American cars. Of course, the *polar* was introduced or refined in an effort to counter the influx of American films (especially after the Blum–Byrnes agreement), but what is more interesting is the ensuing depoliticisation, diasporisation even, of the working class that this genre implies. Add to this the plethora of comedies – sometimes attaining half the yearly output during the 1950s (Chirat: 1985, 61) – and it becomes evident, through the cinema's cultural hegemony, that the effect of the Occupation had been to reduce France to a state of hermeticism in relation to her recent past. Recalling Truffaut's denunciation of this cinema, it can be deduced that it is from this hermeticism that the key term 'tradition of quality' is born. Truffaut's tirade against the *passéisme* and collusionary immobilism of this cinema becomes quite politicised and nationalistic in this light (even if that was not his intention).

Having said this, it must also be borne in mind that even after World War I France's cinema was very reticent to speak about the war. This time, however, France had no Verdun, nor indeed a Great Man (de Gaulle tried to be it for France but the Fourth Republic shunned him). Its only myth was the Resistance, which got quite extensive cinematic coverage in the immediate post-Liberation period. Even so, that image had to be managed carefully as is evidenced by the fact that the authorities in charge of cinema pre-censorship only passed six out of the sixty scenarios submitted during 1944–5. As for the other aspects of the war, they were too unpleasant or unmentionable to be screened. Humiliation and guilt do not make for easy speculation. Small wonder then that the industry followed the general trend of that time of indirect denial and produced a predominantly escapist mode of cinema as exemplified not just by the huge number of comedies, but also by the substantial output of Belle Epoque films.

This brings us to another myth. Critics who decried the post-Occupation cinema for not being politicised are perhaps naive in their protests. France's cinema does not have a politicised, or indeed in that respect an ideological, tradition. The 1930s cinema must be perceived for the brief politicised moment that it was and must be understood within the context of that time. In other words, the advent of sound, the emergence of an important proletarian class, increased Taylorisation, severe social injustice and, finally, the euphoria of the ascendancy of the Popular Front, were just too many conjunctural events during that decade to exclude the working class and its aspirations from the screen. It must also be recalled that pre-censorship was not introduced until late 1937 when the political climate of increased tension led Jean Zay (the minister then responsible for cinema) to impose it not just on films but on scenarios as well.

Guy Hennebelle (1974, 17) argues that the post-Occupation mentality abrogated its political duty not just because of the demoralised spirit of the French, but also because of the determination of bourgeois hegemony to impose silence on both the past (collaboration, Vichy, etc.) and the present (Colonial troubles). With regard to a cinematic reflection of this abrogation, he goes on to say, as do Comes and Marmin (1984, 146), that instead of Neo-Realism (which in its gritty, no holds barred realism *was* a political cinema), what was sustained was a *néopopulisme poétique*, or what Comes and Marmin describe as national populism. In other words, there was no visual sign of the tremendous political upheavals France had just experienced (and was experiencing), merely a reiteration of cinematic codes of the past. With one or two exceptions, they argue, form and content had not changed substantially but just evolved into an apoliticism. Apolitical it may well have been, but this discourse, as much as that of the *Cahiers du cinéma* (which rejected the 1950s cinema as old hat), forecloses knowledge of that cinema and in so doing misrepresents it.

Accusations of political inauthenticity have also been levelled at the 1930s cinema, but these are finally being dispelled and a clearer picture of the cinema of that time is now emerging. As was mentioned above, that cinema was politicised to a relative degree. However, it was not just through the emergence of the working class on to the screen but also through its reflection of the shifting moods of that time that the 1930s cinema provided a transparence on that period's social and political reality. Not surprisingly it was Bazin (1981, 85) who found this cinema unreflective of French society, claiming that a 'French farmer . . . would know more about the life of an American worker than about that of his Parisian counterpart'. Jeancolas (1983, 164), in his otherwise very useful study, expresses the opinion that until the second half of the decade there was a paucity of truth in the cinema. Mainstream feature films, he claims, were mostly escapist and if any political discourse was present, then it was of the Right and not the Left. Bazin's (1983, 20) objection to the cinema of that time was that it was merely a continuation of the naturalist novel tradition which had already been sufficiently adapted in the silent period. Poetic Realism, which he called *réalisme noir*, was really romantic pessimism, a transposition of tragedy (i.e., bourgeois melodrama) into the proletarian class. This implies that the working class was represented in the same patronising light as in Zola's novels, but the plethora of images of male friendship, the presence of popular songs, the meticulous attention to the whole of the working-class topos (the *arrondissementes,* cafés, *caf'conc'*, boarding rooms, etc), its iconography and gesturality in films, not just of the Poetic Realist school but throughout the decade, would attest differently. Indeed, the focus on working-class male friendship, which starts as early as Clair's 1930 film *Sous les toîts de Paris* and becomes a tradition by the mid-1930s, makes this cinema the precursor to the buddy movie (often considered to be a specifically American genre). Furthermore, I wrote above that the point of view had shifted. There is no implicit text in these films, as there was in the silent films and indeed Zola's novels, that the working class is 'less' than the bourgeoisie. In this final respect, therefore the representation of the working-class is politicised.

As far as Jeancolas's weighing up of the first half of the 1930s is concerned, it is worth recalling that, until the advent of the Popular Front, anti-republicanism on the Right of the political class was rife and that even with the Left in power it did not disappear. In the history section of this chapter, I described how the dominance of rightist discourse was brought about by a series of scandals (during 1933–4) and how certain films were exemplary of this anti-parliamentarism of the time, calling as they did for *l'homme providentiel*. Equally, the Stavisky affair was not without an anti-parliamentarian transparence. Marguerite Viel's film *La Banque Nemo* (1934), although based on a play written in 1931, bears a remarkable resemblance to the Stavisky story. In the film an upstart banker, Labrèche (rising from the gutter literally), takes over the bank and gets involved in dubious financial affairs. A former acquaintance and colleague denounces him, but because Labrèche's ne'er-do-wells implicate virtually the entire government, the whole affair is stifled (certainly not a pro-parliamentarian reflection).

Beyond the general aura of explicit rightist discourses in France of the 1930s, there were also the effects of the Depression on French society. The Depression had a twofold, if paradoxical, impact which manifested itself through a desire to escape and an increased nationalism. As I explained in the Introduction, nationalistic fervour is felt most strongly when a nation is under pressure. There is a need to identify, to see oneself as belonging to the nation. This in turn creates the mentality of exclusion. Thus, if on the one hand images of nationalistic sufficiency abounded and the dominant discourses in cinema were of the Right and if, on the other, there was an escapist cinema that was either nostalgic or timeless, then cinema was providing a fairly true, if partial, image of those times. Furthermore, many of the most popular genres in the cinema of the 1930s exemplified the inseparability of these two tendencies.

The genre most exponential of this conflation was the military film which, after being almost negligible in the 1920s, now came into its own. It took many forms ranging from the 'serious' to the *comique troupier* or barrack film. Of the former type, just over a dozen films refer back to World War I (Prédal: 1972, 165–77) including two remakes from the silent era (Gance's *J'accuse* and Poirier's *Verdun*) and, a bit later, a big recon-struction production *Croix des bois* (Bernard, 1932). Far more prolific in this first category were the Empire films. Some sixty-two were made in the 1930s and almost all of them refer to France's colonies in Africa. In the preceding chapter I noted how, after her defeat in the Franco-Prussian war, France expanded her colonial empire in order to build up her image as a major European power and again how, in the 1910s, faced with the fear of war, the campaign to galvanise a national unity was strongly inflected by the notion of France's might. I also noted how nationalism and escapism were inextricably linked in the colonial films after World War I. The predominant message of these films then, as now, was that of France the civilising force. Now, however, the tone had become even more forceful. The French Empire was anthropomorphised (almost) into France's daughter with her own iconic man/son of destiny, Maréchal Lyautey, the charismatic, influential and imperious but diplomatic Governor General of

Maroc who ruled until the revolt in the Rif in 1925 (interestingly, the revolt was squashed by 'Mother France's' other man/son of destiny, Maréchal Pétain).[17] Curiously, any feeling of insecurity that might be present in these films does not emanate from the natives (even when they are revolting). These rebellious types (*Salopards*, as they were known) are quickly repressed. The only 'dangerous' people are the whites, either convicts on the run or adventurers, all of whom succumb to the forces of the law.[18]

The popularity of Empire/colonial films as a genre is nowhere more in evidence than with the hugely successful *L'Appel du silence* (Poirier, 1936) which drew the biggest crowds on record and won the *Grand prix du cinéma* in 1936. As a marker of its authenticity, the film carried Lyautey's personal endorsement – hardly surprising when one stops to consider that its narrative is close to his dream of reconciling Islamic and French cultures. Reconcilement, for both Lyautey and the hero of the film, meant bringing the Islams back into the Christian fold – a crusading colonisation, therefore. The film is an historic reconstruction of the life of an 1870 militaro-colonial hero, Viscount Foucauld, who – after years of free licence as a young officer – throws himself whole-heartedly into France's colonial expansion. In the desert he comes to a mystical understanding that he is in the presence of God (hence the title of the film). Convinced that he is to bring the indigenous people back to Christianity, he infiltrates the different tribes to learn their language and to spread the message of the Bible, only partially successfully since he dies as a result of a betrayal by one of his own. The reference to Christian mythology is evident. Foucauld starts off as the prodigal son, becomes an itinerant prophet and ends up like Christ. The conflation of that set of references with that of France as the civilising force establishes an unassailable sign, the connotations of which are as strong and impregnable as the Maginot Line. Small wonder Lyautey stressed how timely and important the film was (Olive: 1984, 77).

In addition to the Empire films, there were a few other attempts to galvanise the French into a spirit of unity – not necessarily, however, to fight. The presence of two types of narrative, the one pacifist the other not, once again points to this split mentality. The call for rearmament in L'Herbier's *Veilles d'armes* (1936), the heroism of France's officer class in Paulin's *Trois de St Cyr* (1939), the heroism of working-class men and women in Pallu's *La Fille de la Madelon* (1937) and Hugon's *Le Héros de la Marne* (1938), the ability to overcome personal conflict and join ranks to encourage the defeat of the enemy in Moguy's *Le Déserteur* (1939), and the proselytisation of friendship amongst allies – Belgium in Poirier's *Les Soeurs d'armes* (1937) and Britain in L'Herbier's *L'Entente cordiale* (1939) – are the enumerative signs of a collective memory mostly grounded in the authenticity of World War I. But these signs are countered by a memory equally grounded in that time and which produced the pacifist calls in

Cessez le feu (Baroncelli, 1934), *La Grande illusion* (Renoir, 1937), *Paix sur le Rhin* (Choux, 1938, made to commemorate the Armistice) and *Les Otages* (Bernard, 1939). Or, alternatively, those signs were countered by a memory that is vigilant of the present (i.e., Munich and Nazism) as in Mathot's *Rappel immédiat* and Gréville's *Menaces* (both 1938). All may be calling for France to unite, but the objectives are different. The first narrative type calls for a unity prepared for war (albeit unwanted), the second pleads for a unity to prevent war. In the event, neither was heeded.

A sub-genre of the colonial/empire film was the legionnaire film which tended to stress the escapist mode rather than the nationalistic one. This type of film was profoundly pessimistic in that the chief protagonist, the legionnaire, had run away to join a foreign legion in order to escape prison for a murder or to find mental escape from a disastrous love affair. Often, after much heroics on the battlefield, the legionnaire gets killed. There is little doubt that this end is a self-inflicted wish. Alternatively, the legionnaire remains stuck in the desert, a wasted and failed life. *La Bandera* (Duvivier, 1935) and *Le Grand jeu* (Feyder, 1933) are, respectively, exemplars of these two types of narrative. In their desire for death or a proto-death, both types of legionnaire reinforce the myth of the legion as the ultimate escape. They also situate the mother nation nostalgically – as she to whom they cannot return. In these films, the tone has radically changed from the redemption-style narratives of the silent era. Now there is no queston of redemption, only death. The legionnaire is transformed into a false hero seeking oblivion rather than a new start to life. Not surprisingly, the likes of *Bandera*, popular though it was with the audience, only begot a few in the same vein. What dominates is a healthy image of France's Empire, reflecting the fact that it was the second biggest after Britain.

The second type of military film alluded to, the *comique troupier*, has a long tradition in French entertainment going back to the 1880s. It was first seen in vaudeville and the *caf'conc'* and, somewhat later, in the *théâtre du boulevard*. It was a very popular genre (as the number of films attests – over forty in the 1930s), with a fairly immutable scenario. The stupidity of the middle-ranking NCOs is shown up by the pranks of the private ranks (the COs remain unassailed by the farce – as befits, since by law the army could not be ridiculed). Fernandel and Bach were the greatest specialists in this genre, but Jean Gabin (*the icon* of the tragic working-class hero, at least post-1935) was one such *troupier* in *Les Gaietés de l'escadron* (Tourneur, 1932). This genre, emanating as it does from two somewhat different traditions, spawned two types of *troupier*, each with a distinct uniform. The more senior vaudevillesque version sported the pre-1914 infantry uniform of red trousers and blue jacket, whereas the slightly more junior theatre tradition wore the World War I uniform with all its resonances of Pétainiformism (Jeancolas: 1983, 245). What is relevant here is the referral back in time (once again immunising the army from ridicule) which has a double effect. First, it sanitises images of the army (all good blokes having a riotous time together and no mention of their real function, which is to fight). Second, in its nostalgic representation of the army, this genre eternalises it – renders it as sacrosanct as other icons of France (ibid., 150). The army is resignified into a folkloric myth.

This principle of the imagelessness of war points to the continuing stasis in the French mentality still unable to come to terms with the loss that World War I represented to the nation. It also uncovers one of the underlying motivations for the mood of irrationality that coloured the spirit of those times. Jeancolas (1983, 215) speaks of the crushing weight of the ideology of the *ancien combattant* which was both pessimistic and fraternal in that it could accept the awfulness of the last war only if it was the war to end all wars. The rise of fascism made this increasingly unlikely, thus making the *combattants'* bartering with their conscience even more painful. Perhaps no one incarnates this ideology in cinema better than Jean Gabin with his outbursts of anger and despair on the one hand and, on the other, his companionable disposition towards his mates. But one could also quote Duvivier's films as exemplary of this schizoid ideology (*La Bandera* – dedicated to Franco – and *La Belle équipe*, made respectively in 1935 and 1936, and both starring Gabin).

The overriding spirit of Malthusianism which prevailed during this decade did much to fuel the mood of irrationality and insecurity. France as a nation seemed intent on ignoring what was happening in the eastern part of Europe and remained inward-looking, brooding on its own financial crisis. Cinema too tended to look everywhere except at what was happening outside France's frontiers. Other than the military film, escapist films took the form of historical reconstructions with a particular predilection for pseudo-Slav and Russophilia (old Tsarist Russia) subjects. Alternatively films celebrated youth, albeit in relation to the family and family values (youth would have to await the cinema of the 1950s and especially the 1960s before having an independent representation). As might be expected, escapist films also included the old narrative chestnut of the city versus rural life. Spy films were another favourite (including attempts at rehabilitating the myth of Mata Hari), but all the while glossed over the reality of Nazi Germany. Even the most poignantly specific spy film, *Double crime sur la ligne Maginot* (Gandéra, 1937), which helped propagate the myth that France was secure behind her fortification system, is devoid of any allusion to the Nazis. Finally, in terms of myth and escapist genres, there were films showing a prurient interest in the *pègre* (the underworld or gangs of thieves) and blood-curdling *faits divers*. Films in this category romanticised the violence of the underworld – even the most lurid murders did not necessarily detract from the aura of romanticism surrounding the perpetrator of the crime. The flawed proletarian was of as much interest as the decent hard-working one.

That a nation consciously turned in on itself should have, predominantly, a cinema that does precisely the same, is not astonishing. What is remarkable, however, is how similar the inflection of this mood is to that which immediately followed World War I. The present has a vagueness, especially in the comedies and in the *comique troupier*. There is a desire to be elsewhere in time and space. Aligned to this, the spectre of positive and negative otherness is raised once more. Tsarist and Belle Epoque films, films about the Revolution and terrorism in foreign lands, are prime indicators of this need for otherness, positive or otherwise – and of a desire to speculate on the fortunes (or misfortunes) of others. Comedies targeting otherness (Jewish or Black – André Hugon's comic series *Lévy et cie* and the comedian Martin in Mathot's *Bouboule Ier roi des nègres* are two examples) point to a nervous racism and nationalism bent on the exclusion of the other. On another tangent, pacifist films are once more to the fore but they too are predominantly elsewhere in time and space (the 1914–18 war). In this respect, France's cinema was already reflecting a postwar mentality. Although it proved to be premature (France would go to war), none the less, it does provide evidence that the French were more clear about the war they would not fight than the one they would. Viewed in this light, the period of the *drôle de guerre* (from September 1939 to May 1940) did much to render inert any thought that the French might fight, precisely because of the illusion of normality ('nothing was happening', even though the Germans aggressed by taking back the Rhineland and France did nothing to prevent it) and the false sense of security (based on the impenetrability of the Maginot Line). Irrespective of whether or not France had the modalities by which to fight a war, she was caught unawares by it, difficult though this is to understand with the virtue of hindsight.

A quick glance at what was going on in the cinema industry during the 1930s might serve metonymically as an illustration for France's unpreparedness or unwillingness to contemplate war until the very last moment. The 1930s was a period of considerable cross-fertilisation between German and French film-makers. Most of this occurred through refugees coming to France, predominantly as exiles from the Hitler regime. But it is also true that because, in the early 1930s, the producers were in such dire straits and sound was so expensive, a number of French film-makers (and actors) went to Germany to make multi-versions or co-productions.[19] Only the rich American companies, especially Paramount, could counter this activity, but the Depression obliged them to shut up shop and go home.

This left the stage free for Hitler to step into the multi-production arena for purposes of cultural dominance. He invested enormously in the German production and distribution company UFA which, because it had the modern equipment to hand, attracted French film-makers and actors to come and make co-productions or, indeed, French versions of a German film. In fact, co-productions were going on as late as August 1939 (Fernandel in *Héritier des Mondésir*, Valentin). The temptation is to read this as simply a sign of an ostrich mentality. However, this has to be qualified. When one considers, first, that there were German production companies (ACE and Tobis) based in France and second, that there was open hostility expressed in the right-wing press (the dominant press at that time) to those refugees who had come to France and who worked in the film industry, then a somewhat different picture emerges – one of collusion and xeno-phobia. Jeancolas (1983, 319) makes the point that the Vichy mentality predates Pétain's Vichy government. Pinpointing actual dates may not be particularly useful, but 1935 could serve as a watershed date marking the rise of a collaborationist and anti-semitic mentality which was just as strong as the ostrich one. Curiously, this year coincides with the collapse of the big producers in the French film industry. But this was also the year the Paris branch of Tobis dismissed all Jewish personnel. This was the year of Feyder's *Kermesse héroïque* (a Tobis production) which, although situated in a Flemish town in 1616, openly advocates female collaboration with the enemy, despite Feyder's claims that he wanted to make a feminist film (Guillaume-Grimaud: 1986, 84). Finally, this year was notable for the numerous newspaper articles talking of the *courant judéo-balkanique* in the cinema and of Jews owning the film industry.[20]

This rhetoric marks a considerable shift from earlier rhetoric for a national cinema. In the 1920s, calls for a national cinema were made against the invasion of the American product. Furthermore Soviet cinema had been banned by censorship for political but not nationalistic reasons. Since they believed that the public would be influenced by the bolshevising message of Soviet films, the authorities proscribed their screening in public forums (even though they were widely seen in private clubs set up by the PCF). Film critics writing in *Pour Vous* and elsewhere were now targeting either their own citizens (a number of the producers and distributors in the film industry were French Jews) or refugees and Russian *émigrés*, all of whom did much to enhance the image of France's cinema. Without the camera operators, set designers and composers of those two waves of *émigrés* (in the 1920s and 1930s), French cinema might never have entered the modernist age of film so fulsomely as it did, let alone established itself as a quality cinema. This nationalistic rhetoric is complemented by the attempts at erasure of those working behind the screen. For example, the cinema of the 1930s is often qualified as the cinema of the actor. No positive reading of this statement can be made because of all that it excludes. Nor can it bear up to scrutiny. What can truthfully be said is that the cinema products of those years were pluriculturally inflected. When actors became a central consideration again, it had as much to do with the novelty represented by sound as with anything else. Furthermore, sound privileged actors differently from silent films which meant that a renewal of the acting class was possible. This, in turn, also constituted a new attraction. Voice as much as gesture made up the morphology of the person on screen. Sound exposed the vocal weakness of those silent screen stars who lacked a tradition of theatre performance or whose 'foreignness' worked against them (including foreign stars such as Ivan Mosjoukine and Sessue Hayakawa, whose screen acting styles were highly acclaimed in the silent period).

In France, although there were no great French stars who perished (in contrast to what happened in Hollywood, it was secondary actors who fell by the wayside), none the less the advent of sound heralded the arrival of a new wave of actors, all used to a stage tradition in one shape or another (classical, boulevard or music-hall) – a process which, in many respects, marked a return to the practices of the earlier (pre-1914) cinema. This acting class of the 1930s was predominantly French, but to attempt to justify the 'Frenchness', that is the 'national', of France's cinema via that group alone is patently to gloss over all the constituent parts of film production and to misrepresent the fact that the 1930s, just as the 1920s, were remarkable times of cross-fertilisation for France's cinema. The star system had been reborn (again!), but so too had the notion of film-making as teamwork (the *travail d'équipe*) so identified with French film-making practices. Where the influx of stars did have a crucial impact, however, was on the narrative style. Because there were so many talented actors, the tendency was to create a subplot to the main intrigue which would put secondary roles on display, hence the parallel structuring in the narrative so distinctive of the films of this period. In a sense, therefore, the actors did contribute to a 'Frenchness' by adding this new narrative dimension to their cinema.

The Occupation only put a partial end to these practices. Some familiar names disappeared from the screen. This was partly due to the departure for America or elsewhere of film-makers and some of the big stars (Clair, Duvivier, Renoir, Gabin, Morlay, Simone Simon went to the States; Feyder and Françoise Rosay went to Switzerland). But there were other contributory factors. Xenophobia and anti-semitism ruined or put a stop to some careers (amongst film-makers, for example, those of Léonide Moguy and Pierre Chenal, both French Jews, and the half-British Edmond T. Gréville) and took away production and distribution companies belonging to Jews (for example, the father and son distributors Siriztky). A number of *émigrés* moved on, in the main to Hollywood. The great majority of the industry who could, stayed put, which would explain why the look of France's cinema did not change considerably. Also, any new film-makers to arrrive on the scene tended to have worked as an assistant to established, but departed, film-makers and had yet to define their own styles (Becker and Bresson, though they came through this system, are perhaps the two most important exceptions to this last point). Although the look did not change dramatically, the same cannot be said of the content. The four years of the Occupation saw the birth of some twenty new film-makers (thus continuing the trend of the 1930s), but this potentially energising renewal was not repeated in the film texts themselves. Virtually half the output were melodramas (104 out of 220), echoing the earliest traditions of French cinema when melodrama abounded. The dominant themes of this genre dealt with guilt and restitution. In these films, guilt comes as a result of falling away from order (i.e., family order), restitution as a reaffirmation of that order. Natalist discourses abounded too, as did the stress on land as the site of social fixity.

In the total Occupation film output there are fourteen suicides and ten references to the actual war. The suicide rate of just over three per year is not substantively higher or lower than that of the 1920s or 1930s cinema. What is interesting is that it should be perpetuated as a narrative tradition in this most untypical moment in France's history. Not surprisingly, references to the war are most standardly made through scenes of the moment of mobilisation (i.e., the *drôle de guerre* period) and not the Occupation. Colonial films and films showing French heroism dwindle to a mere four apiece. Male friendship – so strongly valorised in the 1930s cinema – is also now virtually absent, appearing as a central theme in only four films. Historical reconstructions (twenty-eight), comedy (twenty-three) and crime (twenty-one) films make up a third of the production. Each of these genres averages around 10 per cent whereas fantasy, the most escapist of all genres, only constitutes 5 per cent of the overall production. Given the climate of the times, this genre could have been expected to be much more in evidence, either as escapism or as a way of by-passing censorship. For the first time in its film history, the representation of the provinces is on a par with Paris. No real surprise there, given the two zones. Otherwise, the representation of other locales remains fairly constant with previous cinema traditions, with ports, 'elsewheres' and the city/rural conflict all averaging around 5 per cent respectively (Siclier (1981) gives a résumé of most of the feature films of this period).

Of all the genres, comedy is the one most evidently on the decrease. Marcel Oms (1975, 67) characterises this cinema of the Occupation as cruel and redolent with a sense of failure. The plethora of melodramas would tend to support this view, as does the increase on screen of adaptations by Georges Simenon – an author renowned for dark and misanthropic (even misogynist) crime stories (his *oeuvre* constitutes 41 per cent of the crime films made during 1940–4). Self-hatred and self-pity do find a resonance in the cinema of this period (as evidenced, for example, in the number of suicides). France was a defeated and occupied country – she was not France. An inability to cope with defeat (rather than a refusal which would have produced a very different tone) is the mood generated by a great number of the Occupation films. The inability to deal with loss which was so strongly expressed in the 1920s cinema has given way, in the face of defeat, to a bleaker pessimism. The loss of identity, implicit in France's occupied status, bore no relation to the loss of humankind in World War I which could be carried with pride. Indeed, psychologically, France as a nation was mourning in shame, not in pride, and would have been doing so even more deeply had it not been for Pétain and Vichy. To mourn in shame must undoubtedly create a schizophrenic mentality. In this respect, therefore, melodramas with guilt and retribution as their central theme partially correspond to the mood of that time. Thus, whilst cinema did not 'deal with' the meaning of Occupied France, it did not necessarily or totally run in the other direction of escapist discourses – to Goebbels' annoyance at times. His outburst at what he perceived as nationalistic discourses in Christian-Jaque's *La Symphonie fantastique* (1941) – a film about Berlioz – is legendary and is inscribed in his own diary for all to read (Bertin-Maghit: 1989, 23).

Film critics and theorists who witnessed this period serve as an interesting reflection of the schizophrenia which that time produced in the French mentality. Some see this period as a golden age of French cinema (e.g., Claude Beylie: 1975, 8), whereas others regard it as rose-spectacled and mediocre (e.g., Guy Hennebelle: 1974, 14). The truth of the matter lies somewhere in between. Certainly, as far as French cinema was concerned, this period marked an apogee in terms of production consumption. French cinema dominated because 'enemy' films were proscribed by the Germans. Furthermore, the French public had shown considerable distaste for German films, so Germany established its own production company in France, Continental. Goebbels was responsible for setting it up, after which he put Alfred Greven in charge. Greven appreciated the aesthetics of cinema and was determined to get the best of the French industry into Continental. To this effect he appointed Clouzot as artistic director and, thanks to enough film-makers (twelve in total and all renowned for their work in the 1930s) joining ranks with the production company, a cinema of some quality was secured for that company. It is instructive to note, however, that Continental produced virtually half of the comedies of that period (eleven out of the twenty-three), which might give some credence to accusations against that company of frivolousness and escapism.[21] Elsewhere, the numerous production companies, so in evidence in the latter half of the 1930s, continued to supply films of the same mixed quality as before (i.e., good, bad and indifferent).

If the Occupation marked the cinema-going audiences' chance to see their home product more fully than ever before, such was not the case shortly after the Liberation. American products swamped the market. As far as France's own production was concerned, given the economic stringencies, a good number of her films (in some years almost half) were co-produced, mostly with Italy. Literary adaptations continued to abound, as did numerous remakes. In this respect French cinema during the Fourth Republic was indistinct in its practices from that of the 1930s. The numerous remakes during the 1930s were obviously due to the transition to sound, but there seems little to justify the average of almost ten per year during the 1950s. On the surface, therefore, there is an aura of uninventiveness about the cinema of this period, which is due partly to a sameness with the past (a great number of the scripts were adaptations written by long-established scriptwriters) and partly to the plethora of comedies (some of which continued the tradition of the comic series privileging a specific actor – Fernandel, Robert Lamoureux, etc.). Although audience taste for Americana and French comedy do reveal a need to escape, it was not necessarily just from the experience of the Occupation, as is evidenced by the fact that these are still the dominant likes of todays' film-goers.

Another clue to the so-called lack of invention is the proliferation of co-productions. Since they were expensive to make, the tendency was to play safe, even though they did permit the implementation of colour on a reasonably large scale (their costs being shared), and by the mid-1950s 50 per cent of films were in colour. By 1954, almost half the films were co-produced, creating a crisis not just with the look of the product but also of identity for France's cinema. A further clue to this sameness can be found in the effect on the product of a standardisation of production due to a harmonisation of technology. Elsewhere, especially when attempts are made to attribute it to 'old hands' coming back and trying the same prewar formulas, this sameness starts to gain a mythic dimension. Certainly they did return (Gance and L'Herbier, for example) and certainly their films were out of touch with the changes, but one could count as many other 'old hands' who returned and revitalised the cinema (Clouzot and Renoir being the most obvious ones). Where film-makers are concerned, perhaps a better reason for the lack of great revitalisation can be found in the dearth of new names amongst talented feature-length film-makers. There were only six or seven in all: Jacqueline Audrey, René Clément, Jean-Pierre Melville, Georges Rouquier, Jacques Tati and Nicole Védrès. Truffaut names Roger Leenhardt, Yves Ciampi, Alexandre Astruc and Marcel Camus along with the other male film-makers in the list, but omits the two women.[22] Of the six or so named, most made films that today are still considered innovative. None the less, in terms of renewal, this represents only a fifth of the film-makers which the Occupation spawned, so the post-Occupation figures quoted are misleading.

What these figures do not reveal are the reasons for this apparent small number of innovative film-makers. First of all, there were actually about thirty or so new film-makers on the ground. However, they were mostly trained as assistants and their venture into film-making was often rapidly eclipsed by the mediocrity of their products. Second, most young film-makers had limited resources. Producers were wary of backing them, which in turn made it impossible for them to get on to the co-production circuit, which was very big in the 1950s. Third, several others, most noteworthily Georges Franju, Alain Resnais (although not exactly young) and Agnès Varda, given the financial constraints, made shorts and documentaries only to emerge as feature film-makers in the late 1950s. Two others, Jean Rouch and Nicole Védrès, turned their talents, respectively, to ethnographic and cultural history documentaries. Finally, controversial film-makers, the most famous one being René Vautier whose anticolonialist film, *Afrique 50* (1955), was banned, hardly got to make films at all.

Given the climate at the time of political immobilism and strong censorship, especially on what was happening in the colonies (it should be recalled that the heritage of the COIC meant that pre-censorship was still in place), it is difficult to see how either this younger generation of film-makers or those who came out of the Occupation period could make innovative films, if by innovative films what is meant is making political films or indeed making them politically. Traces of such endeavours are to be found in the documentaries (some of which were subsequently banned – *Les Statues meurent aussi*, 1953, by Resnais and Marker which showed the effects of colonisation on African artefacts was one), but they are not the stuff of mainstream commercial cinema.

The politicisation of cinema that occurred in the 1930s centred around a new representation of the working class, but for the rest of the political scenario the screen was pertinently silent. The emerging class of the post-Liberation era but more especially the 1950s, or the class that caught public attention, was no longer the working class but the youth class, the class that had been silent during the Occupation except as an adjunct of the family. This class (represented age-wise by the young generation of film-makers) was now in its early twenties by the time of the Liberation and was the new postwar generation. Unlike their forebears of 1918 who thought the war to end all wars had been won, this generation was marked by a bitter disenchantment and a cynical disbelief in what it was told. Thus for this generation the period 1945–55 was one of youth culture. Pétain the patriarch was gone and with him certain taboos. Although the family still represented a strong social and ideological reality, this young generation, which had missed out on a normal apprenticeship to adult life, was intent on breaking with tradition. Sexually and morally, it was a period of grand abandon (for the most part in the cities – rural France did not change in such a dramatic way). To the economic expansion and political impotence of the nation corresponded the hedonism of French youth. Myths were demystified. Wars did not stop wars. Nuclear reality menaced life quite differently, pointing to the triviality of human existence. Sexual liberation was an important indication of young people catching life on the hop. Pop music (later consecrated by the radio show *Salut les copains*), impromptu social get-togethers or *surprise-parties* as they were first known (later to be called *Booms*) and a specialised youth-culture slang – all these were outward signs of a new generation unwilling, because there was no point, to wait.

The emblematic film which catches this impatience and sense of having been cheated by the war is Claude Autant-Lara's *Diable au corps* (1946–7), although Yves Allégret's *Les Miracles n'ont lieu qu'une fois* (1950) could lay an equal claim. Autant-Lara's film is about the illicit love affair between an older, married woman and a teenage boy. Given the date of the film, it would seem in some ways more prophetic than emblematic, since it predates (almost) the new mentality. However, the literary text upon which it is based, Raymond Radiguet's novel of the same title, was published in 1923 and the story is set in the period of World War I. The adolescent of the novel, François, was 15, two years younger than the protagonist in the film (played by Gérard Philipe). For him (as for many of his age, according to Radiguet), the Great War represented a glorious four-year holiday of happiness and self-indulgence. The novel describes cruelly and clinically an adolescent's journey into manhood. His affair with Marthe (played in the film by Micheline Presle) leads to her pregnancy and subsequent death. She is married to a soldier at the front, so her infidelity becomes doubly immoral. This interpretation goes as follows: by betraying her husband, she assails the institution of marriage, and by making a mockery of her husband's heroism in going to war, she betrays her nation. Small wonder she must perish for her illicit lust.

The tone of the film version is even harder. François is resolute in his claims to happiness at all costs and he has nothing but contempt for bourgeois morality, which he treats with complete insouciance. It is doubtless this greater cynical egocentrism and the more pronounced amorality which disturbed the producers (the American-financed Transcontinental) and which made the film into a *cause célèbre*.[23] The bourgeoisie and Catholic groups were outraged at what they saw as an assault first, on the contemporary moral order, and second, on a collective memory of France's heroic past. It is surely this lethal cocktail of anti-establishmentarianism and individual liberty which caused this film to be singled out for a more vitriolic attack than others made previously by Autant-Lara who, whatever the status of his political convictions, has always been a controversial director. He was to reap similar opprobrium with his film *Le Blé en herbe* (1954) which again deals with a love affair (seduction really) between an older woman and an adolescent.

Yves Allégret's film is no less harsh, but the angle he adopts is different. His film reflects the sense of loss and disorientation felt by the generation of 1939. This is France's youth that was cheated by the Occupation and yet tainted by it – a generation caught after the war between bitterness, indifference and revolt, a generation which, during the Occupation, behaved no better and no worse than its elders. This is exemplified by the central protagonist (played by Jean Marais) who is not a Resistance hero but a young medical student who drops his studies and sees through the Occupation thanks to his little black market racket. Weak and cowardly, unpartisan and without principle, nothing shocks, not even the realisation that the woman, from whom he has been separated by the Occupation and of whom he has dreamed throughout, will be unrecognisable to him. Lost loves, dashed hopes – all these truths were familiar to that youth class whose very youthfulness had been sullied by the stigma of the Occupation.

Youth and morality were very much on the agenda during the post-Liberation period and well into the 1950s. The explosion of *ciné-clubs*, the swing of jazz cellars, the intellectual sway of existentialism – these were but the elitist manifestations (the Saint-Germain des Prés generation) of a very strong current of anti-conformity amongst France's young citizens. It is in this climate that nudity, female nudity, came on to the screen (although, historically speaking, it had first been on display as early as Antoine's *L'Arlésienne*, 1922). Before the Brigitte Bardot factor, there was Martine Carol. Martine Carol set the pace, but Bardot outstripped her. Neither was considered a particularly outstanding performer, but both possessed a naive sexuality – or what was conveniently perceived as such – which satisfied voyeuristic tendencies without compromising the spectator. The body was eroticised and handed to the audience (sometimes on a plate), but it was untouchable because it was imbued with an infantilo-innocence that kept the spectator suspended between fantasy and desire.

The sex symbol *à la française* was born in 1950 with Richard Pottier's film *Caroline chérie*, starring Martine Carol. Then came Brigitte Bardot – 'BB' – the icon of French female sexuality and *Et Dieu créa la femme* (Vadim, 1956), the film that sealed her destiny. It also influenced the walk and the look of a generation of female adolescents. In cinematic terms, 'BB' was France's greatest cultural asset and if she had not existed she would have had to have been invented to compete with the Americans' new-style sex symbols. It is in this curious respect that women performers gained a relative ascendancy over their male counterparts for the first time in France's film history. In terms of performance, the 1930s was dominated by male actors (*the* star being Gabin). At that time, forty out of the new influx of sixty actors were men. In one respect, where male actors were concerned, that great influx stymied future talent. But, in another, it did leave room for new women performers to emerge. Certainly in the late 1930s Michèle Morgan was on the ascendancy, but the war took her to America. It should be added too that she was often identified as a star alongside Gabin, with whom she made several films. Thus her stardom, although indisputable, was simultaneously conjugated with the name Gabin. They were seen as the ideal screen couple/lovers. In the 1950s, the women stars were there and far more distinctly on their own, if not necessarily 'in their own right' (i.e. as an antidote to the American sex symbol).

Apart from the films that referred to youth culture and the plethora of comedies, the other dominant trend in cinema, post-Liberation, was for literary adaptations from the nineteenth century and the 1900–18 period, revealing a preoccupation with the past and a nostalgic refusal to confront the present. Given that France was struggling to regain her identity, this unreflexivity can be interpreted as a desire for the good old days when, as myth would have it, France knew who she was. This fairly typical response in difficult periods (as was seen in the early 1920s cinema) should not gloss over the myth-making practices that this positioning reinforces. Thus, not only was there silence on the colonial conflicts, but also after an intial spurt there were very few films dealing with war (let alone *the* war and the Occupation), and even so the tendency was either to ground its meaning in the authenticity of history (e.g., the myth of the Resistance) or, quite the reverse, to place the narrative in an unspecified space or time (as was the case for a spate of spy films). This sense of denial with its implicit hermeticism allowed for films to belie reality and to play at make-believe. The Belle Epoque films gave a false image of an opulent France. Similarly, films of Paris's *haute couture* served as cultural proselytisation, last seen in the modern studio spectacular of the late 1920s, but gave the lie to the deprivation felt by the French in the late 1940s and early 1950s. Films of this style can be seen as deliberately vacuous, although Becker's *Falbalas* (1944) stands as an exception with its subtle satire on a profession whose value as an industry is undoubted, but whose contribution to the moral resistance offered to the enemy is deemed an exaggeration by some (Hackett: 1946a, 50).

This period in France's history was perhaps one of its most difficult morally. Hypocrisy in the light of the Occupation had a very different resonance from the old-style bourgeois hypocrisy pre-1940. Now it touched all classes. Only a minority of people were untainted from some form or other of collusion. In the 1930s, the reactionary social framework – hypocritically and fiercely defended by the bourgeoisie – was none the less there for all to see. Now it was a question of moral respectability for all, but to which few could lay claim – hence the fact that this time the great majority wanted to and needed to turn a blind eye to what had really happened. Instead of exposure, which would have torn the fabric of France's society apart, a myth of national unity was created – a myth which, in turn, was fed into by the myth of the Resistance. Only a few films resisted this fraudulence by serving up psychologically and socially dark and disturbing films. It must be stressed, however, that these films pointed to the mood of that time rather than to the specificity of the Occupation period. In the main, expediency required silence. If France was to recover economic well-being, then it would be at the expense of more moral issues which would have to be seen as 'not there'. If there was an age of masks in France in the twentieth century, then this period, rather than the 1930s, must surely be it.[24]

THIRTY YEARS AT THE MOVIES: IN CLOSE-UP

Only during the Occupation period can France's cinema be deemed not to have been predominantly Parisian. Other than at that time and continuing the practices of the silent era, Paris remains at the centre. Also continuing the traditions of the earlier cinema – the cinema not of the centre (i.e., Paris) but at the periphery – is still Brittany and her ports, Provence and *the* port Marseilles, occasionally other northern ports, otherwise the mountain ranges and, finally, the colonies. By the 1950s, other elsewheres appear, testifying to the new, though not yet widespread, leisure factor: first, the seaside and other holiday spaces, and second, the sporting arena. In this respect, the holiday spaces represented in cinema 'fulfil' the aspirations of the working classes at the time of the Popular Front era – at which time the seaside was evoked in films as a dream, a fantasy, not a tangible reality. Indeed, in the late 1930s, the forty-hour week meant that what was available to the working classes was a trip out on their bicycles to the countryside at weekends and a return with flowers tied to their handlebars (Martin: 1987, 16). Incidentally, this makes even heavier the cruel irony of François's unachieved dreams in *Le Jour se lève* (Carné, 1939). He never gets to the countryside with his loved one, Françoise, let alone ties flowers (*les lilas* he talks of so often) to his handlebars. All he gets to tie there is a teddy bear which, according to Françoise, is his alter-ego. By the 1950s, the seaside was still an illusory inaccessible space to the working classes. Even though they could now see it on the screen, it was still a middle-class leisure space, well into the 1950s, as Tati's *Les Vacances de M. Hulot* (1953) attests.

In that they constitute the topos of otherness within French cinema, it is interesting to note who populates these places at the periphery and to remark – with the exception of the inhabitants of the new elsewheres – how little departure there is, once again, from the silent era. These elsewheres are occupied by the peasant classes, the provincial bourgeoisie, gangsters, merchant seamen, sailors, fishermen, the army, the Foreign Legion and, less frequently, the navy (mostly at sea). In these environs and as far as the working-class male is concerned, it is to be found predominantly in the latter categories (i.e., military or civilian forces), less so in the provincial cities. Clearly the forces are not traditionally places for working-class women. They are obliged to remain within the provinces or the provincial cities. Their immobility corresponds to the male's potential mobility and women are fixed without much say or control. Under-represented in the provinces as a *working* class (in the eyes of the dominant ideology, that is), women of that economic class tend to be either mothers/fallen women, molls or prostitutes. This is not to say that working-class women in Paris are not often represented in this way, especially during the 1930s when prostitution was a common recourse for many women – and not just working-class women. Until women gained legal rights over their property in 1938, prostitution was a recourse for other economic classes as well, hence in the cinema of the 1930s, 1940s and even the early 1950s the syndrome of the 'kept' woman. Whatever the case, women during the 1930s and 1940s are not represented as having much control over their destiny. As far as the new elsewheres of the 1950s are concerned, generally speaking they are populated, if it is the holiday spaces, by the bourgeoisie, and if the sporting arena, then depending on the sport, by working-class men struggling to climb the economic ladder through their talents (usually boxing – e.g., *L'Air de Paris*, Carné, 1954 – or alternatively as a jockey – e.g., *Premières armes*, René Wheeler, 1949).

In terms of genres, still with regard to the silent tradition, although most were sustained, none the less some took a different orientation, and others disappeared to be replaced by other, sometimes more apposite genres. The 1930s witnessed the disappearance of the modern studio spectacular (not surprising, given the costs) and the emergence of a new genre, the operetta (the musical comedy), a genre which was particularly popular at the advent of sound but which did not disappear until the end of the Occupation. Over the period 1930–58, crime films became an increasingly popular, though never dominant genre. Furthermore, these 'polars 'and gangster movies progressively came under the umbrella of social realist films.

Over this thirty-year span, other shifts within the social realist category of films related to the changes in representation in terms of class, age and gender. What was absent (i.e., outside the periphery) was any representation of race (except for musicians in night-clubs). By the 1950s, immigration from the Maghreb and Francophone Africa meant that race had become a 'presence'. However, it was not to enter even the cinema of the periphery until the 1960s with the impact first, of Rouch and Camus's cinema, and second, the advent of both Maghrebin and black African filmmakers (respectively, in the mid-1960s onwards and in the 1980s). Questions of race within the hexagon specifically addressed by the cultural groups in question also had a late start (the 1970s at the earliest).

With regard to other genres, colonial films started to fade in the 1940s and all but disappeared in the 1950s (perhaps the only genre to disappear for political reasons). Again this genre resurfaced in the 1960s, but under numerous different guises. Historical reconstructions and Belle Epoque films remained as stalwarts throughout these three decades. Melodrama, after reaching new heights during the Occupation, progressively gave way to the *drame psychologique* of the 1950s. Finally, after the four year interruption (1940–4) comedy reclaimed its earlier 1930s ascendancy as the most popular genre of all.

Rather than getting bogged down in a systematic analysis of these diverse typologies of genre, what is proposed is a more intensive approach to the cinema of these three decades by looking at it through the optic of social and political representation and transparence and within the framework of sameness and otherness, inclusion and exclusion, reification and subjectivity. It has been noted how social and political unease characterises this thirty-year span and how order was achieved (if at all) more through repression (1930s), oppression (1940–4) and suppression (1950s). Even so, the process of social change was an ineluctable, if paradoxical outcome of political and economic strategies and events. Thus, although the lines of social class were still clearly delineated in the 1930s, none the less alphabetisation of the peasant classes (started during the Second Empire), education of the popular classes including girls (beginning at the turn of the twentieth century), the rural exodus (thanks to education and Taylorisation) and the fraternising of classes amongst the soldiers during the Great War led to boundaries becoming less distinct. Indeed, the process of the dissolution of class lines, started in the post-World War I period, was becoming an increasing (albeit not virtual) reality by the late 1950s.

A first set of representations: social realities, women, and the working class

The representation in film of social issues over this period provides a marker to these shifts in boundaries, though not always or necessarily a transparence. Take, for example, the representation of the working classes. The shifting of points of view from the 1930s to the 1940s has already been commented upon. So too has the subsequent disappearance (almost) of this class in the 1950s, and its replacement by the youth class or, alternatively, by its evolution into a new, modernised gangster class.[25] However, it is patently clear that in reality the working class did not disappear. In mainstream cinema, in the 1950s, it was glossed over in favour of other attractions, youth for one. It was excluded as a social issue because of its association first, in the possessing classes' minds with the Left, the CGT, strikes and unruliness, and second, as much in the minds of producers as in those of that same lot of *bien pensants*, with unprepossessing images of hardship. The working class as a cinematic attraction and issue had faded and lost its glamour.

Carné was to find this out when his attempts to reintroduce the Poetic Realist mood of his prewar films met with little box-office success. Both the pessimism and the stylisation were dated, as was exemplified by *Les Portes da la nuit* (1946). The whole notion of poetic realism just did not sit comfortably with the new times of jazz and modernity. The drabness of the carefully (if controversially) reconstructed Barbès métro and the insalubrious, poky apartments overpopulated by children – though undoubtedly true of that time for the working class and unemployed of Paris – were no longer the images of auto-reflexivity or identification desired by the spectator. The symbolism that had worked so effectively before the war now had no real resonance – it was all too familiar and predictable. Thus, the jaundiced spectator might utter: 'So what if the hero [Diego] meets the love of his life for the first time in a reflecting glass [narcissism, death, etc.]?' 'So what if the couple make love, for the first and last time [but we knew that because of the mirror image], in the children's local hideout [the spectre of the fated couple's puerile love in *Le Jour se lève* arises]?' 'So what if one of them dies?' How, too, could the general public, after four years of living the opposite, believe in the certainty of circumstance, in Destiny forecasting future events or fate playing a role in the narrative? Nor were the messages of revenge over *collabos* and brotherly love in the Resistance ones that rested easily in the consciences of many, particularly if, as in this film, they were identifiable with particular individuals (i.e., in this film there was no anonymous class of resistors or collaborators – they were individuated characterisations).[26]

In the 1930s, although the spectator was privileged to a more positive image of the working class, much of its reality was absent. The insecurity of working conditions for young people hardly got a mention, as did the problems of unemployment and old age.[27] Governmental measures to encourage early retirement and free up places for the younger generation – a policy dear to Léon Blum's heart – never got beyond his investiture speech of 1936. Whilst the demographic ageing of France was not absent from the screen, it was simply not represented as a problem, in fact, quite the opposite if the number of couplings between younger women and older men are to act as a guide. Interestingly, what was a problem in relation to one aspect of France's ageing populace (keeping younger people out of work) was glossed over in favour of another preoccupation, the birth rate, with older men keeping younger men out of the matrimonial bed. There are a few noted exceptions. *Le Temps des cerises* (Le Chanois, 1937), *La Vie est à nous* (Renoir, 1936) and *La Fin du jour* (Duvivier, 1939) make references to this double problem of an ageing France and unemployment (however, this last film, which is about an actors' retirement home and ageing has little, if anything, to do with the working class). In the main, younger women marry older men startlingly frequently. Despite César's confident assurance to Panisse in *Fanny* (Pagnol, 1932) that 'young women belong to young men', it is Panisse (the older man) who gets to marry Fanny who has been left (high and dry and pregnant) for the high seas by her lover Marius, son of César. Nor is it implied in this order of films that the marriage, whilst it may well be of convenience, is sexless.

In terms of difference in representation of this class, the fundamental point is that instead of the earlier silent era's sense of superiority over the working class, in the 1930s films worked towards an idealised version of the working class. Sellier (1981, 9 and 16) makes the point that the greatest evidence of the falsity of this image comes with the representation of working-class sexuality. Illegitimate pregnancies abound in the cinema of these times as much as before, but now it is the working-class man, either lover or father, who is supposedly concerned as to the intactness of the woman. However, as Sellier says, this obsession with virginity and its possible loss is in fact a bourgeois preoccupation. Other sexual images also disturb this idealised representation. The working-class woman as an object of rape coupled with the normality of the working-class man's sexuality erect some troubling positionings with regard to the way in which the bourgeoisie reifies, first and foremost, the working-class male. The working-class male is potent, capable of violence but/and unimpeachably 'straight'. Perversity (i.e., homosexuality) is the reserve of the bourgeoisie, signifying their decadence. The working-class male is both subject (he is the agent of his own passions) and object, to be gazed upon by the bourgeoisie for his otherness, perceived as enigma (because of the unpredictability of his actions). This homoeroticisation of the working-class male is perpetuated within the narrative by the abundant images of male camaraderie or male bonding. *The* icon of this form of reification is of course Jean Gabin. There were others (Fresnay, Modot, Gil, Le Vigan, etc.) but they were hierarchically placed on a scale: Gabin and then the rest. Most of his films after 1935 are strongly inflected by this process of ideation – a process, incidentally, with which he strongly colluded (Vincendeau: 1985, 254).

As part and parcel of this tradition of idealisation, the absence of the workplace marks most of the films of this social realist category. It must be recalled, however, that whilst some films were based on literary adaptations, many others were reinscriptions of the *théâtre du boulevard*. Thus whilst original scripts (which were not there in great numbers, costs being a major cause) and literary adaptations could produce films where work and the workplace were an integral part of the narrative – *A nous la liberté*, *Toni*, *L'Atalante* (Vigo, 1934), *La Belle équipe*, *La Bête humaine* (Renoir, 1938) to quote some obvious examples – the transposition of theatre into a filmic text would inevitably mean that relationships rather than the workplace would be foregrounded. Guillaume-Grimaud (1986, 83) notes a rare, if flawed exception to this practice in Maurice de Camonge's *Grisou* (1938), an adaptation of a play by Pierre Brasseur. Ostensibly about the unsafe conditions in the mining industry, the film documents the working conditions of the miners (men and women), including a fatal accident due to the negligence of a white-collar worker. This documentary aspect, however, is set against a series of love intrigues, initiated in the first instance by a disaffected miner's wife who has obviously married beneath her (in the end she leaves with the clerk who was responsible for the accident which buried her husband alive!). Thus, the potentially political nuances of the dangers of mining ultimately get subsumed into the predictable iconography of the working class at play (the singing and dancing at the miners' dance-hall, the pursuit of romantic happiness, etc.). In the meantime, the *petite bourgeoisie* carries on, unquestioned, with its own affairs.

As a background to his filmed theatre, it could be said that the 'Pagnol' films do show his actors in places of work. However, this is more to give the air of authenticity to his dramatisation than anything else. The intentionality of the decor for *Marius*, *Fanny*, and *César* – the famous Pagnol trilogy directed respectively by Korda (1931), Marc Allégret (1932) and Pagnol (1936) – is clearly to circumscribe an area that is not Paris, to make Marseilles and Provence exotic and 'other', to make that 'other' more than Paris (more interesting, exciting, etc.).[28] Jeancolas (1983, 147) also points to their exotic appeal but argues that the popularity of these films is equally a result of the contemporaneity of the adaptations. *Marius* and *Fanny* had been huge stage successes and the film versions attracted large audiences, eager to see the stage actors on screen. Equally successful, however, was *César*, which was directly scripted for film. However, it should be acknowledged that its success is undoubtedly due to the fact that it came in the wake of the success of the other two and also the increasing cinematic fame of Raimu and Pierre Fresnay. In any event, given the number of 'pagnolades' that came in the wake of these films, it is clear that producers had understood public taste for this type of film.

The theme of this trilogy, illegitimate pregnancy, is a fairly stock one and one that Pagnol appears quite fond of since it reappears in two other films of his of this period, *Angèle* (1934) and *La Fille du puisatier* (1940).[29] Apart from Pagnol's and the bourgeoisie's prurient interest in this 'social fall from grace', which is one of the reasons for its appeal, there are other features that demarcate this series of films from others of the same ilk. The first, I believe, is the fact that the central female character – played by Orane Demazis in the 1930s films and in the 1940s film by Josette Day – makes strong, if not feminist, representations against the male discourses that would position her.[30] In all instances, after the initial terror of finding themselves pregnant, the female protagonists find ways of coping, even to the point of standing up to the authoritarian 'father'. These ways of coping are also assisted by other women (mothers or aunts) giving support. Even proto-women give support. As Vincendeau (1990, 78) points out, Panisse occupies a feminine as well as a masculine position in *Fanny* (he wants to attend the birth, cossets the infant and pays great attention to its health and subsequent development). In *La Fille du puisatier*, it is the aunt (another fallen woman of the past) who at first gives support. Eventually the father of the fallen daughter also occupies a Panisse-like positioning. These strong female discourses, the succour and eventual parental acceptance and nurturing, were quite an exception at that time within this melodrama/ social realist genre. This is perhaps why Pagnol is troubling for feminist critics of today because although on the one hand these strong representations of women are made, on the other, all the traditional male discourses are equally in place.[31] Marius's longing for the sea is more important than Fanny's longing for him. She does not 'understand' this longing but in the end relents and lets him go for the sake of his happiness (*Marius*). Patriarchal modalities are fully in place both in relation to the father/son (César/Marius) and father/daughter (César/Fanny) dynamics. It is César who dictates the letters to his son which Fanny must write. As they discuss the unborn child's future, César and Panisse paterlinguistically take possession of Fanny's womb. Patriarchal language is reiterated when César, in the name of the 'law' of the father, forbids Marius from repossessing Fanny and taking her/his child away from Panisse (*Fanny*, Vincendeau: 1990, 77).

Before going into detail on the issue of the representation of women, a few more points need to be made about that of the working class and, primarily, the working-class male. In its idealised representation in the 1930s, the male protagonist is the sign of sexual and physical potency. He has power over his immediate entourage – power to attract, seduce and dominate men and women of his own class. This power sometimes extends over to other classes, with women actively signalling their interest in his potency and men their agitation. As far as male characters from other classes are concerned, he attracts by way of repulsion, that is, he fascinates but troubles – precisely because of his potency. He troubles also because he is *at* the centre, is *of* the centre and all others are, to differing degrees, not. In particular, the male of the other classes is at the furthest edge of the periphery. Part of what troubles the male outsider too is the male camaraderie existing between the centre and those closest to the centre. The outsider can neither penetrate it to evict the one at the centre, nor be part of the male bonding he sees before him. All gazes serve to eroticise the male working-class protagonist. The working-class hero does not usually get represented as seeking socio-economic advancement. So, to the potency myth gets added the one of working-class solidarity which can stand firm to all that assails it – provided it is not a woman. Women are repeatedly represented as the cause of disbanding male bonding. The bleakest of films in this category must be Duvivier's *La Belle équipe* and Carné's *Le Jour se lève*. Interestingly, critics have closely associated these two films with the rise and demise of the Popular Front. Critics who have read in Duvivier's film an attack on the early optimism of the Popular Front are probably correct (Duvivier was certainly not of the Left). The film was made in June and July 1936 and coincided with the early days of the Blum government and the euphoric strikes calling for better conditions. It should be pointed out, none the less, that Duvivier's portrayal of male friendship gradually being eroded by a woman and by desire for that woman was canonical by 1936, so the film does not limit itself to just that reading. Nor does Carné's film, which has been read as marking the demise and death of the Popular Front. If the men in Duvivier's film do not get to fulfil their dreams of setting up their *guinguette* (a dancing and refreshment café in the country) it is because, whilst economically they can be *solidaires* – as one (the five friends are unemployed but they have a win on their shared lottery ticket which they decide to invest in a common project), sexually they cannot – hence the relevance of the revolver shoot-out between the two remaining male protagonists in the original ending of the film (which Duvivier had to tone down into a semi-happy one), in which all 'perish' because of a woman. In Carné's film, the hero gets cut off, isolated, from his mates because his sexual jealousy pushes him to murder. On a first level of reading, therefore, it is sex before politics (i.e., politicised images of the working class) that drives the narrative.

By the 1950s, this tradition has gone into two different directions, even though what remains as a constant from the 1930s tradition is the representation of male friendship. The more dominant trend is that by which the working-class hero becomes assimilated into another class, the gangster class. The other, somewhat less prevalent trend sees the proletarian hero resurfacing in his place of work and/or in a newly styled buddy-and-road movie that concerns truck-drivers and their ordeals. Clouzot's *Le Salaire de la peur* (1952) becomes such a film – two men are obliged to unite to survive (albeit unsuccessfully) the dreadful ordeal of transporting nitro-glycerine – and Verneuil's *Des Gens sans importance* (1955) starts and ends in that mode. In the gangster films, there is no honour amongst gangs (rival gangs all set out to steal each others *grisbi* (loot) and women – almost one and the same), but there is male bonding within the gang with, once again, a central focal hero. A new dimension to the characterisation of the central protagonist is that he often has a protégé, a proto-son. Exemplary films of this genre are Becker's *Touchez pas au grisbi* and Dassin's *Du Rififi chez les hommes* (both made in 1954) and Melville's *Bob le flambeur* (1955).

These three films are worth a brief exploration together. In all three, the leader of the gang (even if there are several gangs, the spectator is positioned with just one, that of the hero) decides to do a last job, but as a result of this decision, the leader loses his proto-son. Whilst the immediate cause of the proto-son's death is his own imprudence, boastfulness or foolhardiness in trying to outstrip the father-figure, the fact remains that it is the decision to do the last job that sets in motion the ineluctability of the 'death to the son'. From that Oedipal/counter-Oedipal moment on, however, it becomes the woman who is causal in bringing about the demise of the projected job which will cause death or imprisonment for the father-figure. Agency here gets tripartised, but in a closed chain effect: the 'father', the 'son' and the 'woman/whore'. Or put another way, the 'law' of the father (the decision to do a job) is resisted Oedipally (by the proto-son leaking the decision to his woman or breaking one of the father's cardinal rules). This sets in motion events that will lead, on the one hand, to a counter-Oedipal outcome (death of the son) and, on the other, to the betrayal of the father (and implicitly the son) by the woman/whore. In this respect, although this is a new genre, it is in fact a newly styled version of the generational conflict melodrama narrative (that goes back to silent cinema) – newly styled because of the look of the film with its modern gadgets, design and technology, and newly styled in its references to a new social (or anti-social) phenomenon, drugs. Viewed in this light this new genre, all its suspense and thrills notwithstanding, takes over the moralising mantle of the earlier, melodramatic genre.

Whilst the female character may be pivotal to many cinematic narratives, the representation of women remains by and large unchanged over this thirty-year period. Certainly, in the 1950s there was a move towards a more explicit eroticising of the female body. Indeed, Simone Signoret, Martine Carol and Brigitte Bardot are not the same women as Michèle Morgan, Arletty or (especially) Gaby Morlay. However, this change in representation does not necessarily mean that women were represented as having any greater control over their destiny. In *Dédée d'Anvers* (Yves Allégret, 1948), it is significant that it is the male (in the form of her understanding friend/boss, played by Blier) who wreaks revenge for Dédée (played by Signoret) by running over her pimp (played by Dalio), albeit at her bidding. In this film, the prostitute with a golden heart, Dédée, does not have the power to effect change. As her nickname suggests, she (Dédée) is fixed (*of* Anvers, even though she originally comes from Paris). The shooting of her lover by her pimp in cold blood not only destroys all future chance of her happiness, but also guarantees that her life will remain the same.

The same 'no change' prevailed for the earlier screen heroines. Michèle Morgan remains exotic and mysterious, enigmatic and unfathomable (a successful attempt at making a French Garbo). Her beauty is evanescent, not tactile, at least in her 1930s and early 1940s films. In any event, she either enigmatically disappears (*Remorques*, Grémillon, 1941) or is left to carry on in her misery (*Quai des brumes*, Carné, 1938). There is rarely a hint that her destiny might change course, and if it does it will be a manmade change. On this point, *Gribouille* (Marc Allégret, 1937) is sufficiently ambiguous in its ending. Rescued a first time by the father, will she now be rescued by the son? The father, nicknamed Gribouille (i.e., simpleton), was instrumental through his words as a jurist at her trial in obtaining for her a not-guilty verdict of murdering her lover. Her lover had stolen money from his father and was intent on eloping with her. She claims a misunderstanding had occurred and she shot him in self-defence. At the end of the film, a pastiche of these events occurs. Gribouille's son, who has fallen in love with her, steals from his father with the same intention of eloping. Gribouille intercepts him and slugs Morgan over the head. Twice then the father intercedes and shapes her destiny – a fairly standard patriarchal set of affairs, simpleton or no simpleton.

Arletty, predominantly characterised as a *parigote*, attracts in a way that is different and ambiguous. She is usually a representative of the working class and has the gift for quick, witty and acerbic repartee (*gouaillerie*, as the French call it). She does not, however, provoke interest, that is, she is not presented as enigmatic – except as Garance in *Les Enfants du paradis* (Carné, 1944–5). Part of this is due to the fact that she often plays secondary roles and, as convention would have it, is not supposed to upstage the leading woman's role (even though she might well do, as in *Le Jour se lève*). She pleases because her banter teases. But she is also recognisably 'not very different from us' (i.e., she is not mysterious), and this is where her attraction places her ambiguously. Her ability to send up men fulfils both male and female spectators' expectations of her as a comic actress. Both identify with her, but in this double identification she becomes them and the other, that is, she simultaneously remains herself and becomes almost indistinguishable in her banter from the rest of the men. She becomes almost as significant as the male. She shifts, as the half cross-dressing in *Circonstances atténuantes* (Jean Boyer, 1939) exemplifies, when she dons a cap and black polo-neck sweater (icons of the working-class gangster at that time) to go on a robbery.

Eroticism in the female characterisations of the 1930s and 1940s comes down to hints of sexual promise and intimacy. Women are 'unattainable' (e.g., Michèle Morgan, Mireille Balin), but mysteriously and inexplicably 'give' themselves to the hero (usually to Gabin, and only for one night), or they are 'animal' (e.g., Ginette Leclerc, Simone Simon) and insincere in their lust. Alternatively they can be 'foreign' – but of the colonies (e.g., Annabella, Line Noro) – or Parisian hookers (e.g., Arletty, Michèle Morgan – surprisingly, one might think, but here too she remains evanescent and 'unattainable'). In both these latter cases they 'love their man' (to death in the case of Line Noro in *Pépé-le-Moko*, Duvivier, 1936). It would be invidious to draw a conflation between the prostitute and the 'exotically' foreign woman were it not for the fact that there seems to be a case for it. Both are even more outside the centre than the other two categories (unattainable or animal). Legally and racially, they are at the periphery and this is reflected in the unfolding of the narrative. They are without. Thus it is the man who will leave them, normally for a woman in one of the other two categories. If this is the case, then it becomes the turn of the male to be forced to the periphery or to be positioned as victim. However, and this is the significant difference, no matter how he is positioned (peripheral and/or victim), the male still has agency over his destiny and can elect either to disappear or to obliterate himself (Pépé commits suicide not because Nora has denounced him to the police, but because he cannot attain Balin). Alternatively, in similar narrative types (but without the 'exotic' elements) he can simply obliterate the 'animal' or the 'unattainable' woman (respectively in Renoir's *La Bête humaine*, 1938 and Lacombe's *Martin Roumagnac*, 1946).

Throughout these same two decades, women are reduced to a simplistic dualism. They are either the agent of danger or salvation. Most extreme on the scale of salvation is the self-sacrificing woman, epitomised by Gaby Morlay in *Le Voile bleu* (Jean Stelli, 1941). Madeleine Renaud is obliged to sacrifice herself in *Les Remorques* and willingly gives up all security for the sake of France's glory in *Le Ciel est à vous*. At the other end of the scale, Mireille Balin ensnares her man, virtually to the point of impotence (symbolised by her reducing him to tears), although he kills her for it (*Gueule d'amour*, Grémillon, 1937). Whichever way she is represented upon this binary line – mother or whore, nurturer or parasite – woman is central *to* the narrative, but is never *at* its centre. For example, Gaby Morlay is certainly the main character of *Le Voile bleu*, but she is not the subject. What is at the centre, is the myth of woman as 'Total Mother'. Indeed, the film's dedication (with all the proto-pro-natalist and National Revolution discourses inherent in its message) makes this clear: 'Dedicated to all those who foster others' children and to those who have to give them up.' This film, however, with its masochistic and even sadistic resonances, is almost perverse in its glorification of motherhood and mothering. After the death of her husband in combat during World War I, which not only precipitates the premature birth of her child who dies shortly after, but also leaves her infertile, Morlay decides to take up the blue veil of nannying. Widowed and childless she declares she will dedicate her *self* to caring for children. In each household in which she works every child grows to love her to the point where she signifies more as mother than the actual mother herself. Morlay loses her child and becomes the very thing she cannot be, a mother. Separation from each child, once they have outgrown their need for her, means a reliving of the initial loss. However, to this masochistic inflection of the text gets added the equally perverse one of sadism. All the children grow to love *Manou*, as they call her, very intensely (one child actually pretends she is her mother). This drawing of their love, to then walk away from it as she does with each departure, can be read as a revenge on her own loss especially since, in order to be able to leave, she often has to hurt the child. Thus she simultaneously relives the loss and takes her revenge on it. She is both Demeter – 'mother-earth' – and Nemesis – the retributive 'chaste mother'.

Women and death are frequent symbolic associations. They either bring it on themselves or are the cause of the male protagonist's death or demise (a role often played by Gabin). The central cause for these deaths is either love or desire. Yvonne's heart gives out in *Remorques* at the loss of her husband's love. She is represented as possessive and uncomprehending of her husband – a drudge, not to put too fine a point on it – which almost 'excuses' his having an affair. In *Douce* (Autant-Lara, 1943), Douce dies, engulfed by smoke and flames, because she played at love and transgressed social lines. Both Madeleine (*Gueule d'amour*) and Séverine (*La Bête humaine*, 1938) are murdered by their lovers for their 'heartless' ways. So too is Blanche in *Martin Roumagnac*.[32] Lucien (*Gueule d'amour*) and Pierre (*Au-delà des grilles*, Clément, 1948) flee France because they have killed their lovers. The male protagonist of *Pépé-le-Moko* also has to leave his beloved Paris. His desperation at this *dépaysement* is so great that he ends up killing himself. Unable to rejoin the woman of his life (she brings Paris back to life for him) and aware that the alternative is to remain forever stuck in the Casbah with only songs about Paris (sung by Fréhel) and his mistress (the woman he does not want – she who holds no memories for him), the only choice is death.

The representation of woman in the 1950s still fixes her misogynistically. She is either fallen (or about to fall), adulterous, ensnaring or scheming. If the mother is less visible, the proto-mother is still thriving, especially in the *polar* films, where her image is double (in a different way from the one we might expect). In this genre of film, she is endowed with the standard mothering strengths, but the subject of her nurturing – her 'children' – are now grown men who are ultimately less adept at running their lives than she is. Wherever the male protagonist turns, there is this caring, wise and all-knowing mature woman successfully running her business as the proprietor or manager of a Paris night-club or café bar. She is fixed in her 'mothering' role, but appears unfixed as a competent business woman. However, because she is not sexualised (as anything except mother), in her capacity as *femme d'affaires* she does not threaten. She is almost 'one of the boys'. Thus she is simultaneously fixed as mother and not woman but other – useful, because she will not (be allowed to) transgress. That role will fall to the younger woman who is sexualised and does transgress and will be punished. The mother cannot be punished, but the younger woman/whore can be.

There are, however, other less fixing representations in this cinema of the 1950s. Younger women stand up to paternal authority and point to the hypocrisy of adults' double standards. Sexuality is given a different representation, albeit still predominantly from a male point of view. Thus, women are more frequently represented as supposed agents of their own desire. Social issues specifically concerning women are given a transparence. Unwanted pregnancies, the dangers of back-street abortions and the lack of recourse to legal terminations are put on screen. In Astruc's film *Mauvaises rencontres* (1955), abortion is at the centre of a police investigation. A young woman is bullied by a policeman into denouncing the doctor who performed her abortion – in vain, for the doctor has already committed suicide. Even more graphic is the death from an abortion of a young woman, Clothilde, portrayed in *Des Gens sans importance* (Henri

Verneuil, 1955). Her visit to the abortionist is spine-chilling in its realism, as is the inevitability of the circumstances which drove her to it.

It is worth pausing for a moment on this film because of its contemporaneous transparence on social issues, youth culture and the conflicts and shifts of preoccupations between generations. These people of no importance are the working class (in a sense, therefore, the title points to this class's loss of signification in the 1950s films). But as their tale unfolds it becomes clear that their story is as significant as any other. Told in the form of a flashback, it relates the even greater misfortunes that visit upon the male protagonist's life after he gets involved with a younger woman. Jean (played by Gabin) is a middle-aged truck driver who is married with three children. They all live in a small apartment in a *banlieue* of Paris (La Villette, to all appearances). Hardship epitomises his life and that of his wife, whom he hardly sees because he is always on the road. His teenage daughter presciently foresees her father's affair when she implies that he does not need to come home because he gets what he wants, sexually, on the road. Although clearly unhappy, Jean has never been unfaithful. In fact his distressed life is more a consequence of his work. But it is made clear that he brings his tiredness and bad moods home, spreading them equally over his wife and daughter (his two sons are spared his moods). The wife, of course, is completely resigned to the drudge to which she has been reduced over the years. However, the daughter is not.

Sparks fly between daughter and father as she persists in her determination to establish her autonomy and attain a better quality of life. Her father ridicules her ambitions. None the less, it is she who succeeds – she achieves her goal to become a photographic model in advertising. Her first coup is a photograph emblazoned on camembert boxes (the cheese her father likes to eat!). The young woman with whom Jean eventually has an affair, Clothilde, is just the opposite of his daughter in both appearance and make up. She is brunette, his daughter is blonde. She is downtrodden in her circumstances, working as she does as a *serveuse* in a routier café-hotel located in a desolate place somewhere between Paris and Bordeaux. As such, therefore, she more readily resembles Jean's wife than his daughter, despite the fact that these two are of similar age. Even though it is she who chases after Jean and more or less forces the seduction (in the truck, of course), the spectator is never privy to any sense of passion. Indeed, the relationship quickly develops into a carbon copy of the one with his wife, this time with Clo complaining that he is never there. The *dénouement* is initiated by his daughter (already suspicious that her father is having an affair) when she intercepts and reads Clo's letter to her father announcing her pregnancy. The daughter feels totally justified in her action because her father intercepts and reads her letters. She also feels justified in unmasking her father to her mother's face by reading the letter out loud, a vengeful act for which she later apologises.

The Electra and counter-Electra resonances to this scenario in the doubly configurated father–daughter relationship (Clo and Jean, and Jean and his daughter) point to the confusion which these modern times produce in the minds of both generations. Since this is Jean's flashback, it is to his subjectivity that we are party. He perceives his daughter's behaviour on all counts (from cheese box cover to divulging his secret) as transgressing parental authority, that is, the patriarchal 'law'. The daughter's meddling in her father's affairs also refers to the precocity of this new youth generation that is ready at an early age to assume its adultness. The modern daughter is counter-Electra, or is perceived as such by her father. Hence the symbolism of the cheese box with its new endaughtered cover. Formerly his favourite cheese, Jean now refuses to eat it. This refusal gives a double reading. First, he cannot/will not consume the daughter. Second, he rejects the daughter because of his perception of her behaviour that threatens the *status quo*. What then of Clo, the daughter substitute? Before they become lovers, Jean pushes aside her approaches saying she could be his daughter. Displacement of fatherly desire could well be at work here, not that it will save Clo either from her wretched working conditions or from death. It is here, at the interface of these two representations of the younger generation by the older generation (Jean re-evoking, reconstructing in his mind Clo and his daughter) that one can see the ambivalence felt by the latter in relation to the former. The younger generation is both to be feared (daughter) and to be suppressed (Clo), or because it is intimidating in the modernity of its views and rejection of old, established values, it needs quashing.

As was mentioned earlier, female sexuality receives a different and troubling representation during this decade. The same images of vamp or virgin, whore or mother remain, but now there is a more sustained image of woman as agent of her desire/sexuality. It is not the fact that she is agent that disturbs, but what occurs in the representation of this agency. Female sexuality where vamps, virgins and whores are concerned is now represented as the site of perversity. In the earlier films, there is no direct implication that female sexuality is itself the site of perversity. The woman might well be perverse in her scheming ways and drive men to their ruin, but the stress is on her scheming ways which only then are associated with her femaleness (i.e., this sort of scheming is the hallmark of that sort of woman). Female sexuality comes more potently to the fore in the 1950s and at times is even represented as having drug-inducing properties. This shift in the representation of female sexuality as addictive and therefore perverse in itself is troubling because it now means that the female body has legitimately been made the site of narration by and for the male. This representation reaches its apogee in Vadim's *Et Dieu créa la femme* (1956), although it has some notable antecedents. The central female protagonists in *Caroline chérie*, *La Ronde* (both made in 1950 by Pottier and Ophuls respectively), *Lola Montès* (Ophuls, 1955), and Cécile in *Bonnes à tuer* (Henri Decoin, 1954) are all bodies that get narrated in this particular way. Perhaps cruellest of all is Lola (played by Martine Carol), whose sexuality is narrated upon by the ringmaster of a circus as she sits cooped up in a cage in the circus ring. Could the reader ever imagine the reverse happening?

Vadim's offensive but highly successful film *Et Dieu créa la femme* (renamed by some feminists as *Et l'homme créa la salope*) stars Brigitte Bardot as an overactive sexualised nymphette whom nobody understands except for the father figure (played by Curd Jurgens), who decrees from a distance how she shall conduct her life. This older man, a highly successful entrepreneur, has been so profoundly marked by Bardot that he does all in his power to keep her in his sight and to protect her – including arranging her marriage to a man she does not love – so that she will not be forced back to the orphanage. As a minor, she is at risk of being sent back by her foster parents who can no longer tolerate her decidedly physically irreverent behaviour towards the adult world. Hitting from the hip, she sveltly swivels her way around St Tropez leaving no doubt as to her sexual self-absorption. The perception the spectator has of Bardot is of course the privileged one of the father figure. Nobody except him, he says, understands her free hedonistic spirit, which he sees as much like his own – a new form of narcissism which explains first, why he never becomes her lover (although he is in love with her), and second, why he shields her from her husband's gun (!) and is almost fatally wounded.

If Bardot displaying her bodily beauty through baring her legs and curving her body around pillars *and* men is a sign of her free spirit, then it is a very specified sign, located as it is in her bodily text. The fact that the father figure must keep her within his sight makes it perfectly plain that she must be accessible for his viewing. It is also very difficult to speak of Bardot as the character named Juliette because the film is so evidently not about Juliette but about Bardot and Bardot's Body (BB). She is hardly ever absent from the screen – always there to be speculated. In this respect, the viewer is positioned much as the father figure looking at, but not touching, the Body Beautiful (BB). The closing sequence with her frenzied hip-wiggling attempts at Latin American dancing, shot in close-up (waist-down), says more about male voyeurism and the fetishising gaze than female agency. By now the body has become pure object to be carved up (by the camera) for speculation. The body-frenzy equals the body-perverse. The fact too that the film is shot in cinemascope makes Bardot's body even more of a readable text, first, by sculpting her body on to the frieze of the screen, and second, by giving the spectator panoramic vision on her body.

It is reported that Bardot did not rate herself as an actress – she found it too tiresome to try and be a great performer and preferred instead to be

sexy (Sallée: 1988, 29). This is an opinion not confirmed by her performance in Godard's *Le Mépris* (1963), the opening sequence of which could
be seen as a rebuff to Vadim's territorialisation of her body (Bardot
narrates her own body as the camera slowly pans over it). The fundamental
problem with Vadim's film is precisely that it counters Bardot's expressed
desire to be sexy and with it the implicit connotations of agency. She is
sexual, yes, but she is not subject. She is the wild animal that has to be
tamed first, by the father who 'locks her up' (in his gaze) and then by her
husband who almost kills her (the gun shots) and slaps her into submission.
The affinities of this imagery with the *mise-en-scène* of *Lola Montès* (circus
and cage) are evident for all to see. The message is equally clear: women
who 'try' to agence their desire (subjectivity, sexuality) will be punished for
their 'transgression(s)' – for this is how women's attempts at agencing
appear to the dominant, patriarchal ideology. Brilliant Bardot (BB) was
very clever to respond by retiring early (in 1973) and taking all her 'manmade' millions to bestow on animal welfare. What a snub, indeed.

A SECOND SET OF REPRESENTATIONS: MORE VIRTUAL
REALITY, THE NATIONAL REVOLUTION AND NOT
SPEAKING ABOUT THE WAR

As the above section has endeavoured to demonstrate, cinema does function as a virtual reality, as a model-making tool of perceived realities. The
parallel worlds it creates are those that emanate from the human mind
rather than from a one-to-one reflection of reality itself – reality being
either too small and limited or, conversely, too huge and frightening for
human imagination. In this respect, cinema has the power either to sanitise
reality or to shock us into a new understanding of reality or, indeed, into an
understanding of a new reality. Clearly it is the former tendency that will
predominate – cinema is after all a popular cultural artefact and therefore
conservative in its representations. The majority audience goes to be
entertained, not instructed. But there are inevitable consequences to this.
Misogyny is continually normalised. Images of the working class – whatever the point of view – are safely inscribed into an otherness that is
fetishised into unmistakable icons and morphologies. The bourgeoisie is
often stereotyped unflatteringly as mean, moralising and rapacious, but
that is as much a convention as is the iconography of the working class. All
are conventions consolidated, in the main, by the literary tradition that
inflects French cinema so strongly.

There are, of course, exceptions. In *L'Amour d'une femme* (Grémillon,
1954), a woman's professionalism leads her to walk away from love, but
not before being besieged by moral conflict, torn as she is between her
vocation as a doctor and her love for a terrorist. Grémillon also made *Le
Ciel est à vous* (1944) which again addresses the courage of a woman. It is

noteworthy that in both films traditional roles are reversed. The woman is either aviator or doctor.

In Becker's films women are also represented in their own right and their characterisations have strength and depth. His representation of youth similarly shows young women confronting equally important issues as young men (*Antoine et Antoinette*, 1947, *Rendez-vous de juillet*, 1949, and *Edouard et Caroline*, 1950). Becker believed that the Occupation marked a certain emancipation of the young woman.[33] The example he cites of her taking a lover before getting married can today seem rather limiting and unfortunate until one realises just how much young women were controlled by not just the 'law' of the father, but also the law of the state (women were not enfranchised until 1944 and married women only stopped being minors in 1938). Sexual independence, therefore, was a form of assertiveness, even though it rarely benefited the woman. Becker saw himself as a *cinéaste social*. Interested in people as a whole, his films study them with the detailed attention of an entomologist (an approach that is continued in the 1970s onwards in the work of Bertrand Tavernier with his intimist portraits). Becker's *Casque d'or* (1952) dwells lovingly on the passion shared by Marie (Simone Signoret) and Manda (Serge Reggiani). Marie and Manda are unquestionably agents of their own desire – an assertiveness which is signified by the fact that their passion is literally kept separate, sanctified away (in a rural hideaway) from the rest of the mostly insalubrious goings-on in the Parisian underworld to which they both belong. Only the spectator is privy to their tender attachment as they silently declare their love. In a different mode, intimate observation is also at work in Becker's *Touchez pas au grisbi* (1954) which is as much about ageing as it is about the goings-on in the gangster underworld. Max is no longer the 'great' gangster he was. He is growing old, not just as the glasses he wears at the end of the film attest, but also because ten years earlier he would have saved his friend and got the loot (*grisbi*) back. It is also about Max's intimate daily gestures of dressing and undressing, of sharing his thoughts with his buddy, of caring for his *môme* Marco, his proto-son, etc.

Becker's mentor, Renoir, had similar attachments to people. His prewar films are especially enlightened in their observations of the working and proletarian classes. *Toni* (1934), *Le Crime de M. Lange* (1935) and *La Bête humaine* (1938) are amongst some of his most sensitive treatments of those classes' struggles and hardships as well as being revelatory of their solidarity. Renoir was a great champion of republican ideals and his films have consistently analysed human behaviour, particularly in relation to class and to individual as well as group aspirations. Renoir is often singled out as one of the giants of the French cinema of this period (in a similar way that Godard has been canonised as guru of the last thirty years of French cinema). In Renoir's case, much of this is is as a result of his lionising by the *Cahiers* group. Whilst certainly a film-maker of exception, the point needs to be made that he did suffer a very uneven career (especially in the 1930s) due not only to controversy over his work, but also to public distaste for some of his films. Some were great hits, some great flops. Exemplary of the first are *La Grande illusion* and *La Bête humaine*, and of the latter *Toni* and *La Règle du jeu* (1939, a film which drew the wrath of the crowd at the time) – all 1930s films. The success of the first two films cannot be detached from the effect of the Gabin factor.

Although *La Grande illusion* is now rated as one of the twelve best films ever made, at the time Renoir could find no one willing to produce it. Eventually, thanks to Gabin's intervention – he very much wanted to play the role of Maréchal – a producer was found. A year later, Gabin again secured Renoir a viable producer when he took the central role in *La Bête humaine* – anecdote has it that Gabin wanted to drive a train. Gabin was once more involved in the success of one of Renoir's postwar films, *French Cancan* (1955). With regard to the two failures, in the case of *Toni* this was due to both the subject matter and the unpolished look of the film. In the case of *La Règle du jeu*, failure was due to subject matter alone. Renoir's decision to use non-professional actors and to record on location in *Toni* (a film financed by Pagnol, incidentally) produced what film historians see as one of the precursors of Italian Neo-Realism. The way in which the camera details the hardships of immigrant labour in the south of France, the naturalness of the improvised dialogue and realness of the different native and non-native accents – all align the film to that movement. But the actual narrative, based on a true story of a *crime passionnel*, inflected as it is by fatality, also brings this film close to the tradition of Poetic Realism. It is not being suggested that the blend of these two modalities is what caused the film's failure, rather that its very failure, in 1935, points to the paradox inherent in film reception. Disliked then because of its 'rawness' (which gave it an amateurish, unpolished look) and 'unattractiveness' (no film stars to attract), this film – thanks to the admiration of the *Cahiers* first and foremost – is now canonised as seminal to Neo-Realism. Similarly, *La Règle du jeu*, which was totally rejected by the audience of the time (mostly because of its seemingly exponential demonstration of bourgeois decadence), is now valued as a *mise-en-scène* of the interaction of social classes.

Renoir is an important film-maker, but he should not be made the 'victim' of historicism. His films of the 1930s, in their concern with social issues and their socio-realistic representation, rejoin Clair's and Vigo's of that same period and align with these film-makers in what Jeancolas (1983, 219) typifies as a reaction against the anti-republicanism so rife in France at that time. Nor are these three film-makers alone in their preoccupations. There are also individual films which focus equally sharply on these classes that are not at the centre. Thus Georges Lacombe's *Jeunesse* (1934) depicts the relentlessly bitter hopelessness of the life of working-class youth in Paris, and both Pierre Chenal's *La Rue sans nom* (1932) and

Jean Grémillon's *La P'tite Lise* (1930) deal with the miseries of society's outcasts (criminals, wastrels and prostitutes).

During the thirty-year span under consideration and within this category of films of exception, other social issues are no less sensitively addressed. The plight of children is represented with perspicacious psychological realism, whether they are underprivileged as in Marie Epstein's *La Maternelle* (made in 1931 in collaboration with Jean Benoît-Lévy – a remake of Gaston Roudès' 1925 film of the same title), borstal kids in need of rehabilitation rather than more incarceration (*Le Carrefour des enfants perdus*, Joannon, 1943, and Carné's *La Fleur de l'âge*, 1947, a film inspired by an actual insurrection at the Belle-Ile penitentiary), exploited cheap youth labour (Yves Allégret's *Une si jolie petite plage*, 1948) or, finally, social outcasts (e.g., orphans, vagrants and delinquents) in a boarding school for difficult children (*La Cage aux rossignols*, Dréville, 1944). Sensitive sexual issues also enter into this arena of socio-realist films of exception. Impotence is at the centre of Gréville's *Remous* (1934), proto-incest (a step-mother's passion for her step-son) at the core of Feyder's *Pension Mimosas* (1934), and lesbianism is at the heart of Jacqueline Audrey's *Olivia* (1950). Less sensitively treated but painfully realistic is the collapse of a marriage and the murderous resentment it causes as the wife takes revenge on her husband in Decoin's *La Vérité sur Bébé Donge* (1951), a film which begs the question: what is a couple?

Bresson's films of this period (as well as those of the next epoch) point to the individual, rather than society, as the first root cause of the impossibility of the environment as a living reality. His harsh asceticism transposes on to screen an austere realism which forces a confrontation between protagonist and spectator alike and their human condition. The filmic language Bresson employs is austere. So too is the episodic nature of his films' narrative structure. Austerity is also omnipresent in the quasi-Jansenist vision of life and death which these films reveal. Bresson's films trace the spiritual/unconscious progression of an individual either away from misrecognition of the object of desire (*Pickpocket*, 1959) or towards freedom (*Journal d'un curé de campagne*, 1951). There is nothing heroic about Bresson's protagonists (not even the Resistance escapee in *Un condamné à mort s'est échappé*, 1956). Nor is there anything artificial about the film-maker's style. It is within this unadorned style, where the camera observes impassively the movement of the characters, that the essence of Bresson's realism lies. The Bressonian protagonist remains as impassive as the camera. The facial expression barely changes. The protagonist does not perform a role but speaks it in a monotonous voice. An indifference governs the relationship between protagonist and the spoken word. The Bressonian protagonist interprets nothing. Rather, her/his complexity is revealed by the camera as it frames the gestures, above all those of the hands. In other words, it is through the physiology/materiality of existence that the protagonist's soul, which is initially represented as imprisoned by her/his body, is revealed. To this effect, Bressonian space is constraining. The camera moves hardly at all and is almost without exception angled horizontally (i.e., at 90 degrees). The frame is often static and in medium shot. The image itself is flattened and thus deprived of its third dimension. Time is stripped of any chronology and is maintained suffocatingly in the present. The purely episodic structure, the exclusive use of the cut, and the use of ellipsis are the main editing processes whereby Bresson creates the present moment. In a way, it is as if one image in the present is replaced by another which is also in the present. These images accumulate and push or transport the individual inexorably towards her/his destiny (often, but not exclusively, death). It is not just the inevitable force of destiny which this disinterest with the past or present suggests, it also functions to suppress psychological realism (which would allow for the spectator to identify, rather than be maintained at a distance). No facile explanation or interpretation of the protagonist's behaviour is offered, hence the non-expressive manner of the actors' delivery. In this cold, unemotional environment the isolation and alienation of the protagonist can be felt in all its brutal realism.

Renoir, Cocteau, Bresson, Becker – these, then, were some of the few film-makers whose work of the 1930s into the 1950s was heralded by the *Cahiers* group, leaving of course a great number unmentioned or dismissed. But, despite the *Cahiers* group's dismissiveness of the much-maligned cinema of the 1950s, there were films that attempted to give a transparence on contemporary France within both the comic genre and a range of socio-realist films.

Virtual reality is also apparent in André Cayatte's polemical films (*films-à-thèse*), which he started making in the 1950s. Alhough perhaps not the most gripping cinematographically, in their focus on social and judiciary issues they do have the merit of confronting the ostrich and amnesiac consciences of the French. His films were also very popular with audiences. Cayatte called these films 'socially true stories' and many of them addressed the imperfections of the French legal system. Cayatte had been a lawyer, and so was well placed to cast an investigative eye. Euthanasia and the difficulty jurors encounter in judging it dispassionately is just one controversial subject Cayatte raises in *La Justice est faite* (1950). The film also calls into question the system of jury selection and its function. In *Nous sommes tous des assassins* (1951), it's the turn of the death penalty to come under attack. Juvenile delinquency and their causes are examined in *Avant le déluge* (1954).

What is interesting, especially in these last two films, is Cayatte's endeavour to broaden the debate on miscreance. In the former film, the various murderers on death row reveal to a newcomer how they came to kill their victim. The narratives dwell on the complex circumstances –

social and psychological – that drove them to murder. How is it possible to justify the death penalty when there are so many complex impulsions and motivations that push a person to murder? This is the first question which the film poses. A second, even more ethically worrying question becomes: what if the person sentenced is innocent? In *Avant le déluge* (which is loosely based on a real occurrence), fear of a third World War (because of Korea) pushes five middle-class adolescents to rob, murder and assassinate. But that fear is only the tip of the iceberg. Social egotism amongst the possessing classes, anti-semitic prejudices, collaboration mentalities and the way this all gets passed down to future generations are considerations that are woven into the complex narrative of this film. Wrongful imprisonment and dubious police practice were to have been at the centre of a 1951 film based on a true story, *L'Affaire Seznec*, had the minister of Justice not intervened to oblige the *Commission de censure* to ban it. Cayatte was to have a mild revenge on this intervention in *Le Dossier noir* (1955). False confessions as a result of police brutality, police pressure to find a guilty person at all costs and incompetence of the pathology laboratory in a post-mortem make up this dark indictment of the judicial and investigative institutions whose comportment has vital consequences for the running of a society (a sinister image not seen again until the cinema of the 1970s).

Even darker social realism is to be found in a considerable number of films during the five-year period after the end of the war. The films of Clouzot and Decoin are the most remarkable in this context in their fierce, almost cynical pessimism, but the work of Yves Allégret and Jean Duvivier in that period comes close on their heels. The fact that one or two of these particular films are Simenon adaptations (e.g., Duvivier's *Panique*, 1946 – remade in 1988 by Patrice Leconte as *Monsieur Hire* – and Decoin's *La Vérité sur Bébé Donge*, 1951) should not mislead us into believing that film-makers were simply pursuing a tradition of black pessimism already in evidence in late-1930s cinema and in the Maigret adaptations made during the Occupation. This pessimism now has a new bitterness. To the hopelessness that was collectively shared in the earlier cinema corresponds an individuated, bleak, no exit reality. Each character experiences her/his misery (whether self-induced or not) alone. After the Liberation euphoria, what *was* there to celebrate after all? Acutely unpleasant economic stringencies and a lack of identity.

With the scriptwriter Jacques Sigurd, Yves Allégret made three extremely black films in quick succession which very clearly refer to this immediate present – *Dédée d'Anvers* (1948), *Une si jolie petite plage* (1948) and *Manèges* (1950). The dereliction felt in *Une si jolie petite plage* (which it patently is not – the north of France in winter) marks not just the environment, but also the characters of the film. All the characters are revealed as participants in this morose tale of a young man (played by

Gérard Philipe) who returns to the hotel where he worked (was exploited) during the summer when he was still with the *Assistance publique* (state orphanage). Steadily and coldly the film reveals how this orphan of France (i.e., with no identity) becomes a victim of the meanness that surrounds him but which pushes him in turn to make a victim of an older woman, a singer whom he murders.

Manèges is perhaps the bleakest statement of all in terms of its exposure of ruthless greed played out in the person of a daughter–mother duo. Played by Simone Signoret and Jane Marken, this duo seeks economic and social mobility through advantageous marriages for the daughter (the 'kept' woman syndrome already alluded to). The daughter lands her man (Bertrand Blier) and then sets about fleecing him of his fortune. When he is virtually ruined she begins to look for another choice victim. Her desire for more money and status take on hysterical proportions to the extent that her greedy desperation catapults her into a near-fatal accident which leaves her paralysed from the neck down. The film is constructed around a double narrative told in flashbacks – a criss-crossing of realities spelt out over the now inert and inarticulate body. First comes the husband's version of events that have led to his wife's paralysis – blinded by love, he had noticed nothing. Then comes the wife's version: because she can hardly speak, she insists that her mother tells her husband the truth, not to salve her conscience, but as revenge – a discourse central to a number of narratives in films immediately after the Liberation. So, in this respect, Allégret's film is consonant with the time. However, the vengeful woman is also a canon of traditional narrative cinema, so equally there is nothing new in this narration.

What is striking about this film is its extreme representation, which seems to point to the extremes felt at that particular time. This film makes clear that even if she is totally incapacitated, a woman can still wreak revenge – female discourse as revenge – and man is powerless to prevent her and can only abandon her to her fate once she has 'spoken' her revenge. Allégret was not alone in his misogynistic tales. It was a tradition much in evidence in the mainstream feature films of the early 1950s, which reveal an increase in socio-ethical malaise. The impossibility of dealing with the meaning of the Occupation and the impossibility of coping with present hardships led, it would appear, to a rise in the images demonising women. Working from Doniol-Valcroze's 1954 survey of films of this period and their representation of women, it would seem that in the forty films listed as having been made between 1949 and 1953, the central female protagonist is a vengeful person fifteen times (i.e., 38 per cent of the time), and a prostitute seventeen times (i.e., 43 per cent of the time).[34]

One final point on these cinemas of exception concerns comedy, the filmic genre most prone to stereotypes (especially on questions of race, gender and class). There are historical reasons for its predominant fixity which make the exceptions all the more remarkable. At the beginning of the 1930s, the advent of sound posed a problem for producers as to what sort of comedy should be launched. It was unlikely, they thought, that the formulas that worked for the silent era – based as they were on visual effect and the musical accompaniment – would attract the spectators. For this reason they turned their attention to what was liked in the theatre, which was overridingly the *comique troupier, boulevard* comedy and vaudeville – three types of comedy that are very evidently based in stereotypes and firmly rooted in the stereotyping process. These trends continued well into the 1950s and beyond.

Not surprisingly, the bourgeoisie is a target feature common to a great many of the comedies, as it still is today. As a class it is either a butt to ridicule or a loser to the less fortunate or less intelligent. There are twists, however, when it comes to the bourgeoisie being confronted by the criminal class. There, the bourgeoisie tends to win, proving that crime does not pay (*Circonstances atténuantes*). But if of criminal inclination itself, the bourgeoisie is likely to get away with it – which is just a reversal of the stereotype of moral rectitude evidenced in its other encounter with criminality, leaving the spectator with the comforting image of the bourgeoisie's inherent hypocrisy. The exceptions to these traditions occur when the prevailing mode and mould are broken. Thus, although the exaggerated comic styles of Fernandel, Bach and Bouboule were mainstream attractions in the 1930s, and whilst Fernandel continued to attract well into the 1960s with his grimaces, tics, gesturality and Marseilles accent, there were other comedians, following in the tradition of Max Linder, whose understated style showed the way for an alternative non-vaudevillesque type of comedy. In the 1930s and 1940s respectively, Michel Simon and Noël-Noël best exemplified this restrained tradition of performance. Simon's performance as Boudu in Renoir's *Boudu sauvé des eaux* (1932) gently ironises bourgeois values and moral respectability. In *Les Casse-pieds* (Dréville, 1948), the central character, played by Noël-Noël, deftly makes the point that no one is exempt from being a tiresome bore at one juncture or another, including himself.

The comic cinema of this period, because it breaks so fundamentally with all the rules whilst simultaneously remaining deeply rooted in the comic traditions, is surely the work of Jacques Tati. Tati's films, *Jour de fête* (1949), *Les Vacances de M. Hulot* (1953) and *Mon Oncle* (1958) are remarkable for their economy of style and apposite gesturality. Using a minimum of dialogue and a maximum of visual effect and natural sound, Tati creates an observant satire on contemporary France as it moves into becoming a society of consumption. These three films reflect what ails the bourgeoisie, rather than point accusingly at it. Thus, in *Jour de fête*, the gawky, ungainly village postman (played by Tati) is persuaded to modernise his old Peugeot bicycle *à l'américaine* but with disastrous consequences for the day of the fête. Tati's gesturality is the first comic spring of this and his other films. His movements are unpredictable, peripatetic and angular. They set in motion comic disaster after comic disaster. In reality, his films are a series of gags, timed to perfection, but they do also put in place a narrative of sorts: the goings-on in a village (*Jour de fête*), summer holidays by the sea (*Les Vacances de M. Hulot*), a day's outing in Paris (*Mon Oncle*). So, although these gags are vaudevillesque in their heritage, none the less, there is more to them – what these gags reveal, through their interaction with other people or the environment on the screen, is not just a first, but also a second-order narrative. *Jour de fête* shows how social habits of a lifetime routinise and prevent us from perceiving things differently. *Les Vacances de M. Hulot* takes bourgeois conformity to task, this time demonstrating – via Hulot/Tati's clumsy awkward body hurtling itself into situations he does not read correctly – how closed and unindividualistic the codes of bourgeois morality and respectability are. Through a series of juxtapositions first, between parts of modernised Paris and, as yet, untouched buildings and *quartiers*, and second, between clean, aseptic modern gadgetry, technology and design and Hulot/Tati's cluttered home and old *vélomoteur*, *Mon Oncle* raises the whole question of consumption, of slavish conformity to modernism, and of the dehumanising effects of the industrial world as manifested by the reconstruction programme in Paris. The message of this film becomes not a defence of tradition, but a clear indictment of progress at any price.

These cinemas of exception do not prevail, however, over the general rule of trivialisation. For example, suicides in the 1930s cinema (so much *à la mode*) were mostly the privileged death of the working-class protagonist. But the root cause of this self-inflicted end was, more often than not, thwarted love or betrayal in love and not the more realistic reasons of the impossible working conditions and the hardships of unemployment – two realities that severely afflicted that class. As for the condition of children during that same period, a film which is remarkable for sanitising the plight of an orphaned child is Marc Allégret's *Sans famille* (1934, remade in 1958 by André Michel). A somewhat Oliver Twist story, it relates how a kidnapped infant (from a rich English family) ends up in France, and is abused by all and sundry until he is befriended by a wandering minstrel (an ex-tenor of great fame dying of some fatal disease). After his singer-mentor dies, he ends up back in London only to fall in with a gang of thieves (*à la* Fagin). Eventually, by the time he is an adolescent, he is restored to his rightful mother. The child/adolescent remains totally self-composed throughout this life of deprivation and loneliness. The only bright spots in his life as a vagrant are his time with the minstrel and a brief visit on a barge with a sickly boy who, unbeknown to him, is none other than his brother (when his 'unknown' mother, also on the barge, asks him to stay with them, he refuses!). What the narration does tell the spectator is that if you have breeding (even if you do not know that you have it), it will show through. These laundered images (*images d'Epinal* as they are known in French) are totally devoid of psychological realism primarily because they gloss over what being an orphan represents in relation to a sense of identity. Reassurance for the spectator comes in the very implausibility of the tale. Epstein's film, *La Maternelle*, functions precisely in the opposite direction, showing how a young orphaned child eventually finds a sense of identity for herself working in an infant school in a poor quarter of Paris.

Whereas many of the images of the 1930s sanitised social issues, those of the 1950s took a quite cynical and prurient path in the work of some of the new generation of film-makers (although older film-makers were not exempt – Decoin's *Dortoir des grandes* 1953, gives a fairly scabrous image of lesbianism in an all-girls' boarding school). Films by Ralph Habib and Yves Ciampi (for example), under the guise of tackling social problems, disintegrate into exploiting female sexuality and sanitise away the *real* problem. Habib's *La Rage au corps* and *Compagnes de la nuit* (both made in 1953) are, respectively, supposed to be about nymphomania and prostitution. Ciampi's film *L'Esclave* (also 1953) purports to deal with drug addiction. Instead of tackling the relevant issue, each film removes it. Drug addiction is removed by being represented as the problem of women *chanteuses* of Saint-Germain des Prés. Prostitution is relocated into pimping, or into a certain class of masters. Nymphomania, by being overexposed, becomes naturalised. Implicit in *La Rage au corps* is the notion that some women just want more sex than others. By constantly displaying the nymphomaniac *à l'oeuvre*, her behaviour becomes normalised – it becomes no longer an illness. In short, Habib's films serve to trivialise serious issues into basic soft porn. The spectator/voyeur has both the excitement of erotica and the moral superiority that s/he would never 'do this' (i.e., become victim to the pimps' exploitation or want too much sex).

The tradition of the drug scene and *chanteuses* goes back to the 1930s cinema (most famously, Fréhel in *Pépé-le-Moko* and *L'Entraîneuse*) and was represented then as the 'edifying spectacle of the miseries of the "lower classes" (Vincendeau: 1987, 113).[35] In other words, we watch it from a position of superiority. Now, in Ciampi's film, the salutory lesson appears to be a warning: 'this will happen to you if you get hooked into the *chanteuses* scene'. But there are two problems with Ciampi's representation. First of all the male protagonist, a song-writer, is an 'innocent' victim of his addiction – innocent because he was treated with morphine for an accident. It was only subsequently that he was dragged into the world of drugs by a *chanteuse* who became his lover. Because this is not an everyday tale of the possible it therefore becomes not a social problem *per se*. Second, whereas in the 1930s films, we only saw the results of drug addiction (on Fréhel's physique), in the 1950s films we are party to it in all its luridness, no holds barred. Thus the spectator is watching a film that, on the one hand, has ghettoised drug addiction, and on the other, has displayed the sordidness of this disease which in no way implicates the voyeur/spectator. Given bourgeois hostility to the Saint-Germain des Prés of the 1950s, this film confirms their impression of that quarter's debauchery (mental and physical) and removes the problem of drug addiction as a social phenomenon requiring attention. In other words, there is no shift in positioning from the 1930s, just greater prurience.

Apart from Tati's films, comedy in the 1950s marked an almost total abrogation of virtual reality. There was a spate of films starring Gérard Philipe as a 'rakish-but-charming' feckless seducer (e.g., *Fanfan la tulipe*, Christian-Jaque, 1951, a remake of Leprince's 1925 film of the same title, *Monsieur Ripois*, Clément, 1954, and *Pot-Bouille*, Duvivier, 1957). *Boulevard* comedy of pure badinage was a particular specialism of André Hunebelle (eighteen films between 1945 and 1958) with such titles as *Ma femme est formidable* (1951), *Mon mari est merveilleux* (1952) and *Les Femmes sont marrantes* (1957). But because it was a genre much enjoyed by the general public, other directors were not slow to join the gravy train. Christian-Jaque made *Adorables créatures* (1952), a film which centres around a number of sketches portraying a couple's mutual adultery, a scheming young woman landing her rich sugar daddy, an older woman with a predilection for younger men, etc.

Autant-Lara's film about social climbers (in this case the husband – and he dies of apoplexy) and marital infidelity, *Le Bon Dieu sans confession* (1953), was made with this same public in mind, as were the numerous films made by Sacha Guitry during this decade (*La Poison*, 1951, or how to murder your nagging wife successfully – hence feminisation of *poison*; *Je l'ai été trois fois*, 1952 – three times a cuckold; *La Vie d'un honnête homme*, 1952 – a twin brother takes over his deceased, but reprobate brother's business and decides to take over his way of life as well; finally, *Assassins et voleurs*, 1956 – shows how to become successful at killing and stealing). Farcical films starring Fernandel abound, averaging four a year. The dominant criterion of all these films (and of many more besides) is pleasure. All are marked by the same stamp of facileness and are seemingly content, through their sanitised images, to erect the myth that all is happiness. When it is recalled that comedy (which includes musicals as a sub-genre) made up almost half the production of the 1950s, and that the great majority of the comic films displayed a voluntarist myopia to social realities, then it is not difficult to perceive what the collective mentality required of its nation's second most important industry (as it was then). To obscure through pretence is not the sign of a healthy nation but of one that is doubtful of its identity and moral ground, one that is insecure and, although aware that there is a conflict of realities, one that feels that silence is the only response. It is perhaps in the light of this state of affairs that one can better understand Renoir's call for a moral renewal in France's cinema.

The last part of this chapter will be concerned with the war period (1939–45) and its unsignifiability after the war, as well as production during Vichy and its relationship to the National Revolution. The plethora of books (relatively speaking) on the Vichy/Occupation period attests to the disquiet this period causes – a disquiet equally manifest in the many contradictory conclusions the different authors come to. Some say there was no Vichy cinema (Siclier: 1981, 225), that is, that there was no propaganda cinema extolling the virtues of the National Revolution. Others claim that there was – and quite a lot, albeit subliminally (Bertin-Maghit: 1980, 104). Yet others gloss over it by saying it was French cinema's moment of renaissance (Courtade: 1978, 222). Others again say that there was some, but that it already predated Vichy, that is, Vichy was already part of the French mentality (Jeancolas: 1983, 298). This division on the transparence on the National Revolution, however, is not matched by the opinion of these same film historians (and others) on the postwar film products about the Occupation. In this instance, there is a consensus amongst them that the reality of the Occupation was left unspoken until Marcel Ophuls' *Le Chagrin et la pitié* (1970) and that the sacrosanct image of the Resistance was untouched until Jean-Pierre Melville's *L'Armée des ombres* (1969).

Immediately after the war, France's cinema produced quite a number of films about the war, chiefly about the Resistance (although it was not to become a genre/sub-genre until the 1960s). In this respect, for a brief period France's cinema did not show the same *pudeur* as it did after the 1914–18 war. But then it was a different war that it was now showing, not the earlier one of bloodshed and terrible loss of life, but an imaginary war, one in which France did not fight except as a *résistante*. In the post-Liberation period of 1944 and in 1945, eleven films about the war period were made, eight of which were about the Resistance. Overall, this production amounted to almost 15 per cent of the total film output (seventy-six films from August 1944 to December 1945). By the end of 1947, however, the production of these films was on the wane. From 1944 to 1958, out of the thirty films made about the war period in France's history, twenty-one were produced between 1944 and 1947 (i.e., 70 per cent). Interestingly, the 'greatest' period for this kind of film was 1959–73, a fourteen-year span during which fifty films were produced (even though this still only represented 4 per cent of total production). In the next fourteen years, 1974–88, production returned to the earlier figure of thirty films (which brought it back to the same percentage figure for 1944–58 of 2 per cent of total production).

The apparent dearth of films on the Resistance (fifteen between 1944 and 1947 and then nothing until 1952 – two films – and again nothing until

1956 – two films) was not due to a lack of scenarios, but to political expediency. Out of sixty scenarios submitted by January 1945, only six were authorised by a special pre-censorship committee set up by the *Commission militaire nationale*. The ostensible reason given was quality control and prevention of collaborators' participation. A further, unspoken reason, however, was France's need for national unity, which could only come about by a careful reconstruction of her shattered image. The Resistance was crucial to that reconstruction and to national unity. For that reason the myth of the Resistance had to be managed carefully. What is striking in these first films, supposedly about the Resistance, is their lack of authenticity (Comes and Marmin: 1984, 101). They are either spy stories which rehash old narrative lines of prewar films (*Le Jugement dernier*, 1945, is quite similar to *Double crime sur la ligne Maginot*, 1937) or films whose location provides an imprecise contemporaneity (like many of the Occupation films). This lack of authentic reference (the one exception being the quasi-documentary *La Libération de Paris*, 1944) reflects a different kind of *attentisme* from the Occupation period. Clearly it would take time to find an acceptable image grounded in authenticity that would simultaneously be capable of presenting a picture of a unanimously resistant France.

Interestingly, it fell to one of the new generation of film-makers, René Clément, to make *the* mythic film of the Resistance, *La Bataille du rail*, 1946.[36] This film, however, is not without its problems in its representation. Whilst it did offer a truer image than previous films of resistance activity (sabotage of the railway network to prevent the Germans transporting armaments and other supplies across France), it also made possible a *post hoc* identification with the Resistance – precisely because of its documentary look which privileged no particular railway worker. The French could all become Resistance fighters with hindsight.

The ordinariness of the Resistance fighter is reiterated in Clément's next film, *Le Père tranquille* (1946). Written by Noël-Noël, the film stars him as the central, eponymous character of the film. This quiet, undemonstrative personage, despised by his son for his inaction against the German occupiers, is in fact none other than the head of the local Resistance. Legitimation does not stop there: it covers all generations of ordinary people – even if only adjunctively. Thus, both his son and daughter have Resistance credence, the son because he joins the *maquis*, the daughter because she loves a man with Resistance connections. This trivialisation of French women's role in the Resistance by marginalising them in this way may well be connected to the political instability of the time and may not be unrelated to woman's recent enfranchisement, which was perceived as a threat to the republican spirit. For whatever reason, the real importance of women in the Resistance would have to wait until the 1960s before it made its way on to the screen (in Clément's *Le Jour et l'heure*, 1962, and

Melville's *L'Armée des ombres*, 1969, both starring Simone Signoret). For the moment it was to remain fairly token, as another film of this time, *Jéricho* (Daquin, 1946), makes clear (the woman here represents female Resistance because, she is in love with a *maquisard*).

In other respects, however, *Jéricho* does make a greater attempt at authenticity than *Le Père tranquille*. Based on a real event, the freeing of prisoners from an Amiens prison by allied bombing (the RAF), it reveals how not all the French were heroes. The prisoners concerned are those who have been randomly rounded up by the Germans in retaliation for Resistance attacks on their military installations. Supposedly representative of Occupied France, the group is composed of Resistance fighters (Catholic and Communist), black-marketeers, the courageous and uncourageous bourgeois, etc. This specific polemicising sets the film apart from *Le Père tranquille*'s troubling sanitisation of French comportment during the Occupation, but it joins ranks with Clément's film in its call for national unity under de Gaulle – a curious attestation to the climate of the times when it is recalled that Daquin was a Communist (the threat of civil war must have been very strongly felt for his, albeit implicit, endorsement of de Gaulle's leadership, although not all the Communist factions were hostile to de Gaulle during the Resistance).

The other main Resistance film, Melville's *Le Silence de la mer* (1949), is only such with hindsight. In terms of the timing of its release, it came out too late. The French mentality had 'moved on'. The Fourth Republic was born with all its attendant problems and the rallying call of the Resistance no longer had any resonance. In fact, 1946 was the watershed for Resistance films. Two other films, both by Dréville, also arrived too late on the scene – *La Bataille de l'eau lourde* (1947) and *Le Grand rendez-vous* (1949). The significance of these three films for the historian lies not with their audience appeal but with their relationship to authenticity. Dréville's 1947 film (a co-production with Norway) records an actual event that had occurred in occupied Norway and features some of those who took part in it (authenticity again as per the post-World War I films). The film relates the attempts of the Resistance to foil German efforts to seize a stock of heavy water intended for the manufacture of an atomic bomb. The second Dréville film refers to another real event, the American disembarkation in Algeria. In fact, of the three films mentioned, it is Melville's film that is the most fictional and yet it is the one that is referred to in histories of cinema as being a far more authentic image of resistance to the occupying forces than any of its antecedents. This provides an intriguing insight into what resistance/the Resistance has come to signify.

Melville's film narrates the resistance spirit of two French people, an uncle and his niece, to a German officer who has been billeted in their home. The German, convinced that culture can unite the two countries, tries repeatedly to engage in a conversation with the two, only to meet with stony silence. Their mutism is their resistance. If this film is the image of authentic resistance, then it implies that authenticity is less about fact than about correct positioning. This quasi-existential reading of the Resistance and the endorsement of this film as *the* film of the Resistance have come about, it seems to me, because of the *mise-en-abyme* of resistance itself which this film connotes. First, this film is based on a book written by Vercors, a pseudonym adopted during the war by Jean Bruller, an illustrator. Bruller took this name when he founded the clandestine publishing house *Editions de Minuit* as a protest against the German censorship of writers concretised in the *liste Otto* (a list established by Otto Abetz and sent to all publishing houses in Occupied France proscribing authors who were Jews, Communists or Socialists). Written in hiding in 1941, Vercors published his book, *Le Silence de la mer*, in 1943. But Vercors was not just a pseudonym: it was also to become one of the most famous *maquis* stakeouts. Here already, therefore, are four texts of resistance: Vercors/Bruller, the writer and symbol of the intellectual resistance, the clandestine publishing house, the clandestine publication, and Vercors the site of *maquis* resistance.

The second order of resistance texts concern the film. First, there is the film-maker, Melville, whose original name was Grumbach. He took on this pseudonym (in honour of the author of *Moby Dick*, a book whose central theme addresses the nature of evil) at the time of the Occupation when, in response to de Gaulle's call, he joined the Free France movement. Second, there is the film. Melville made it in 1947 without the permission of the pre-censorship board (by then located with the CNC). The clandestine book now becomes a film made in clandestineness. The conditions of production are also redolent with resistance resonances. Melville had minimal resources (since it was a clandestine product). With his limited budget and access only to mediocre film stock (bought on the black market – a non-resistant resonance), he made the film with a skeleton crew (which met with union outrage – another non-resistant resonance). When it was first made, Vercors himself did not want it screened because he felt its timing was still too close to the events of the Occupation. Eventually, in 1949 Vercors and a committee of Resistants finally approved the film and it was screened. It now had the cachet of Resistance legitimacy. So to the first order of intertexts concerning Vercors, comes this second order of intertexts: the first text of resistance, the clandestinely made film, becomes a second text, the authenticated text of the Resistance. Later this film became a third text of resistance when it was hailed by the *Cahiers du cinéma* group as resistant in its style to the *tradition de qualité* and, alongside another Melville film, *Bob le flambeur* (1955), as a trail-blazer for the New Wave. Of such connotations myths are made. But let us return to the war.

During the Occupation period itself some 220 films were made, out of which approximately 9 per cent could be deemed to have had clear Vichy or Nazi connotations.[37] Films in the Vichy category were pro-natalist, pro-filial obedience, pro-rural life and anti-city. In other words, they were replete with National Revolution messages. Similarly, there were films in this category that attacked every political grouping that was not Vichy. The other category (Nazi) targeted Jews as the source of what ailed France. They either owned too much of the country's capital, cinema industry, etc. or they were corrupters of youth – *Les Corrupteurs* (Pierre Ramelot, 1942, commissioned by the *Institut d'études sur la question juive*) was the most virulently anti-semitic in this regard. Freemasons were similarly targeted as debauchers of France's youth and as much the cause as the Jews for France losing the war – *Forces occultes* (Paul Riche, 1943) provided the most reactionary propaganda in this case. These two films merit attention because of the image of the nation's mentality that their narratives construct. Propaganda works by playing on myths that are powerfully ingrained in a nation's consciousness, and also through that consciousness's tendency to function atavistically. These films start from the accepted tenet of anti-parliamentarianism – a position widely held by France's right-wing political and military classes. Thus they appeal to a mentality that is resolutely grounded in pre-Republicanism when the nation was governed not by Freemasons and Jews but by the legitimate supreme authority, the King and the aristocratic classes (including the military). In this atavistic mode, it is easy to mobilise myths of endangerment to France's security in the form of the grasping, avaricious Jew and the ruthless, self-seeking Freemasons, as indeed these two films do. From there it is but a small step to a legitimation, within the nation's consciousness, of the systematic elimination of Jews and Freemasons.

Claims by some film historians that these two films were not widely seen (Chirat: 1983b, 51 and Siclier: 1981, 39) are contested by Jeancolas (1983, 355 and 357). *Les Corrupteurs* was shown as a feature short accompanying Decoin's hugely successful *Les Inconnus dans la maison* (1941). Decoin's film was made for Continental and was the German production company's first success since setting up in occupied France (Comes and Marmin: 1984, 119). As for *Forces occultes*, 450 copies were made and distributed around France – hardly an insignificant number (Jeancolas: 1983, 357). The evidence points to the fact that they were seen and widely so.

Elsewhere in other less identifiably Vichy films, any direct or indirect criticism of the bourgeoisie in films was to be read as an attack on the successive governments of the 1930s and the Third Republic in general which together had got France into her present predicament. These particular films were not based on contemporary France but on an imprecise contemporaneity, a fundamental contradiction which reflects the French mood of *attentisme* of that time (politicians today still hate most of all to be accused of *attentisme*, presumably because of its Occupation stigma). The mood was 'wait and see'. But conjuncturally alongside this refusal to get involved was the ineluctable fact that France's fate and that of her people was being decided. By staying outside, anything became possible, not least of which Pétain's *Etat Français* and its National Revolution.

Earlier in this chapter I pointed out how Vichy, in its anti-republicanism, was not a new phenomenon within France's political culture – quite the reverse – and how periods of dictatorship (Napoleon I and III and now Pétain) made the possessing classes feel more secure in the legitimacy of their ownership than did the different Republics. What dictatorships imply, however, is the ascendancy of the patriarch over the mother-nation and with it the infantilisation of the country's citizenry. It is not difficult to see how, at the interface of anti-republicanism and infantilisation, myths can easily be mobilised. Lacking a belief in republican principles means losing the mother-nation. However, a citizenry cannot be without identity, otherwise anarchy or civil war will break out, so the citizenry seeks solace in the father, behind whom it groups. This is what happened in France. Thus Pétain could rely on the myth of national harmony symbolised by his own person to consecrate his National Revolution and call on France morally to regenerate. What he was actually calling for was the restoration of a rigid social conservatism and a society where everyone remained in their place. This is manifest in his claims that only an inventory of past values would give France the necessary strength for renewal.

Apart from the clearly Vichyite/Pétainist films already alluded to (and listed in note 37), there are two areas in which cinematic production reflects the *arrièriste* ideology of Pétain's National Revolution. A nostalgic romanticism for the former national glory, as exemplified by the Second Empire and the Belle Epoque, finds strong representation in film, as do narratives favouring regionalism and decentralisation in relation to Paris. Of course, neither of these two discourses is Pétainist purely and simply. As I have already noted, they are ones that go back to the discourses of post-World War I cinema. What is different is the focus of these discourses. No longer are they just a case of escapism in the face of loss, they are also an expression of a need to come to an 'understanding' of what has happened – an understanding which comes down to the following bald statement: because republican governments rejected the values of the past and the merits of peasantism, France's glory is in tatters.

Oms (1975, 67) sees in the historical reconstruction and Belle Epoque films an attempt to uncover the meaning of history and to question the significance of nationalism. I cannot read them as assertively as that and would be more inclined to interpret them as an expression of unease in the face of a lost nation, a sense of being not at the centre, but outside, on the periphery of France-as-Nation/France-as-History. Films set in the past tend to valorise France's past national treasures such as Berlioz and his music (*La Symphonie fantastique*), Louis XVIII (*La Duchesse de Langeais*, de Baroncelli, 1941), Napoleon I and III (respectively in *Le Destin fabuleux de Désirée Clary*, Guitry, 1941, and *Lettres d'amour*, Autant-Lara, 1942). Elsewhere, in Cayatte's *Au bonheur des dames* (1943) for example, films celebrate the munificence of Belle Epoque capitalism and patriarchal philanthropy which in this instance – thanks to the likes of Aristide Boucicaut (founder of *Au bon marché*) – produced the huge departmental stores on the Paris boulevards.[38]

Curiously absent from this historical reconstruction tradition is Joan of Arc, surely *the* icon of France-as-History. She was in fact present in the press and on stage (even though the plays predate the war, going back as far as those of Péguy, who died in 1914), but her absence from the screen is remarkable. After all, the anglophobic resonances which her myth could engender would not have made a film about her necessarily proscribable by the pre-censorship board. The myth of Joan, is however, susceptible to a simultaneously nationalistic and anglophobic response in an audience. Thus, any potentially ambiguous polemicising in a film would be censorable. However, there is no evidence that attempts were made to submit scenarios on her life which would lead one to read this absence, this inability to renew her myth, as a sign of France's sense of otherness, of *dépaysement*.

The disorientation (*dépaysement*) felt by the French also finds an echo in the rural/city conflict films, and there are the usual prodigal or proto-prodigal son/daughter narratives – *Monsieur des Lourdines* (Pierre de Hérain, 1942) and *Patricia* (Paul Mesnier, 1942) being exemplary of these two aspects of the genre. But as one would expect, it is even more explicitly represented in those films set in an indeterminate present. *L'Assassinat du père Noël* (Christian-Jaque, 1941) is a film that temporo-spatially conflates these two types. A baron returns to his castle in the Savoie after a long journey around the world. Mystery surrounds him and eventually the rumour is spread that he has leprosy. The daughter of the globemaker in the village determines to become his servant and offers her services. Instead, the two fall in love, the baron turns out not to have leprosy and all ends well.

This first-order narrative tells of the unadvisability of going away (the baron's last lines are, 'why go all the way round the world when the ideal woman of my dreams is right here in my home village') and of the importance of stability within the community to a sense of well-being. However, there are second- and third-order narratives at play in this film. Both the father, Cornusse, and his daughter live in imaginary worlds of their own construction. Cornusse, with his globes, constantly invents stories of his travels (especially to China) with which to regale the village children (of which there are many). His daughter, Catherine, makes dolls, carries them around in her arms and dreams up fairy stories of an ideal prince. Whilst the images of Catherine appear to denote motherhood, in point of fact they connote quite the opposite. In her fantasy-land, she is closed off from reality and seems, at times, close to hysteria. Her hints of hysteria are counterpointed by the apparently real hysteria of Mother Michael, the slightly deranged nun who, by her vocation, is equally child-less. However, both speak the truth (have visions) which, mythically, is the lot of the mad. The village is in a siege mentality. It is cut off by the snow. A body wearing Cornusse's Santa Claus outfit has been discovered and a precious ring has been stolen from the church's nativity scene. Mother Michael denounces the culprit long before she is believed and he is apprehended. Catherine has a presentiment that her beloved baron is in danger. He is found bound and gagged in Cornusse's shop. He had happened upon one of the thieves, the now-dead Santa Claus. Suspicion falls on everyone, particularly on the schoolmaster – a Socialist and a brutish boor. In the end the culprit, the chemist, is apprehended. Miraculously, the ring is found. It had been hidden in Cornusse's shop sign – a glass globe (what and where else!) – which the children had stolen and then broken when playing with it in the snow. The smashing of the globe, of course, reinforces the first-order narrative about the merits of com-munity stability.

Through its symbolic representation (the dolls, the ring and the crib), the second-order narrative refers to the fertility imperative. Motherhood, therefore, is another sign of stability (i.e., non-hysteria). The third-order narrative juxtaposes alienation as truth with knowledge as danger. Three outsiders – Catherine, Mother Michael and the baron – all utter the truth. Their otherness, *dépaysement*, peripherality, is where truth lies. The one with knowledge, the schoolteacher, is seen as a menace who terrorises not only his pupils but also Catherine, to whom he makes brutish advances. Knowledge destabilises; truth, whatever its source, re-establishes order. The nostalgia for stability to which the three narratives refer can be interpreted on the one hand, as Pétainist in their discourses, and on the other, as reflecting the climate of the time. With regard to the first interpretation, it must be stressed that the reactionary ideology that attempted to prevent the rural exodus, the stress on fertility and the effect of education on the rural exodus, are as much 1920s and 1930s discourses as they are Pétainist. Certainly, they do not disturb Vichy ideology, but then very few, if any, films of that period did. As for the second interpret-ation, it is in the very location of these narratives – in an indeterminate present – that we can read the sense of disorientation caused by the overall impact of the Occupation.

If these images remained undisturbing to the Vichy ideology, what of films set in the past that could have been made into vehicles for subliminal counter-ideological messages? The fact that, in the main, there weren't any says a great deal about the innate conservatism of the cinema industry itself and far less about individual acts of courage amongst the industry's personnel. There are three films in the retro-nostalgic mode that are mostly cited by historians as being Resistance films: two Carné films *Les Visiteurs du soir* (1942), *Les Enfants du paradis* (1944-5) and Delannoy's *Pontcarral, Colonel d'Empire* (1942). The problem is, as with *Le Corbeau* and *Le Ciel est à vous* (two controversial films set in the indeterminate present), that these films lend themselves to a double reading. Thus *Les Visiteurs du soir* is a fairy story where love triumphs over evil. Until its closing shot, when the Devil turns the lovers into statues only to find that their hearts beat on, it is nothing more than a fairy story. The closing shot potentially creates a schism between signifier and signified and thereby a shift in the sign. The beating heart could now signify France's will to fight on despite the oppressor. A fairy story becomes a Resistance story, maybe. The case is less arguable, in my opinion, for *Les Enfants du paradis*. This film is a melodrama, a love story set against and within the arena of melodrama itself, the *théâtre du boulevard*. Garance's single utterance, '*j'aime la liberté*', is not enough to make it a Resistance film, any more than the production difficulties it encountered or the fact that Carné had Jews working on his film crew. Nor, necessarily was it Carné's intention that it be read as such, since he held back the film's screening until the Liberation.

Again, *Pontcarral* may well have some signs that could point the spectator to read it as a Resistance film, but only in the closing shots. Set in the beginning of the nineteenth century, the film narrates the exploits – both military and amorous – of Colonel Pontcarral (a characterisation loosely based on Marshal Bugeaud). His allegiances are to the Emperor (Napoleon I) and later Louis-Philippe. The Colonel is an honourable man, a man of the Empire who leads his regiment into the Algerian campaign in 1830. Algeria was invaded by France in 1830 and was the first country to constitute part of its new Empire. Pontcarral is therefore part of France's glorious past. So far it is difficult to read a Resistance discourse in all of this. What potentially prevent this film from falling into a Pétainist discourse, however, are its concluding shots. These were added by Delannoy and were not part of the original text (published in 1937, by curious coincidence the year of the World Exhibition in France). These shots show a memorial plaque in the desert commemorating Pontcarral's death in 1835. Filing past it and saluting are soldiers, but not any ordinary soldiers. These are the French-trained indigenous soldiers, the *Spahis*. In other words, France's modern Empire (represented by the *Spahis*) is saluting the founder member of France's new Empire (started in 1830 and represented here by Pontcarral). A bold image for France with Resistance connotations one might be led to believe, and one that might hold, provided one did not know one's history. The Resistance imagery starts to fade when it is brought to mind that the man in charge of Algeria in 1942 was General Giraud, a man loyal to Pétain and an avowed Vichyite. But Giraud was perceived as something of a hero in popular imagination because he had escaped from a German prison. He was made High Commissioner (replacing the assassinated Darlan) by the Allies anxious, after invading northwest Africa, to secure a neo-Vichyite regime in north Africa sympathetic to their cause. De Gaulle had expected to be appointed, but the Americans who accepted Vichy as the legitimate French government (which de Gaulle refused to do) chose Giraud instead. He maintained all of the regime's repressive legislation, including the decrees against Jews, and the systematic arrest and expulsion of de Gaulle's partisans in north Africa (McMillan: 1985, 141). In the closing shots of *Pontcarral* there is an implicit reference to Giraud and his soldiers – a troublesome sign indeed of/for the Resistance given the inevitable connection with Pétainism. This may be the benefit of hindsight speaking and a more generous reading might allow that, if anything else, these shots connote the very real lack of clarity (deliberate or not) that surrounded that time.

I said earlier that in the late 1930s, France's cinema was already manifesting a postwar mentality – a curious cart before the horses situation if ever there was one. Thus the conflicting messages of films of that time of pessimism and pacifism on the one hand, and on the other, of patriotism and national unity, show a clairvoyance and a more lucid foresight of what was to come than most films of the Occupation or Liberation periods could ever hope to reveal. This war which nobody could vouchsafe to speak about truthfully would need the end of another hidden war, France's fight with her colonies, before a clearer image could emerge. All of this is the province of the next chapter, and it is to this and the last thirty years of French cinema that I would like now to turn my attention.

NOTES

1 See Lagny, Ropars and Sorlin (1986), Lagny (1989) and Vincendeau (1985).
2 See Bertin-Maghit (1980 and 1989), Garçon (1984) and Jeancolas (1983).
3 For more detail on this fascinating period of political exchange see Larkin (1988, Chapters 3 and 9) and McMillan (1985, Chapters 10 and 11). Incidentally, McMillan (1985, 103) attributes the coining of the term not to Thorez (as Adereth does) but to the Radical Gaston Bergery (in 1933, so predating Thorez), a politician who was to evolve from being a staunch anti-Fascist to an eventual Vichyite.
4 Duvivier was amongst the directors who left France during the war and went to the States. He took *Untel père et fils* with him. The Americans had no trouble in perceiving its propaganda value and it was adapted into an English version and shown with a new title, *Heart of a Nation*. No ambiguity there.
5 See Adereth (1984, Chapter 4), Larkin (1988, Chapter 6) and McMillan (1985, Chapter 14).
6 Cinema theatres were also venues for resistance. Audiences first hissed and later (when the German authorities insisted that the lights be kept up) sneezed and coughed through the Newsreels showing German soldiers or Hitler. Allies bombed cinema theatres that were reserved for German soldiers (*SoldatKinos*).
7 Nor was the Fifth Republic without a Vichyite presence. Jean-Louis Tixier-Vignancourt, head of Vichy radio and cinema, sought the Presidency in 1965 and

eventually became a deputy in 1966. It is noteworthy that the ranks of the extreme Right had swollen in the 1960s due to the arrival in France of the *pieds-noirs*.

8 For the cinema world, seventy-three dossiers were submitted to the *Comité de la libération du cinéma français* (CLCF, the commission appointed to conduct the *épuration* of the film industry) but only twelve sentences were handed down ranging from the death penalty to short prison sentences. Otherwise there were brief suspensions from the industry. Two deaths were noted – the execution of the film-maker Jean Mamy (under the pseudonym of Paul Riche, he made *Forces occultes*, an anti-masonic film in 1943) for denouncing certain colleagues, and the suicide of Pierre Guerlais (the producer of Autant-Lara's *Mariage de chiffon*, 1941 and *Douce*, 1943) whose fraternising with the Germans during the Occupation was denounced by the commission (CLCF). The scriptwriter Jean Marquès-Rivière was condemned to death but escaped. Film-maker Pierre Caron and actors Robert Le Vigan and Maurice Rémy exiled themselves (terrified for his safety, Le Vigan, who had received death threats for his collaboration with the enemy, almost literally ran off the set of *Les Enfants du paradis*; Siclier: 1981, 115). Some actors' careers were ended – Mireille Balin, Corinne Luchaire and Josseline Gaël – and other people in the industry were suspended for a while – Arletty, Albert Préjean, Tino Rossi, Ginette Leclerc, Henri-Georges Clouzot, Henri Decoin. Some were sent to prison (Sacha Guitry and Pierre Fresnay) and then resumed their careers. Two production companies went through the *épuration*, Orange, whose productions were heavily sub- sidised by the Germans, and Nova Films which was directed by Jean Mamy (alias Paul Riche). See Bertin-Maghit (1989, Chapter 11), and for a full list of those sanctioned see his Annexe (430–6). See also Chirat (1983b, 78–97).

9 For further discussion of these issues which are central to French political culture see Hanley et al. (1989, 101–9) and Larkin (1988, 43 and 142–6).

10 See Jeancolas (1983, 55–61 and 92–7). Jeancolas makes the point that program- ming in the early 1930s was not dissimilar to that of the early silent cinema with 3–5 shorts followed by a feature film. He adds, however, that as purchasing power diminished (effects of the Depression), the audience wanted more for their money. By 1932 the double bill had been introduced and, in some cases, a mixed medium of cabaret or music-hall.

11 For more detail, see Abel's (1988, 1–24 and 145–67) excellent account and Jeancolas (1983, 190–207).

12 In fact, both films can be read as pro-National Revolution texts, the one through the notion of individual heroism and the other through the notion of bourgeois small-mindedness denouncing the corruption of democracy (i.e., Republicanism). Perhaps what was really being targeted by these criticisms was Clouzot's seeming inhumanity – there is no room for compassion in his films.

13 Nineteen issues of *L'Ecran français* were produced during the Occupation. Authors included Louis Aragon, Louis Daquin, Paul Eluard, Raymond Queneau, Jean-Paul Sartre, Pierre Seghers. (See Olivier Barrot's (1979) useful study of this review's history. With regard to the fascist press, it is now well known that Lucien Rebatet (an alias for François Vinneuil) was the film critic for *Je suis partout*. What may be less well known is that the editor of the robustly pro-German and antisemitic *Le Film* was P.A. Harlé, formerly editor of the influential trade magazine *Cinématographie française* (Jeancolas: 1983, 307). Harlé subsequently resumed his post as editor after the war, only relin- quishing that role when the magazine was merged with *Film français* in the mid-1960s.

14 The debate on who invented depth of field has been going on for a long time with the main contestants for the honour being Orson Welles (with his film

Citizen Kane, 1941) and Renoir. Bordwell and Thompson (1980, 278–9) talk of depth of field in relation to Renoir's film *Le Crime de Monsieur Lange* (1935) but Salt (1983, 269) makes the point that, although the technology for it was in place in the late 1930s, Renoir did not achieve deep focus. I will quote Barry Salt in full for the interested reader: 'All in all, any distinctive look that some French and German films of the period have is due far more to set and costume design than to features of their photography and scene dissection. Throughout the later 1930s just as in Hollywood, European photography continued to be at, or near, maximum aperture, and the faster film stocks were not used to achieve smaller apertures and hence greater depth of field. For the last time, there is *no* "deep focus" in Jean Renoir's films, just extensive use of staging in depth, sometimes beyond the limits of sharp focus. And occasionally he uses a surreptitious focus-pull to sharpen the back-ground slightly when the main interest in the shot moves there and vice-versa.'

15 Curious then that Truffaut should have made *Jules et Jim* (1961), his first film in cinemascope, in black and white until one realises that the insertion of real World War I footage may have demanded the use of black and white so as not to break the deliberate sense of seamlessness and timelessness in the film. In another respect, it was not apparent that the French were overzealous for colour. By the mid-1950s, only 50 per cent of French production was in colour, and black and white films were topping the list of receipts: *Gervaise* (Clément, 1955) and *La Traversée de Paris* (Autant-Lara, 1956). It is also true that television was not the great threat to France's film industry as it was to the States' industry and colour was not introduced to French television until 1967. For the record, only two colour films were made immediately after the war: *Le Mariage de Ramuntcho* (Marc de Vaucorbeil, 1946) and *La Belle meunière* (Pagnol, 1948). Finally, of course, there may have been purely financial reasons on Truffaut's part.

16 I'll quote his most damning, not to say vitriolic paragraph. 'There are less than seven or eight scriptwriters who work regularly for French cinema. Each of these scriptwriters has only one story to tell and since each one aspires to the success of the "two greats" (Aurenche & Bost), it is no exaggeration to say that the hundred or so French films made each year all tell the same story: it is always about a victim, most generally a cuckold.' (*Cahiers*, no. 31, 1954, p. 23).

17 Lyautey dreamed of reconciling Islamic and French cultures – an ambition he never fulfilled. However, the modernising of Casablanca from a village into a great port and the exploitation of poorly treated land into fertile farms (by French *colons*) were two of his great achievements, earning him the nickname 'Lyautey Africanus' (Brogan: 1989, 269). None the less, he did achieve his ambition in a mythic sense when he was appointed General Commissionaire for the 1931 Colonial Exhibition in Paris. Elsewhere, as a testimony to his importance in the French colonial mentality, he appears, acted by Gabriel Signoret, in L'Herbier's *Hommes nouveaux* (1936), a film dedicated to showing the well-doings of colonial France and there was to have been a film *Lyautey l'africain*, due to commence in March 1939 (Jeancolas: 1983, 257), but which presumably was never completed (in any event there is no trace of it).

18 Pierre Sorlin (1991) has written an informative essay on French colonial films in the 1930s.

19 Exiles to France, many of whom fairly quickly moved on to Hollywood, included Fritz Lang, Richard Pottier, Erich Pommer, Robert Siodmark, Max Ophuls, Georg-Wilhelm Pabst, Billy Wilder, Robert Weine, Eric von Stroheim, Alexandre Korda, and the actress Dita Parlo. French film-makers who went to

Germany included Henri-Georges Clouzot, Jean Grémillon, Edmond T. Gréville and Henri Roussell. French actors who went through the Berlin studios included Annabella, Florelle, Jean Gabin, Henri Garat, Albert Préjean and Françoise Rosay.

20 For more information on this, see Jeancolas (1983, 116ff) and Léglise (1970, 67ff).

21 Richard Pottier who had exiled himself to France was one of the most prolific (five films), a fact that would attest to Greven's apolitical, if not a-nazi, stance. It is documented that he probably feigned ignorance of Jean-Paul Le Chanois's real identity and half-Jewish parentage (Jean-Paul Dreyfus). The Continental output included Christian-Jaque's notorious *Symphonie fantastique* – notorious because Goebbels saw in the depiction of Berlioz as a magnificent musician a cultivation of France's nationalism. He wanted the French to see only light films empty of all polemic (Bertin-Maghit: 1989, 23). The twelve directors were: Fernandel (two films), Jean Dréville (one), Christian-Jaque (two), Henri-Georges Clouzot (two), Henri Cayatte (four), Richard Pottier (five), Maurice Tourner (five), Maurice Gleize (one), Georges Lacombe (one), Henri Decoin (three), Pierre Caron and René Jayet (both with one apiece). For more detail see Jacques Siclier's (1981) very useful study of the film output during the Occupation.

22 Again pointing to the mysogyny of some of the *Cahiers* contributors. Truffaut cites these names in his Introduction to Bazin (1981, 11).

23 For more detail see Chirat (1985, 137ff).

24 I am referring here to John Martin's (1987, 90 and 118) characterisation of French society in the 1930s as the age of masks.

25 Siclier (1990, 40) identifies one attempt at representing the working class in an Yves Allégret film, *La Meilleure part* (1955), a film about workers on a damn site in the mountains.

26 This film was initially intended to star Gabin and Dietrich. However, they dropped out of the project and Carné had to 'make do' with an inexperienced pair to play the fated lovers, Yves Montand and Nathalie Nattier. In Carné's mind it would seem that he never saw it as anything other than a Gabin film because the predictable 'Gabin explodes' scene is left in, even to the point of using 'Gabin-speak'. Diego losing his temper at the snivelling *collabo* yells at him '*est-ce que tu vas te taire?*', repeating it again and again louder and louder, but sadly with none of the vigour and venom of the Gabin delivery in *Le Jour se lève* and so many of his other films.

27 It is interesting and perhaps not coincidental that, in my research for this chapter, I have only come across women writers on this period raising this point with any consistency. See Geneviève Guillaume-Grimaud (1986) and Geneviève Sellier (1981).

28 For a very full analysis of the 'Pagnol' trilogy see Vincendeau (1990, 67–82).

29 It is to be hoped that the universal appeal of this theme has found its apogee and thus nadir in Corinne Serreau's *Trois hommes et un couffin* (1985).

30 Anecdotally it is worth mentioning that at the time of the trilogy's staging and filming as well as that of *Angèle*, Pagnol was married to Demazis. Later, at the time of making *La Fille du puisatier*, he was married to Day.

31 In *Angèle* and, more especially, *La Fille du puisatier*, the single mothers are represented as not needing men to help them cope. Angèle's story is much harsher than Patricia's, however. Once persuaded to come home to her father and mother, she is locked away by her tyrannical father and left at one point to drown.

32 The film *Martin Roumagnac* was little more than a vehicle for Gabin, his famous

'Gabin-speak' ('tu vas te taire?', etc.) and his repeated outbursts of anger and violence against his lover, played by Marlene Dietrich. In my own humble opinion, I feel this duo would have been better advised to have plumped for Carné's *Portes de la nuit* (of the same year), the film they were originally supposed to make. The thinness of the story line – Martin/Gabin gradually ruining himself for a woman of easy virtue (Blanche!) but with class – reduces this film to a poor simulacrum of the prewar lover-killer films starring Gabin.

33 Becker raises these points in an interview with *Cahiers du cinéma* vol. 6, no. 32, February 1954.

34 See Doniol-Valcroze (1954) 'Déshabillage d'une petite bourgeoise sentimentale', *Cahiers du cinéma*, vol. 4, no. 31, pp. 2–14. Misogyny seems rife through this period. For a sample list of films I would refer the reader to *La Marie du port*, Carné, 1950, *Méfiez-vous des blondes*, Hunebelle, 1950, *Caroline chérie*, Pottier, 1950, *La Ronde*, Ophuls, 1950, *La Poison*, Guitry, 1951, *La Jeune folle*, Allégret, 1952, *Le Rideau cramoisi*, Astruc, 1952, *Adorables créatures*, Christian-Jaque, 1952, *Mina de Vaughel*, Clavel, 1952, *Le Bon Dieu sans confession*, Autant-Lara, 1953, *Mme de . . .* , Ophuls, 1953. Although not of this period (1949–53), we should not neglect the powerful revenge story in *Les Diaboliques*, Clouzot, 1955 – a sure indication that this is a tradition that will not go away.

35 Amongst the *chanteuses* focused on in Vincendeau's essay are Fréhel and Piaf. Lys Gauty, singer of *La Chaland qui passe*, which was controversially inserted into Vigo's film *L'Atalante* after his death, also figures in this essay, as do the *chanteuses* perhaps less known to the Anglo-Saxon reader, Yvonne George and Berthe Sylva. For other readings on this topic see Adrien Rifkin's essay, 'Musical moments', in *Yale French Studies*, no. 72, 1987.

36 There is some ambiguity surrounding the inception of this film which might serve to explain why it joins ranks, in the end, with the myth-making practices so tied into the Resistance. Even though this film was commissioned by the *Coopérative du cinéma* in conjunction with *Résistance Fer* (Hackett: 1946b, 51), it was also made under the auspices of the *Commission militaire nationale* (see Adolphe Nysenholc, 'Propagande de guerre et de cinéma', *Revue Belge du cinéma*, no. 8, 1984, p. 29).

37 In the pro-National Revolution category we can list: (1) in the pro-natalist vein – *Vénus aveugle* (Gance, 1940, and dedicated to Pétain), *Le Voile bleu* (Stelli, 1942), *La Nuit merveilleuse* (Paulin, 1940), *Escalier sans fin* (Lacombe, 1943), *Péchés de jeunesse* (Tourneur, 1941), *La Loi du printemps* (Daniel-Norman, 1942), *La Fille du puisatier* (Pagnol, 1940), *Le Premier rendez-vous* (Decoin, 1941), *Le Carrefour des enfants perdus* (Joannon, 1943); (2) in the conflict of generations, filial obedience and back to the earth vein – *Untel père et fils* (Duvivier, 1940), *Le Cap au large* (Paulin, 1942); (3) in the individual heroism vein – *Le Ciel est à vous* (Grémillon, 1943) *Premier de cordée* (Daquin, 1944) and totally separately in a vein all on its own but there because of the ambiguity of its message, *Le Corbeau* (Clouzot, 1943). In the Nazi category we can list: (1) in the anti-Jew and anti-masonic vein – *Le Péril juif* (produced by the Institut des études juives and attributed to Pierre Ramelot, 1941 – Jeancolas: 1983, 344), *Les Corrupteurs* (Ramelot, 1943), *Forces occultes* (Riche, 1943), *Les Inconnus dans la maison* (Decoin, 1941); (2) in the anti-all that is not pro-Vichy vein – *Monsieur Girouette* (Ramelot, 1942), *Résistance* and *Patriotisme* (two fictional shorts, 1944); (3) in the pro-German vein – *Fort Cambronne* (1943). For more details see Jeancolas (1983, 319–60), Bertin-Maghit (1989, 135–52), and for a résumé of some of the scenarios see Siclier (1981).

38 This film was an adaptation of a Zola novel. It is, however, quite a travesty of

Zola's message and, incidentally, a sanitised reconstruction of Aristide Boucicaut who is the real person upon whom Zola's character, Mouret, is based. Boucicaut's principles were based on modern capitalism and enlightened paternalism. His first principle was to rotate stock quickly. To accomplish this, clients had to be made welcome and personnel feel cared for. Free entry to the store, prices clearly marked, return and exchange of goods, low profit on goods – all were measures employed to entice clientele. Accommodation for female personnel and the principle of commission were just two of the methods he used to guarantee quality staff service and returns. Zola obliterates much of this in his anti-capitalist stance. He hated Napoleon III for bringing France into the age of capitalism and his novel shows the scheming Mouret outbidding and buying out all the local small shopkeepers so that his store can reign supreme. In the film, Mouret's characterisation is quite muddled. He is depicted as a ruthless businessman with a heart of gold who eventually becomes a true philanthropist thanks to falling in love with the niece of one of the small shopkeepers he has effectively ruined. In both fictionalised texts, Boucicaut/Mouret is represented as a capitalist *tout court*. In fact, in capitalist circles of the time he was seen as a Red (i.e., quite left wing in his thinking).

BIBLIOGRAPHY

Abel, R. (1988) *French Film Theory and Criticism: A History/Anthology Volume II, 1929–1939*, New Jersey, Princeton University Press.

Adereth, M. (1984) *The French Communist Party: A Critical History (1920–84)*, Manchester, Manchester University Press.

Barrot, O. (1979) *L'Ecran Français 1943–1953: Histoire d'un journal et d'une époque*, Paris, Editeurs Français Réunis.

Bazin, A. (1981) *French Cinema of the Occupation and Resistance*, trans. Stanley Hochman, New York, Ungar.

—— (1983) *Le Cinéma français de la Libération à la Nouvelle Vague (1945–1958)*, Paris, Cahiers du Cinéma, Editions de L'Etoile.

Bertin-Maghit, J.-P. (1980) *Le Cinéma français sous Vichy, les films français de 1940–1944*, Paris, Ça Cinéma.

—— (1989) *Le Cinéma sous l'Occupation*, Paris, Olivier Orban.

Beylie, C. (1975) 'Réévaluations', *Les Cahiers de la cinémathèque*, no. 8.

Bordwell, D. and Thompson, K. (1980) *Film Art: An Introduction*, Reading, Massachusetts, Addison-Wesley Publishing Company (second reprint of 1979 original).

Brogan, D.W. (1989) *The French Nation: From Napoleon to Pétain 1814–1940*, London, Cassell Publishers Ltd (originally published by Hamish Hamilton Ltd, 1957).

Buchsbaum, J. (1988) *Cinéma Engagé: Film in the Popular Front*, Illinois, University of Illinois Press.

Chirat, R. (1983a) *Le Cinéma français des années 30*, Renens, 5 Continents, Hatier.

—— (1983b) *Le Cinéma français des années de guerre*, Renens, 5 Continents, Hatier.

—— (1985) *La IVe République et ses films*, Renens, 5 Continents, Hatier.

Comes, P. and Marmin, M. (1984) *Le Cinéma français 1930–1960*, Paris, Editions Atlas.

Courtade, F. (1978) *Les Malédictions du cinéma français*, Paris, Alain Moreau.

Garçon, F. (1984) *De Blum à Pétain*, Paris, Editions du Cerf.

Guillaume-Grimaud, G. (1986) *Le Cinéma du Front Populaire*, Paris, Lherminier.

Hackett, H. (1946a) 'The French cinema during the occupation', *Sight and Sound*, vol. 15, no. 57.

—— (1946b) 'The French cinema since the Liberation', *Sight and Sound*, vol. 15, no. 58.

Hanley, D.L., Kerr, A.P. and Waites, N.H. (1989) *Contemporary France: Politics and Society since 1945*, London, Routledge (new edition).

Hennebelle, G. (1974) 'La Grande trahison du cinéma français de 1945 à nos jours', *Ecran*, no. 21.

Hillier, J. (1985) *Cahiers du Cinéma: The 1950s*, London, Routledge and Kegan Paul.

Jeancolas, J.-P. (1983) *15 ans des années trente: le cinéma des français 1929–1944*, Paris, Stock.

Lagny, M. (1989) 'Epistémologie de l'histoire', in *Histoire du cinéma: nouvelles approches*, Paris, Publications de la Sorbonne.

Lagny, M., Ropars, M.-C. and Sorlin, P. (1986) *Générique des années trente*, Saint-Denis, Presses Universitaires de Vincennes.

Larkin, M. (1988) *France since the Popular Front: Government and People 1936–1986*, Oxford, Oxford University Press.

Léglise, P. (1970) *Histoire de la politique du cinéma français, Tome I: Le Cinéma et la IIIᵉ République*, Paris, Lherminier.

—— (1977) *Histoire de la politique du cinéma français, Tome II: Le Cinéma entre les deux Républiques (1940–1946)*, Paris, Lherminier.

Magny, J. (1991) 'Le Septième art selon André Bazin', in Hennebelle, G. (ed.) *Histoires des théories du cinéma, CinémAction*, no. 60.

McMillan, J.F. (1985) *Dreyfus to De Gaulle: Politics and Society in France 1898–1969*, London, Edward Arnold.

Martin, J.W. (1987) *The Golden Age of French Cinema: 1929–1939*, London, Columbus Books.

Olive, J.-L. (1984) '*L'Appel du silence* ou le traumatisme français de Foucauld à Saganne', *Les Cahiers de la cinémathèque*, no. 40.

Oms, M. (1975) 'Le Charme discret du cinéma de Vichy', *Les Cahiers de la cinémathèque*, no. 8.

Prédal, R. (1972) *La Société française (1914–1945) à travers le cinéma*, Paris, Armand Colin.

Sallée, A. (1988) *Les Acteurs français*, Paris, Bordas.

Salt, B. (1983) *Film Style and Technology: History and Analysis*, London, Starword.

Sellier, G. (1981) 'Ces singuliers héritiers du cinéma français des années trente', *Cinéma 81*, no. 268.

Siclier, J. (1981) *La France de Pétain et son cinéma*, Paris, Henri Veyrier.

—— (1990) *Le Cinéma français 1: de La Bataille du rail à La Chinoise*, Paris, Ramsey.

Sorlin, P. (1991) 'The fanciful Empire: French feature films and the colonies in the 1930s', *French Cultural Studies*, vol. 2, part 2, no. 5.

Vincendeau, G. (1985) 'French Cinema in the 1930s: Social Texts and Contexts of a Popular Entertainment Medium', unpublished Ph.D. thesis, University of East Anglia.

—— (1987) 'The *mise-en-scène* of suffering: French *chanteuses réalistes*', *New Formations*, Winter, no. 3.

—— (1990) 'In the name of the father: Marcel Pagnol's "trilogy", in Hayward, S. and Vincendeau, G. *French Film: Texts and Contexts*, London, Routledge.

3 EMBLEMATIC SHOTS OF THE MODERNIST ERA OF CINEMA: WOMAN, THE WORKING CLASS AND NOT TALKING ABOUT THE WAR

Woman under patriarchal vigilance: *Angèle*, Pagnol, 1934

Woman as social climber: *L'Entraîneuse*, Valentin, 1940

Woman as destroyer of working-class solidarity: *La Bête humaine*, Renoir, 1938

Gabin in his 'pre-fetish star' mode as a comic in *Les gaietés de l'escadron*, Tourneur, 1932

The working-class male moves into gangster-chic: *Touchez pas au grisbi*,
Dassin, 1954

Postwar acquiescence: *Les Miracles n'ont lieu qu'une fois*, Allégret,
1950

Silence as resistance: *Le Silence de la mer*, Melville, 1949

Chapter 4

From ideology to narcissism: French cinema's age of the postmodern 1958–91

In the Introduction to this book, the point was made that within every art movement and art form there are two apparently codifiable trends: mainstream and avant-garde art. Mainstream art recodifies the dominant praxis – makes anew what is already there. In this respect it is either heavily dependent on its immediate predecessors or else it harks back to earlier art forms. Thus it is not unequivocal to say that mainstream art opposes change and as such serves to preserve the dominant ideology. In its unidirectional reflection, this art can be qualified as symptomatic and unoppositional. In its most extreme forms this can lead to academicism or to mannerism. Conversely, avant-garde art, as its name suggests, is art before its time – art looking forward not backwards (as mainstream predominantly does), attempting to break terrain with its implicit subversion of the old codes and conventions. Symptomatic, mainstream art runs the danger of semiotic reductionism. Conversely, oppositional art displays itself as redolent with semiotic expansionism.[1]

Cinema as a cultural production presents no exception to this aesthetic dualism of mainstream versus avant-garde art. Either it reflects a given image or series of discourses and, as such, is politicised from without – in this respect it is co-opted into the dominant ideology and, as such, contributes to a dominant matrix of social and political perceptions – or it refuses that role of reflection and the secure iconography that goes with it, and by so doing subverts the political and aesthetic hegemonies, in which case it is politicised from within. The postmodern cinema, from 1958 to the 1990s, is consistent with this trend. Before considering the two trends of cinema's postmodern age, I shall briefly discuss what the term postmodern implies.

The postmodern as an effect is a reaction against the established forms and canons of modernism. As an effect it also represents the erosion of the distinction between high and popular culture. The postmodern does not, however, refer to style; rather, it refers to a periodising concept 'whose function is to correlate the emergence of new formal features in culture with the emergence of a new type of social life and a new economic order' (Jameson: 1983, 113). In other words, it is a conjunctural term at the interface between artefact and the new moment of capitalism. In the case of France this moment dates from the birth of the Fifth Republic, again justifying the nomenclature for this age of cinema as postmodern. This new moment of capitalism is varyingly called modernisation, post-industrial and post-colonial society, consumer society, media society, etc. What is significant is that the term postmodern is consistent with the way in which Western contemporary society defines itself – that is, in relation to the past (e.g., post-industrial) but also in relation to social practice (consumer) and technology (media). Equally significant is the deliberate omission (by the French at least) of the 'ism', *le postmoderne*. This suggests that postmodernity is not a style or, in any event, cannot be labelled as an historical style in the way that classicism and modernism are. In its consistency with Western definitions, the postmodern looks back, is retrospective, is not defined as other, but as *post*modern, as coming after. In its lack of history it rejects history, and because it has none of its own – only that of others – the postmodern stands eternally fixed in a series of presents. In relation to the contemporary cultural aesthetic, the postmodern in its mainstream mode manifests itself through mannerism and stylisation. In cinema, fixity triumphs over disruption (Hebdige: 1979, 119), formalism and retro-discourses over film-making practices and meaning construction.

The postmodern age is more akin to a cult than to a movement. The very absence of the 'ism' warns us that this is a non-collective phenomenon which, by implication (because it is not part of a group), addresses the cult of the individual. Curiously, this contemporary hedonism recalls the aesthetic culture of the Symbolists at the end of nineteenth-century France – a neo-romantic nihilism wherein the individual artist became a cult figure (the life of the artist turned into a work of art, a way of life marked by uselessness and superfluousness). The *'fin de siècle'* mood of that time was a reaction to the political, intellectual and moral crises taking place at the national level, and the art that period produced was – even when in an oppositional mood – non-collective and individuated. Bourgeois values were rejected but simultaneously art turned in on itself. The death of ideology, as represented by the end of the Second Empire and the crushing of the Commune (1870–1), left the artist in the presence of a spiritual void. The concern for the artist now became a question of how to fill the nothingness of the abyss. The response was aestheticism, art as an end in and of itself, a contemplative art which led to a self-sufficient formalism. In other words, only form – not meaning or content – could fill the void.

The *'fin de siècle'* mood of this, the twentieth century, is once again conditioned by the death of ideology – not just on a micro-level in France, but on a macro-level – this time engendered by the apocalyptic events of the Holocaust and the dropping of the Bomb. How to go on, knowing what we know? Such is the wailing cry of Beckett's characters. How to invent, when invention can lead to such wholesale self-destruction? Such is the morose message of Kiefer's canvases. In answer to these daunting, perhaps unanswerable questions, postmodern culture bifurcates. The majority tendency is unoppositional, symptomatic postmodernity (a uni-directional reflection) providing a conservative cultural production – in other words, mainstream culture. The minority is avant-garde and oppositional.

It is convenient to see the avant-garde postmodern age of cinema as a logical, though not exclusive outcome of the writings of the *Cahiers* group. This is in fact a very poor approximation of the truth, but even if we accept this simplified version of the advent of oppositional avant-garde, this avant-garde itself is not without its problematics because the tendency has been to conflate the two moments of its production (early and late 1960s). This has meant that the first New Wave (1958–62), which was anarchic only in relation to the cinema that had preceded it (*le cinéma de papa*), has become imbricated into the more ostentatiously political cinema of the second New Wave (1966–8). In terms of the number of film-makers involved in production, the New Wave cinema (mark one) in France came of age in 1958–9 with the intention of putting into practice the theories of style advocated by the *Cahiers* group during the 1950s. This cinema rejected the cinema of the modernist age and focused its attention on the importance of the auteur and *mis-en-scène*. In short, the collective was out and the individual in. With *mis-en-scène* prioritised, the potential for pure formalism was there for all to see. The New Wave film-makers manifested their avant-gardism not just through their subversion of the mainstream cinema of their predecessors but also through their concerted attempts at a complete rupture with modernist cinematic codes, both narrative and visual. There was no *récit*, no realistic story as such (i.e., no beginning, middle and end) and no literary adaptations as in 'high art' literature (i.e., if any it was popular and pulp fiction that was adapted). The time became the 'now-ever-present' of the 1950s and 1960s. The discourses were contemporary and about young people. By the second New Wave there was no positive reflection of the dominant ideology to be found. Mercilessly, bourgeois myths were taken to bits and denormalised. The consumer boom, nuclear war, Vietnam, student politics, adolescence – all were subjects for treatment. By now, the consumer boom (already criticised in the first New Wave) was not about comfort and a better way of life but about prostituting the self in order to be better able to consume. The most important consumer durable of that time, the car, was exposed as the machine of violence and death into which our covetousness had transformed it – a minotaur of our age (*la déesse*), the consumer durable that consumes us.

In terms of the visual, this New Wave cinema (mark one and two), unceremoniously deconstructed the institutional iconography before the spectators' eyes. The establishing shots (which safely orientated the spectator in terms of space and time) were excised. A fast editing style (achieved by jump cuts and unmatched shots) replaced the seamless editing style that had prevailed before. The camera abandoned the studios and went out into the streets and suburbs of Paris (Paris was the one icon that did not disappear, although now she was 'truly' represented). This cinema, therefore, was as much about the process of film-making as it was about desanitising the sacred cows of the bourgeoisie. Film-making practice (the technology of the media) exposed social practice (consumption). This last point is quite important because it prevented this cinema from fulfilling its potential for self-reflexiveness. Had this cinema focused purely on form (the process of film-making), on what could be termed the gesture of representation, then the implicit self-reflexiveness would have led to the unyielding formalism (one might almost say to a necrocinephilia) associated with the '*fin-de-sièclisme*' of the nineteenth century and which came to typify much of the mainstream cinema of the 1980s.

This avant-garde postmodern cinema of the New Wave was short-lived. With a few exceptions (Godard being *the* exemplar, but amongst contemporaries Varda and Resnais could be cited although they are not specifically New Wave), New Wave film-makers continued their careers in more mainstream cinema. The 1970s would briefly see a new type of oppositional cinema in the work of women film-makers – mostly, at least initially, associated with the women's movement. And throughout this thirty-year period, as in the previous ages, individual film-makers would continue to produce oppositional cinema (Bresson being a prime example). The major difference with previous ages is the prevalence of individuated work as opposed to the notion of the collective. In previous periods the avant-garde of the 1920s regrouped film-makers under their varying umbrellas and the socio-realist and poetic-realist film-makers of the 1930s constituted a visible movement and worked as teams. Only exceptionally could one talk of teamwork with the New Wave film-makers (Truffaut being the most obvious example).

The brief popularity of this New Wave cinema (in its first years it was virtually as popular as mainstream cinema) coincided with the political culture in which it found itself and with the most politically tense moments in France's history of that period. The first period of popularity, 1958–62, coincided with the radical effect on institutions of the advent of the Fifth Republic and its new constitution. This time also marked the bloody decolonising of Algeria. The second period of popularity, 1966–8, coincided with the progressive disenchantment with de Gaulle's authoritarian presidential style, unrest on social and educational levels due to a lack of resources to accommodate the expanding urban society and student university numbers, workers' concern at their conditions, and lastly concern with the rise in unemployment, all of which culminated in the events of May 1968. In some respects, therefore, this cinema was being kept alive

Fetish 'stars' of the New Wave: Jeanne Moreau
and Jean-Claude Brialy

Arguably the biggest comic of French sound cinema:
Louis de Funès

B.B. – Brigitte Bardot takes the money and runs for animal rights

by the instability of France's institutions at those times of great political upheaval – an instability which the New Wave (though not a political cinema) so clearly reflected through its praxis.

FRANCE 1958–91

Although cinema of this age lacks an 'ism', this is not the case within the political arena. In the last thirty years France has experienced two long periods of a single president in power – de Gaulle (1958–69) and Mitterrand (1981– and still in power at the time of writing). The terms Gaullism and Mitterrandism serve as proof of the reality of the president-ialisation of the Republic in that both the 1960s and the 1980s are eras typified by the name of the head of state. Not surprisingly this presidential stability has meant that the Fifth Republic has been one in which constitu-tional matters have played a dominant part in the political agenda. This thirty-year period has also been marked by two radical swings within electoral voting patterns which in effect put these two men into power and allowed them to leave their names as political signifiers. The first, in 1958, was a sharp swing to the Right. This swing led to the collapse of the PCF, a situation from which it has never really recovered.[2] The crisis in Algeria was a prime mover for this swing in the vote. In May of 1958, Corsica had been invaded by Algerian-based French troops, and in Algeria itself the generals in command had formed themselves into a military junta and were preparing to launch their plan, *Operation Resurrection* – a plan to occupy Paris should parliament refuse to hand over control of the government to de Gaulle. The then government of the Fourth Republic felt it had no alternative but to call on de Gaulle to stabilise a situation which was putting public safety gravely at risk. De Gaulle agreed to become the necessary arbiter on the Algerian question and was invested on 1 June 1958. However, he only agreed to this investiture on condition that parlia-ment would grant him the constitutional reforms he deemed necessary to a national recovery (Larkin: 1988, 266). The panic caused amongst the general public by these events, therefore, was a major cause for the swing to the Right in voting which produced 206 seats for the Gaullists and an overall majority for the Right of 416 seats out of a total of 578.

No such drastic situation brought about Mitterrand's and the Left's victory of 1981. However, the vote for the Left did come about as a consequence of Gaullism and the overriding effect of the constitution of the Fifth Republic. De Gaulle's constitution, in a nutshell, effectively shifted the emphasis of power away from the legislative body and invested it more fully in the executive – that is, in the presidential body. Political stability could only come about, de Gaulle reasoned, if a nation was secure in its self-esteem and if the state made possible a crystallisation of social bonds (ibid., 281–2). To this effect, he perceived the desirability of a strong executive that could give 'direction and coherence to the disparate demands of a divided electorate' at the same time as a representative parliament (the legislature) – albeit with lesser powers than in the past – would guarantee democratic safeguards (ibid., 282). The changes in the constitution strongly reflected de Gaulle's idea of France and his firm belief in the nation-state. His idea of France was 'both an ideal and a political device designed to legitimate the authority of the French state and unify the French people' (McMillan: 1985, 158). It must not be forgotten that in the late 1950s, France was still deeply divided internally as a consequence not just of the Algerian crisis but also of earlier, yet unerasable moments in her history – most notably the 1940s Occupation and the Indo-China crises of the 1950s. De Gaulle saw patriotism as the unifying force in French national life. Patriotism and the nation-state were key, closely inter-connected concepts to de Gaulle's thinking. These concepts were to take him further still in his radicalising reforms so that by 1962 he had instituted through popular referendum the election of the president by universal suffrage. This close bond between state and citizenry – exemplified by the president being the universally acclaimed choice of the electorate – was, according to de Gaulle's thinking, a double-edged contract between the representative of the nation-state and the nation itself, and a contract that would guarantee national unity.

Essentially, de Gaulle's constitutional reforms (1958 and 1962) come down to five major principles. The executive power was separated from the legislature. Both the executive and legislative powers were to be elected by universal suffrage. The government would be responsible to the legislature and an independent judiciary was to be maintained. Finally, the relation-ship between France and her overseas territories was to be reformed. In so far as the president was now elected by universal suffrage (thanks to the 1962 constitutional reform), de Gaulle felt he had secured the legitimacy of the presidency to represent the nation-state. The president was the people's choice and symbolised the contract between the state and the citizenry which in essence was one of mutual interpellation: the nation could call on the president and the president could call on the nation.

De Gaulle was convinced that colonial France had had its day. The 1958 constitution, introduced by him, offered overseas territories the choice between independence or subsidised dependency. At this juncture this meant little more than the devolution of power to those territories through secession. However, the Algerian crisis did much to refocus France's thinking and when the government offered better conditions of separation (independence with co-operation) numerous territories opted for this particular path of independence. By 1962, however, several others had chosen complete independence (Larkin: 1988, 306). Although these moves to independence were bloodless, such was not the case for Algeria. In the eight years it took France to resolve the crisis, excluding the civilian toll,

243,000 Algerian and 17,456 French fighters and soldiers lost their lives (ibid., 278). These figures would not be known until well after the signing of the Evian agreements in 1962 – agreements which gave Algeria independence but which in themselves came about in an equally silenced way in so far as they were barely debated and were not voted by the parliament but directly by the electorate in a referendum (the president calling on the nation). Given the state of insecurity felt by the nation (which was considerably increased by the planned putsch and subsequent assassination attempt against de Gaulle in 1961), the result was a massive 'yes' (91 per cent of the French electorate) to Algeria's independence. Few would deny that this colossal consensus was motivated far more by the desire to be rid of the problem than to have any understanding of its implications.

The loss of the Empire, which had essentially been a sixteen-year process (1946–62), did not in the final analysis discredit France's image in the eyes of the superpowers and her former allies, both important reference points for de Gaulle (his dislike of America and mistrust of Britain notwithstanding). In terms of appearances, France was moving with the times. Apart from this modern liberalising image projected by de Gaulle's policies, freeing France from her territorial responsibilities meant greater economic resources were to hand to invest in the hexagon (mainland France) itself. The drive towards modernisation and efficiency, already initiated in the 1950s (thanks, of course, in part to the Marshall plan), could now be enhanced even more. Even the franc was modernised and called *le nouveau franc*. Economic rationalisation and investment in the industrial sectors enabled productivity to soar during the 1960s (McMillan: 1985, 164). This new, modern France was to clean up her cities and to replace insalubrious sanitation with a health-hazard-free sewerage system. Housing developments in the *banlieues* (especially of Paris) were to give comfortable modern shelter to the increasing urban population. To facilitate economic stability further, taxes were lowered to create a greater purchasing power. The consumer boom was truly ready to take off.

This modernisation of France was not, however, a nationwide success story. Although by the end of the 1960s French farmers were supplying 42 per cent of the EEC's total exports of food and raw materials, the top 10 per cent of the farmers were producing 60 per cent of the output. One reason was the continued effects of parcelisation (dividing farms up amongst heirs) which, during the 1950s, was still widely practised despite Vichy's consolidation law of March 1941. A major factor in this law's inability to put a stop to parcelisation was its slow implementation. Farms could not be worked efficiently which led in its turn to a disaffection with farming and, subsequently, to a rural exodus (by 1968 the rural population had declined to 34 per cent). Thus, by the time the consolidation law was taking proper effect, demographic movements had in many respects rendered the law virtually redundant because the rural exodus brought in its wake an increase in the size of farms. But this demographic movement also meant that only those farmers with the resources could properly modernise their farming methods. In the main, only the young generation of farmers was prepared to take the risk of credit to purchase new equipment. The older generation of farmers, whilst it might possess a newly bought tractor (in the 1950s the number of tractors increased fivefold), felt that further investment was beyond its means and that credit would cut heavily into cost-value so that profits would be marginal. Curiously, although agricultural policy was to exercise successive governments' ingenuity, this time (unlike in the 1930s) no attempts were made to stem the rural exodus, presumably because of the need for industrial workers. This demographic movement finds only a very partial reflexiveness in cinema, and unlike the previous two cinematic eras, this era is significant for its lack of 'back to the land' films and a dearth of narratives extolling the virtues of rural life over the evils of the city.

The apparent prosperity of the 1960s was not making for a happy nation in a number of other social areas, and this *was* reflected in much of the cinema of the 1960s. In the 1960s, supermarkets increased twenty-fivefold (from forty to over a thousand). This aggravated the trend – already noted in the 1950s – of forcing small shopkeepers out of business. Elsewhere, mechanisation and improved technology put the artisanal class in a very unfavourable position. Nor was the working class spared. Automation in industry took away their privileged position as skilled workers and reduced them to semi-skilled status with a repetitive job on an assembly line (ibid., 167). Out in the suburbs the modern, low-rent flats (known as the *HLMs* or *habitations à loyer modéré*), although providing shelter for a proportion of the growth in the urban working class, brought about an increased sense of isolation amongst both men and women. The spaces were totally unsocialised, drab concrete masses in the main with no centralised shopping or café area to meet. Women at home felt cut off from life and workers now had to become commuters, adding extra time on to their working day. Furthermore, the four-week paid holiday (introduced in 1963) did little to compensate for this loss in leisure hours and as late as 1969 less than half the working class (43 per cent) took a holiday away from home (ibid., 168). Nor did taking a holiday represent any upward movement in social status – the working class stayed (i.e., were economically obliged to stay) amongst their own. Even if in other areas of leisure consumption (TV, radio, hi-fi, etc.) credit made the accumulation of previously inaccessible consumer durables possible, the working class still remained socially fixed whilst the middle classes continued their social mobility practices. This reality was further evidenced by the effects of the slow implementation of reforms in education. In the belief that education can give a child the cultural capital s/he needs to advance socially, in 1959 the school leaving age was raised to 16. However, this liberalising law did not come into effect until 1969. This meant that no true social change in terms of upward mobility was felt during the 1960s and was unlikely to be felt until at least the mid-1970s. The fact that changes in voting patterns in the late 1970s and again throughout the 1980s did occur would tend to indicate that social change was indeed facilitated, albeit in the long term, by education.

This first age of the Fifth Republic, the age of Gaullism, was about economic regeneration, modernity and the birth of new institutions. All of this contributed to make the Fifth Republic as a whole the greatest peacetime period of nationhoodness for France, at least in this century, if not in her entire history. None the less this age was not without its less favourable political effects on the relationship between the state and the citizenry. Before examining these effects I shall address the issue of nationhoodness. De Gaulle not only sought for political stability, but also perceived national unity as central to his mission and his vision of France. What is of interest is that all the strategies he adopted were in relation to 'otherness'. Thus his foreign policy focused on what he perceived were the common interests of the French nation as opposed to those of other nations (he was far from being pro-European but was keen to see the franc aligned with the Deutschmark, hence the new franc). He wanted France to rank amongst the great nations which meant having nuclear status. To his mind this meant having greater independence from America. France's eventual withdrawal from NATO (because she was allowed no share in its direction) was similarly a stance against America.

Culture was another area where France was to stake out her difference even to the point of being transformed into a political institution by the creation of a Ministry of Culture (the first Minister was André Malraux). Cultural chauvinism is nothing new in France's history, none the less, its elevation to an institution in its own right was a bold strategy indeed towards securing national unity – it was one area which, surely, would find no one in dispute. The way in which culture was administered, however, was revealing of a mentality that wanted to be modern, but conversely of a personality that could not relinquish control – a problem that would surface in its totality in 1968–9 and for which (as much as anything else) de Gaulle would be dismissed by 'his' electorate. Culture was disseminated to the provincial cities and put on display in newly established *Maisons de la culture*. In other words, it was sent out from Paris to the regions for the uninitiated to consume – hence the significance of the places that housed this culture: *Maisons de la culture* (for *the* culture read Parisian culture). Even culture, therefore, was centralised.[3]

Historians have qualified these strategies for national unity as de Gaulle's politics of grandeur. They have also described his time in office as dictatorship by consent. Certainly the Left felt that de Gaulle's new style of presidency, with so much more control centralised in his own person, effectively rendered it unparliamentary as an institution. De Gaulle's response was that election to the presidency through universal suffrage was a legitimation of the president's function as representative of the nation-state. This led him moreover to consult less and less with parliament and more and more with the citizenry via the use of referenda. Any sensing on his part that parliament would block his measures would result in his going directly to the people. It was not only through the use of referenda as a political weapon that de Gaulle sought to curb parliamentary power. The legislature itself was divested of former powers that now became the prerogative of the executive. De Gaulle's reasons for imposing the tighter controls on parliament were based in his firm belief (emanating from a century and a half of republican history) that no French government could ever enjoy an overall majority. De Gaulle's constitution also witnessed the fact that he never believed the Left would accede to power. How else to explain measures – sanctified by the articles of the constitution – to facilitate the government pushing through bills against all odds? Thus, firm legitimate leadership and governmental stability were the linchpins of de Gaulle's political practice – a practice which succeeded in emptying the political arena of any real debate (because he would either go directly to the electorate, or his government would push through legislation).

The effect of Gaullism was also felt by the political class in that it brought about a bipolarisation of political parties, something hitherto unheard of. In this respect, Gaullism acted as a federating force of the Right that obliged the Left to respond in order to survive. The long-term effect was one which de Gaulle never anticipated: the consolidation of a credible centre-left party, the Socialist party (PS), that could be elected to power. The other long-term effect has been a progressive divestment of power amongst the citizenry as exemplified by such factors as the limited choice of 'yes'/'no' in a referendum and the two-person race in the presidential elections. This has led, on the one hand, to a depoliticisation of the electorate, through a bipolarisation of the political debate, and on the other, to a strong consensual support for the Fifth Republic, through the personalisation of politics thanks to the presidentialism of the Fifth Republic.[4] It is remarkable, given France's history of political cultural instability, that this consensus has met with dissension only twice in its thirty-year history – and even so only on a minor scale. The first time occurred with the brief eruption of May 1968 and the second with the rise of the National Front in the 1980s. The first dissension marks an electorate of protest, the second what Shields (1991, 72) terms the electorate of refusal. Viewed in this light, the accession to power of the Left in 1981 was not an anti-republican vote (i.e., it was neither a voice of protest nor of refusal) but rather the opposite. It provided proof that the constitution sanctioned the transfer of power from Right to Left. The elections of 1981, if anything, finally and fully legitimated the Fifth Republic (Cole: 1990, 7).

Larkin (1988, 280 and 359) refers to the Gaullist era as *La République des citoyens* and to Mitterrand's as *La république des professeurs* (a third of his ministers in 1981 were teachers – surely a Pétain nightmare). These are bold epithets which in the case of de Gaulle are not without their ironic resonances since his last call (but one too many as it transpired) on the electorate lost him the presidency when they voted 'no' on his 1969 referendum. Before moving on to Mitterrand's era, I shall briefly consider the twelve years that separate these two dominant moments in the Fifth Republic's history. They may not be as significant, but in relation to cinema they are certainly not without their importance. The two presidents, Pompidou and Giscard d'Estaing, who filled those interim years helped to move on the Gaullist agenda, albeit in different ways and with different scenarios in mind. Pompidou, a Gaullist who favoured development of big capital, used the state as an industrial spearhead and was fully committed to the ultimate logic of economic expansion – exposure to foreign competition. He felt this was necessary not just for France's future, but also to secure the popularity of Gaullism now that de Gaulle had gone (Hanley et al.: 1988, 43). His lasting legacy, however, will doubtless be his concerted pursuance of a building programme that was massive in scale yet notorious for the graft scandals that surrounded it and unfortunate in the concrete property developments that were spread all over the major cities, chiefly remarkable for their size and ugliness. Given Pompidou's professed admiration for art, especially modern art, this legacy of ugliness may or may not surprise. It is perhaps appropriate that he should have attached his name and his efforts to the building of a museum of modern art that is a concrete erection adorned with plastic tubes and glass, the Pompidou Centre, and that he should have done so at the expense of the demolition of virtually the whole of Les Halles area.

In the 1974 presidential elections, brought about by Pompidou's premature death, Giscard d'Estaing narrowly defeated Mitterrand on a ticket of '*Change sans risque*'. Though not a Gaullist, he headed a coalition of centrist parties (*Union Démocratique Française* or UDF), Giscard's presidential style was quickly to go down the Gaullian way. On the surface he espoused liberal policies, but over the seven years of his mandate he revealed his deep-seated conservatism (earning his presidency the epithet of Orleanist). Indeed his election motto points to this dualism.[5] He believed in steady material progress in an atmosphere of political and social consensus which could only be guaranteed by a pluralistic and democratic society under the 'aegis of enlightened leaders' (ibid., 46). What Giscard effectively put in place was a cultification of the presidency. Charisma (de Gaulle) turned into cult. The mythic, epic, presidential style embodied by de Gaulle was transmuted into the personalisation of the presidency. The demagogue was replaced by the pragmatist – dictatorship by consent now became autocracy by default. A politics of modernisation turned into a non-politics of *attentisme*. Inevitably, political pluralism (so in evidence in the previous Republics) in any valid sense of the term was all but dead.

Sadly for Giscard (in election terms), pluralism was dying out not just in the political arena but also in the social one. The improvements in the standard of living (for example, by 1973, 63 per cent of French families owned a car) brought in their wake a cultural homogenisation that started to blurr class distinctions, which in turn set in motion a further depoliticisation of the electorate. With the gradual disappearance of the working class (by the 1980s one one-third of the work-force were industrial workers), what had gradually emerged over the previous twenty years was a growth of the middle classes which, by and large, were no longer subject to the same influences that, until recently, had informed political culture (Gaffney: 1991, 21). This has meant, today as then, that former allegiances to political parties are no longer felt as binding, but conversely that allegiances to political candidates are (especially presidential candidates). This is a factor which has largely determined the PCF's demise and the rise of the National Front (mostly thanks to the charisma of its leader, Le Pen) and which has made possible Mitterrand's victories in the 1981 and 1988 presidential elections.[6]

It was stated above that the Fifth Republic came of age with the 1981 presidential and legislative elections which proved that alternation was possible. Two other factors – the female and the youth vote – also contributed to this maturation. Gaffney (1991, 27) makes the point that by the 1980s women began to vote for themselves and not according to the prescription laid down by the father figure (father, husband or male partner). Undoubtedly, the feminist movement did much to liberate the female suffrage as did the increase in the proportion of women students accessing universities. By 1977 the proportion was 47 per cent, having risen from 25 per cent in 1930 (Larkin: 1988, 343). Equally important to this sense of independence was some of the legislation for women voted through under Giscard (the legalisation of the birth-control pill in 1974, the 1975 Simone Weil Act legalising abortion and the 1975 Act legalising divorce by common consent). Given that the majority of the female vote went to Mitterrand in the 1981 presidentials, Giscard's liberalising policies were not without their bitter-sweet irony. In that same vein of irony, the youth vote also let him down in the 1981 elections. In 1974, Giscard extended the franchise to 18-year-olds, but once again the majority youth vote went to Mitterrand. One last liberalising Giscardian measure of note, in the context of this study, that was also to backfire because it opened the floodgates to pornographic films, was the abolition of cinema censorship in 1974.

The third-time-lucky presidential candidate, François Mitterrand, was well aware that his electoral victory in 1981 was only partially a mandate for the Left and implicitly an electoral reaction against the prevalent lack of political pluralism and Giscard's autocratic presidential style. Elected on a ticket of radical reform that was committed to social justice and equality, Mitterrand's winning slogan '*La Force tranquille*' gave every indication that these changes would be implemented judiciously. The economic climate of the time, however, meant that the major planks of his and, subsequently, the Socialist government's manifestos would cost dear. Reflationary policies at a time of recession are fairly irreconcilable economic realities. The basic economic policy was to create increased domestic demand and to provoke, through state structural intervention, a steady expansion of the economy. To increase demand, the basic wage was raised, the working week shortened, an extra week's paid holiday introduced and welfare payments increased. To these not insignificant costs were added the enormous ones of state structural intervention (i.e., nationalisation and *dirigisme*). The cost of nationalising major industrial companies and the main commercial French banks, so that the government could control investment in industrial development and give direction to that development, might well have seemed an acceptable price to pay for modernisation. But the reality of the recession meant that France was spending to create economic growth when other countries were tightening their belts. The nationalisation programme, coupled with the introduction of social and economic measures in the work sector, produced a massive shock to the economy, pushed inflation above 14 per cent and caused unemployment to rise from 7.4 per cent to 8.7 per cent (Shields: 1991, 76). These policies of reflation were adopted in the belief that the economy would recover by 1983. Such, however, was not to be the case, and by 1982 the Socialist government found itself in a position of having to introduce austerity measures much like those of its other European partners. Indeed, the economic policies pursued under the austerity programmes (of which there were two) were not dissimilar to the Barre Plan of the late 1970s. Thus disaffection with the Left quickly set in (almost as rapidly as it did with the Popular Front some fifty years earlier) and Mitterrand spent the next four years of his presidency as France's most unpopular president of the Fifth Republic. By 1986 the electorate, tired of austerity plans and worried about unemployment, voted the Right back into parliamentary power. The constitutional *non sequitur* had at long last occurred.

This constitutional oddity was in fact to prove Mitterrand's saviour. From being the most unpopular elected president of all times, he progressively regained stature as he proved time and again his ability to respect the wishes of the electorate by not intervening in the parliamentary affairs of the right-wing government (headed by Jacques Chirac as Prime Minister). He became the *président-arbitre*. Although this period of what was called cohabitation marked a decrease in presidential powers, it did not decrease the importance of the presidency in the eyes of the electorate. To this effect, the dominant strategy in the run-up to the 1988 presidentials was what has become known as presidentialism which, in effect, is a consolidation of a practice begun by de Gaulle but reified by Mitterrand. Central to this strategy is that the candidate must be perceived as being more than just the representative of her/his party. Cohabitation had allowed Mitterrand to position himself as 'president of the French people' which, by implication, meant that he was attached to the citizenry and autonomous from the Socialist party. He, more than any of the others, was able to convince the electorate that he was the most multi-dimensional candidate and that his credentials as a man of state were unimpeachable.[7]

In the eleven years to date of Mitterrand's two presidencies, the major markers that can be pointed to reflect his concern with justice (he is after all a lawyer), freedom of the individual (as exemplified, on the legal front, by the abolition of the death penalty and by measures in favour of equality for women), constitutional continuity (but not at any price – although he was prepared to respect the conditions of cohabitation, none the less by changing the voting pattern to proportional representation, he ensured that the Right did not get an overwhelming majority which would have forced his resignation), and social justice (as exemplified by better working conditions and rights and by his less successful policies on immigration).[8] Elsewhere, Mitterrand and the Socialist governments' policies on regionalism and culture serve as testimonies to a desired decentralisation of the power base and a cultural pluralism that is not centred exclusively in Paris. Economic planning was devolved to the regions and urban planning to the municipalities. Perhaps most symptomatic of innovativeness in cultural decentralisation was the renaming of the *Maisons de la culture* as the *Centres culturels* or *Centres de recherche et d'action culturelle*. These now became centres of innovation, cultural exchange and self-expression as opposed to the mission stations of French national culture that Malraux had envisaged (Larkin: 1988, 370).

The thirty years of the Fifth Republic have witnessed a twofold process, the first of which affects the presidency and can be summed up as a movement from the historicisation of the presidency through to its personalisation and, finally, into presidentialism. The second process affects the legislature and more specifically the political class (and thereby parliament). In essence the shift in balance over the past decade has been towards the right of centre in terms of political positioning (thanks to the important presence of the National Front, but also to the failure of the Left to implement its programme of reforms at the beginning of the 1980s). As Garnier and Janover put it, the electorate is now faced with two types of conservatism – the one (the Right) reactionary, the other (the Left) progressive (quoted in Shields: 1991, 86). In any event the political class can be said to have evolved from a position of bipolarity into one of predominantly centrist discourses – or what some political historians call a lack of ideology.

The period of the Fifth Republic has seen greater political stability than ever before and this in turn has meant that constitutional matters have been those to dominate. None the less, this period in France's history has been one where – two waves of modernisation notwithstanding (with all the resonances of rebirth they bring with them) – earlier myths and institutions have been put to death. The Fifth Republic has witnessed the 'death' of the Empire (1962), the 'death' of republicanism and the ascendancy of presidentialism (1962 onwards), the 'death' of political pluralism and the advent of bipolarisation followed by the 'death' of ideology (1962 onwards), the 'death' of the *communard* spirit (as exemplified by the non-events of post-May 1968), the 'death' of Socialism (1983 onwards) and, finally, the 'death' of the PCF (1984 onwards). This morose scenario found a ready reflection in the 1988 presidential elections where all candidates ultimately fought on a ticket of continuity rather than change. Mitterrand's campaign was perhaps the most outstanding at selling this message through positioning himself as the site of all Republics past that could guarantee France its unity and continuity as exemplified by his slogan '*La France unie*'.

The two sets of antagons that typify the political culture of this thirty-year period – modernity and morosity, instability and stability – find a ready reflection in the French cinema. In the introductory preamble to this chapter I mentioned that the cinematic praxis of the New Wave cinema reflected the instability of France as a nation in a period of radical institutional change. This cinema revealed the instability of a nation whose new mythologies (with the exception of de Gaulle's own myth) were yet to be invented, even though the pretence was that they were already in place. The subversion of aesthetic discourses, as exemplified by this cinema, brought into question the ideological nature of cultural signs (the car, modern design, etc.) and exposed the process of institutional mythologising (note how Godard's *Alphaville*, 1965, foresaw the depoliticisation that presidentialism would bring in its wake). In this respect, but only in this respect, the New Wave cinema of the 1960s can be seen as 'political' and innovative.

However, although that decade saw the rebirth of cinema/the birth of a new cinema, it also witnessed a/its 'death'. Ironically, its demise can be traced to the very event which should have enabled it to renew itself yet again – May 1968. The events of that month marked both the end of the potential for change through mass revolt and the first death throes of an oppositional cinema, its final 'death' occurring in the late 1970s. This coincidence of events (which is of course no arbitrary coincidence) offers a pattern for understanding why 1981 did not bring about a much-expected radical departure in cinematographic art. May 1981 was, after all, heralded by many commentators as the beginning of a new era. The Fifth Republic was to remain, but her institutions would undoubtedly undergo substantial renewal to reflect the new ideology (of the Left) – at least, this was the expectation. However, radical change did not occur in 1981 any more than in 1968. It did not occur precisely because, whilst the discursive myths by which the institutions were apprehended changed (president and government of the Left), what these myths actually signified did not. The institutions themselves remained unchanged (the length and function of the presidency, executive versus legislative powers, etc.) Viewed in this light, it may well be that Mitterrand's recent decision to consider putting constitutional reform back on the agenda (for example, a five-year presidency to correspond with the five-year legislature) represents an attempt to put an end to this lack of change and incipient morosity. But these are other considerations that have yet to be voted and may only be a repetition of former presidents' *voeux pieux*.

TECHNOLOGIES AND THEORIES OF STYLE

The impact of new technologies on style can best be summarised under the following snapshot formulas: spectacle of sound, virtual video with computer-assisted editing versus real/reel celluloid with its classical editing technique (cut and paste), and the rhetoric of colour. Technological progress with sound has pushed it from its first mono boundaries into stereo and now into Dolby sound. Not since the advent of the talkies has sound brought such attention to itself. In its search for authenticity through a perfectioning of sound recording, sound has almost fallen into the trap of formalism, that is, of making itself into its own aesthetic product. It is unsurprising in this context, therefore, that since the early 1980s the sound track has become a focus for theoretical investigation.[9] One might find it curious, in the light of the realist debate, that three-dimensional sound should survive and flourish with audiences whereas three-dimensional vision so singularly failed. Doubtless the reasons are first, technological (three-D images launched in the 1950s were quite primitive in relation to what computer technology can now achieve), and second, economic (to achieve three-D visual parity with sound would prove very expensive). Other reasons come down to audiences' aural sophistication in that they are accustomed to stereo if not quadrophonic sound in their own home (radio, hi-fi, compact disc, etc.). Furthermore, audience acceptance of aural reality coincides with the fact that it does not suspend or intrude upon the illusion of reality that the imaged screen provides, rather, in most cinemas it confirms it. Steve Neale (1985, 101) points to the drives and pleasures which the soundtrack facilitates for the spectator as s/he is positioned as the invisible aural voyeur – image *and* sound as spectacle, in concert to double the pleasure.

Interestingly it is sound which is currently keeping video at bay – at least in terms of filmic screenings. For the moment, editing sound on to film, with its perforated strips, produces a richer effect than the multiband sound editing on to video. It is simply easier to manipulate little bits of sound, for example by overlapping them, juxtaposing or setting them off against each other. However, it is doubtful that this state of affairs will last. Once virtual editing is available, sound editors will be only too pleased to move on to this light, hands-on technology. Virtual montage is a process whereby original elements of sound and image are installed (recorded) on to disc, each with its specific address. They are then available to be called upon at will by the editor. All the permutations at her/his disposal are recorded in the form of address combinations that are saved in the computer's memory. Thereafter the film is scored via the desired composition of addresses. Several versions can be made and stored without having to worry about recutting the whole film and starting again from scratch. Mixing sound can take place at the editing table, if desired, so that the editor gets to hear the real sounds at the same time as s/he is editing the visual film (interestingly this is the reverse of what happens with traditional editing: images can be projected as the soundtrack is being edited). The implications of this new technology are enormous. By scoring addresses differently, a film can be made to shift in intention from a feature film to a documentary, or to an instructional film. The ramifications for artificial intelligence are plain for all to see, to say nothing of the repercussions in the scientific and educational domains.[10]

Turning to the third aspect of technologies of style, the rhetoric of colour, Steve Neale (1985) gives a fascinating account of the value of colour in filmic representation which I shall summarise because it has a bearing both on the technologies and the theories of style. What follows is a brief enumeration of the three major points he makes. In the first instance, colour – because it provides spectacle and was initially identified with it – was originally reserved for non-realist films (cartoons, the western, costume romance and the musical). Colour, it was felt, was not codeterminate with realism, rather, it was a feature that distracted the spectator's eye and detracted attention from the narrative. The advent of colour on television brought a change in attitude. Documentary film, news and current affairs programmes were broadcast in colour, a process which gave colour film the legitimate cachet of realism. Thus the signification of colour in cinema shifted. However, it now took on a dialectical function. The key terms centring the discourse about colour became nature-realism/ spectacle-art – two contradictory sets of terms, but also two sets that are incapable on their own 'of containing fully, in descriptive terms, some of the effects to which they refer' (ibid., 151). Simply expressed, if colour was used as spectacle, it could not refer to its realist function. If its aesthetic mode prevailed, then nature was occluded. Crucial to the realist mode was the subordination of colour to the narrative and a desired symbolic organisation whereby colour fitted the dominant mood or emotion. Mainstream cinema has tended to follow this practice with only avant-garde (negative postmodern) cinema, in the main, exploring the symbolic properties of colour to the full.

Neale's second point about colour is possibly the most important of all (certainly where feminist film theory is concerned). Referring to the contradiction between the two sets of terms Neale says:

> It is at this point that a further element, one which is just as constant, just as persistent, enters into the ideological equation. That element is the female body. Since women within the patriarchal ideology already occupy the contradictory spaces both of nature and culture (since they therefore evoke both the natural and the artificial) and since also they are marked as socially sanctioned objects of erotic looking, it is no wonder that from the earliest days of colour photography they function both as source of the spectacle of colour in practice and as a reference point for the use and promotion of colour in theory. The female body both bridges the ideological gap between nature and cultural artifice while simultaneously marking and focusing the scopophilic pleasures involved in and engaged by the use of colour in film.
>
> (ibid., 152)

The female body at the site of contradictory terms is not a new revelation. Virgin/vamp, mother/whore are familiar reductionist representations of the female text. But what is significant in this reading is that, at the same time as the female body bridges the gap between the two sets of terms within the discourse on colour, she both marks and contains 'the erotic component involved in the desire to look at the coloured image' (ibid., 155), that is, she is simultaneously positioned as subject (she 'contains') and object (she 'marks') of the erotic. In mainstream cinema, it is doubtful that this double positioning (as subject/object) will lead the female body, through its visual treatment, to assume agency (i.e., the subject will not supersede the object). However, it is clear that in non-mainstream cinema such agencing could occur (for example, the stylised coloration in Varda's *Le Bonheur*, 1965, counters the subjectivity of the narrative which is male). That it occurs so little is disturbing. But this point leads to the third and final point raised in Neale's discussion which concerns colour's potential to subvert.

Calling on Julia Kristeva's writings on colour, Neale argues that because colour is so closely associated with the psychic and erotic pulsions (including desire and suppression of that desire), it is 'capable of escaping, subverting and shattering the symbolic organisation to which it is subject (ibid., 158), that is, colour can counter its subordination to the narrative. Colour operates on three levels simultaneously: the objective, the subjective and the cultural – (what Kristeva terms the 'triple register' (ibid., 156). Within the domain of visual perception, the 'objective', according to

Kristeva, refers to an outside whereby an instinctual pressure is articulated in relation to external objects. This same pressure motivates the 'subjective' and causes the eroticisation of the body proper (seeing is responding). Finally, the 'cultural' functions to insert this pressure under the impact of censorship as a sign in a system of representation. The cultural operates to contain what happens between the objective and the subjective, that is, its intentionality is containment of the subjective and erotic processes. That the cultural is not always successful in its purpose should not surprise. Pornographic films are surely prime examples, even though it is equally the case that all films have the potential to subvert the cultural's function of censorship. There are, however, other ways in which this sign can be suspended, deconstructed even, this time through the de-eroticisation of colour (a point that will be developed later).

Turning now to theories of style, interestingly, the renewal of film theory did not come via film criticism (as it did in the 1950s) but through other disciplines starting with structural linguistics and semiotics (early 1960s), continuing through into psychoanalysis and philosophy (late 1960s and the 1970s), going on into history (1980s) and, finally, arriving at the 'death' of theory (late 1980s) as signified by the impact of deconstructionism.

The significance of the new trend of essayists and philosophers turning to cinema to apply their theories cannot be underestimated. Not to put too simplistic a reading on their importance, it is doubtless their work which has legitimated film studies as a discipline and brought cinema into the academic arena. What is equally significant is the fact that this thirty-year period of theory was initiated by the popularisation of the first theoretical framework to be applied to cinema, namely structuralism. Although the principle of structuralism dates back to the beginning of the century primarily in the form of Ferdinand de Saussure's linguistic theories, they remained 'undiscovered/unknown' until they were brought into the limelight by Roland Barthes, the essayist of *Mythologies* fame, who was subsequently adopted as the pope of structuralism.[11] In his *Cours de linguistique générale*, Saussure sets out the base paradigm by which all language can be ordered and understood. The base paradigm, *langue/parole*, was intended as a function that could simultaneously address/speak for the profound universal structures of language or language system (*langue*) and their/its manifestation in different cultures (*parole*).[12] Saussure made the vital point that the governing conventions in relation to this language system are very arbitrary and that there is no necessary correlation between the word (the signifier) and the object/idea being designated (the signified). This arbitrariness is manifest in the differences between languages. Saussure maintained that this linguistic system could function as a general science of signs (semiology), that is, it could address many other sign systems precisely because of the arbitrary relationship between signifier and signified (Cook: 1985, 222).

In the final analysis, the purpose of a structural approach is to explain, through a reconstruction, the rules by which an 'object' functions at the same time as it addresses the interface between the sign system (signifier) and cultural artefact (signified). Claude Lévi-Strauss's anthropological structuralism of the 1960s (which looked at American Indian myths) continued in a similar vein, although he adapted it to a structuralist analysis of narrative rather than to a system of signs. This approach became extremely popular during the 1960s to the point where, to adapt a phrase, you could say '*montre-moi ta structure, je te dirai qui tu es*'. There are two essential points to be made about this popularisation of structuralism – the first is historical. By cross-theorising cinema with linguistics, the Structuralists brought back into view the notion of cinematic language, not heard of since the 1920s. This led to a re-examination of the theorists of the 1920s, bringing them out of the oblivion to which the *Cahiers* group had assigned them. It was also a theoretical movement that wanted to move away from the auteur approach that canonised individuals but lacked a truly theorised approach.[13] The second point is socio-political and refers to the underlying strategy of structuralist theory itself which was to establish a total structure. It should not be forgotten that this popularisation of structuralism coincided with the advent of de Gaulle to power. His calls for national unity (in the face of the Algerian crisis), the era of economic triumphalism and the consequent nationalism that prevailed (at least in the mind of the General, if not the electorate) were in themselves symptomatic of a desire for structures to be mobilised to give France a sense of national unity. Thus, the desire for a total structure, as exemplified by structuralism, can be read as an endeavour to counter the real political instability of the 1960s caused first, by the radical changes in the institutional framework, second, by the difficult process of resolving the Algerian crisis, and finally, by the increasing unrest of a depoliticised electorate and a disaffected youth class. Structuralism, in one respect total theory, reflects – certainly with hindsight – the Gaullian concern with the nation-state.

Symptomatic of this desire for order in film theory were Christian Metz's endeavours to situate cinema within a Saussurian semiology in his *Essais sur la signification du cinéma* in which he mobilises a total theory approach in the form of his *grande syntagmatique* (i.e., cinema as a system of signs or a typology of syntagmas). His endeavour was to uncover the rules that governed film language and to establish a framework for a semiotics of the cinema. The trouble with this approach is of course its desire to be total and all-embracing. In the end the problem becomes one of the theory overtaking the text and of theory occluding other aspects of the text and, therefore, being very limiting. What gets omitted in this theoretical approach as it is applied to film is the notion of pleasure and audience reception. What occurs instead is a crushing of the aesthetic experience through the weight of the theoretical framework. Its potential for authoritarianism and prescription did not suit the mood of the late 1960s and especially post-1968. From then on, the shift was away from structuralism and into psychology.

Structuralism did not, however, die. First, it became resignified in the expression post-structuralism that typified the 1970s theoretical period with the advent of both psychology and feminism. Second, in the 1980s it took on a more rarefied (some might say precious) reformulation in the deconstruction debate (without a system of signs to deconstruct, deconstruction cannot really operate). Finally, it is currently on the ascendancy again with the re-emergence and re-evaluation – after twenty years of oblivion (by French theorists at least) – of Lévi-Strauss's structuralist approach. It needs to be said that within Anglo-Saxon theoretical writings, for some time the structuralist approach has been perceived as one of the many modalities by which to examine cinema and has joined ranks with other formerly teleological (Marxism to name but one) and non-teleological approaches to serve as elucidator (rather than coloniser) of the filmic text in all the complexities of its determinants. As a result of this greater internationalism of film theory, it now looks as if a broader-based structuralism is poised to make a modest re-entry into French theory. But this is jumping ahead – I shall return to post-1968.

Post-1968, critical film theory bifurcated. In the main, essayists of the semiological structuralist school went down the psychoanalysis route – most appropriately, in the earliest instances, Christian Matz. Elsewhere, film critics pursued a Marxist-Leninist path bent on questioning the impression of reality that the cinematic apparatus produces and advocating instead materialist film. What is significant in terms of the history of French film theory is not just that this bifurcation should emanate from a post-structuralist positioning but also that it should pick up on and develop theories of the 1920s. The psychoanalysis route continues the idea of the first avant-garde and its notion of the subjective cinema, that is, the filmic representation of the unconscious. The advocacy of materialist film follows more closely upon the second avant-garde concept of pure cinema where film signifies in and of itself.

In terms of the Marxist-Leninist/materialist film debate, the two journals most seriously implicated in it are the *Cahiers du cinéma*, which post-1968 espoused a more theoretical and Marxist position, and the newly created, deliberately Marxist *Cinéthique*. The cinema and reality debate was, in the final analysis, played out between these two.[14] But although both played at adversarial roles, they had more in common than they cared to admit. *Cahiers* adopted an antagonistic position in relation to this relatively upstart journal because it felt that *Cinéthique* was considerably less well informed on film than it was. *Cinéthique*, because it started in Marxist theory, felt it had more political kudos than the until-then apolitical

Cahiers. Both claimed a dialectical and historical materialism as their theoretical base and their starting point was that production practices erase the fact that work is the real producer of the film. Furthermore, they were in agreement on the fundamental principle of putting into question the narrative-representative-industrial system – in other words of pointing to the fact that behind the apparent reproduction of an objective reality, cinema reproduces the dominant ideology. They were also in agreement over the function of materialist film, which was to expose the ways in which cinematic praxis positions the spectator as receptive to the ideological nature of film (i.e., cinema as reflector of the dominant ideology). Where they disagreed was in the degree to which the system of representation should be deconstructed (the word was in the air) in order to foreclose an identification of the spectacle with objective reality. The *Cahiers* critics felt that *Cinéthique* was too extreme (and incidentally not rigorous enough in its analysis) in its paring away at the cinematic process and that film would end up being no more than pure autoreferential texts which, given *Cinéthique*'s commitment to placing the reality debate into the class question, would ultimately be counterproductive rather than counter-cinematic. Whatever their differences, it is within this theoretical tendency that the seeds for deconstruction were truly laid.

As for the psychoanalysis route, Metz's *grande syntagmatique* pointed to the problems of attempting to put in place a total theory – it excluded more than it included and gave no space to the interaction between spectator and screen – and for this reason he and other structuralists turned to psycho-analysis. Following on from Jean-Louis Baudry and perhaps Raymond Bellour, Metz drew on the analogy of the screen with the mirror as a way of talking about the spectator/screen relationship. In any event these three authors, to name but the dominant ones in this area of film analysis in France in the 1970s, drew on Freud's libido drives and Lacan's mirror stage to explain how film works at the unconscious level. It is Bellour who talks about cinema as functioning simultaneously for the imaginary (i.e., as the reflection, the mirror) and as the symbolic (through its film discourses). Metz, for his part, talks about spectator positioning and the voyeuristic aspect of film viewing whereby the spectator is identified with the look. He also sees this identification as a regression to childhood, which brings us back to the Lacanian mirror stage. What these authors are saying in a nutshell is that at each film viewing there occurs a re-enactment of unconscious processes involved in the acquisition of sexual difference (mirror stage), of language (entry *of* the symbolic) and of autonomous selfhood or subjectivity (entry *into* the symbolic order and rupture with the mother as object of identification). In the first instance, therefore, the cinema constructs the spectator as subject. In the second, it establishes the desire to look with all that that connotes in terms of visual pleasure for the spectator.

Psychoanalysis did not limit itself to the study of this double phenomenon that emanates from a spectator/screen analysis – the film texts
themselves were also treated as material for interpretation. However,
within this school of theory, the inevitability of the meaning of the mirror
stage (fear of castration at the sight of sexual difference with the mother)
was never brought into question any more than the implications of scopophilia (the drive to pleasurable viewing) for masculine erotic desire and the
male fetishising gaze. Not surprisingly, gender representation remained
fairly unspoken at least in relation to *différence* (sexual difference).
Conversely, talk of male representation/characterisation as a reiteration of
the Oedipus story was not uncommon. Bellour's 1975 essay on Hitchcock's
North by Northwest is a classic in this context.[15] Needless to say, psychoanalysis in this mode does not advance the elucidation of female representation and spectatorship (any more than mainstream cinema's use of
colour).

Before concluding this section on the psychoanalysis aspect of theories
of style, I would like to recap on some of the problems which the lack of
debate around women in French film theory has caused, not least of which
is the development, in the late 1970s, of theory into a negative formalism,
deconstructionism. Although there was an active women's movement in
France in the early 1970s and important female theoreticians (Irigaray,
Cixous, Kristeva, etc.), none of that activity has filtered across into French
film theory. If one sums up what the basic tenets of psychoanalysis in film
imply, then there is room for concern at this lack of cross-over. According
to 1970s film theory, women are simply not there except as mother and
object. Bellour's concept of cinema as a metonymic functioning for the
imaginary and the symbolic confirms a phallic reading of cinematic praxis
that excludes the female except as object to be viewed and object of desire.
The furthest such a theory could countenance in terms of gender representation is the notion of homoeroticism (male spectator's identification with
the screen 'hero', for example), so the desiring text, the agent of desire,
still remains male.

Vincendeau (1988) sees this lack of cross-over as emanating from two
critical issues, both specific to the French context. The first concerns the
status of feminism, the second that of theory. Feminism in France died an
unnatural, or at least premature death at the beginning of the 1980s. But
this in itself would not be enough to explain the dearth, during the 1970s,
of French feminist theory in film. After all, by the mid-1970s both the
United States and Britain had already begun to incorporate feminist theory
into film analyses. Furthermore, the feminist movements of this period in
these three countries (as elsewhere) came about as a direct result of the
post-1968 mood of disenchantement with leftist (male) ideology. This is
where Vincendeau's second critical issue comes into play. It concerns the
status of theory in general as a legitimate discipline and film theory's desire

not to be excluded from that cachet of legitimacy. To assert feminism as a theoretical approach in its own right – to posit the feminine as central, as subject rather than object of investigation – would, for film theory at least, create resistance in such a patriarchal society as France. I say 'film theory at least' because, as Vincendeau points out, the tendency in France was to accept (i.e., elide) feminism into sociology where it seemed more 'appropriate'. Vincendeau also makes the point that women academics and film-makers saw the cachet of legitimacy as their only way forward, so that for these women theorists and film-makers alike the claim, by the end of the 1970s, was that the feminist cause was over and done with. And indeed, as is evidenced in the film products themselves, from the late 1970s onwards, the more women got to make films the less they showed an interest in feminist theory.

I shall now return to the first critical issue and offer, albeit conjecturally, some further reasons for the 'death' of feminism. Post-1968 witnessed a disaffection with the ideology of the Left. In some respects this disaffection could be read as the beginning of the funeral rites of Marxism. Earlier in this chapter, I pointed to the morose scenario that the Fifth Republic has so far left in its wake. The 1970s could be seen as an initial period of bereavement with ideology, to be followed by a later one in the 1980s. The birth of a group calling itself the *Nouveaux philosophes* which was formed by ex-*soixante-huitards*, all male, was a first indicator of this death of (male) leftist ideology at least. The philosophical text by Bernard-Henri Lévy (a former *soixante-huitard*), *La Barbarie à visage humain* (1977, and very popular at the time), which pointed to the lack of distinction between Fascism and Communism, seems a clear enough symbol (even though the text is terribly problematic) of the sense of an end of all ideologies, or of a blurring of all ideologies. The tendency, throughout the 1970s (especially the late 1970s), therefore, was to see all overt ideology as *passé*. Feminism in France could not have timed things worse. This is a first, preferred reading.

A second reading would, I feel, produce something a bit more coherent. In terms of theory, the 1970s spawned a number of new terms (*nouvelle philosophie* being one), the most important of which were post-structuralism and postmodernism. Three texts of another ex-*soixante-huitard*, philosopher Jean François Lyotard, written during the 1970s will serve as a metonymy for the process of this ending of ideology that is exemplified by these two key terms. First, in *Discours, figure* (1971) it is structuralism that comes under virulent attack. No more 'total theory'. The post-structural moment is born and implicitly, therefore, a fragmented theory. Lyotard's next critique in *Economie libidinale* (1974), in its quasi-dismissal of Marxism, points to the death of an ideology that had sustained the Left, including Lyotard for so many decades. Political modernism was dying, enter the age of the postmodern condition. The coincidence of

Lyotard's third text, *La Condition postmoderne* (1979), with the death of feminism in France is not as innocent as at first appears. Although the postmodern condition points to a crisis in Marxism, it does not represent an overcoming of modernity, but rather a challenging of the rules and a continuous critique. Thus the postmodern condition is always diagnosing, turning every which way for solutions. It is for this reason and in this way that postmodernity has become the melting pot of previously fragmented disciplines – something had to be put into the vacuum created by the death of Marxism and total theory. In reality the death of Marxism in France has brought about a crisis for masculinity and it is this effect that has led to the reclusion/occlusion of feminism. In its struggle either to revive a new Marx or to kill him off definitively, postmodernity in France has deflected attention from the feminist questions that were being raised in the 1970s. In the death throes of its own ideology, post-Marxism has effectively silenced the French feminist.[16]

Whilst post-structuralism and postmodernism have occluded sexual difference within French film theory, other developments in the 1980s have similarly done nothing to address this issue which is considered, in other nation's film theory, to be a central one in the overall debate on cinema. Deconstructionism, in its questioning of codes and formalism (which like structuralism means excluding the spectator from consideration and therefore the whole notion of the look), ignores the question of the power of representation (Gidal: 1989, 43). In its attention to form, which gives it an 'idealist motivation', and because it holds that any 'political or sexual-political representation is problematic' and, therefore, deconstructible, deconstruction 'functions as an alibi for any politics and polemic against representation' (ibid., 43). All is fodder for the deconstructionist machine. Deconstruction reproduces at the same time as it deconstructs stereotypical forms of oppression and in so doing justifies and normalises them. Godard's films of the 1980s are redolent with this problematic. How is it that a camera probing a pubescent girl's body, as in *Je vous salue Marie* (1983), is materialist film as art? And how is it that the 'orgy' scene in *Sauve qui peut la vie* (Godard, 1980) can be read as a deconstruction of capitalist consumption practices and not as a classic metaphor for the female body as object and the perfect site for the Sadean text? I shall leave these questions as floaters.

The 1980s saw the advent of new critical review journals in France that addressed cinema differently from the tradition of the 1960s and 1970s. These journals, of which the best known are *Iris* (a journal of theory on image and sound), *Hors Cadre* (an interdisciplinary journal) and *Vertigo* (a journal of cinema aesthetics and history), refer to cinema's history and aesthetics as well as to the materiality of film (the material status of the image, the construction of sound, the structure of dialogue). This welcome departure has allowed silent cinema to re-emerge as an important cinema, no longer to be doomed to neglect. This advocacy of a more pluridisciplinary approach, though currently to the forefront, does however have a recognisable forefather in the person of Jean Mitry, whose theory rested on three points: language, aesthetics and history. For Mitry, whose starting point to any debate on cinema was epistemological (practical knowledge of the field), cinema must be analysed not just in and of itself but also within a pluricultural context and across history. Thus theory is based in knowledge. With regard to language and aesthetics, as opposed to Metz, Mitry believed that cinema cannot be compared to language (nor for that matter to literature), but rather to language in a philosophical and psychological sense. By this he meant that cinematographic language refers, in the first instance, to temporal and spatial signification. The meaning emanates from an image in movement in time and space. Hence the great importance he placed on editing as the essence of film narrative. In this light, film language is perceived as film-*écriture*. In this way, therefore, Mitry's thinking is in direct descent from the *cinégraphie* of the 1920s and the *caméra stylo* of the 1940s. It would not be untruthful to state that whilst, on the one hand, Mitry's writings represent a continuation of long-standing theoretical debates (a prolongation which is historically important), on the other, they also represent the most explicit all-encompassing source of key areas for modern film theory as exemplified in France and elsewhere. As Andrew (1984, 15) makes clear, Mitry's contribution to the advancement of contemporary theory is not inconsiderable, even if it has in part evolved out of an interrogation of his key concepts 'driven by a desire to get beyond them'.

At present in France, therefore, there is a twofold trend in film theory, the one, more epistemological and exemplified by Mitry, the other, more formalist and abstract and emanating out of the postmodern school of thought. In this bifurcation of theory, there is a key to why contemporary cinema of the 1980s looks as it does. Both theories are pointing backwards. The first is a 'positive' regard backwards, looking at what is there as a continuum, seeing the present as deeply inflected by that past and defining itself in relation to what it is and perceiving that topos as the basis upon which to examine the language and aesthetics of cinema. The other is a 'negative' regard, defining itself by what it is not, *post* modernity, suggesting that all is concluded before and therefore perceiving itself as posthistory – after history. But even to study the history of cinema, as the 'positive' regard proposes, is already to suggest that its moment is over. To this ambiguity gets added a further paradox. The study of history does not imply any necessary learning process. As will become clear, looking back was what most afflicted the cinema of the 1980s, but the cinema of the 1960s and 1970s equally showed a concordance with the theoretical signs of their times. It is these cinemas that I shall now consider.

FROM A *'JEUNE'* CINEMA TO A CINEMA *'POUR JEUNES'*

A mapping of French cinema over the last thirty years in terms of its relationship to mainstream and non-mainstream production, will provide a useful paradigm to guide us through a closer examination of the cinemas of the period. In terms of continuity, there are two points to be made. The first is the constancy over the whole period of the dominance of two genres: comedy in pole position followed by the *polar*/thriller. Second, is the continuation of the *tradition de qualité*, that is, literary adaptations scripted by well-known scenarists and made by well-established film-makers – often ex-New Wavists (Truffaut being exemplary in this instance). As for discontinuity, during this postmodern age, there appear to have been three avant-garde and three mainstream moments. The first avant-garde 'coincides' with New Wave (1958–62), the second with the post-1968 militant cinema, the third with the mid-1970s formalist cinema. The three mainstream moments revolve, to a greater or lesser extent, around key terms. The first is a moralising cinema that was partially in evidence in the 1960s. The second is a cinema of authenticity, strongly associated with the 1970s. The third is the cinema of pastiche, started in the early 1980s, which continues through till today.

Coexisting within the first two periods, the 1960s and 1970s, there were three types of cinema. From 1958 to 1968, the tripartisation consisted of an avant-garde, a New Wave and mainstream commercial cinemas. Post-1968, the avant-garde oppositional cinema generated first, a militant avant-garde, and later, the materialist and ultra-formalist cinema that has also been termed the *Cinéma nouveau*. During the 1970s, the tripartisation took the form of avant-garde, civic and mainstream cinemas. The civic cinema, also known as the authentic cinema, was a by-product of both the moralising cinema and the post-1968 militant cinema. This cinema recuperated contemporary events and provided history with some sort of presence. But what is intriguing is that this authenticity was present in all three types of cinema of this period. Thus much of mainstream cinema also reflected a social contemporaneity.

In the 1980s, the authentic cinema evaporated in the face of pastiche. The avant-garde lived on, albeit on a very small scale. What disappeared was a cinema that came between the oppositional cinema of the avant-garde and mainstream symptomatic cinema. The primary reason for this evaporation of authenticity in cinema was tied in with the overall meaning of disaffection with ideology. When the Left came to power in 1981, they did so on a platform of social reforms. The Left's discourse was embedded with the rhetoric of social justice and as such was far removed from the politics of liberalism that had so valued capitalism, free-market ideology and, implicitly, the individual. In simple terms the socialist platform amounted to a credo in society. But by 1982–3 – and to the electorate's mind at least – this credo, because of the effects of recession, had all but evaporated, and to all appearances the Left was instituting policies that did little to distinguish it from the Right. It is in the centring of these discourses that one can perceive the evaporation of authentic cinema. As with the political arena, the 1980s witnessed a centring of cinema's ideological discourses from the 'left-Marxist inflected' and 'anti-American hegemonic praxis' films of the 1960s and 1970s, from a political cinema that was politically made to an apolitical cinema that was designer- and consumer-led. With rare exceptions, the cinema of the 1980s and early 1990s has been one that says 'since there is nothing here (no ideology, etc.), let's imitate'.

One last point on this mapping needs to be made and concerns the postmodern aesthetic. Earlier in this chapter I spoke about the bifurcation of postmodern culture into two tendencies: symptomatic (or unoppositional) and negative (or oppositional). Whether symptomatic or oppositional, the postmodern aesthetic relies on four tightly interrelated sets of concepts: 'parody and pastiche', 'prefabrication', 'intertextuality', 'bricolage'. What separates the two tendencies is that the oppositional postmodern aesthetic experiments with these concepts and innovates through subverting their codes, whereas the symptomatic merely replicates them. Hence the need for two distinguishing terms for the first concept – 'parody and pastiche'. Parody is the domain of oppositional cinema. Pastiche pertains to the symptomatic in that it imitates previous genres and styles, but unlike parody, its imitation is not ironic and is not therefore subversive. In its uninventiveness, pastiche is but a shadow of the former thing (parody). Postmodern art culls from already existing images and objects and either repeats or reinvents them. In cinema, images or parts of sequences which were fabricated before are reselected. In much the same way that prefabricated houses are made up of complete units of pre-existing meaning, so the visual arts see the past as a supermarket source that the artist raids for whatever s/he wants. A film could be completely constructed out of prefabricated images (and even sounds), especially within symptomatic cinema. Beineix's *37,2 degrés le matin* (1985) is a case in point with images coming from directors as far apart as Huston, Cassavetes, Bergman and Malle, amongst others. Intertextuality refers to the signifying practice of a text in the sense that it is a first text referring, through its construction, to another or other pre-existing texts. Thus, for example, Besson's *Subway* (1985) refers to punk subculture and television designer-violence in its look. In its narrative, it refers to the myth of Orpheus and also, in its up-dating (Orpheus in the 1980s), to an earlier up-dating of the myth by Cocteau in his film *Orphée* (1949). The denouement of the narrative refers to the end of Godard's *A bout de souffle* (1959). And so on. Finally, bricolage is an assembling of different styles, genres or discourses. In oppositional postmodern art, this takes the form of replicating within one discourse the innovations of another. For example, the deconstruction of time and space that occurs in the New Novel is replicated in the films of Duras, Resnais and Robbe-Grillet through a use of montage that disorientates. The most common replication in cinema is the plasticity of video and painting which can be found in many of the 1980s film-makers' work and not just among those of the oppositional cinema.

Glancing back over the past thirty-odd years, therefore, one can see how cinema reflects both the political and the social agendas that extend over these years and how theory and technology inflect the cinemas that are sometimes of the centre, at other times of the periphery. Similarly, according to the climate of the times, certain genres disappear only to resurface when there appears to be renewed public demand or when political conjuncture permits or militates for their revival. In the previous chapters a persistent theme has been a demonstration of how national cinema is a creator of myths that are vested in actors and concepts as signs pointing, in general, to a normalised and sanitised hegemony.

To develop briefly this last point, it is worth looking at the way in which the '*jeune*' cinema – which was an alternative name for the New Wave – came into being and how, in turn, it came largely to be a myth (mostly out of economic exigency). I have said before that there is no such thing as immaculate conception with regard to cinema. There are changes, but they are more the outcome of an evolutionary process than of any stark revolutionary moment or cataclysmic event. In the last chapter we saw how, during the 1950s, youth had come centre-screen as a preoccupation, giving proof to its emergence as a new social class. By the late 1950s in France, this class was very visible and it was Françoise Giroud, editor of the then centre-left weekly *L'Express*, who coined a term for this new socially active adolescence by calling it *La Nouvelle Vague*. Within French cinema, the appeal of the youthful, handsome, sometimes reprobate (in his characterisations) Gérard Philipe (to say nothing of his untimely death, in 1959, at the age of 37) and, especially, the tremendous success of 28-year-old Vadim's *Et Dieu créa la femme* (1956) and the mythologising effect it had on Brigitte Bardot, meant that producers in the late 1950s wanted work made by 'young ones' – both on the screen and behind the camera. This demand helped propel a new wave of film-makers on to the scene. This was not the exclusive reason, however, and it is timely to point to the demographic fact that the older guard of film-makers, who had held the reins in the 1950s, were ageing fast or dying off. This helped to create a gap for the new wave of film-makers. In any event, these new film-makers became associated in people's minds with the New Wave; producer hype did the rest and the rest is history. In the collective memory, all that remains of *La Nouvelle Vague* today is this group of film-makers – a misnomer made myth.

Misnomer or not, an important effect of this demand for a '*jeune cinéma*' was that it created the myth that those making it were all young and, because some of the more notorious first films that hit the screens were made by the *Cahiers* group, that these new film-makers had not come through the normal circuit of assistantship to established directors, but were uninitiates where camera work was concerned and had come to cinema from their critics' desk at the *Cahiers*. The facts attest a little differently. The average age of the film-makers loosely grouped into this so-called '*jeune cinéma*' was 32 (as a measure of the wide range of ages Resnais was 46 and Chabrol 23 in 1958). During the period 1959–60, among the sixty-seven film-makers making their first feature-length film, only 55 per cent came from backgrounds not directly attached to film-making (in the sense of shooting films), and the remaining 45 per cent was composed of short-film directors like Varda and Resnais and assistants (e.g., Deville and Molinaro). However, for a while producers were convinced that the '*jeune cinéma*' was the place to invest. It has to be added that the improved status of the *avance sur recettes* and the low-budget nature of this cinema helped to make investment doubly attractive to producers. The financial risk was far less, or so it seemed. Such was the economic attraction of this cinema that, between 1959 and 1963, 170 directors made their first feature film. But, as we have already seen, producers are notorious for equating winners with repeats. Thus what was novel in 1958–9 had become rebarbative by 1962. Narratives repeated themselves. So too did the unpolished cinematic style. Whereas in 1958 cinematic incompetence was seen as a quality, by the early 1960s it had become an irritant to the spectator. The snob value of going to see the latest New Wave director's film soon wore off, for two reasons. The first, repetitiveness, made the idea of going to see 'another New Wave film' resonate with tedium. The second was the deterrent factor of the widespread exposure in mainstream cinema theatres to the formalistic abstraction and intellectualism (pseudo or not) seemingly inherent in and endemic to this new cinema. Producers, believing that they were on to a winner, screened their 'New Wave' products in mainstream cinema theatres – and not art cinemas where they properly belonged (if at all). When one considers that film-makers in the New Wave group were experimenting with cinematic language and, in some instances, that their work was inflected by the precepts of the New Novel and the Brechtian theory of distanciation, one can see how this distribution strategy was not the best way to avoid alienating mainstream audiences. Small surprise, therefore, that by 1963 very few of the New Wave products ever made it on to the screen. Whilst commercial greed on the part of producers has contributed to making the New Wave seem bigger and more important than it was, these same producers must also shoulder some of the responsibility for its demise, through overkill.

Critics, especially of the Left, have seen the New Wave cinema as apolitical because of the predominance of the need to narrate the self.[17] The alienation expressed in these films, they argue, is personal and not political. These critics maintain that the confessional nature of such apparently diverse films as *Les 400 coups* (Truffaut, 1958), *Hiroshima mon amour* and *Muriel* (both Resnais, 1959 and 1963), *Pierrot le fou* and *Alphaville* (both Godard and made in 1965), is nothing more than characters acting as *metteurs-en-scène* of their own fiction. These same critics perceive the New Wave as a pseudo avant-garde because it is not a political cinema and have derided it as being a cinema emanating from an anarchy of the Right. However, the rather loose bandying of the term avant-garde elides the fact that there was an avant-garde, but it was not in the New Wave. The problem arose out of lumping together, under the banner of New Wave, film-makers who may well have made their first feature film in the late 1950s, but whose work, apart from that temporal conjuncture, bore only the remotest resemblance to the New Wave style and preoccupations. In this respect, Varda and Resnais, for example, get incorrectly positioned as New Wavists.

According to the critics, this cinema has had two deleterious effects on the immediate future of cinema in that first, it discouraged television film-makers from coming into films, and second, it prevented a 'real' underground cinema (Jeancolas: 1979, 127–9). Thus on the one hand they were saying that this cinema did too little, and on the other, that it did too much – all of which endows the New Wave with too much importance. I have already discussed in the previous chapter how France does not really have a political cinema as a tradition, but that there are moments of exception (as in the 1930s, for example). In terms of 'real' underground, France has never had a tradition in the way that the United States or Germany has so it was unlikely that the New Wave would have spawned such a movement anyway, although part of the changes that this group introduced did facilitate the emergence of several 'underground' groups after May 1968. A further defence of the New Wave must be that its 'ethos' did inspire film-makers, underground movements and the emergence of new cinemas elsewhere in other countries and as such represented a moment in France's cinema history when cross-fertilisation was once again a two-way process. Rather than underground, we should speak of experimentation where French cinema is concerned, and as we have already seen, these moments are fairly rare. France's greatest sustained periods of experimentation were probably pre-sound (in its earliest heyday at the beginning of the century and again in the 1920s), after which experimentation became more sporadic and at times accidental. In fairness to the New Wave, it would seem useful to slow down and widen the debate and look at the overall discernible pattern of the last thirty years or so.

Although cinema in the late 1950s was being made then (as always) by an elite emanating predominantly from the white male bourgeoisie, one of the most fortuitous and long-lasting effects of the New Wave was that it forced a reconsideration of production practices. These film-makers were the first to suggest, by their huge influx into the industry, that a democratisation of the camera was possible.[18] This accessibility to the camera would eventually, in the 1970s, allow formerly marginalised voices and people into film-making (e.g., Women, Blacks and Beurs).[19] The second important effect came through the fact that they were the driving force of an auteur-led cinema without which it is doubtful that a renewed politicisation of French cinema, in the late 1960s and early 1970s, would have come about. The New Wave made two significant contributions, therefore, as the following events, post-1968, made clear.

In May 1968 cinema professionals went out on strike and set themselves up as the *Etats généraux du cinéma* (Estates General of Cinema) – a name that resonates with ancient, idealistic revolutionary discourses. In the fervour of the debates of that time they came to the 'realisation' (as did so many other professional groups) that they were workers, that is, that they were part of and not *the* total system of production. They had a function within the industry in a similar way that a factory floor worker on an assembly belt is merely a part of the production. The Estates General attacked cinema as a bourgeois institution and vowed to put in place another kind of cinema that went away from dominant ideological praxis and towards a political cinema that was non-hierarchical and cheaply made and that addressed the real lives of the working class as well as the issues affecting it. To this effect the film-maker no longer saw himself (*sic*) as auteur but as *travailleur* (not, the observant reader will note, as *ouvrier*). In their belief that cinema is a popular art form and in their stand for an anti-hierarchical and egalitarian cinema, these Marxist discourses bear some resemblance to those emanating from the *Ciné-liberté* group in the 1930s which also wanted to give a voice to and a transparence on those who are traditionally marginalised (not just by cinema, but by the dominant ideology).

The Estates General produced a thirty-six point *Déclaration des droits du cinéma* in which they declared the abolition of the CNC – a rather utopian assault against the establishment and doubtless motivated by the general feeling of discontent with state institutions over the Langlois affair. In February 1968, Henri Langlois, the director and one of the co-founders of the *Cinémathèque*, cherished by cinephiles, film-makers and many of the *Cahiers* group, was ousted and replaced by a government nominee. The state, because it subsidised the *Cinémathèque* so heavily, felt empowered to intercede in what it considered to be Langlois's gross mismanagement of its holdings and budget. The outrage was not inconsiderable. Malraux came under personal attack in numerous press articles, film-makers and cinephiles demonstrated to demand Langlois's reinstatement. They then formed a committee for the defence of the *Cinémathèque* and eventually obliged the government to back down. Langlois was finally reinstated on 22 March 1968.

Although nothing came of the Estates move to obliterate the CNC, there were three areas where their demands met with positive results. First, there was a restructuring of the CNC's commission on the *avance sur recettes* to include more film-makers on the board. Second, the profession was opened up to everyone through a small grants system administered by a body specially created to oversee projects – the *Groupe de recherches et d'essais cinématographiques* (GREC). These grants would facilitate first-time film-makers to make shorts (films lasting thirty minutes to an hour) which would then serve as their ticket into the industry. The third, and by far the most lastingly significant effect within the profession itself, was the creation of the *Société des réalisateurs de films* (SRF), a body that would eventually secure the *droits d'auteur* agreement (film-makers' rights over their films) so long sought after.

Looking back over the cinema of the 1960s, starting with the New Wave, we can see how this cinema – its love of certain American icons notwithstanding (Hawks, Hitchcock, Welles) and its Oedipal intentions on the *'cinéma de papa'* put to one side – did put in place a counter-cinema in relation to the standardisation effect of American technology and film practices. This counter-cinema was manifested in such practices as the hand-held camera, refusal of the studio, editing practices alien to the seamlessness of American-style products, a no-star system (even though their non-stars soon gained fetish status – Belmondo, Brialy, Moreau). It did not de-Parisianise itself, but it did secure a social place and space for the youth class. It was not politically engaged, but it was anti-bourgeois in sentiment (especially Chabrol's early films) and motivated by a desire to present the point of view of the individual in society. In some respects, from the point of view of content, this positioning recalls the tenor of the 'political' cinema made in the 1930s when the targeted point of view was that of the working class. The difference here is that the point of view in the New Wave was that of the youth class and one identified (rightly or wrongly) with the film-makers themselves (*'jeune cinéma'*).

The first decade of the Fifth Republic coincided with the 'death' of one father, *'le cinéma de papa'*, at the beginning and, at the end, with the 'death' of another, more real father figure this time, de Gaulle. These two parricides are not unconnected. In the eyes of the younger generation, as exemplified by the *Cahiers* group, the sclerotic paternalism of the film industry had stifled creation and experimentation. In the political world, *l'homme providentiel* of 1958 had transformed himself, by the second half of the decade, into an institutionalised monarch whose oppressive psycho-logical and moral paternalism the young and the intellectuals (at least) could no longer bear. De Gaulle, in wanting to save his country, had effectively suffocated the nation (Martin: 1984, 81). In both instances repression bred rejection if not contempt.

A film by Godard presciently articulates these two realities. *Le Mépris*, which came out in 1963, is about the 'death' of cinema, or of a certain mainstream cinema – the demise of the big-budget studio system movie as normative (including the 'death' of Hollywood as indeed is happening today). The film is also about the 'death' within the film of the then icon of the Fifth Republic, Brigitte Bardot. In this film within a film, Bardot/ Camille meets her death as a result of the contempt she feels for her scriptwriter husband's paternalistic reification of her body. Her contempt begins when she is forced by him to get into the American producer's car – with all the resonances of currying sexual favours which that forcing implies. It ends with her death in a car accident – but not before she has rejected her husband – and with the death, in the same accident, of the American producer. The Fifth Republic as it was is 'dead' and so too is hegemonic cinema.

The 'deaths' of the fathers brought about two different but complemen-tary types of liberalism. Post-1958, in New Wave films, cinematographic language was once again brought to the fore and the literary tradition took a back seat. Realism was the starting point, not the object of the exercise. Cinematic taboos were broken: the camera (being so lightweight) could take any angle it wanted, and this same camera could give the sense of spontaneity associated with live television as it raced around the streets of Paris picking up on people's conversations. Taboos around sexuality were also destroyed: free love was very much on the agenda (the fact that women were represented as agents of their own desire will be qualified later on in this chapter) and the couple was introduced under a completely new guise as a psychologically complex construct, addressing as it did such issues as power, identity and lack of communication.

Post-1962, this liberalism expanded further. However, it was no longer the exclusive domain of the consecrated auteurs of the New Wave. Now even mainstream cinema took on social problems of a wider concern, primarily the effects of modernisation and the consumer society on ordin-ary individuals. In both instances, this cinema has been loosely referred to as a *retour au réel* or naturalist cinema. Within the tradition of the New Wave, Godard's trilogy (*Vivre sa vie*, 1962, *Une femme mariée*, 1964, and *Deux ou trois choses que je sais d'elle* 1966) is well known in this respect. But films by less radical even mainstream film-makers can also be cited as participating in this '*retour au réel*'. In this context, mention must be made of the controversial film by the moderately radical Robert Enrico *La Belle vie* (1962 but not released until 1964 because of its references to Algeria).

It is a film about a young couple's difficulties in affective and social readaptation upon the husband's return from two and a half years' military service in Algeria. Fairly mainstream are Alain Jessua's *La Vie à l'envers* (1963) and *Jeu de massacre* (1966) which, in different ways, show the male protagonist withdrawing from society – from consumer self-satisfaction in the first film and from the vitiating effects of the media world in the other. Though less mainstream, it is appropriate to mention René Allio's film *Pierre et Paul* (1968). In this film, a middle-aged man, content with life and with no particular political affiliation, suddenly realises that he has fallen foul of the consumer society. Like so many other consumers, he has consumed on credit. This revelation of financial ruin through dupery mixed with concupiscence (robbing Peter to pay Paul) leads the protagonist to avenge himself by smashing up his apartment and shooting indiscriminately into the crowd below.

It would be a mistake to see all mainstream cinema of the 1960s as falling into this moralising category. Much of this cinema followed on in the tradition of the 1950s. This cinema was still star-led. The retro-mode continued to favour cloak and dagger films. De Broca's *Cartouche* (1961) is very much in the *Fanfan la tulipe* mode, but the most prolific film-maker in this genre was André Hunebelle. Literary adaptations of the nineteenth-century novel abounded and so too on a less serious side did the adaptation of historical novels, erotica included (Bernard Broderie's *Angélique* series). The *polars*/thrillers also had their retro-resonances with the continuation of Maigret adaptations suitably starring Gabin wherever possible. This retro-mode also nods to Becker's *Touchez pas au grisbi* and Melville's *Bob le flambeur*. Similarly the proto-family is still very much in evidence. Father/son now grows to grandfather/father/son, with the ageing Gabin ever present alongside Ventura and Delon (as in Verneuil's *Le Clan des Siciliens*, 1969). The son continues to defy the father. This hexagonal referentiality is matched, primarily, by Melville's continued nods to the American *film-noir* genre of the 1940s (*Le Doulos* and *Le Deuxième souffle*). It is also matched by the emergence of the more modern Americanised look of the *polars* such as Clément's *Plein soleil* (1960) and Deray's *La Piscine* (1969). Finally, it is matched by the creation of a new genre, or rather the re-emergence in modern dress of a sub-genre of the thriller – the spy series – which was conceived to counter the impact of the Bond series. These were the fairly interchangeable *OSS 177* series, the resurrection of *Fantômas* and the more challenging *Monocle* films. Series (with the exception of comedy) had all but disappeared from the French screen since the 1920s. Now they were back in vogue and were, by and large, as chauvinistic in their hexagonal superiority as in earlier times – xenophobia once again revealing a nation ill at ease with itself. Thus, although, there were contemporaneous and moralising discourses within mainstream cinema, none the less, this cinema of the first age of the Fifth Republic was still doing its level best to remain safely hermetic.

Post-1968, cinema in general moved closer to contemporaneity, both in terms of the social and the political arena. May 1968 allowed (at last) a political cinema to emerge, but it also enabled commercial cinema to rouse itself from its enforced anaesthesia under de Gaulle. Some political cinema was quite radical both in its conception and in its politics. Martin (1984, 86) qualifies it as militant cinema. Other political cinemas were codified much as any other mainstream cinema product and produced a spectacularisation of politics that ranged from a civic cinema (ibid., 82) to a cynical exercise of mixing in the right ingredients to create the flavour of the moment.

Militant cinema rejected the inherent facility of civic cinema in favour of a conception of cinema as a weapon of direct politics, as a political tool in its own right. The very names of some of the collectives point directly to the desire to signify as political. Godard and Guérin's Dziga-Vertov group refers to the 1920s Soviet film-maker and his avant-garde formalism (including deconstruction). The Medvedkine group, which grew around Chris Marker and came out of an earlier group called SLON (*Société pour le lancement d'oeuvres nouvelles*, which became Iskra in 1973), refers to the 1930s Soviet film-maker who shot, developed and projected filmed documentation on the spot (in a train which became known as a *ciné-train*). Not surprisingly, both collectives were of the Left, although the Dziga-Vertov group was highly critical of the PCF (as a result of its ambiguous stand during the events of May). The Dziga-Vertov group was committed to 'making politically a political cinema', but its collectivism is less transparent than in the work of the Medvedkine group (i.e., the Godard touch is very visible in the films which the Dziga-Vertov collective produced). A women's film collective, Musidora (named after the silent screen star of *Vampires* fame) also grew out of this momentum, but was short-lived. Otherwise, on the Left there were the more sectarian groups Dynadia (later renamed *Unicité*) which supported the PCF, the Maoist CRP (*Cinéastes révolutionnaires prolétariens*) and the left-wing *Cinélutte*.[20] Although both Dynadia and CRP limited their perception of cinema to its instrumentalist value of furthering their respective political causes, all the other groups went beyond this in their commitment to a militant cinema as a way of moving the aesthetic debate foreward, even though few of these advances crossed over into mainstream cinema.

Not all of this militant cinema was group- or collective-based. Marin Karmitz made two films in this period about workers, the second of which, *Coup pour coup* (1971), is given over entirely to the experience of women workers who recount their strike and occupation of the factory and their anger at the sell-out of their cause by the Communist union leaders. A militant, rather than a 'reasonable' treatment of the abortion issue was given in *Histoire d'A* (Charles Belmont and Marielle Issartel, 1973). Not only did the film give strong support in favour of liberalising the anti-abortion laws, it also gave examples of the different methods used and the names and addresses where women could go for such assistance. The film was banned by the censorship commission, but over 200,000 spectators saw it clandestinely which makes it one of the most seen militant films of this period.

The veteran René Vautier, whose work was a precursor of a certain kind of militant cinema with his documentaries made in the 1950s on Algeria from the FLN's (i.e., rebel/marginal) point of view (e.g., *Afrique 50*, 1955), was back on screen with two feature films on the Algerian question, *Avoir vingt ans dans les Aurès* (1972) – which reflects on the daily reality of French soldiers living that war – and *La Folle de Toujane* made in collaboration with Nicole le Garrec (1974) and which is a deeper examination of the psychological effects of this war by those who experienced it. The success of Vautier's first feature film (*Avoir vingt ans*) makes the point that militancy and attraction are not mutually exclusive. Vautier was also one of the first to take militant cinema out of Paris and make it regional. He set up *L'Unité de production cinéma Bretagne* (UPCB) in 1972, out of which he produced *La Folle de Toujane*. A couple of years later, Allio set up a centre for Occitane cinema: the *Centre méditerranéen de création cinématographique* (CMCC). Thus, another legacy of the post-1968 militant cinema was a renewed impetus for regional cinemas (those not of the centre, i.e., Paris) unseen since the 1920s and one or two film-makers' work in the 1930s (Pagnol and Renoir). These regional cinemas did not transpose Parisian actors into the 'authentic' locus to simulate the 'authentic' accent, gesturality, etc., but used the indigenous authentic to deliver their message. This legacy remains today in the form of independent regional collectives – collectives that have been rescued from financial difficulty by the state and that have subsequently become funded by the municipality (the case for CMCC) and, finally, by *Centres culturels*, initiated by the Minister of Culture, Jack Lang.

Civic cinema of this same period was not without its significance either in that it too gave a greater transparence on the present. Jeancolas (1974, 15) gives three reasonable explanations for this: first, the shock waves of May 1968, second, the generalising effect of television (by 1966 60 per cent of all householders had a television set, by 1972 this figure had grown to 75 per cent), and third, the successful spate of American and Italian films whose narratives were located in the present. Here in this cinema we are no longer limited to the centre (Paris). In this civic cinema, suburbs and new towns are on the landscape. The provinces are quite faithfully represented. This cinema is concerned with socio-political problems including the immigrant class, women and their respective rights. Political scandals and affairs are readily referred to with a minimum of disguise. High finance and fraud in many domains (e.g., sport and the construction business), sexuality and sexual liberation (including, in the late 1970s, the question of male homo-sexuality) are openly addressed. Workers' issues, especially their relation-ship to production (not fully seen since the 1930s, mainly in Clair's films), are also put on to the screen. The contemporaneity of the different social classes and the types of jobs they have give evidence to a contemporary social landscape. Journalists, radio and television people, advertisers, cops with problems – are all part of this (middle-class) 'authenticity'. Previously taboo subjects such as the Occupation, the real face of the Resistance, Algeria are allowed to be aired, and these films in particular reflect a cinema of disbelief in the recent past as does some of the cinema that moralises on the censorship activities of the Gaullian regime. Also within this civic cinema is a display of the politics of paranoia, particularly in the *polars*/thrillers. This paranoia was not unjustified given the climate of the times when police powers – including the brutality of the CRS during the May 1968 demonstrations – were still very unrestricted and the state had total autocracy over the audiovisual media. Finally, racism is at long last brought on to the agenda.

This civic cinema was not all of mainstream cinema. In the conformist mainstream cinema, comedies especially and *polars* (still the dominant genres) continued to throw back comforting pictures reflecting the immuta-bility of social hierarchy. The retro-mode was still in evidence (including comedies and *polars*) but on a diminished scale. These films favoured the pre-Vichy period and the Occupation. Critics of the Left have tended to see this nostalgia – at least that inherent in the Occupation films – as an attempt to reconcile the Gaullist Right with the Vichy Right, and call this cinema *fascisant*. This is rather a reductionist reading and points, as David Nicholls says (1982, 98), to a paranoid belief that the Left would never legitimately get into power. In this respect, it also reveals a nostalgia for May 1968 and the revolution that did not happen. Another objection to this reading is that the retro-mode was more evidently absent during the 1970s than at any other time in French cinema's history. A more accurate reading would be to see the retro-mode as a typology of film that appeals to wide audience taste. Generally uncontroversial, retro-films comfort the spectator in a number of different ways depending on the subject matter. France's history, family dynasties, scurrilous bandits, nineteenth-century 'classics', Belle Epoque – are all 'appropriate' topics for viewing by audiences wishing to escape the present. Sanitised images they may be and as such they do reinforce the *status quo*, but that is a far cry from *fascisant*. What can be considered disconcerting in retro-films, in general, is their implicit politics of refusal, characterised by a total lack of curiosity.

It was not until Giscard d'Estaing came to power, in 1974, that a fully fledged age of liberalism dawned in France. Giscard had no party *per se* but a consortium of centrists. Nor did he have a platform based on doctrinal lines but instead a number of liberalising policies. If he espoused any ideology at all it was rooted in American-style capitalism and the cult of money. He seemed the modern man set to draw France out of her Gaullist turpitude. Amongst his policies, one had a direct consequence for cinema – the abolition of censorship in 1974. The age of liberalism had arrived, but with it a plethora of pornographic films – not necessarily a curious eventuality until one considers the history of the time and other reforms that policies brought in. The improvement of women's legal status and the legalisation of abortion certainly reflected Giscard's heeding of the claims of the women's movement in France which post-1968 had become extremely vocal and consolidated in its demands. Directly within cinema there is a manifest attestation to the presence of women on a political front by the greatly increased number of women making feature films, particularly in the second half of the decade. During the whole of the decade, some thirty-seven women film-makers made their first feature films (but this only represented 10 per cent of the total 'new talent').[21] Thus the question remains, given all this socio-political framework, why so much porn?

Until 1974, pornographic cinema had been very marginal. Now it had moved from being a cinema of the periphery to a very central one. During the period 1975–9 this cinema averaged 50 per cent of all French production screened. Giscard had said 'no more censorship' (in cinema or in prisons – a curious conflation) and he was kept to his word. There are three important things that critics have said about this rise, if not in the popularity, at least in the exhibitionist practices of this newly popularised genre, none of which can be separated out from the feminist issue – or so it seems to me. First, Martin (1984, 94) argues that pornographic and erotic films are a sociological phenomenon that is typical of liberalism. He goes on to say that in a society that is intent on frenetic consumption and pursuing the proto-American ideal of get rich quick, sex will also be grabbed on the quick. Second, in addition to Martin, Jeancolas (1977, 259) argues that implicit in this consumption of porn is a reflection of a society that is ill at ease with itself, surrounded by false desires (created by the drive to consume). In this respect, porn cinema functions much like advertising in that it awakens a desire, distorts it by giving it magical proportions (in much the same way as an advertisement promises the spectator exotica or improved performance if s/he will only purchase 'x' product), and then gives false satisfaction because the film cannot fully deliver (no apologies for the dreadful puns). Third and finally, the effect of this proliferation, along with the way in which it is packaged, is to normalise desire. Or so the argument goes. Maybe. But I believe there is more to this than meets the eye.

Pornography is not just about desire, if indeed desire is the right word. It is also about man's profound mistrust, even fear of women's sexuality. Pornography, therefore, is a means whereby men can control it, position women as they want them positioned – particularly as desirous of the phallus. So rather than normalising desire (which it may well do, but I doubt), pornography is a form of policing desire, of making women conform to a specifically phallic conception of them. Clearly, with the rise of the women's movement, males' anxiety about their position and renewed fears about female sexuality came very much to the fore. Pornography in this regard and especially its proliferation can be read as a phallocratic response to the possible loss not just of the 'phallic' (language, machismo, etc.) but also the female object of desire (woman no longer positionable/fetishisable by the male gaze). It is instructive in this context that some male porn filmmakers should adopt a female pseudonym as if to reassure the male spectator that women really do 'desire' like this (if 'women' film-makers say so, it must be true). What is worrying though is the implicit revenge on feminism that this artifice proposes. By adopting a pseudo-feminist position, through the simulacrum of sexual equality ('liberated women are free to make this sort of film as well as men'), feminism gets recuperated into male mythology (a bit like the intention behind the myth of the burning bra).

This whole cycle of events got going in 1974 when the film *Emmanuelle* (made by Just Jaeckin – 'just joking'?) was exhibited in a number of fashionable Parisian cinemas.[22] Even though *Emmanuelle* was not strictly porn (sexual acts were simulated rather than real), it got lumped into the general catch-all word. In sixty weeks the film had topped 2 million viewers in Paris and it was the top film of 1974.[23] Pornography had not just come of age: for that year at least it was France's leading national cinema product – a curious state of affairs if there ever was one. What makes the picture even murkier is the role the state played in the subsequent five years of this 'genre's' history. By the following year, *Emmanuelle*'s erotica had turned into hard-core porn with Jean-François Davy's *Exhibition* which again was screened in top cinema houses (it ranked eighth that year, closely followed by Jaeckin's *Histoire d'O* in ninth place). Public outrage demanded government intervention. Public opinion was so strong that in 1976 it even pushed Paris courts to condemn one film (*L'Essayeuse*) to the stake. The government could not reintroduce censorship because it would be accused of taking reactionary measures (which would go counter to Giscard's very carefully groomed image of liberal modernity). So the government went down the fiscal route and did three things. It imposed a heavier tax, an 'X' certificate on porn films and on cinema theatres specialising in screening them. It also imposed an extra tax on imported porn. Thus the government in an invidious way became both the pimp and the protectionist for French cinema. The extra tax went to subsidise the *avance sur recettes* and the imposition of still further tax on imported films guaranteed that porn films became an indigenous industry. The government also ensured that, for a while at least, porn was big business, since 'X' cinemas were specifically designated as such and would thereby attract the appropriate viewers/voyeurs.

As has already been mentioned, genres come and go (some more evidently than others) and by 1979 this particular industry/'genre' was on the wane. The reasons are of interest. The first is economic: because of the increase in taxation (not just on porn films but also on film receipts in general), ticket prices had risen to the point where audiences were becoming disaffected. Television of course played its part. A further reason was the transformation of the geographic implantation of cinemas. Cinemas in the suburbs and in working-class districts closed down for lack of economic viability and cinema venues became very centralised. Porn did not turn audiences off, but economic exigencies and lack of immediate accessibility made this cinema, briefly of the centre, return once more to the periphery. By the 1980s porn films were attracting around 5 per cent of the cinemagoing audience, representing a return to the normal state of affairs (Martin: 1984, 94).

Whereas the 1970s cinema marked an opening up of the social sphere under its observation, that of the 1980s marked a closing down. A major reason for this was the fact that cinema had truly become demand-led. However, because this audience was predominantly that of the youth class (15–24-year-olds) and accounted for 51.3 per cent of the entries (Bonnell: 1989, 26) – the rest being made up of middle-class professionals and intellectuals – the overriding factor became entertainment value. In terms of subject matter, therefore, what predominated were films that reflected either that youth generation or that generation's taste. A diminished audience in terms of heterogeneity leads – as all advertising agencies know – to a diminished market in terms of choice. A standardisation of the product was the direct result, bringing in its wake a progressive ideological normalisation. The cinema's primary focus in the face of this lack of subject matter was films about adolescence and young adulthood, including placing that adolescence in the relative nostalgic atmosphere of the 1950s (it should not be forgotten that by the 1980s a significant number of the 1970s new film-makers were in their mid-forties).

Civic cinema did not disappear immediately, but was soon on the wane and what little there was (produced in the early 1980s) tended to have reference points that were more international and less specific (political assassinations, political corruption in general, international espionage). In that they imitated the American genre more closely both in look and in the lack of topical references, the same can be said of the still immensely popular *polars*. The '*retour au réel*' of the previous decade lived on but only in appearance. Any idea that it reflected society by giving a transparence on those marginalised by cinema is largely a myth – the exception being the newly emergent Beur cinema. Thus, although another new wave of women film-makers came on to the scene (around twenty or so), very little of their work or indeed that of their slightly older counterparts could be called women's, or indeed feminist cinema. The women's cinema – what there was of it – was the work of the 1970s. Subjects that could now be treated in this post-feminist period included male and female sado-masochism, anti-colonialism, the family – that is, to all appearances, male perversions or Judeo-Christian constructs (although a woman's voice was speaking). Elsewhere, mainly in the *polars*, marginals were no longer invited to have a more centred voice. They were either demonised or criminalised. The 1980s, it would appear, was not the decade to be an outsider. The age of liberalism was over. So too, it would appear, was the age of ideology – a surprising assertion given that the Left had at long last acceded to power and that it has remained in power for a third of the Fifth Republic's existence. Given that the period after 1981 did not bring about the radical political change anticipated, is it that surprising, one wonders, that cinema was equally unmoved to innovate and renovate?

The culture of the 1980s was predominantly the pastiche culture. After all, it was the decade that launched the term 'Le Look' in fashion ('*montre-moi ton Look et je te dirai qui tu es*'). French cinema was no exception and seems to have been made up of two dominant characteristics: the *cinéma du Look* and the *cinéma rétro-nostalgie*. In the first case, the image was the ontology. A sort of BCBG on celluloid, the *cinéma du Look* was belief in the image as pure surface seduction, the image for and of itself. The image was the message. This was due in part to a resurgence of American cultural imperialism not just on the cinema screens but also on the television channels in the form of advertising, video-clips and popular series. It was also due to the fact that the majority of films produced were made with the television market in mind. Thus this cinema adopted the iconographic forms of hi-tech and designer-violence (*Miami Vice* is exemplary in this respect). In the second case, the 1980s cinema adopted a form of cultural nostalgia. This cultural nostalgia manifested itself in films harking back to earlier cinema genres and traditions, hence the plethora of neo-*films-noirs* like Boisset's *Bleu comme l'enfer* (1985) or Swaim's *La Balance* (1982) and of literary adaptations, especially of Pagnol's novels. It also harked back to earlier types, for example, Tavernier's neo-Renoir/Becker *Un dimanche à la campagne* (1983) and the Fernandelesque *Trois hommes et un couffin* (Coline Serreau, 1985). Thus, whilst nostalgia culture harked back to earlier myths and thereby functioned cryptologically as transparence for past ideologies, the *cinéma du Look* refracted purely and solely upon itself. Narcissus had come of age.

French cinema of the 1980s, therefore, was essentially non-oppositional. It displayed itself symptomatically in that it was both retro-nostalgic and hi-tech – two modalities that did not mutually exclude each other. In its nostalgic manifestation, French film gazed back to earlier styles and genres in cinema. As hi-tech, French film was designer-film, contemplating itself as pure style. These films, so redolent with designer-hyphenated images (designer-violence, designer-clothes, and designer-stubble – the hyphen signifying reliance), revealed an obsession with and a dependence on the image. In both instances the image was fetishised and necrophilia was at work. Retro-nostalgia contemplated its own filmo-cultural heritage and hi-tech was fascinated by its empty brilliance. With regard to the latter category, it is worth briefly mentioning the example of *Bleu comme l'enfer* because of its extreme fetishism with the image as object. In this film, which is almost entirely constructed out of scenes of violence, what is in evidence is the extremes to which those images of violence will be pushed. In this very conventional (in terms of cinematic narrative codes) love-triangle, designer-violence is nowhere at its best until the final gory and gruesome denouement where husband (a cop, played by Tcheky Karyo) and lover (Lambert Wilson) fight over 'the woman' by hurtling sticks of dynamite (the inflamed phallus) at each other somewhere in the wastelands of the Alpilles (hell it might be, but *High Noon* it isn't).

Films of earlier generations are now pastiched and are devoid of that element of parody which would breathe an air of irony into them. The remake of *Le Diable au corps* (Marco Bellochio, 1986), first made in 1946 by Autant-Lara, will suffice to illustrate this point. The original filmed version of this story of an illicit love affair presented a cynical amorality that the remake fails to recapture or to make anew within 1980s post-liberalism. The more recent version tells the same story but without the cutting edge of the Autant-Lara film. There is only one major difference. The sex scenes which were discreetly ellipsed (the adolescent in his lover's bed 'the morning after'), because of censorship, are now inserted. Absence has become presence, the ellipse has been visually filled, and suggestion eroticised. That is all. But 'putting in the sex bits' does not a new film make. Forty years on, the lifting of censorship notwithstanding, the cinematic process gazes vacuously backwards.

Similarly, genres are mimicked and not renewed as the spate of *polars* (25 per cent of the output) demonstrates. Extremely popular with the public, many of these films hark back to the stereotypes of the American *film-noir* of the 1940s. Equally, the more evidently nostalgic films echo, stylistically, the cinematographic language of the 1930s and 1950s, and institutionally, the sexual conventions of the 1940s and 1950s. The sexual revolution (of the 1960s and 1970s) is over, the family and the extended family is back and with it the patriarch. *Conseil de famille* (Costa-Gavras, 1985), presents all the clichés of happy family life. Father and associate (a close friend of the family who lives in) – safe blowers by trade (shades of *Touchez pas au grisbi*) – loving wife and two adorable kids (a little bit of sibling incest on the side) live in perfect harmony. Business prospers and the father insists on adopting all the bourgeois trappings such as expensive holidays by the sea, private education for the children, and *chez les jésuites* for the boy – a mistake because the boy will 'turn moral' and grass on his father. But even this Oedipal gesture fails to ruin happiness. After serving his prison sentence, the father returns and everyone becomes one happy family again. *Trois hommes et un couffin* (Serreau, 1985), which has earlier prototypes in John Ford's *Desert Son* (1948, starring John Wayne) and Henri Verneuil's *Le Boulanger de Valargue* (1952, starring Fernandel) and in which three men get landed with having to care for a baby, is equally regressive in its re-awakening of traditional family values and celebration of paternity.

As far as age representation is concerned, youth prevails to the point where youth-as-image is fetishised. Political cinema has evaporated and if any ideology is being reflected in these films it is that of youth 'neoculture' (rock-video-disco). It might be tempting to state that there is small surprise in this given that the cultural group being targeted with this unthinking/uninventive/auto-referential celluloid is predominantly the youth culture. By diffusing images of their own particular culture, they are sending back images of 'sameness'. In this way the media, under the pretence of doing precisely the opposite, effectively defuses (whether intentionally or not) any potential politicising of this group. Youth sub-culture has become recuperated and the images, in defining this group's own culture, become a mask for repression and self-deception ('*montre-moi ton Look et je te dirai qui tu es*').

In terms of subjects, themes and style, the spectator of today is reviewing and reliving the whole of modernist cinema (1930–58). But today's post-modern cinema also cannibalises itself as it regurgitates images and discourses of its own age. With a few exceptions, there are no social or political films. Some of the major issues of the 1980s go unheard. Unemployment and racism (except in Beur cinema and a handful of films), Aids, sexism, drug addiction, nuclear policies and France's international role in the Middle East and elsewhere, are all subjects which pass almost completely under silence. This dearth of subjects coincides with a cinematographic mannerism which manifests itself in the first instance, by a prurient necrophiliac fixation with images and genres of a by-gone cinema, and in the second instance, by a servile simulation of television visual discourses. It is in this sense that postmodern film-makers of today display a disdain for culture with a capital C. All culture, 'high' and 'low', is assimilable/quotable within their texts so that the binary line is erased. This would not necessarily be a bad thing if they were to make some meaning of it. Instead, in their formalism and mannerism they aim purely and simply for the well-made image. They invent nothing. Viewed as a whole, the 1980s cinema has signalled the arrival of the *fin-de-sièclisme* mode.

I speculated earlier on how the New Wave, though not through any necessary intentionality, reflected the instability of France as a nation in a period of radical institutional change and how, with hindsight at least, it reveals the fragility of a nation whose new mythologies had not yet been invented. In the post-1981 period, the regressive and narcissistic character of cinema – fixed as it is in its reflection of institutional myths which go back thirty years and in its affirmation of the intellectually deficient neoculture/post-culture of the present – reveals a nation devoid of its own ideology and a society with a highly restricted culture lacking any clear sense of identity. Without identity, French cinema on the whole is holding up a single image – a simulacrum in the form of mass media discourse (predominantly clip and '*pub*' and nostalgia culture). Small wonder that Disneyland has come to the suburbs of Paris – the *guinguette* of this particular *fin de siècle*.

I shall now take a closer look at these cinemas of the past thirty years, starting from the peripheries and moving to the centre.

TWO GENRES OF THE PERIPHERY: OCCUPATION AND COLONIAL FILMS

During the de Gaulle era, some sixty feature films about the Occupation period were made (compared with only eleven under Giscard). The peak years were 1958–62 when thirty films were produced, half of which were either specifically about the Resistance (nine in all) or directly referred to it through their narrative (six). This exaltation of the Resistance is hardly surprising given de Gaulle's prominent role as leader of the Free French during World War II. This time, of course, the resurrection of the Resistance 'as a good thing' was once again not without its political expediency. De Gaulle's designation of power in 1958 was a popular decision, but he still had to convince the electorate to vote for his constitutional reforms and consolidate his own legitimacy (through universal suffrage). There is no intention to point to a propaganda conspiracy here, but it is clear that, with pre-censorship still in effect, scenarios not extolling the Resistance would be unlikely to get past the final post of censorship. Whatever the case, the indications are that producers had seen a winner in cashing in on de Gaulle's iconographic prestige and milked it for what it was worth. Post-1962, the genre started its move back towards the periphery. But by then de Gaulle had the cachet of legitimacy and television too – the medium he was henceforth to exploit as his propaganda sheet.

It was not until the 1970s and the new age of liberalism that the 'truth' about the Occupation and the Resistance could come out. Equally pertinently, this exposure was not limited to the more marginal militant cinema but extended to the mainstream cinema that we have categorised as civic. Two films, *Le Chagrin et la pitié* (Ophuls, 1970) and *Français si vous saviez* (Harris and de Sédouy, 1973) – although not strictly feature films in that they are composed of edited documentaries and interviews – were the first to raise questions about the way the French conducted themselves during

that period. If anything, they obliged a reappraisal of that time hitherto
sacralised in myths of the Resistance. Ophuls' film was produced by the
makers of the second film and would have remained a peripheral film if a
number of myths had not, in turn, grown up around it. Originally intended
for television, Ophuls' four-hour documentary film was turned down by the
ORTF. The rumour ran that the ORTF had forbidden its transmission. But
as Ophuls himself says, the ORTF was not obliged to buy the film and if it
was guilty of censorship, then it was one of inertia rather than cunning
(quoted in Jeancolas: 1979, 209). In any event, public demand grew and
screening had to be moved from the small *art et essai* cinema into a bigger
theatre.

As far as mainstream civic cinema is concerned, amongst the films made
about the Occupation period, mention must be made of Louis Malle's
Lacombe Lucien (1974), first because of the controversy surrounding it and
second because it attracted such a large audience (it ranked sixth in 1974,
the year of *Emmanuelle*), testifying to public interest in the topic if nothing
else. The critics (mostly of the Left) accused the message of this film of
being *fascisant* in its portrayal of a young man who by accident joins the
milice (or as Lucien repeatedly says, *police allemande*). Although the
polemic around this film has long since abated, I think it is worth putting in
place a counter-argument because this will not be the first time in this
discussion of the civic cinema of the 1970s that the accusation of 'politically
incorrect' political films will be heard. I would argue that this film, amongst
other things, is a film about the *discours fascisant*. It points, in the first
instance, to the fact that Fascism is an 'attraction' – the first time Lucien
encounters it he is positioned as an outsider looking on (as voyeur). If
Fascism attracts, it is paradoxically because the image is eventually
vacuous. Fascism was born out of a need for a sense of national unity. But
that national unity was perceived monoculturally – all 'others' were to be
excluded/exterminated. Fascism in this respect is a mass movement whose
ability to thrive is based on the appeal of revolutionary methods without
any revolutionary programme. In other words, Fascism has the manifestations of ideology but no ideological content. The Final Solution is
nothing to do with ideology but with a sadistic revenge on the 'others'. In
the second instance, Malle's film echoes Wilhelm Reich's definition of
Fascism as the substitution of one sort of mysticism for another: the sado-
masochistic mysticism of nationalism for the masochistic international
religious mysticism. Lucien's gradual ensnaring of the Jewish tailor's
daughter, France, clearly exemplifies the sado-masochistic dynamic of
Fascism. Finally, the film exposes the fiction swallowed by those without
identity but who are desperate to have one, namely, that the language of
the father/Führer will invest them with power. It is for this reason
that Lucien's joining the *milice*, though aleatory in its timing, is not
accidental.[24]

Turning briefly to the other genre of the periphery mentioned above, the colonial film, the first point to make concerns the virtual invisibility of Indochina. On the rare occasions that it is the central focus of a film, as in Coutard's *Hoa Binh* (1970) and the collective film *Loin du Vietnam* (1967), the tendency is to look at its more recent history and relate it to the American intervention in Vietnam. Alternatively, if France's role is referred to, Indochina becomes reduced to a militaro-racist text (*Fort du fou*, Joannon, 1963). The one exception is Pierre Schoendoerffer's *La 317e Section* (1965), a careful, virtually unpartisan reconstruction of his own experience of the Indochina war when he was an army cameraman (his fictionalised version was shot by Coutard). The title of the 1967 collective film, *Loin du Vietnam*, would appear to sum up aptly producers' interest in that part of the ex-Empire. Elsewhere, if a colony can be said to dominate, then it is Algeria that comes first, but only during the 1960s and 1970s. Again as with the previous genre, in the 1960s, as one might expect, the few films that made it to the screen toed the official line. But, as Jeancolas (1979, 162) points out, the attempts on de Gaulle's life and the OAS terrorist activities in France would make this type of film perfectly consonant with the official climate of the times.

By the 1970s, however, the colonial film was showing a more anti-militarist point of view (with the exception once again of the more 'neutral' Schoendoerffer and his film *Crabe-Tambour*, 1977). *Avoir vingt ans dans les Aurès* (Vautier, 1972) was the first film to speak out fulsomely against French intervention in Algeria. The most significant aspect of this film is its representation not just of the French army troops' disenchantment with the Algerian war/conflict but also of their total disbelief in their function in it. Not a patriotic sentiment in sight. Boisset's *R.A.S.* (*Rien à signaler*, 1973) is categorically anti-military in its depiction of brutality by the military (to their own). Finally, Heynemann's *La Question* (1976) denounces the use of torture by the French army against the Algerians. Other films of the 1970s concerned with ex-colonies attempt to reflect the effects of colonialism on the indigenous people. To quote one last example, Ciampi's *Liberté I* (1961, the title means Independence Year One) looks at the difficulties faced by an ex-colony (Senegal) once it has received its independence. Corrupt structures do not disappear with the colonialists, Ciampi's film tells us, but remained ingrained in the practices of the indigenous bourgeois class.

By the 1980s the connotations were different. Colonial films were now about the personal experience or semi-autobiographical recollection of an ex-colonial. Up until this time very few films addressed this particular aspect of ex-colonialism.[25] Interestingly many, but not all, of this last generation of colonial films were made by women – a voice of marginals speaking about marginalities, including their own. Algeria, Nouméa and Senegal are the colonies/ex-colonies at the centre of, in respective order, *Outremer* by Brigitte Rouan (1990), *Bal du gouverneur* by Marie-France Pisier (1990) and *Chocolat* by Clare Denis (1988). All three reflect an anti-colonial mentality which the film-makers try to explore through the subjectivity of the female protagonist. This they do by addressing the 'marginal' of colonialism, that is, central to their discourse is the notion that the coloniser is the alien not the colony. Women as marginals themselves have their marginality even more strongly represented in the colonies, where the futility of their lives becomes strident. Each film recalls the central protagonist's childhood through traces of the lives of the respective families – a microcosm through which to examine the dynamics of colonialism. Paternalism here (the family), paternalism there (the colony). These films are not just a protest against the effects of colonialism but are also a deep questioning of the coloniser's *raison d'être* (why am I here?) and of the post-coloniser's role in relation to these countries (why am I still here and making movies?).

TWO CINEMAS OF THE PERIPHERY: THE AVANT-GARDE AND WOMAN'S EROTIC GAZE

Over the last thirty years, the avant-garde has followed a similar pattern to that of the previous avant-garde (begun in the 1920s). It has moved from the periphery to a brief moment in the limelight (late 1950s, early 1960s when it was associated with the New Wave) and then gradually regained the periphery. Another important point is that those film-makers who are making oppositional cinema now are predominantly those who were there at the beginning (Varda, Resnais, Godard and Bresson) – the ranks of the avant-garde swelled somewhat in the 1970s (to include Duras, Hanoun, Robbe-Grillet and briefly Eustache with *La Maman et la putain*, 1973) only to contract again in the 1980s. There is currently little sign of any new-comers to the scene, although some critics are touting Léos Carax as a harbinger of a new avant-garde. *Cahiers du cinéma* has recently devoted an entire special issue to him and his latest film *Les Amants du Pont-Neuf* (1991) and see in his work a new cinema emerging.[26] However, whilst his work displays the outward signs of invention, it shows none of the inner investigation of film language as sign. The plasticity of his images in *Mauvais sang* (1986) is remarkable and memorable, for example, yet the same can be said about Beineix's *Diva* made six years earlier, and the visual virtuosity of *Les Amants du Pont-Neuf* is not tenough to sustain a fundamentally flawed narrative or even counter-narrative.

If any cinema can be said to be breaking any moulds, it is the recent arrival in mainstream cinema of a black humour type of cinema that may be the augur of something new. This is a biting satiric comedy that does, it seems, set questions. Etienne Chatiliez's two films *La Vie est un long fleuve tranquille* (1987) and *Tatie Danielle* (1990) signal a new departure in their mordant disquisitions on family life, and so do Eric Rochant's *Un monde sans pitié* (1990) and *Aux yeux du monde* (1991) in their examination of the aberrational effects of the 1980s on the human psyche. Two swallows do not a renewal make, however. As Jean-Pierre Jeunet and Marc Caro's madly fantastic allegory about the 1930s, *Delicatessen* (1991), makes clear, renewal is difficult to sustain and can verge upon the grotesque. What is significant is that the renewal is being attempted in comedy, the most conservative of all the genres. Perhaps as with Tati it will be short-lived. Or, alternatively, as we enter into this new decade and then the millennium, perhaps it will spill over into other genres and French cinema will experience a new cycle of invention. But this is speculation. Let us return to the avant-garde.

Although all the avant-garde film-makers mentioned above have contributed to the counter-cinematic praxis, lack of space and indeed the genesis of this book (which is to see France's national cinema as a whole) does not permit me to develop upon this oppositional cinema at great length. Resnais, Duras and Robbe-Grillet's work (though not to be seen as one and the same) explore the movements of the unconscious mind and the distorting processes of memory. The work of Resnais will have to serve as exemplary because, of the three, he has been the most prolific (albeit with only thirteen feature films to his name compared with Godard's fifty!) and his work spans the three decades under review. It is also noteworthy that his first two films were scripted by the other two. Resnais makes the subject matter of his films an occasion for stylistic experimentation. His whole cinematic practice is one of dislocation then reorganisation of the image sound and text. His films place in counterpoint an easily understandable story with multiple signs that are totally resistant to that narrativity. Just to cite, by way of illustration, a Resnais film per decade, *Hiroshima mon amour* (1959), *Providence* (1976), *La Vie est un roman* (1983) – all of which have as a basic construct a series of imbricated texts, some readable, others not – is to make the point about his cinematographic style. In each film someone's story gets revived and relived in a series of different ways and in different contexts and times. Two love stories converge and dissipate in the face of each other ultimately to be confined to oblivion much as Hiroshima's (the Atomic bomb) and Nevers' (the Occupation) histories (*Hiroshima*). Clive positions his family in his novels but also narrates them as he truly perceives them, only to discard them once they appear to him in flesh and blood as they 'really' are – totally distinct from his double fantasies (*Providence*). Life is a novel, one man's folly, an animated cartoon fairy tale and a teachers' conference; life is geologically inscribed (across time and texts) and functions as much within the imaginary as within the real (*La Vie est un roman*). Resnais's films incessantly place before us, in all the attendant formations and manifest complexities imaginable, the mnemonic infrastructure of the mind. Whilst, on the surface, it appears that a cinematic socio-psychologism is at work here, it is also the case that sub-textually there is a cinematic theoretical psychoanalysism endeavouring to unravel, unlayer mental functionings crucial to our survival and without which we would undoubtedly perish (as exemplified in different, real or metaphorical ways in *Van Gogh*, 1946, *L'Année dernière à Marienbad*, 1961 and *L'Amour à mort*, 1984).

Godard is undoubtedly *the* icon of the avant-garde cinema and his films have had the most radical effect on other cinemas – not just the French but also most of the other cinemas both mainstream and experimental. It is he, along with Varda, who has the most contemporaneous of discourses. His films of the 1960s are virtually alone in reflecting that period's sense of discomfort at the sclerotic state of a society where the '*génération du baby-boom*' was being governed by an old man whose principles and mores had more to do with those of his grandparents than his own. In this regard, *Weekend* (1967), although it is about the evils of the consumer society, is also about the effects of republicanism on civil liberties. In the film, the discourses of republicanism are counterpointed with capitalist consumption, the rhetoric of ideology with human practice, and together they produce the following readings. *Weekend* is a cautionary tale about revolutionary texts – it is also a deconstructed road movie and as such subverts, anarchises even, the genre. Three texts are up for scrutiny: the Jacobin (in the form of St-Just), the revolutionary Communist (the garbage-men) and the anarchist (the hippie anarchists). The reader will note that Godard excludes the Girondin revolutionary text – the one of 1789 or the one of 'reason' – and sees only that France's republican heritage is based in the Jacobin tradition. The Jacobin revolutionary text (i.e., 1792, Robespierre and the guillotine) leads to terror and the endpoint of the Sadean text (murder), that is, to an indifference to and abuse of human rights and its necessary corollary murder (mass-murder in the case of the 'Terror'). The revolutionary Communist text as enunciated in the film with its belief in guerrilla warfare leads to blood-thirsty acts of sabotage (at least in the thinking of its enunciators). The anarchist text leads to an erection of *the* revolutionary man into totem and taboo (as totem he can break all taboos and so can kill, rape and plunder and even indulge in cannibalism). In other words, the total Sadean text becomes dream fulfilment (sex, murder and consumption). Nor is the bourgeois capitalist consumer couple, Corinne and Roland (played by icons of the popular cinema, Mireille Darc and Jean Yanne) excluded. Corinne's sex-scene narration at the beginning, Roland's setting fire to Emily Brontë, and Corinne's consumption of her husband's body are all parts of the Sadean text. Capitalism rejoins the Jacobin text. Let us not forget that capitalism has as its first syllable 'cap' meaning head and that capital refers simultaneously to money and to death. Capital, Godard's film tells us, kills legitimately.

Godard's films of the 1980s show the effects of his radical work during his 1970s Dziga-Vertov phase – use of video montage technique, exploration of the plasticity and painterliness of the image, renewed investigations into the sound–image relationship (or lack of). They also show that he has moved away from making political films politically and moved into a more subjective counter-cinema. *Sauve qui peut . . . la vie* serves as an example. Ostensibly this film is about the difficulty/impossibility of bringing love and work together and by extension of bringing man and woman together living and working as equals. Simultaneously this film details, in five episodes, male and female sexual fantasies. The social and political ramifications of the first set of positionings (love and work together) act in counterpoint to these fantasies. We see that men and women cannot work and love together (the central couple Denise and Paul have split up because Paul cannot work with Denise and Denise can no longer love Paul). We see that work means capital exchange. The prostitute Isabelle makes her money trading 'love' (i.e., sex) for money. Men are the source of capital (Paul has to pay alimony and child support to his wife, pimps beat up Isabelle for not paying her dues). And so on. Aligned with these socio-political realities are the fantasies. The women have theirs in their minds, those of the men are exteriorised (not difficult to see why – fantasies as genitalised). Isabelle fantasises a lesbian encounter while a man is speaking out loud his fantasy in which she is participating. Big business men buy Isabelle's willingness to co-operate in their Sadean orgy and she concocts a shopping list. Not difficult to see in all of this that capital 'fucks' legitimately.[27]

Varda's importance in moving along cinematic practice has also had wide reverberations for other countries' cinemas (especially women's cinemas).[28] In all her films, Varda's uniqueness resides, on the one hand, in her sense of detached awareness, and on the other, in her ability to film from an unexpected and original perspective. Like Godard, she brings topicality on to the screen, although her topicality is of a very different order. Having first realised the topicality of an issue and the need to translate it into film as a marker of a particular generation or movement, she then proceeds to document that issue in a non-conflictive way. It is in this respect that Varda's films can be seen as non-ideological and yet replete with socio-economic realism. She films with a detached objectivity which she achieves, in the first instance, through the use of counterpoint (in the Faulknerian sense of running two narratives contiguously), and in the second, through a truncation of time, space and narrative. To this effect Varda remains detached from her characters. They have no depth in that she does not supply them with a psychology any more than she dramatises the narrative. It follows from this detachment that the characters are not always central – their story is as significant as the next person's.

Varda subverts the cinematic codes and in so doing denaturalises the dominant (male/Hollywood) ideology by opening up institutional myths and smashing the icons that support them. Myth is the signifier of ideology and within the dominant ideology transmits, amongst other images, the image of woman. The function of myth is also to normalise, that is, to render invisible what is visible. The myth construction of women in cinema goes back to the earliest cinematic practices of Hollywood. As Claire Johnston (1976, 209) says, 'in the case of women the dominant ideology presented her as eternal and unchanging'. Eternal and therefore ahistoric, woman is presented as spectacle, as object of and for the male gaze. She does not represent herself, she is fetishised. Varda counters this naturalisation of woman (i.e., that it is natural to reify/objectify woman) and opens up the 'myth of woman' through cinewriting the process of her invisibilisation. In *Cléo de 5 à 7* (1962) she shows the process of the reification of woman through language. Cléo is shown trapped, reflected in the image construction of others who narrate her. This is an image construction in which she in fact colludes by talking about herself in the same terms and by her constant self-referentiality through mirrors. By the end of the film, however, she asserts her self and abandons the rhetoric of both language and reflection that would fix her by leaving behind those who narrate her through their portraits of her.

Varda also takes film genres to task by disrupting their codes. In so doing she creates an alternative, counter-cinematic text for the spectator to reflect upon. In her film *Sans toît ni loi* (1985), the road movie – predominantly a male genre – is up for disruption. Genre-wise a road movie unravels in chronological time and space and the point of view is that of the roadsters. The purpose of the trajectory is ideological (for example, by exposing a social injustice) and implies self-discovery. Varda's film totally dismantles time and space because the whole film is one long journey (going from left to right) cut up by a series of flashbacks (eighteen in all) which give no precise idea of where we are in relation to the chronology. Subjective codes are disrupted in so far as it is everyone else's point of view except that of the roadster, Mona. Gender convention is broken. Mona is female and, as her name connotes, is both unique and alone (mona meaning one). She is also eternal and outside history (Mona Lisa, *the* female icon of ahistoricity in modernist art). Counter to the tradition of the road movie, the film is not an ideological film. Rather it shows different people's reactions to Mona's independence. Finally, there is no hint of self-discovery. In her filth and solitude, Mona has already acquired her identity, her marginality, and therefore gazes uninterestedly past the others – including us. In her refusal of all social discourses, which her mutism reinforces, she defies identification, will not be made other. In the eighteen portraits which each contributor provides of her, they fix their gaze not on Mona but on their perception of Mona as a figure of desire (or repulsion). As such, each portrait offered up to the spectator is revealing of the relator and not the one related. The effect is to empty the mirror of ascribed meanings since these portraits, emanating from or fixed as they are in male discourses, cannot produce her identity. No one can fix her because she has placed herself outside that which can be defined. Mona's response is, in effect, the perfect one to woman's ahistoricity. I will represent myself as nothing – as '*sans*'.

Since women film-makers of the 1970s and 1980s (and through to today) do not identify themselves as a group (despite the Musidora collective of the early 1970s) or as feminists (except, to my knowledge, Varda), there is little point in arguing the case for them – Serreau: '*je ne suis pas une femme qui fait du cinéma*'; Diane Kurys: '*ça m'exaspère qu'on parle de films de femmes*'; Isserman: 'we resist any collective image or any attempt to make us into a school'.[29] What does bear remarking upon are the traits their cinema have in common because something of a pattern emerges in cinematic style and diegetic predilection. Many of the films are semi-autobiographical or are preoccupied with human relationships and the way in which the world is perceived and represented. Sexuality and power relationships are often central to these films and are often addressed from the woman's point of view. Alternatively, the point of view is neither male nor female and more that of the camera – that is, the eye of the film-maker (a woman). In either case the male gaze has been displaced which allows for desire to be represented differently. The displacement clears the way for the emergence of a female eroticism which can be mono-sexual/lesbian, as in the love affair between the two married women in *Coup de foudre* (Kurys, 1982), bi-sexual, as in the triangular relationship between two men and a woman in Serreau's *Pourquoi pas!* (1977), or heterosexual, as in *L'Amant magnifique* (Isserman, 1986).

Alternatively, films can act to de-eroticise desire, again keeping men out as beholder of the gaze. Breillat's *36 fillette* (1989) does this. In this film, a 14-year-old girl, Lili, is determined to lose her virginity which is represented in the film as a burden and an embarrassment for her (the title of the film refers to a girl's garment size and points to Lili's predicament: she is *fillette*/adolescent, but also of a 'voluptuous' size, 36). After an almost-affair with a 40-year-old man for whom she experiences almost-attraction and caring, she opts to lose her virginity to a pimply youth for whom she has no feelings. The lack of point of view/subjectivity disturbs, however, because it creates an ambiguity around Lili's assertion of her right to sexual autonomy and begs the question of her motives (is she doing the right thing for the wrong reasons, or vice versa?). The film also works to deromanticise both virginity and its loss – a second intentionality which again functions to perturb received (i.e., patriarchal) notions about sexuality. Female nubile sexuality was very much a preoccupation in male film-makers' work in the 1980s. What distinguishes Breillat's film from theirs, of course, is this double intentionality of disengagement which serves to displace the voyeur.

Female eroticism can also allow for desire as a negative value – desire as fetish – to emerge. Rape as witnessed and experienced by a woman is central to Bellon's *L'Amour violé* (1977), which examines how it affects her perception of herself and her sexuality. Rape in this film is represented for what it is, an act of male violence intent on the annihilation of female eroticism. Desire as fetish is very clearly inscribed in Breillat's *Tapage nocturne* (1980) and Claire Devers' *Noir et blanc* (1986) where sado-masochism is voyeuristically represented from a female point of view. In the first film, sado-masochism is entered into by a woman film-maker. In the second, the relationship is between two men, one black and the other white – hence the title of the film, but also because it is shot in black and white. In both films the physical violence repels and attracts and points to the potential of female eroticism as 'perverse' fantasy. Devers' film is particularly disturbing to the spectator, and intentionally so, because in its extreme violence it addresses so many complicated layers of social reality and sexual fantasy. A middle-class married white male chooses to become the victim of a black masseur. The film portrays the escalating levels of pain through which the white will put himself and the 'understanding' complicity of the black – whose understanding leads him to refuse to participate at times. The outcome, death, comes as no surprise in one sense, but the horror of its graphicness (literally a ripping to pieces on a huge piece of rolling machinery – chains and all) is 'devastating' to the spectator who none the less 'keeps on watching'. Sado-masochism as an attraction; class and race difference as a fascination; male fetishism with violence as misplaced homo-erotic desire; the gaze as mutilation: Devers' intention is to place us in all those positions because the point of view is that of the camera. She plays relentlessly on our fantasies. We anticipate, guess what will happen next (since the violence is on an escalating scale). In this representation of sado-masochism as spectacle she questions visual power – we are placed in Foucauld's panopticon from which we can see everything. Absolute sight means absolute power, which in turn means death – the death of the subject. Desire at its most terrible.

Although there may well have been economic reasons for Devers shooting her film in black and white, the absence of colour does have further counter-cinematic connotations which relate to the scopophilic drive. Looking at this film along the lines of Neale's analysis of the value of colour, by shooting it in black and white Devers makes clear that woman is absent as object of desire. By removing 'woman' as marker and focus for scopophilic pleasure, she denaturalises the naturalisation process that traditionally occurs in narrative cinema with representations of the female text. Equally she subverts the 'cultural's' function as censor (to contain the spectator's subjective and erotic processes) because the illusion she creates is not 'cut to the measure of desire' (Mulvey: 1981, 214). In this way, Devers confronts us with the moral ambiguity of looking and does not let us off the hook but obliges us to recognise the dual process of voyeurism and fetishism inherent in our positioning as spectator. Whilst scopophilia is developed in its narcissistic mode by cinema in general (pleasure in identi-fication), this film also makes clear the potential of scopophilia in its fetishistic mode (which is the second stage of the scopophilic drive: the gaze as erotic fixation) to act as a source of sado-masochism.

In terms of style it is in the cinematic representation of this different point of view or, alternatively, suspended point of view, that a distinct cinematic style can be discerned – and it is one that has to do with rhythm. Annette Insdorf (1978, 52) notes a penchant in women film-makers' work for long takes to allow relationships with space, as much as those between people, to be established. The camera work, with its fluid long takes, allows for the sense of a woman's body to emerge rather than being fragmented, to be subject rather than object. Similarly characters are given time and space to establish themselves as subjects – subjects also of the wide range of emotions that enter into the notion of desire. To quote Breillat, 'hesi-tations, the smallest details; all these are not erased, but are filmed almost in real time'.[30] In this regard, this cinematic language represents a filling of the gaps that are mostly left out in the traditional (male) representations of desire (which fragments and fetishises the woman as object). Thus, if they are not feminist films, at least they show a perpetuation of the represen-tation of female subjectivity first 'seen' in Germaine Dulac's cinema, most significantly in *La Souriante Mme Beudet* (1923).[31]

THE CINEMAS OF THE 1960s AND 1970s: MORAL DISCOURSES AND CIVIC CINEMA

The moral fiction of the 1960s predominantly hit out against the bour-geoisie and the effects of conspicuous consumption and was, in part, the legacy of the New Wave. Godard has already been mentioned. Among the more mainstream film-makers, Chabrol, Mocky and Rohmer stand out as key in this domain. However, theirs is not the only form of attack. Indeed two basic approaches prevail in this cinema. The first, as exemplified by the above-mentioned film-makers, assails the bourgeoisie from within. The second, exemplified by Malle and Allio, points to the bourgeoisie's ridicule by confronting that class, most often from without, with non-conformist behaviour.

In his films, Chabrol provides a social document of contemporary France that is far from flattering in its continuous criticism of bourgeois morality. He exposes the weakness of this class that will do anything to preserve appearances. This morality of respectability is the very key that sets off the predicament that his characters find themselves in because it leads them to behave stupidly. Thus in his first film, *Le Beau Serge* (1958, credited as the first New Wave film), a young student's attempts to rehabilitate his old schoolboy friend from his alcoholism and to restore him to his marriage (i.e., to come back into the 'normal' fold of things) fail miserably. In Chabrol's next film, *Les Cousins* (1959), two cousins – both law students living together in Paris – once again represent this opposition in behaviour in which, this time, one is dissolute but successful (in exams, with women, etc.) and the other hardworking to the point of failure. He fails his exams because he knows too much and gets muddled, and he loses the woman to whom he has professed his love in a poem. His plan to kill his cousin for all his successes (including 'taking his woman') seriously backfires when the dissolute one kills him instead, albeit by accident (the gun goes off when he is playing around with it).

The trenchant bitterness of Chabrol's films not only points to the stupidity of people but also shows how, in the thwarted atmosphere that bourgeois morality creates, individuals can be driven close to madness. Not surprisingly, since it is the basic tenet upon which bourgeois hegemony resides, the site in which this stupidity and/or madness comes out is often the conjugal arena. In *La Femme infidèle* (1968), *Que la bête meure* (1969) and *Le Boucher* (1969), for example, the mediocrity of one of the characters is matched only by the obsessional preoccupation of the other. In *La Femme infidèle*, the husband tracks down his wife's lover and kills him. She realises what he has done but says nothing and the suburban couple continue to live on in silent complicity. *Que la bête meure* traces the story of a bereaved father's revenge on the man who killed his son in a hit-and-run accident. Finally, in *Le Boucher*, the eponymous butcher – an emotionally and sexually repressed individual – becomes enamoured of a 'spinsterish' schoolteacher. He visits her daily and relates his life to her. However, after the brutal murders of two young women, the schoolteacher works out that he is the killer. She does not denounce him, but when she realises that 'he knows that she knows' she panics and locks herself up in the school (in a frantic scene worthy of Hitchcock, whom Chabrol much admires). The butcher finally breaks in and commits suicide, knifing himself before her very eyes.

Chabrol's obsession with the very fine line dividing good and evil, morality and madness, stupidity and frustration, and the way that social/bourgeois hypocrisy papers over that crack, has remained constant throughout his work. Social hypocrisy of a slightly different order can be found in the films of Mocky and Rohmer of this decade. Mocky's films, especially his comedies, are as caustic as Chabrol's but he targets in a more all-encompassing way the aspects of contemporary life which he finds abhorrent. He extends the standard target of the bourgeoisie to include the army, the police and the church. For good measure he adds the media – particularly the press (*Snobs*, 1961) and television (*La Grande lessive*, 1968). Mocky is no less aggressive in his sociological films, in which he examines questions of sexuality in the so-called age of sexual liberation.

The more permissive sexuality of youth is under scrutiny in *Les Dragueurs* (1959). In this film, where two young men try but fail miserably to pick up a date for the night, Mocky exposes the sexual mentality of the young as neurotic on the one hand, both in its desperate attempts to get a fix and in its fear of not getting one (as exemplified by one of the youths), and on the other, as the cause of great anxiety to individuals who feel pressured into this cruising game but who would prefer to believe still in the romantic notion of meeting the love of their life (which is the case for the other youth, played by Charles Aznavour). In the next two films in this vein, Mocky treads in what were considered dangerous, taboo waters in the early 1960s. The long-term effects of marriage on a couple's sexual drive are the subject of *Un Couple* (1960) and the first sexual encounters by adolescent girls that of *Les Vierges* (1962).

Rohmer's films are more intellectually intimist than those of either Chabrol or Mocky. He focuses his attention on human relationships, on the individual's struggle between love and reason, and on the unsoundness of what motivates our behaviour. In his first set of films (the *Contes moraux*), it is the male point of view that is privileged. By the 1980s (in his *Comédies et proverbes* series), it is more ostensibly the woman's point of view that is privileged, a position that neither Chabrol nor Mocky would ever seek to emulate. Rohmer's moral fiction does not particularly address the social questions of the time but it does paint the social mores of a certain intellectual middle class and provides an intimist portrayal of the practices of self-deception. Subjectivity is at the core of his films and indeed cinematic practice, for it influences the way he makes films. For example, in *Ma nuit chez Maud* (1969), although the film is narrated by the central protagonist, Jean-Louis, none the less question marks are placed incessantly on who has control of the narrative. Although Jean-Louis says one thing, the picture we form is quite different. As Norman King (1990, 236) points out, Jean-Louis's 'persistent attempt to control the event is undercut by what we see'.

Of the film-makers whose work most readily represents the other tradition of this moral fiction of the 1960s – holding up a mirror of non-conformity to challenge the safe images of the dominant ideology – Malle and Allio will serve to exemplify this tendency. As early as his second film, *Les Amants* (1958), Malle had the refusal of a female protagonist to conform to bourgeois values as the centrepiece to his film. In this film, the wife of a wealthy businessman decides to abandon husband, daughter and lover to go off with her newly acquired lover who rescued her when her car broke down. Prior to this moment the woman (played by Jeanne Moreau), bored with the ease of her bourgeois trappings and her husband's unattentiveness, takes up with a polo-player and spends time in Paris with him attending parties and the like. This substitution of one set of bourgeois realities for another is represented as far from satisfying for her. However, her suspicious husband sets in motion a new departure in her life when he insists on inviting the man he believes to be her lover to spend the weekend with them. Moreau is obliged to drive back from Paris, but her car breaks down and a young man in a dilapidated Citroën gives her a ride home. He too is invited to stay. That night they make love and the next day they depart together. Again, cinematic style is matched to the storyline. There is virtually no dialogue and the shots are left to express the woman's subjectivity as she experiences first her boredom and then her sense of freedom, albeit agenced by another (her new lover and, indirectly, her husband). The amorality of her decision was of considerable shock value at the time. However, because her decision to reject wifehood, motherhood and economic ease is not completely without its own problematics (she departs with another), it would appear that Malle is offering a more complex reading than just that of the woman as chattel to the bourgeoisie. Through the very process by which she comes to leave, Malle is addressing the middle-class belief in the 'reality' of the newly liberated woman and exposing it for the partial myth that it is.

Allio's female protagonist also asserts a choice in his film *La Vieille dame indigne* (1965). After sixty years of devoting her services as wife, mother and housewife to her family, upon the death of her husband Berthe decides to sell everything and lead a life according to her desires. She visits friends, goes on holiday, eats in restaurants – takes all the pleasures she had denied herself or had been denied by the strictures of a society that says to be a married woman means devotion to the family and self-abnegation. The moral outrage of her family, so replete in the certainty that their values are superior to hers and 'naturally' correct, completes the picture. Their indignation at her obvious pleasure makes clear that a woman's right to self-determination is not a *chose acquise* in a society that is controlled by men or by the patriarchal law.

In this moral fiction, other realities prevail, and they are ones that are not unconnected with the effects of the dominant ideology on the outsiders, the less privileged, those without a voice whose protest can only be registered by self-destruction. A mood of pessimism is reflected in this cinema of the postmodern age that points to the alienation felt by those who are not part of the consumer society or who have been profoundly affected by it and by a society which they perceive as lacking in a system of values to which they can adhere. Alienation pushes the protagonists to opt for death. In *Ascenseur pour l'échafaud* (Malle, 1957), a war veteran whose sense of values has totally dissipated after his return to civilian life chooses to get caught for a murder he committed as a gesture. In *Mouchette* (Bresson, 1967), an adolescent girl commits suicide because she can no longer continue to accept the constant abuse and neglect she receives in a totally uncaring environment.

Another set of outsiders, cultural minorities – the immigrant classes of the post-Liberation period and early 1960s, mostly Blacks and Maghrébins brought in to help bolster France's ailing working force – receive only very little transparence in the 1960s. At this stage, cultural minorities were not yet a 'real', politicised factor. This politicisation did not occur until the 1970s when the effects of recession took their toll and marked immigrants out as what ailed France. None the less, racism was already on the rise in the 1960s, especially as a consequence of the Algerian war and the subsequent decolonisation of France's Arabo-African empire.[32] Not only was there little transparence on racism during this period, but also the tendency, when cinema addressed the issue at all, was to look outside the country to economically deprived minorities elsewhere. Thus Marcel Camus denunciates the apathy towards racism in *Orpheu negro* (1958) – a transposition of the Orpheic myth into the streets of Rio de Janeiro into which Brazilian Blacks are yearly allowed to descend from their hovels on the hill for the three days of the carnival to dance and sing. Jean Rouch, in *Moi un noir* (1958), traces the effects of colonialism in reducing indigenous tribes to a new kind of poverty-stricken proletariat. Finally, in Claude Bernard-Aubert's *Les Tripes au soleil* an imaginary space is invented – a fictitious Latin-American town – to act as a back-drop for a moralising didacticism on interracial hatred (between Blacks and Whites). Only one film (to my knowledge) commends itself by locating the issue of racism in France, Paris to be precise. It is Michel Drach's *On n'enterre pas le dimanche* (1959) which focuses on the difficulties of an interracial relationship in a society that reproves and is openly hostile to such pairings. By the 1970s, cinema had become more aware or able to be more open on issues affecting these cultural minorities and a handful of films finally addressed questions of everyday racism.

The 1970s has to be seen as a period of considerably greater openness and transparence on the socio-political culture of France as a nation than at any other time in this cinema's history as is attested by the fact that its civic cinema has numerous modes of address: films of protest, a 'political' cinema, anti-historicism cinema, films that give reflections of non-heroisation and a transparence on racism, sexuality and the couple. Nor is the conventional mainstream without social-political inflections that occasionally demarcate it from the mainstream cinema of previous ages. Within civic cinema and the numerous films that look either into the social or the political arena, there is an expression of a new individualism that is strongly tied in with the question of civil liberties and their assertion or violation. Social justice, politics, the role of the police, the impact of the media – all are issues central to this cinema. There is also a renewed focus on the working class and other groups marginalised by society. This *cinéma-vérité* style of filming, in its focus on and attempt at reproducing the subjectivity of the working class, is reminiscent of the cinema of the 1930s with the major difference being that, although male friendship is still in evidence, the group has all but evaporated. Thus, the notion of class solidarity has been dissipated. Equally, whilst the individual is at the centre, he (*sic*) is neither leader (because the group is predominantly absent), nor heroised. In this new cinema on the working class, the actors in the main are not well known or, alternatively, are not professionals. This was a deliberate choice on the part of film-makers making this cinema, most of whom were Left of centre and for whom such a process would go counter to both their desire for authenticity and their politics.

Not surprisingly, this cinema on the working class is the one that most readily puts in question the whole of society. The working-class protagonists in these films are represented as victims not of any particular individual but of a system that operates to alienate, exclude and oppress and against which this class does its best to assert its rights. Two responses prevail in this cinema. The one is to opt out, the other to opt against. Of the first response, not all films convince and some run the risk of valorising marginality, making it heroic and therefore mythic. Faraldo's film, *Bof* (1970), runs into this problem. Whilst, along with other films of this type, it does hit out against the moralising and intimidating practices of the paternalistic factory-cum-business establishment, it goes for an easy solution by having its protagonists, a father and son duo, pack their jobs in and head for the south of France to live an alternative life-style – a sort of 'familial sexual communism'.[33] What is missing in this film is any sense that their gesture is more than a *boutade* against the age-old cliché that work (especially factory work) is a form of poorly paid slavery. The problematic with Faraldo's film is the double enunciation in the idealism of the solution – it founders on its very unreality at the same time as it heroises the gesture (i.e., 'don't we all wish we could do that?') – which means in effect that what should have been at the centre of the film's considerations, the signifying process of the rupture, gets diasporised.

An example of 'opt out' films that does not fall into this stereotyping of refusal/rupture is Philippe Condroyer's *La Coupe à dix francs* (1974). This film shows the opting-out process as a complex one. But, embedded in this dark and pessimistic film, there is also a stronger political message of a refusal to compromise as the primer and the finaliser of this process. In this film, based on a true story, a young worker with long hair – an apprentice carpenter (connotations of Christ) – is continually subjected to the humiliating looks, taunts and spying of the *bien pensants* in his provincial town. His work place is just as alienating, with his employer treating him no differently from the townsfolk. As a defence he immures himself in his solitude. His boss's order to get his hair cut represents a compromise that he cannot make, a final humiliating blow that would render him without independence of mind or identity. His suicide through self-immolation is the extreme opt-out, but the political resonances of this refusal to compromise and his gesture of rupture act powerfully as judge and jury on the society that marginalises him. His suicide is a rejection of society's aggress-iveness and by extension, a declaration of its undesirability as a living reality. His self-immolation is doubly political because of its brutal self-aggression on the one hand, and on the other, its extreme unacceptability within Western society.

In the films in this cinema on the working class that 'opt against' the alienating effects of society, what is revealed is either a progressive recog-nition on the part of the protagonists of the structures that oppress them or a situationist exposure of the reality that surrounds them through the acts of the protagonists who are marginalised by society and its structures. Doillon's film, *Les Doigts dans la tête* (1974), illustrates the first of these responses: recognition. An apprentice baker, Chris, goes on strike when the exploitative hours and harsh realities of work-production-capital, as exemplified in his boss's intransigent ways, become insufferable. But it is what happens afterwards that is important. He holes up with three com-panions in a small room – his girlfriend, a friend and a middle-class young Swedish woman who is passing through town. The ensuing dynamics of the group lead the three French protagonists to reflect on their situation in relation to their bosses, their work, their refusal to work, the greater mobility and freedom of the Swedish woman, on how they live, and so on. A second encounter, this time with a unionist, gives the three other things to reflect upon. Will joining the union mean just another set of structures? Opting against has led to a clarification of what is there, and although it appears probable that they will rejoin the system, it will be with an awareness and most likely mistrust of those structures that oppress and alienate.

Vergez's *La Virée superbe* (1973) exemplifies a situationist stance in that no awareness can even enter into the reality of these marginals of society. In this film the group of *loulous* are represented not as drop-outs, as the police who constantly survey them believe them to be, but as youngsters who cannot get out of the '*zone*' (the insalubrious ex-urbs and suburbs of Paris). They are stuck in the desolate and empty building plots with nothing to do but hang out in seedy cafés or charge up and down riverside roads on their motorbikes (hence the ironic title of the film), mess about in fairs, try to pull small-time robberies and more than likely end up in prison. Through showing the situation as it is experienced, this type of film denounces the notion that these marginals have elected to 'opt against' the societal structures and asserts rather the reverse, that is, that their margi-nality is symptomatic of the failure of the system.

Because the climate of the times post-1968 should have made a heroisa-tion politically undesirable, it is worth discussing briefly a film which appears to be in this category of film on marginals, but which at a closer examination clearly is not. Bertrand Blier's *Les Valseuses* (1974) is a film about two *loulous* who decide that their mission in life is to go around the country proving their virility (hence the slang reference in the title of the film, *valseuses* meaning testicles) and robbing to assuage their appetites. It is not just their contemptuous behaviour towards everybody, especially the bourgeoisie, or their sexual aggressiveness that belies the credibility of this film as a realist representation of that class. It is also the contempt with which they reject work, and ridicule those who do, that reveals the 'lie' about the point of view.[34] The dupery 'this is a film about marginals' is clear for all to see but one that reassures in that it sends back comfortable stereotyped images of 'what that class gets up to'. This presumably explains why it was so popular, although the attraction of two actors (Depardieu and Dewaere) emerging into the 'known' category probably also contributed to its success (in any event, it came second in box-office receipts in the same year as the hit porn film *Emmanuelle*). To all effects we are back to the images of the proletariat as the dangerous classes that abounded in the silent cinema and that of the 1940s. It is not just the archaism of Blier's film that should concern, however. In its fabrication (i.e., pretending to be what it is not), it is pastiche parading as parody. As we see, Blier was a man before his time, or his film was at least. With its double problematic this film can be seen as a precursor to what dominated the cinema of the 1980s – archaism and pastiche or, in other words, the post-modern-neo-culture.

There are two further important aspects of the civic cinema of the 1970s that require examination: that which delved into the political arena on the one hand, and on the other, that which has been called the cinema of the 'everyday'. The civic 'political' cinema has often been criticised for its lack of politicisation, for spectacularising politics, for selecting isolated events – all of which it is argued let the spectator off the hook and positioned her/him as a consumer.[35] Even though much of this cinema uses political reality either as a backdrop or as central to its narrative, it is accused of by-passing ideology and making politics a matter of drama and adventure. The argument goes as follows: rather than a political cinema, it is a new kind of thriller that depoliticises because it entertains. The use of stars only serves to reinforce this effect. Finally, it is argued, this cinema is as much part of the dominant ideology as any other. Hard words for a cinema that was extremely popular and had a film in the top ten virtually every year. Yet, because cinema is both consumer- and supply-led, this spate of political films could be seen as a cynical exercise in cashing in on the popularity of the American political thriller (especially the post-Watergate cycle of paranoid films).

However, leaving aside the economic, supply-led argument, it is surely significant that there was clearly a demand for this type of film. After so much silence, audiences were wanting to be entertained by politics. The political culture of the time certainly fed into this new demand. The effect of de Gaulle had not only been to empty the political arena of ideological discourses, it had also led to the personalisation of power. Once the patriarch of France had departed, gaps opened and there were spaces to talk about politics. Henceforth, political machinations, financial scandals, underhand speculation in real estate and graft in the building industry were all stories that the press was uncovering at the time. They also pepper the cinema of the 1970s. Thus, the Ben Barka affair receives a barely disguised reconstruction in Boisset's film *L'Attentat* (1972). In this affair, Ben Barka, the exiled leader of the Moroccan opposition, disappeared after being kidnapped in Paris in October 1965 at the behest of the Moroccan minister of the Interior but with the collaboration of the French intelligence. The murder of a socialist poster-sticker in Puteaux in 1971 is the trigger for two films about political chicanery, *Il n'y a pas de fumée sans feu* (Cayatte, 1972) and *Défense de savoir* (Nadine Trintignant, 1974). The murder in 1975 of a judge who was investigating several areas of underworld corruption in Lyons and who uncovered links with the political world and money-laundering practices with Swiss banks gets almost immediate coverage in Boisset's *Le Juge Fayard, dit 'Le Shérif'* (1976). The Aranda affair (1972), in which a ministerial attaché leaks documents about France's arms trading with Libya to the press, is equally quick to get mention on the screen in Molinaro's comic thriller *L'Emmerdeur* (1973).

The great success that Costa-Gavras's first three 'political' films met with (*Z*, *L'Aveu*, both 1970 and *L'Etat de siège*, 1973) gave proof to the fact that the cinema-going audience was not parochial in its interests but could be equally intrigued by the politics of 'elsewhere'. All three films are based on real events (the assassination of a Greek minister, a Stalinist trial and the kidnapping of an American diplomat) and all three star Yves Montand, the fetish star of the genre. The success of this film reflects a nation that was maturing politically, partly because modern technology meant that news travelled faster than ever before, but also because 1968 had been a watershed year for awareness, including an awareness about international politics. The anti-Vietnam movement and the women's movement were international consciousness-raising movements. By the late 1960s the baby boom had come of age, had 'rebelled' against the 'father' (de Gaulle) and was asking questions of institutions of authority. It is symptomatic of this internationalism that *Z* was universally acclaimed, almost as if it was *the* emblematic film of that generation and an era that refused to be hood-winked and lied to by its 'elders and betters', that is, by those in power.

The reading of Costa-Gavras's films by critics mostly of the Left is curiously quite other.[36] A first criticism levelled at them is that they are all safely not 'about' France and therefore disengage the spectator from examining her/his own complicity in 'the political'; second, that the use of stars renders the characters they are portraying somewhat less credible; and finally, that their style is too mainstream (aka Hollywood). This is perhaps to misread Costa-Gavras's intentions which were to use a political event to show how the state machinery could crush an individual. His films were to act as mediators between state and citizenry and to make the point that civil liberties are not a given. The failure of his fourth 'political' film, *Section spéciale* (1975), which did focus on France (Vichy France) was confirmation for the Left that their reading was a correct one. A different reading could go as follows. The nation had already seen *Le Chagrin et la pitié* (or heard about it at least) and *Lacombe Lucien* (a box-office success) and was aware that the Occupation was not a simple black and white affair. The problem with Costa-Gavras's film was also the absence of the formula for his 'political' films. Without a central individual protagonist with a human face (preferably Montand's) vying against the state, the process of subject/audience identification (a part key to the success of Costa-Gavras's other films) became more fraught – indeed, it did not occur.

The reflection of history in the cinema of the 1970s also reveals a civism in its deliberately anti-historicism approach. History is no longer spectacularised but grounded in the reality of everyday life. The history now is the history of the ordinary people, no longer great men (*sic*) and great moments. History becomes popular history and not biopics. Thus the films of Allio and Tavernier, Comolli and Téchiné, are films that give a new politicised reading of history. Allio's *Les Camisards* (1970) and *Moi, Pierre Rivière* (1976) examine two types of persecution, the first religious, the second judicial – as, in this last respect, does Tavernier's *Le Juge et l'assassin* (1976). The issue of social class is at the heart of Allio's *Rude journée pour la reine* (1973) and Téchiné's *Souvenirs d'en France* (1974) and is just one of the preoccupations of Tavernier's *Que la fête commence* (1975). More explicitly political in their reference are Comolli's *La Cécilia* (1974), which analyses the reasons for the failure of a small socialist commune in Italy at the end of the nineteenth century, and *L'Ombre rouge* (1980) in which the Communist methods during the Stalin period are examined.

The brutality of justice as barely distinguishable from the brutality of a murderer is the focal point of *Moi, Pierre Rivière* and *Le Juge et l'assassin* (both based on true events, the first in 1835, the second at the end of the nineteenth century). In the former film, the eponymous protagonist, a peasant farmer in Normandy, kills his mother and two siblings. In the latter film, a demented former sergeant spurned by the woman of his affections tries to shoot himself. The bullets in his head serve only to increase his dementia and, once he escapes from the asylum, he goes on a rampage killing little girls and boys. A local judge (the story is set in the Jura) decides to catch this madman. He is represented as a product of the political and religious culture of his time and, in his moral hypocrisy, as no better than the murderer he pursues and persecutes. If anything he is worse in that he stands for a society that willingly sends its children to their death in mines and factories (Tavernier makes the point that during the time it took the murderer to kill twelve children, 2,500 had perished in their work place). Both films argue that a social order based on concupiscence and exploitation can only breed stupidity, injustice and an indifference (particularly to the plight of ordinary people), all of which in turn leads to an institutionalisation of violence (both moral and physical).

Moral violence perpetrated by the social order is the message behind Allio's portrait of Jeanne in *Rude journée pour la reine* and Téchiné's portrait of Berthe in *Souvenirs d'en France*. It is perhaps not surprising that the two film-makers chose to represent this violence through the portrayal of women or that, in both instances, upward mobility is central to these two women's narratives – be it imaginary, as in the first case, or real, as in the second – because it is not in their power to obtain it by themselves but only through the agencing of the male and his money. Patriarchy and capitalism make ready bedfellows and jailers. A suitable metaphor for the workings of social order. Jeanne (played by Signoret) is a cleaner who is no longer in her prime. She lives in the suburbs with her oppressive husband and equally suffocating relatives. Her only escape from the present is in her fantasies that take her back in time or displace her elsewhere and position her as 'someone important' – the wife of an Austro-Hungarian king, an aristocrat in the court of Versailles, the wife of a President, etc. All her fantasies, however, are fed by the pulp fiction that she reads and the products she consumes off the television, that is, by mass-media popular culture. Thus even her fantasies are ultimately not hers (unlike the smiling Mme Beudet in Dulac's film), but those of a consumer society based on capital and patriarchy.

Souvenirs d'en France refers in its title to the *France profonde* of the bourgeoisie and is also an intentionally ironic pun since the whole genesis of the narrative is people putting their backgrounds behind them. The film starts in 1936 (Popular Front time), although prior to the story proper there is a flashback to the early 1900s to situate the narrative. It tells of a young man from the Spanish immigrant class determined to better his life. He becomes a blacksmith, marries the local baker's daughter and, by dint of his hard work and that of his sons, transforms his forge into a factory. Back to 1936. His wife's newly acquired status makes her hostile to her son's affections for Berthe (played by Moreau) the laundress. However, they marry, so she too joins the ranks of the bourgeoisie and, like the baker's daughter before her, soon gets co-opted into that class. Berthe the Resistance heroine becomes the lady of the factory and when she persuades the workforce not to continue their strike (we are now in 1968) in exchange for greater participation it is clear 'her humanism notwithstanding' through the arguments she uses that she has become assimilated into that class and, through her discourse, has become the tool of that class used to restore order. As Prédal (1984, 170) says, she is more servant than mistress of her condition.

Much of the cinema of the 1970s abounded with contemporary social issues. As with the cinema reflecting history, it is equally inflected with the ordinariness of the characterisations. This ordinariness, however, can run one of two ways and, because of the implicit identification for the spectator, can either lead to the fabrication of the myth of ordinariness (which reassures) or to a signification of ordinariness (which questions). In its first manifestation, as myth, the attraction is that, with a bit of luck, we might find ourselves in that 'ordinary' person's position (after all Delon and Montand started out as ordinary and poor before they got their lucky breaks). In this respect, what makes these protagonists' ordinariness so appealing for the spectator is that, whilst they are 'just like you or me', they are also transparently not, because they act in ways we would not dare. In its second manifestation, as signification, ordinariness as a site for speculation can shock and not allow the spectator to disengage. Into the first category of ordinariness at its most facile go all of Claude Lelouch's films starting with *Un homme et une femme* (1966). So too do Jean Yanne's caustic comedies that slate, *à tour de rôle*, the media and the women's movement (respectively, *Tout le monde il est beau il est gentil*, 1972 and *Moi il y en a vouloir des sous*, 1973). As an example of the less facile but still in this mode of ordinariness, mention should be made of the films produced in the second half of the 1970s starring Annie Girardot in the role of the assured professional woman whose assuredness gets thrown by the arrival on the scene of a man. In this respect, *Tendre poulet* (de Broca, 1978) is the exemplary film of this recuperation of the feminist discourse. This is mainstream cinema at its most popular and most ordinary.

In the cinema that questions, issues are raised about the family (no longer necessarily a stable reality), the couple and sexuality. It is worth pointing to a couple of films that address taboo aspects of sexuality and which bring those taboos or social reaction to them into question because of the very siting of them in the arena of ordinariness (something which the *Cages aux folles* trilogy – about the homosexual world of camp – very patently does not).[37] Catherine Breillat's *Tapage nocturne* is a hard-hitting film (literally) that investigates a woman film-maker's exploration of her sexuality and desire for something other than the traditional coupling, both of which eventually lead her into a sado-masochistic relationship. There are, of course, problematics – especially for feminists – about this representation of female sexuality and desire. But if one adopts a neutral position, it becomes clearer that the point Breillat is trying to make is first, that this kind of relationship is one that is not rarefied, and second, that female sexual fantasies do exist (something that is hardly ever touched upon in cinema) and/but they can disturb as much as those of the male. Cayatte's film *Mourir d'aimer* (1971) is not just about sexuality but also about the hypocrisy of justice. It narrates the true story of an incident, which occurred in 1968, of a young schoolteacher (played by Girardot, ordinary but powerfully moving) who falls in love with one of her pupils, still a minor. She gets pushed to suicide when her lover's parents take her to court where she is not just sentenced, but also humiliated as perverse and submitted to harassing psychology. Again social reaction is being exposed for what it does. For its own moral security the social, and in this case, judicial order must deny that this too is a form of sexuality that is not uncommon. To believe that it is not rarefied would disrupt. A certain cinema of the 1970s, therefore, questions the rigidity of sexual mores, the hegemonic belief that all is the same (family, coupledom) and anything else exceptional perversion. By the 1980s, this unpacking and questioning for the most part had disappeared and was replaced by a virtual cynicism about sexuality. The age of liberalism was short-lived indeed.

Concern with adolescence and the troubles they experience, either at/with school (*Passe ton bac d'abord*, Pialat, 1979) or more generally within the social system itself (*L'Horloger de Saint-Paul*, Tavernier, 1974) are issues that become quite commonplace in this cinema of ordinariness. So too does the question of education and its effects on children (*B.A. BA*, Abraham Segal, 1971). Whilst the family is less in evidence as a nuclear unit, there are films where parents are divorced and mothers (occasionally fathers) are raising their children by themselves (*Une histoire simple*, Claude Sautet, 1978). Concern too with justice and more specifically the death penalty (which Giscard opposed but never abolished because public opinion was against it) is at the centre of quite a few films, only a couple of which could be deemed to reflect an ordinariness (*La Machine*, Paul Vecchiali, 1977 and *Le Pull-over rouge*, Drach, 1979), the others being either star-led and/or overmelodramatic. By the 1980s, of these various issues, single-parenthood excepted, most had evaporated or had been probed (*sic*) from a different, predominantly prurient point of view.

Everyday racism – racism as ordinary everyday reality – appears in a number of films in the 1970s: *Elise ou la vraie vie* (Drach, 1970), *Soleil O* (Med Hondo, 1970), *Mektoub?* (Ali Ghalem, 1970), *Dupont Lajoie* (Boisset, 1974), *Voyage en capital* (Ali Akika, 1978), *Passagers* (Annie Tresgot, 1971), *En l'autre bord* (Jérôme Kanapa, 1978). What appears to dominate is a point of view of the 'other'. In five out of the seven films mentioned the subjectivity is intentionally that of the class that is oppressed and/or the object of racism. In the films by Boisset and Drach, the point of view is either 'neutral' (Boisset) or that of a woman sympathetic to the 'other' (Drach). Hondo, Ghalem and Akika address the difficulties of being on the periphery from virtual first-hand experience. In *Soleil O* and *Mektoub?*, a Mauritian and an Algerian (respectively) arrive in Paris only to meet with standard reactions of mistrust and abuse as they try to find accommodation and work. These reactions are represented in this normalised way (standard) to show how ingrained they are in the mores of the 'legitimate' citizenry. In *Mektoub?*, racism as a vicious circle is metonymically expressed through the protagonist's (Ahmed Chergui) illiteracy and his desperate attempts to get himself regularised, that is, to acquire the appropriate papers. The state has no place for those who do not fit in. Since it is bound to the concept of citizen identity being validated first and foremost by papers, the state will ensure the exclusion of those who cannot prove their identity and thus legitimate their presence there. The film also shows how racism as refusal and rejection of 'otherness' acts in complicity with the state machinery. Each road Chergui goes down, whether in search of a room or a job, meets with a dead end so that in the end, inevitably Chergui gets arrested by the police. *Soleil O*, as its ironic title would indicate, is about the progressive darkness and despair the protagonist feels as his illusions and hopes for a brighter future in Paris gradually evaporate under the relentless effects of racism. *Passagers* paints the similar progressive disillusionment of a young Algerian and the effects it has on his personality. Woman as victim of both racism and sexism is central to *En l'autre bord* and *Voyage en capital*, where sexism is not just an outside reality (white men) but also an inner one (men of their own race) – a threefold oppression therefore: men, the dominant white class and the state.

Because the subjectivity of these films is intentionally that of the 'other', what does not get glossed over is the complicated nature of the source of racism, that is, that it not only emanates from the notion of otherness, but is also politicised because of the collusion between state and citizenry in their determination to exclude. This is what is problematic to differing degrees about the other two films. Boisset and Drach show racism at work, but it is too specified. In Drach's film, *Elise ou la vraie vie*, the racial conflict is between white and Algerian workers in a car factory. The year is 1958. Time and space, therefore, are placing racism within a very specific context. Elise falls in love with a fellow worker in the factory, an Algerian who is a member of the FLN and who falls victim to the racism of his co-workers. Drach's film, however, does make the crucial point that everyday racism is the effect of a depoliticisation of the workers, which is half-way to placing the question of racism in a broader socio-political context.

In Boisset's *Dupont Lajoie* this awareness seems critically absent. There are problems right from the beginning of the film starting with an artificial realism in the *mise-en-scène*. The *petit bourgeois* Parisians are holidaying in a camp site near a building site and temporary living quarters for the Algerian builders. In a first altercation with the Algerians, the group of campers quickly reveal their racism and sense of moral superiority. Later at a local fair one of the campers, Lajoie, takes a fancy to a young woman and drags her off. In his attempt to rape her he kills her. Terrified by what he has done, but not too terrified so he cannot act, he takes her body and dumps it on the building site. The first assumptions made, *of course*, are that an Arab is guilty. Because the police seem to be dragging their feet, the campers form a lynch mob and go on the hunt for the 'guilty' man. The sub-text to the lynch mob's sense of legitimacy is less that he has murdered her and more that an Arab has touched one of 'their' women – a first phobia about the 'other' being his greater sexual potency. Boisset, therefore, has put in place two stereotypes about the 'other': socio-racially inferior and sexually dangerous (potent rapist predator-cum-murderer). He has also asserted that the site of that racism is the mentality of the *petite bourgeoisie* – which gives two readings: within each one of us there lurks a racist or, conversely, this is the act/attitude of a specific class which in turn confirms another sense of superiority (the spectator is not of that class). The specificity of the event and its location, the *mise-en-spectacle* of stereotypes and the 'unproblematised' encoding of the universality or, conversely, the class specificity of racism – all of this ends up normalising racism and examining neither its source, nor its illegality nor indeed its political inflection. Boisset's intention was to make a political film on racism, but in the final analysis it remains a film about one racist moment.

MAINSTREAM CINEMAS OF THE 1960s AND 1970s: COMEDY AND *POLARS*

What remains to be discussed in relation to this cinema of the 1960s and 1970s are the two dominant genres: comedy and the *polars*. Although, generally speaking, much that is produced tends to offer a less immediate reflection on contemporary discourses, within both genres there are points of intersection where they do address these discourses, and moments of overlap between them that reflect a similar concern with or acknowledgement of the modalities of the time. I have already mentioned Malle's and Mocky's comedies and their differing comic styles (anti-conformist and caricatural respectively) with which they moralise on the contemporary consumer society. Amongst the *polars*, Becker's *Le Trou* (1960), based on the true story of a man falsely imprisoned for murder and his attempts to escape, carries on in this vein, this time in its questioning of justice. Otherwise little in these two genres is controversial, though some of it is not without its ironic comment.

Essentially, these two genres offer up discourses that are either modern (or apparently so – and it is in this appearance that irony is more in evidence) or reactionary. This clash between the reactionary and the modern points to the conflict in the first instance, of two generations (de Gaulle's and the youth generation), and in the second, of two realities (*la tradition française* and *la chose américaine*). How this manifested itself in the *polars* of these two decades will serve to clarify this point. On the reactionary front, it is the retro-mode that dominates. In these films, the same themes of dishonesty amongst thieves, male friendship and proto-father/son relationship (with all its Oedipal resonances) are there as before. So too is the impenetrable, dour but intelligent Maigret. On the modern if minority front of the *polar*, the contemporary American influence is felt as much through the narrative as the visual style. In terms of narrative, it is now the couple that comes centre stage and is often the cause for the crime (*Plein soleil*, *La Piscine*, for example) and the proto-father/son that moves back stage (an exemplary exception being *Le Clan des Siciliens*). In terms of style, American fetish objects (*la chose américaine*) such as swimming pools and yachts are simultaneously the object of desire and the scene of the crime. Within this simultaneousness a double irony prevails. An ironising of the subject's desire for the object is joined with an ironising of the object of desire itself. To want it leads to death, the object itself becomes the container/instrument of death. This double irony undoubtedly reflects the ambivalence felt by a nation moving into the age of consumerism at the same time as it was experiencing a period of ideological and political confusion (an anxiety which was equally in evidence in the xenophobic nature of the spy thriller).

In the modern comic tradition, discourse on *la chose américaine* retains the same double irony present in the *polar*. However, before engaging in that debate, let us look first at the reactionary discourses. Comedy in the 1960s still reaps its laughs at the expense of the stereotyped 'other' – often the woman (turned out as an exotic and savoury dish in Jean Léon's *Aimez-vous les femmes*, 1964).[38] These films, seemingly based on human relationships and conjugal misunderstandings, incessantly privilege the man over the woman. Thus, in *Le Farceur* (de Broca, 1961) the bored disenchanted wife (Hélène) decides to have fun with the successfully seductive Edouard-the-Joker. When the two decide to run off together, both have second thoughts. It is the difference in doubts that is revealing. Hélène fears the potential loss of comfort and luxury that her husband offers her, Edouard the potential loss of freedom. In *Allez la France* (Dhéry, 1964) a rugby fan almost misses his wedding when he dashes over to England to see a Five Nations cup match between France and England. He has not told his bride-to-be of his jaunt, however. He gets tangled up in all sorts of farces including getting his front teeth broken and rescuing Diana Dors from an aggressor. Although the whole comedy hinges on whether or not he gets back in time and intact, the subtext reads quite differently – marriage means loss of this sort of freedom (rugby matches and rescuing beautiful women) and an entry into conformity (as is symbolised by his enforced silence once he has his teeth repaired – in order to heal he must not speak). Mocky's *Les Compagnons de la marguerite* (1967) sets an equally misogynous agenda for women. A husband fed up with his wife (who is a TV addict!) conceives of an ingenious wife-swapping plan. By forging documents, he can by-pass the divorce court proceedings and make the exchange. Other dissatisfied husbands come to him for his service and so successful is he that he sets up his own company. Burlesque satire it may well be, but women remain as a pure commodity.

Elsewhere on the comic front and in this reactionary mode comedy types such as thriller comedies (*Le Diable par la queue*, de Broca, 1969 and *Tontons les flingueurs*, Lautner, 1963) and burlesque comedies (*Oscar* and *La Jument verte*, Autant-Lara, 1959) all tend to valorise the family and the notion of order. The notion of the family is iterated in comedies centred on children. Children had not been seen in any quantity since the silent cinema days. The cinema of the 1930s and 1950s tended to dwell on the other representation of children, as victim. Children-based comedy starts to re-emerge as a popular genre (as exemplified by the extremely successful *La Guerre des boutons*, Robert, 1962, although it will not truly gain momentum until the 1980s.[39] Given de Gaulle's natalist policies, a greater representation of children in the cinema of the 1960s might have been expected, even though social trends indicate otherwise. The 1960s was the age of the postwar baby boomers who were less intent on procreating than their forebears. This trend continued into the 1970s as a result, amongst other things, of the legislation concerning women's reproductive rights. Whatever the socio-demographic trends, the genre has grown in importance since its revival and, by the 1980s, it has broadened its frame of reference to include adolescents (not surprisingly given the youth audience).

No less reactionary are comedies that deal with the Occupation period. It has now become possible to 'laugh about the war'. *La Vache et le prisonnier* (Verneuil, 1959), starring Fernandel, provides a series of vaude-villesque sequences for the grimacing comic who, in his endeavours to escape the enemy, reveals that the German soldiers are stupid (they make way for him to cross a bridge with his cow – Marguerite, who else!), the SS either benign or a phantasmagoria (when stopped by a couple of SS men they too turn out to be escapees) and the French police at the border brutes (they send him scurrying back into enemy land). Two 'Resistance' com-edies of the late 1960s – *La Grande vadrouille* (the popular Gérard Oury's top-selling film with 13 million spectators) and Rappeneau's *La Vie de Château* (both 1966) – secure the myth of the indefatigability and resolute-ness of the Resistance whilst permitting the spectator to smile at the way in which the central protagonists become *résistants malgré eux*. This is turn secures the collectivising myth, already commented on in relation to the early 1950s cinema, that within the heart of every French man and woman there beats a true *résistant*.

Modern comic discourses essentially have two modalities, both of which have as a frame of reference Americana or the American modernist dream. The first, Americana, can be found, for instance, in Demy's musical comedies which represent an attempt to incorporate the American musical and comic traditions into French cinema with the intention of opening up the French tradition to enable a new kind of comic film to emerge. The bitter-sweetness of Demy's films – especially the totally sung

Les Parapluies de Cherbourg (1964) – undoes the happy romantic ending associated with American musicals (except *West Side Story*, of course). In this film, boy meets girl, they fall in love and promise eternal love, but he gets drafted to Algeria. Unable to wait, she finds another love and leaves Cherbourg. She returns one day (with her husband) and happens upon her former love back at his job but wounded from the war. Demy's musicals push the genre to the limits of unreality, becoming parody used to ironic effect. Demy achieves this first of all by the colliding interplay between sound track and the diegesis. A banal but true-to-life love story (realism) gets turned into a musical novel (artifice). A second way by which he achieves this distortion is through the forced coloration of the decors and costumes which change in accordance with the psychological mood of the central characters. In other words, Demy makes colour function in the subversive way described in the technologies of style. Realism is undermined by artifice and vice versa. However, the musical comedy seems destined not to become a French genre and has all but disappeared. Apart from Demy's work, there are only one or two films that come to mind (Varda's feminist musical *L'Une chante l'autre pas*, 1977 and Besson's designer musical *Subway* 1985).

The second modality of modernist discourses reflects upon the French 'obsession' with *la chose américaine* – with *the* dream object being the American car. It is not only the French who get ironised in such comedies as *La Belle américaine* (Dhéry, 1961) and *Le Corniaud* (Oury, 1965), but also the American object itself. In the first film, when a young couple, Marcel and Paulette, miraculously get to purchase a '*belle américaine*', it is like a dream come true. However, the beautiful dream car becomes more of a hindrance than a help even where social mobility is concerned. Its ostentatiousness costs Marcel his job and, although there is a brief upward swing, it is not long before the couple find themselves locked up in jail and the victims of numerous other misadventures. By now Marcel is convinced that he must sell the car 'because it is of no use' (i.e., it only brings him/them bad luck). It is only when his friends find a practical purpose for his *belle américaine* that he is persuaded not to let go of his dream (notice how Paulette has slipped to the sidelines). Thus, *she* is transformed into something practical *à la française* – an ice-cream van. The couple's future is assured.

In the other film, *Le Corniaud* (a term meaning imbecile), the dream machine again becomes the site for satire. As with the other film, the ironic play is double (targeting both the French adulation of the dream object and the *chose américaine* itself). Ordinary Antoine Maréchal (played by Funès) cannot believe his 'luck' when he gets the opportunity to drive a Cadillac after his 2CV is smashed to pieces by a big businessman's luxury car. The trouble is, he has to go to Naples to pick it up and come back through customs. When this supposed simpleton (*corniaud*) realises that there are drugs stashed in the car, he decides to see through his commission but with the help of the police. The Cadillac is delivered, but so too are the gangsters, into the hands of the police. At first, then, the Cadillac is an object of which *le corniaud* is a 'victim' (his adulation of *la chose américaine* gets him into the fix in the first place), but then the tables turn and he is in charge of *her*, using *her* as bait to catch the dealers. Thus *la belle américaine* becomes functional, has a practical purpose. Twice, therefore, *la belle américaine* becomes the 'ice-maiden'.[40]

The socio-political inflection present in much of the 1970s civic cinema also finds a place in the *polars* and comedies of the more readily identifiable mainstream cinema of that decade. Sautet's realist portraits in both genres unmask the mentality of the neo-bourgeoisie, the new rich class of the economic boom of the early 1970s. The narratives of his extremely popular films (often ranking in the top five or, at least, top ten French films) function to remove the social mask and reveal to the protagonists the true nature of their lives, which they may not be willing to accept. Thus, in the *polar* genre's *Max et les ferrailleurs* (1971), the eponymous protagonist – a cop – is exposed for the mediocrity of his own set of values based as they are in immediacy and in his being right. He is committed to arresting criminals, but in his tunnel/monovision he will even go so far as to set up a robbery of his own and use a gang led by a former friend of his to carry it out. In the closing moments of the film he shoots a fellow police officer who insists, against Max's orders, on arresting Lily (Max's mistress). His total lack of scruples, in this ultimately unnecessary killing, also point to his inability to perceive any moral line between being a policeman and taking the law into his own hands. By way of comparison, in the comedy genre, *César et Rosalie* (1972) and *Vincent, Paul, François et les autres* (1974), both bitter-sweet comedies, show male protagonists who are unable completely to come to terms with the truth. César fails to see that taking his wife for granted and his self-satisfaction at his successful business do not necessarily mean happiness. The three protagonists in the other film, now in their mid- to late forties, find that it is hard to come to terms with not having accomplished their youthful ambitions and ideals and easier to deceive themselves than to face the fact that they have compromised all along the line.

Popular comedy of this decade tends to concentrate on the male as central to the diegesis rather than the female. The incompetence of men is represented as endearing (*Le Distrait*, Pierre Richard, 1970, *L'Emmerdeur* and *Le Grand blond avec une chaussure noire*, Yves Robert, 1972), as is not growing up – boys will be boys (*Les Zozos*, Pascal Thomas, 1973, *Un éléphant ça trompe énormément* and its sequel *Nous irons tous au paradis*, both by Robert, 1976 and 1977). Even the new phenomenon of the *café-théâtre* alternative comedy (with Coluche and Michel Blanc among others) did not produce any less of a misogynistic representation of women in the films they made with the director Patrice Leconte. The *Bronzés* series (the collective genderising of *bronzés* does not disguise the fact that the central focus is men), which they launched in 1977, is about holiday adventures either at the *Club Méditerranée* (*Les Bronzés*) or in the ski resorts (*Les Bronzés font du ski*, 1979) where the main sport is for men to 'land' (mostly) as many women as possible and for women to 'catch' their man. Only the timid Michel Blanc goofs up (but incompetence is endearing). Comedy, therefore, remains predominantly conservative and unchanged in its sexual transparence (and that still includes the *Cages aux folles* series with its stereotyped camp – which gay people do like to see, but which does little to advance the image of gayness).

If comedy is the genre that comforts in its mostly unflinching repetition of stereotypes, thus reinforcing the illusion that society is safe because unchanging, in some respects this is less true of the *polars* of the 1970s where the politics of paranoia are fully to the fore. Its ubiquitous presence in the *polars* attests to a prevailing preoccupation with the belief that police and politics are hand in glove. Justice is class-based and favours the rich and influential only. Radio/television is the voice of the state. People who meddle and get too close to the truth are essentially expeditable. And so on. This sense of paranoia in its turn breeds, at its most extreme, a kind of social schizophrenia in which the protagonists no longer know where the truth lies – the modern mechanisms, whereby 'truth' is either hidden or mediated away, making certainty impossible. It should be recalled that a sense of schizophrenia is not alien to France's cinema. We have seen how it occurred after both World Wars and how, although in both cases it was linked with a desire for denial, the cause of that schizophrenia was different, occurring in relation to loss and guilt respectively. This time, however, there is no evident cause such as war to unleash this reaction. Therefore it might seem curious that this cinema should reproduce a sense of schizophrenia. Certainly, the myth of man-machine can be pointed to as a part cause – technology outstripping human endeavour – but that was a myth already raised at least as early as Godard's *Alphaville* (1965).

Another reason that can be mobilised is the death of the 'father' which could give two contrasting readings. First, it is now safe to express the destabilising effects of virtual censorship. Second, the loss of the father has led to a feeling of leadershiplessness, even powerlessness. Another reason that can enter into this conundrum concerns France's changing identity over the 1960s, during which time she was on the one hand, whittled down from an Empire to a hexagon (just the mainland) and on the other, elevated to nuclear status. Furthermore, over that same decade, the effect of conflicting political discourses of modernism and monarchism, of freedom and alienation of the citizenry – both of which could not be reconciled in the French mentality – must be invoked. Finally, it is also relevant to mention the change in the nature of protest in the 1970s, because it does point to a more reflectively self-conscious society, to a society that is consciously looking at itself and that will therefore be more aware of the schizophrenic ambience that surrounds it. The shift from the violence of protest of the 1960s to a more gentle, unaggressive protest (as described in some of the films about marginals) pointed to an internalisation and individualisation of reactions against various forms of oppression and to an understanding that it was the nation that was the first site of schizophrenia, not the individual mentality.

To return to the *polar*. In broad terms it is possible to discern three types of *polars* overall. The above-mentioned politics of paranoia is a first type of *polar* that falls into a category with which we are already familiar, the authentic cinema. After that comes the retro-mode and, finally, the heroic mode, both of which more readily belong in conformist mainstream cinema. The heroic mode breaks down into two types. In the first instance, there is the cop who is too conscientious for his own good (*Dernier domicile connu*, Giovanni, 1970) or too good to be true (*Il était une fois un flic*, Lautner, 1972). In the films of Giovanni and Lautner the cop will go to any lengths to 'get his man'. Giovanni's cop is the victim of his own competence and integrity. Because he successfully apprehends the miscreant son of an influential lawyer, he gets shunted on to a sideline where there is little for him to do. But even there he is oversuccessful in the tasks he is assigned. As a result he gets a 'big one' and has to trace the last whereabouts (hence title of film) of a crucial witness in a mobster murder case. Despite numerous attacks by the mobsters trying to 'protect' their own, he eventually tracks down the witness. Mission accomplished, the murdered is convicted. But the witness is killed for his testimony as a direct result of the cop's success. Justice is sweet, but policing has a human face. In Lautner's film, the cop goes to the extent of creating a proto-family so that he can catch his criminals. In the end he nets his criminals, marries his 'wife' and adopts his 'son'.

In the second instance, there is the cop or, this time too, the gangster whose comportment is heroic. Verneuil's two films with Belmondo (his own fetish star for this genre) *Le Casse* (1971) and *Peur sur la ville* (1975) enter into this category, as do Mocky's *Solo* (1970) and Deray's *Le Gang* (1972). Verneuil's two films place Belmondo as heroic from opposing ends of the *polar* spectrum. In *Le Casse* he is a gangster and in *Peur sur la ville* he is the indomitable cop. The heroism here is less to do with the narratives (indeed in the first film, Belmondo is rotten to the core) than with Belmondo's very physical prowess. The spectator would know that Belmondo performed all the stunts himself (no stuntman for the body-built actor!). So it is the heroism of his stunts that attracts. Deray's *Le Gang* enters the heroic mode because it is about solidarity amongst gangsters (hence the title).

Mocky's *Solo* is undoubtedly the most offensive in this series of films heroising gangsters or cops and points to a phenomenon that will be far more widespread in the *polars* of the 1980s – vigilante vengeance upon a detested social class. In this latter respect, it must be stated that over the two decades there is an important shift in the class targeted by self-appointed justicers. It changes from the bourgeoisie and the elite industrialists (favourite targets of Mocky) to marginals and *loubards* in the 1980s. The despised class now becomes essentially a non-class – having no status, it is an easy class to attack. However, it should also be pointed out that Mocky's type of heroisation is very much in the minority in the 1970s. In his film a gangster dies for his brother who is part of a revolutionary group of avengers. In trying to prevent his brother and the group from committing further massacres, he gets embroiled and eventually participates in the very massacre he is trying to stop. As a result he gets singled out as the leader, pursued by police and gunned down, but in the meantime he has facilitated his brother's escape.

Heroisation in all of the above types of film is spectacle and, inevitably, reductionist, but it does nothing to prevent their enormous popularity – due, it must be said, mostly to the use of fetish stars like Belmondo, Ventura and Delon, but also to a 'tradition of quality' associated especially with Deray, Lautner and Verneuil. To a degree, the same can be said of the retro-mode, a mode in which Deray dominates (the box-office as well) with stars like Belmondo and Delon. *Borsalino* (1970) brings the two stars together in a fantasised reconstruction of the adventures of two Marseilles gangsters of the 1930s, Carbone and Spirito. Renamed Siffredi and Capella, the intrepid duo – greatest of friends after initial animosity – decide to take on the various bosses who control the city. Having eliminated them all, they take over, only to realise that a new generation of *caïds* is more than likely to follow in their footsteps. At the point of realisation, Capella decides to leave Marseilles (not for nothing does his name mean 'head'), but he gets gunned down. Siffredi disappears, only to return in a sequel in 1974, *Borsalino et cie*. Rather than a realistic portrait of 1930s gangsterdom, this film is a buddy movie (aka *Butch Cassidy and the Sundance Kid*, made in 1969 and released in France the same year as *Borsalino* which came top, the American film ranking tenth).

Deray's *Flic story* (1975), starring Delon and Trintignant (another fetish star), takes us back into the late 1940s and through to the mid-1950s. It traces the nine-year saga – based on the memoirs of a former detective of the *Sûreté nationale*, Roger Borniche (whose revelations also inspired Deray's *Le Gang*) – of the pursuit, arrest and execution of a dangerous but intelligent criminal. This time, instead of the brash and bravura of the duo in *Borsalino*. the spectator is party to the vying of two intellects as the one tries to ensnare the other in the physical and mental traps set in this cat and mouse *flic* story. Delon the *flic* eventually 'gets his man', but the ensuing months of interrogation blur lines and a certain complicity and understanding grows between them. It is not difficult to see in this equalisation of intellect and humanising of the characters (murderer and cop) another form of the process of heroisation already alluded to. Respectively, Deray's two films valorise brawn and brain, *polar* clichés which have entered the mythological canon of this film genre and which do little to distinguish them, any more than those of the heroic mode, from the American products of the same order. This is not a negative value criticism, because box-office returns indicate that the French prefer to see their own stars embodying these clichés rather than their American counterparts, as is attested by the fact that on average three to five films in the top fifteen are French *polars* – only once (in 1972 with Coppola's *The Godfather*) does an American gangster/thriller movie outdo an indigenous product of the same genre.

Nor should it be inferred that the French are pure consumers of clichés. Counter-heroic films were also being made that were equally popular. Because it brings the counter-heroic and the retro-mode together, Enrico's *Le Vieux fusil* (1975), will suffice by way of illustration. Incidentally, in that year it came second to Verneuil's *Peur sur la ville* and Belmondo's heroic muscle-flexing stunts. Set in Pétain's Vichy France (in Montauban near Toulouse) in 1944, this film depicts the limits to which outrage will push an individual. Not at all heroic, a middle-class middle-aged doctor (played by Noiret) avenges the brutal slaughter of his wife (played by Romy Schneider) and the child whom he had sent for safety's sake to his estate in the country. In his mistaken belief that Pétain's *milice* will only seek reprisals in the town, he effectively sends them to their deaths because, as it turns out, the *milice* (now on the defensive) do not care where or whom they target. When he rejoins his family he finds that they and the whole village have been massacred. Step by step, one by one, the doctor picks off the *milice*. Filling them with terror, he sets traps into which they ineluctably fall and he hunts them down with his old gun. The chronology of this revenge is interspersed with flashbacks to his life with his wife and daughter in the provincial town of Montauban. How could 'this' be happening (his tracking down and killing) when 'that' (his life with his family) was all he had known and expected to know? Why should 'that' (the *milice*'s massacre) have happened when all his life he had been outside politics and engaged only with his profession (which implicitly meant saving lives)? What is it that causes a benign, well-tempered doctor to turn into a determined, ruthless even, avenger-murderer? These are some of the questions raised by the counterpointing of the past with the present. Like *Lacombe Lucien* before it, this film raises questions about that period rather than offering answers, and as such enters into the arena of authentic cinema.

Although paranoia and schizophrenia (sometimes to the point of madness) are often either backdrops to or guiding forces in the narratives of the authentic mode of *polars*, there is an attendant realism to them that makes it impossible to reject the implicit pessimism in these films. Within this cinema, apart from the obligatory presence of the CRS, the police detectives are pictured as complex constructions whose very ambiguity does not allow for the facile fingering of them as purely corrupt and sadistic, even though at times they often behave as such. Films of this order expose corrupt police practices and by the end of the 1970s, it is even further suggested that a certain institutional malaise is being experienced by the police – a malaise that creates rivalries between different crack police brigades so that mistakes do occur and police get killed by their own (*La Guerre des polices*, Davis, 1979). But malaise, mental and moral disintegration are not just the province of the police. In *polars* where police are not at the centre of the narrative there is also evidence of a victimisation and schizophrenia that points to a society that has suffered secrecy long enough on the one hand and, on the other, is ill at ease with itself in its newly acquired affluence. Just to mention three films in this vein, Enrico's *Secret* (1974), Boisset's *Folle à tuer* (1975) and Deray's *Un papillon sur l'épaule* (1978) to some degree or another all touch upon the fine line that separates a person from madness. The solitude that paranoia (however justified) induces in an individual is the starting block for the descent first into a schizophrenic apprehension of the surrounding society and then into madness. It is instructive that in the three films, characters at one point or another end up in a mental institution not because of any imputed false perception of the world, but as a result of forces outside of them and beyond their control that put them there because of the potential truth of that perception. They act, therefore, as an allegory for the process of paranoia described above. *Secret* and *Papillon sur l'épaule* tell of an individual who, by stumbling upon something the powers-that-be want kept secret, ends up in a mental institution. *Folle à tuer* makes the point that those who are locked up in institutions may not necessarily be the mad ones after all. Rather, their madness may well be the result of their inability or unwillingness to cope or live in a mad society.

PASTICHE CULTURE: A LAST LOOK AT THE CINEMA OF THE 1980S

The cinema of the 1980s and early 1990s is pastiche culture. Once again this is not an immaculate conception. Occasionally during the cinema of the 1970s there have been one or two cases of a cinema that has had something in common with the cinema of pastiche associated with the cinema of the 1980s (and early 1990s). I have already mentioned Blier's *Les Valseuses*. The comedy genre, because it remains so unchanging (and only exceptionally renewed), is almost inevitably a cinema of pastiche and as such need not detain our attention here. But, the *polar* of the 1970s did not entirely escape stepping into the postmodern neoculture, as I pointed out with

Mocky's *Solo* which is not an isolated case. Patrice Chéreau's *La Chair de l'orchidée* (1975) and Hugo Santiago's *Ecoute voir* (1978) both pass over the logic of a narrative for the look and, with regard to the second film, the sound of the film. Without any regard to intrigue (what intrigue there is can be reduced to a series of incoherently unrelated narratives), the heavily expressionistic images of Chéreau's film serve as sole signifier for the corruption of a crumbling society. In Santiago's film, the plot device is ultimately a series of encounters linked together into a thriller genre. A private eye (Catherine Deneuve) sets about thwarting a plot to take over the country and the minds of the citizenry by controlling the media. This barely disguised reference to Giscard's *télécratie* sets up the potential for an allegory. The bi-sexual 'proto-Marianne' (Deneuve is bi-sexual in this film and in 1985 she becomes the new figure-head for Marianne), fighting against the Orleanist autocrat, could have been read as liberalism (as defined by her sexuality, dress code and profession) exposing the purported father of liberalism (Giscard) for his true nature (an autocrat). But Santiago allows that to slip away and for his film to become a film about crime films, a reflector of crime films' style rather than a renewal – the essence of pastiche.

With a few exceptions already discussed, lack of renewal and a reflecting backwards are the hallmarks of the 1980s cinema. All is style, be it retro-nostalgic or hi-tech – the two dominant styles of this cinema. Both categories of films look back to earlier prototypes and it is in this walking back to the future that the whole inability to invent and create resides. Within these two categories I have noted seven different typologies of film, although clearly a film can bear more than one generic resemblance. What is there is revealing. On the nostalgia front one can list: remakes, literary adaptations, screwball comedy mostly valorising the family, or at least paternity. At the interface between nostalgia and hi-tech, because they will be astride the two categories, come the *polars* (the thriller and the *film-noir* genre). The hi-tech films almost exclusively concern the 13–25 age group and can be categorised as follows: adolescent-teenage movies, lost generation movies (rebels with or without a cause), psychological movies.

All genres, almost without exception, revivify earlier institutions and myths and as such reify them. For example, the family is represented in much the same favourable light as it was during the 1940s and 1950s when the need then, as now, was to procreate (*Conseil de famille* and even on a subliminal level *Trois hommes et un couffin*). Alternatively it is represented as an ideal fervently wished for, for example, *La Baule-les-pins* (Diane Kurys, 1989). Literary adaptations and remakes abound. *Les Misérables* (Robert Hossein, 1982) and *Manon des sources* (Claude Berri, 1985, and all the other Pagnol adaptations he has made) are simultaneously literary adaptations and remakes. *Un amour de Swann* (Volker Schlöndorff, 1983) is just another example of the retro-tendency that serves to consolidate a variety of myths. These films point to the good/bad old days, rural revivalism and turn-of-the-century gentility – that is, all that we can no longer aspire to be or possess, or conversely, all that we are satisfied is no longer our lot in life. But these retro-discourses are precisely not about the past, but about our ideas or cultural stereotypes about the past.

Historicism, however, is not very much to the fore, which is rather curious given the bicentenary of the Revolution. There was *the* film *La Révolution française* (Robert Enrico and Richard Heffron, 1989), a costume drama superproduction which gave a sufficiently official version of 1789. Elsewhere there was the feeble comedy by Jean Yanne *Liberté, égalité, choucroute* (1985) and *Chouans!* by Philippe de Broca (1987), an ahistorical and somewhat anti-republican film in its portrayal of revolutionary zeal as virtual psychosis and in the fact that the two lovers, from opposing sides (monarchical and republican), go off to live in freedom in America. Incidentally this film is also an adaptation of a Hugo novel and a remake of the first Chouan film that goes back to silent *ciné-romans* days (*Jean Chouan*, Arthur Bernède, 1925). Otherwise all that remains as a bicentennial sign is *Danton* (Andrej Wajda, 1982), a French film but an adaptation of a Polish play that says as much about the conflict between Lech Walesa and General Jaruzelski as it does about the one between Danton and Robespierre. The only other sign is *Adieu Bonaparte*, a Franco-Egyptian production made by Youssef Chahine in 1985. This film, about Bonaparte's 1789–99 campaign in Egypt, is ultimately not about the Revolution *per se* but first, about revolutionary idealism in the form of France's desire to export the Revolution, and second, the birth of Egyptian nationalism.[41]

It is worth pausing for a moment on this 'lack of history' because of what is reveals about France in relation to France-as-nation and France-as-history. Over the past thirty years, in relation to history, France's cinema has evolved from a representation of history as dissimulation (1960s), to one of revelation (1970s) and, finally, to one of diasporisation. Brisset (1990) suggests that this lack of representation of history in the 1980s cinema reflects the general apoliticised mood prevailing in France. The argument goes that the French are more preoccupied with economic astringencies than with images of their history. Whilst not disputing that reading, I think it has to be added, first, that ideologically the Fifth Republic has gradually fallen into a state of somnolence from which there are no signs as yet that it is ready to awaken. Ideologically asleep, there is little need for France to wave national myths (unlike during the early de Gaulle years) of the order of the Revolution. Second, there are financial reasons. Historical films cost a lot to make and are rarely blockbusters. In fact, France tends to make one blockbuster or *film-choc* per year for the one-off audience (usually a literary adaptation *à la* Berri or an 'animal' film such as *L'Ours* and *Le Grand bleu* – all big hits). Third, the Fifth Republic coincides with the age of postmodernity. Postmodernity implies the rejection of history or, rather, the disappearance of a sense of history – a disappearance largely assisted by the new media technologies which, through their informational function, fragment time into a series of presents. Jameson (1983, 125) cites the media exhaustion of news and how it relegates recent historical events as quickly as possible into the past. One could just as easily mention computer technology whereby the three big finance markets (Tokyo, London and Wall Street – not even New York you will note) have dissolved the twenty-four hours that separate the Pacific state from the Atlantic one. All of these objects are also artefacts of a consumer society. As far as France is concerned, the consumer society was born in the Fifth Republic, since when the logic of consumer capitalism has prevailed (ibid., 125). But the effect of this has been for us to become hooked on obsolescence and to remain forever fixed in the present because in 'the next three minutes' we will be offered 'something new' that is not new, of course, but is different (take, for example, style which changes so quickly that it catches up on itself). For three decades, the pursuit of the logic of capitalism has propelled France (and other countries in the West and in the Pacific zone) into the logic of sameness and exhaustion (or vacuity even) of ideology and ideas. In this state, not only is it impossible to achieve an aesthetic representation of the past, but also current experience – at least in mainstream cinema – resonates with a peculiar emptiness. The '*société de consommation*' of the 1960s and 1970s has now become the '*société de pub*'.

This coyness with history is similarly echoed in films about the Occupation period. Apart from a couple of comedies (the very popular *Papy fait de la résistance*, Jean-Marie Poiré, 1983 and the farcical flop *Fucking Fernand*, Gérard Mordillat, 1987), the Occupation gets marginalised as a back-drop for the callisthenics of Belmondo in Henri Verneuil's *Les Morfalous* and for the personal story of a *pied-noir* in Alexandre Arcady's *Le Grand carnaval* (both films made in 1983). As if pointing to the unaddressability of the past, both films are located in Algeria. Back in the hexagon, Truffaut's *Le Dernier métro* (1980) is a *mise-en-scène* of nostalgia for the Paris of the Occupation and a *mise-en-abyme* of theatre (theatre within theatre, play within play) that allows performance to be at the centre of the diegesis – Occupation as theatre. Symptomatic of what is problematic in this film are the throw-away lines ('I'm not going to drop my trousers so he can see I'm not a Jew') and images (do we really believe that the Jewish girl with the yellow star emblazoned on her coat actually managed to be sneaked in to see the theatre performance?) that purport to refer to 'what it was like' but which clearly refer to stereotype before reality, to spectacle (exposing, seeing, watching) before history.

In all of this postmodern ahistory and with regard to other films on the Occupation, it seems curious that there should be a number of films (I have noted five) in which women finally get to signify as having had an important role to play in the Occupation period, even though only one film has woman characterised as a Resistance fighter (*Blanche et Marie*, Jacques Renard, 1985).[42] Why now? Why in the postmodern era when history is being rejected? One convenient answer would be to say that because woman is traditionally placed outside history, nothing could be more appropriate than that she should emerge now and within those specific films. That is, because history no longer exists, it is timely to represent woman especially since, out of all the 'history' films, this is one period from which she has been conspicuously absent (except in Clément's *Le Jour et l'heure*, 1962 and Melville's *L'Armée des ombres*, 1969, both starring Simone Signoret). Another way of reading this would be to see the phenomenon as part and parcel of the recuperation of feminism by post-modernist discourses, that is, it is now all right to talk about courageous women because feminism is dead (in France, that is). A third way of interpreting this representation would be to consider it alongside the notion of legitimacy, that is, of cinema deluding itself that it is making an historical film historically since at least two of the films, *Blanche et Marie* and *Une Affaire de femmes* (Chabrol, 1988), are based on factual events (respectively, rural resistance and the execution of an abortionist).

But because there is no history, it can also be made up. Thus, since 'no texts' exist, hagiographies such as Camille Claudel's 'story' (*Camille Claudel*, Bruno Nuytten, 1989) or those of 'unknown' saints whose 'stories' should be known – say, *Thérèse* (Cavalier, 1986) or *Bernadette* (Delannoy, 1987) – can be fabricated or prefabricated. That is, a bit of passion here, a bit of madness there (a precursor of course is Truffaut's film *L'Histoire d'Adèle H.* – the reader will have noted the *histoire* in the title and its implicit referral to invention). Hagiographies are especially 'interesting' if women are both passionate in their respective ways about the object of their desire and touched by madness.

So much for history. Contemporary political history gets just as little airing and the few films that do take on a political theme are set within a vague present. Two films based on novels by Françoise Giroud (of *Nouvelle Vague* neologism fame) are worth mentioning for their vagueness and also because Giroud was for a while the Minister for Women's Affairs under Giscard's presidency and has worked for television. In *Le Bon plaisir* (Francis Girod, 1983) the tale revolves around a president of the Republic who discovers that a former lover of his has had a child by him. Will he be exposed and have to resign, especially since his ex-lover (Catherine Deneuve) seems disinclined to let him off the hook when a third party gets hold of a compromising letter? Thanks to intrigue and money, the security of the state and its institutions remains assured. It is not just the vagueness of the when and the who that concerns, but the fact that such a 'scandal' would be unlikely to threaten political power in France (in the United States, where morality is much valued, it would be a problem). It is well known that presidents of the Fifth Republic have had 'mistresses' in their earlier political life, so to make political intrigue out of this situation is at best a bit pointless, at worst a bit scurrilous. The representation of women is one that links up with the second film, *Le Quatrième pouvoir* (Serge Leroy, 1985), which also lends itself to a troubled reading of the image of women. This time the film relates the machinations of a woman television presenter (Nicole Garcia) who is consumed with ambition. In both films, the women are represented as vengeful and unscrupulous, as if signalling a death to the neo-romanticism of the New Wave (which Giroud 'invented' after all) and a backlash on the liberalism of the Giscard presidency. As we shall go on to see, vengeance is present in the other two categories of genres either as a dominant trait (in the *polars*/thrillers) or as implicitly explicit (in the hi-tech/youth films).

Before coming to these last two categories, one last point needs to be made on this lack of contemporary political transparence within mainstream cinema and, for the greater part, non-mainstream cinema and it addresses a specific exception to this practice. Just as in the 1970s there was a cinema of the periphery that moved closer to that of the centre in the form of a brief spate of women's films (films made by women about some aspects of women's issues, sexuality and the couple predominantly), so too in the 1980s another cinema of the periphery, that of the French Maghrébins (what I termed earlier Beur cinema), has moved from the outer periphery and has been recognised as a cultural cinema in its own right. This cinema does reflect part of the socio-political reality of France: racism, unemployment, drugs, the distressing conditions of the HLMs and suburbs for Arab inhabitants as exemplified in the two films by Mehdi Charef *Le Thé au harem d'Archimède* (1985), *Camomille* (1987) and in Abdelkrim Bahloul's *Le Thé à la menthe* (1984). The images are not all negative, however. This same cinema also gives cultural representation of Beur hopes and desires. Critics have heralded it as the new popular realism of the 1980s (echoes of the 1930s), an epithet which could be a good or a bad thing – the tendency of some cinema of the periphery to get co-opted is legion enough. It is not yet clear whether this cinema, like that of others of the periphery, will get recuperated or returned to the outer margins or if it will be able to sustain its visibility in a way that women's cinema in France has failed to do. I do not want to make an invidious comparison between the 'women's problem' and the 'Arab problem' especially since neither of these two cinemas limits itself to just that. Nor is it necessarily a bad thing to be on the periphery if visibility of a kind can be sustained. The point I am trying to make is that women's cinema was on the periphery, came into a more central position and then disappeared back to the margins. And yet women making cinema have predominantly left the periphery of women's cinema (or avoided it altogether) and are making films whose intentionality is avowedly not feminist. They have elected to move towards the centre. Only a few have not. Cinema of the periphery can reach mass audiences without having to change its fundamental position. What remains to be seen is if the Beur tradition can continue (a similar question currently applies to the new Black cinema in America) and not to be recuperated by mainstream cinema or film-makers.

Turning to the next category of genres, the one interfacing between retro and hi-tech – the *polars*/thrillers – it is clear from a first glance that it echoes the ambiguous characterisation of the American prototype of the 1930s and 1940s. It is interesting that, on the whole, this genre eschews referring back to the three emblematic French gangster movies of the 1950s (*Du Rififi chez les hommes*, *Touchez pas au grisbi* and *Bob le flambeur*) when that was a genre that invented itself. In this almost mid-Atlantic product of the 1980s, police and detectives (private or otherwise) are less than virtuous – even slightly corrupt. Halfway between light and dark (chiaroscuro), these knights of the night are as cynical and sceptical about the world as were their American forebears and as hard-bitten and rough with 'their' women as before. The environment in which they move, however, is ambiguous in a different way from before. It is now the melting-pot of postmodernity. On the one hand, many of the objects that surround them – especially their cars and coats (literally that in which they put themselves) – are of a bygone age (*Poussière d'ange*, Niermans, 1986), thus assimilating them with the earlier iconography of, say, Sam Spade or Philip Marlowe or even Eddie Constantine (Eddie Constantine, incidentally, is a French parody of an American parody of a private detective). Conversely, at arm's length from these 'heroes' are all the electronic and technological artefacts of our modern hi-tech society. Retro-man looking at hi-tech consumer undurables – the perfect postmodern condition. Elsewhere as a sign of moving with the times, there are some spectacular blood-curdling special effects unseen before in this genre in France – doubtless a by-product of the popularity of Clint Eastwood's *Dirty Harry* series. Normal, run-of-the-mill brutality is also reassuringly in evidence: the *bottin* treatment (using the telephone directory to hit suspects on the head), head butting and body blows are there for all to see in Swaim's *La Balance, Police* (Pialat, 1985) and *Les Ripoux* (Zidi, 1985). At first, the image of the cop or detective (a few modern devices apart) appears to remain unchanged from earlier representations, but this is just an illusion mobilised by the prefabricated nature of the image. Slightly seedy, a bit *pourri* (which, incidentally is where the back-slang *ripoux* comes from, *pourri* meaning rotten), somewhat brutal, the detective – his rapier-like wit notwithstanding – is often portrayed as mildly ineffectual or even ambivalent in successfully bringing about justice (an illustrative example would be Miller's *Garde à vue*, 1981). The current popularity of the *polar* in France is most certainly ascribable to this ambiguity and ambivalence of the cop or detective. On the surface this representation seems to continue the 'humanising' trend started in the 1970s, but the picture is not so untroubled as might at first appear.

The first obvious point to be made is that the myth perpetrated here reaffirms existing prejudices and thus normalises the image of police as ineffectual, brutish and corrupt. Rather than seeing the 1980s as a continuation of the 1970s image, it would seem that the image has developed into one where the police become, globally, agents of a repressive and negative education (to use Gramsci's terminology). In the 1970s, the detectives were given either a more human face (sometimes dying for their pains) and/or a complex characterisation even if they were also agents of repression. Thanks to the films of the 1980s, we now 'know' that the police as a whole are as susceptible to corrupt demeanours as those self-same persons they pursue in the name of justice. These films no longer 'question' the role of the police, as they did in the 1970s. In the very act of confirming the corrupt practices, the *status quo* of the institution itself remains unchanged: 'this is how it is'. Furthermore, limiting the construction of the cop's characterisation to the negative value only does not ultimately change anything: 'this is how they are'.

The second point concerns the kind of transparence on society which these *polars* give. The genre drops the 1970s tradition of referring to contemporary reality such as the political scene, police malaise and error, including fighting each other at cross purposes. In general the French *polar* has now fallen under the influence of the American and Italian thrillers to the extent that it has become ultra-codified so that it cannot breathe. The film might well be redolent with ambiguity and cynicism as it starts off, but it is unable to sustain the clichés/codes and so, not knowing where to go, often ends in a blood bath or with some unrealistic compromise. Deville's *Eaux profondes* (1981) best exemplifies this point. An older man (Trintignant), passionately in love with his much younger wife (Huppert), puts up with her amorous dalliances with younger men but only because he has a 'secret' weapon that keeps the more persistent lovers at a distance. He insinuates that he has murdered one of her previous lovers. However, when the guilty person for that murder is arrested, he has to reassert himself and make fiction reality. Two murders later and after endless attempts to expose her husband as the murderer of her lovers, the wife eventually reconciles herself to living with him. The unconvincing compromise apart, the phallocentrism in this film, even perverse phallocentrism – the legitimation of which is signified by the denouement ('it's OK to do in other phalluses as long as mine remains strong') – is perfectly consonant with the 'maleness' of this genre, as is the ultimate subjugation of the woman/wife. Retro-discourses join up with retro-cops.

To this effect, it is clear that the true subtlety of the *polar* has gone. But what has also been marginalised is the national specificity of the genre. In the discussion of this genre in the previous chapter, the point was made that French cinema in the 1950s did manage to produce an indigenous product albeit, of course, inflected by American *film-noir* discourses. The argument there was that the working class of the 1930s had been transposed into a new gangster class but that resonances from the earlier representation – especially male friendship, but also the proto-father/son relationship – gave this new genre a French specificity. This latest generation of *polars* has lost that idea of a social community. Now, all that remains is an iconography of Frenchness – a dialogue that refers, albeit vacuously, to France's past, French stars and, in terms of narrative, a Poujadist mentality (the little guy (*sic*) against the big one).[43] What does get introduced into this landscape as a new signifier of Frenchness is the drug underworld almost always associated with an Arab 'community' (*La Police*, Pialat, 1985 and *Tchao pantin*, Berri, 1983), which represents a displacement of the problem. Diaspora joins up with retro-discourses and retro-cops.

The fourth aspect of these *polars* 1980s-style that demarcates them from earlier forms of the genre is that, under the guise of giving 'true' transparence on society (aka the Arab drug underworld, the violence of young *loubards*, etc.), they are in fact reinforcing sacred cows normally associated with rightist discourses and the *bien pensants* class. Two key terms sum up this so-called realism: insecurity and the right to legitimate defence. The reasoning goes as follows: because insecurity is caused by the presence of marginals (Arabs, *loubards*), it is up to either the police or the citizen to ensure their erasure. It would seem that marginals have now replaced the mob and the dangerous classes of the silent cinema. This attitude manifests itself in the *polar* by a new thematic departure. Vengeance has now entered the *polar* diegesis. The individual as vigilante or posse is now the postmodern hero of the *polar*. Thus, a former cop will avenge the death of his son who died from a drug overdose (*Tchao pantin*); a fiancé will avenge the manslaughter/murder of his fiancée (*Tir groupé*, Missiaen, 1982); a husband will avenge the murder of his family (*Légitime violence*, Leroy, 1982). The perpetrators of the murders are all outsiders (*loubards*, Arabs) and therefore outside the law and expeditable by these self-appointed justicers. The surviving victims of the crimes have legitimacy on their side in that they are the 'father' (father, fiancé, husband) – therefore, the 'law' (of the father) – who has been dispossessed. In this respect, the title of the last film cited aptly sums up the notion of legitimated vengeance.

This 'vengeful' cinema brings us back to a not dissimilar reading of the mood of ahistory in contemporary cinema – social unease and a sense of insecurity. Even though Fabius's policies of economic modernisation (*une politique de relance économique*, 1984–6) marked a move away from the economic austerity policies introduced by Mauroy in 1982/3 and were proving successful, the mediatised mood of the mid-1980s revolved around this idea of insecurity. Indeed it should not be forgotten that insecurity was the key word that proved to be Jacques Chirac's electoral ticket to the Matignon in 1986. In the previous two chapters, we have seen how in periods of social malaise (generally brought on by an unhealthy economic climate) extreme positions get adopted by a so-called silent majority. Fear of the 'other' is the most rampant manifestation of this malaise. The groups targeted are inevitably those with the least power and, therefore, those most visibly targetable as 'other'. In making the marginals in society (and I include Arab drug dealers in this category) a predominant target for erasure, the 1980s *polar* reflects this misrecognition of the true source of malaise and subsequent displacement of fear. This is completely the reverse of the 1970s *polar* which questioned the corrupting effects of capitalist and political power. In the 1980s, film follows media hype.

With regard to the last three genres loosely designated under the category youth and hi-tech, as one might expect it is the image of youth that predominates. I say 'image' rather than 'portrayal' because, essentially, it is only a part of youth that is held up for inspection. These films most generally depict the youth generation in relation to their (normally heterosexual) sexuality. It is particularly important to point out that, in terms of the fetishisation of youth, it is most especially the nubility of young women and teenage girls which is put on display. Many of the stars are young girls (14–17 years of age) thrown into dubious sexual activities. The spectator-viewer-voyeur's gaze is transfixed upon their sexuality which is either just barely dormant and at the stage of pubescent awareness (*L'Effrontée*, Miller, 1985, *Charlotte forever*, Gainsbourg, 1986 – both starring Charlotte Gainsbourg), or proto-incestuous (*Noce blanche*, Brisseau, 1989) or, finally, unremittingly voracious (*37,2 degrés le matin*, Beineix, *La Puritaine*, Doillon – both 1986). In either case sexuality is the agent of disorder, even death. In other representations the Laura myth (*Laura*, Preminger, 1944) is revivified. In *La Lune dans le caniveau* (Beineix, 1982) and *Police* (Pialat, 1985), the central protagonists (both played by Depardieu) become haunted and then obsessed/tormented by a young woman who remains (even if sex had been exchanged, as in *Police*) *insaisissable*. Young female sexuality, therefore, is represented as the predominant cause of disruption (of male hegemony). In terms of reactionary iconography, it is hard to imagine a more retrograde perception of woman/the female sex. Virgin, she is Lilith the temptress who rejected Adam. Non-virgin, she is Eve the seductress who tempted Adam into his fall from grace.

Gender representation in the psychological films is equally problematic and regressive where women are concerned. Madness and incest are two of the more favoured psychological environments into which women are plunged (remember the hagiographies). In neither instance is the point of view female. The gaze is masculine, either that of the lover or the father.

The gaze is uncomprehending since it fixes the loved one as object of desire. The lack of psychological vraisemblance, therefore, is hardly surprising. For example, in both *37,2 degrés le matin* and *Péril en la demeure* (Deville, 1984) a very basic equation is drawn between the woman's nymphomania and her hysterical behaviour. That the men willingly indulge the woman's sexual appetite is by-passed. The fact that this simplistic proto-Freudianism is reminiscent of many American movies of the 1950s with their very rudimentary representation of psychological disorder is not enough by way of explanation of these images. It is as if, after first recouping it in the 1970s, an historical revisionism of the women's movement is now taking place – as if it were a *point de détail* (to quote a well-known Le Pen saying referring to another kind of historical revisionism). This total lack of a desire to understand is most vibrantly manifested in Beineix's film *37,2 degrés le matin* (which is a bit worrying given its continued enormous crowd-drawing appeal and the fact that it is much liked by many young female spectators). This film is not a film about a young woman's progressive descent into a hellish madness, although it pretends to be just such. It is not a study in madness, or for that matter a film about man-as-victim of a nymphomaniac. Rather, it is a male fantasy of the 'supreme fuck'. It is a film constructed out of a series of video clips of madness interspersed with 'fucking' or, if you want to go with the overt diegesis, a hi-tech designer clip-film about nymphomania. The image of woman as sexually armed and dangerous brings us back, if not to porn, to some very ancient and reactionary phallocratic fixations about women. Besson's *Nikita* (1989) is supposedly of the *polar* tradition but because of the way in which it fetishises the protagonist it belongs here. Nikita starts off as a deranged *loubarde*. By the time the police agent Tcheky Karyo (uncle Bob) has finished with her, her violent temperament has been 'tamed' to make her into the secret police's top hitman (*sic*). In this film, the supreme male fantasy is fulfilled. Woman becomes gun (i.e., phallus). The dream of Narcissus is complete.

Perhaps one of the greatest sexual myths is the taboo of incest. It is not incest that is taboo (otherwise, Malle's *Souffle au coeur*, 1971, would have encountered more trouble than it did), but talking about it. Hence the shock value of two films devoted in their entirety to fathers discoursing about their incestuous rapports with their daughters: *La Puritaine* and *Charlotte forever*. In this latter film, Serge Gainsbourg actually directs himself and his daughter as the incestuous pair (Gainsbourg's daughter was only 14 at the time of the film's release). The similarity between the two films is quite striking. The discourses are delivered in close hermetic spaces: the theatre for Piccoli on Bonnaire (aged 17 at the time) in *La Puritaine* (the father is a director, she an actress), the father's apartment for *Charlotte*. These spaces are not – as this hermeticism might suggest – womb-like, rather they are cold and gloomy. In these spaces, the fathers recreate the bodies of their respective daughters. They narrate the body in a fragmentary fashion in the same way that a voyeur looking through a small opening would see a woman's fragmented body. This naming of the parts – because it can be endlessly replayed – is used by the fathers to enhance their sexual fantasies. The resultant fragmentation serves to delay the gratification of the total gaze and the notion of final possession (so in a sense the gaze is fetishised too). The coldness of the space and the fragmentation of the body entomb the daughters' sexuality, their bodies frozen by the eye of the father. *Noce blanche* fetishises the incest taboo in an equally disconcerting manner. It is, at first, a reworking of the Lolita myth but without the sex (hence the title). It is also a 'remake' in reverse order of Malle's *Mourir d'aimer*. In this film, a middle-aged male school-teacher falls in love with a teenage woman pupil. This time it is the young woman (rather than the older person) who dies, because love is never consummated and because the schoolteacher withholding sexual consummation (he does all he can to suppress his feelings, he is married, etc.) sends her on her way. Although sex never occurs, their passionate encounters make it clear that if they did have sex it would be 'amazing'. The point here is that the suspension of sex is the only thing that keeps this film going. It is a film about incest-potential and suspended potency.

The female body as the locus of deviancy, and woman as victim of her own sexuality, are both age-old myths. To see them revivified and ascribed to teenagers displays a new kind of misogyny – a misogyny which, through its assault on nubility, erects as its final goal the desexualisation of all women. The treatment of pre- and post-pubescent female sexuality in comedy films, where it is presented as a commodity to be got (in a series of *comique troupier* films) or given away (in a series of films made by the ex-porn 1970s film-maker Max Pécas), is no less disturbing as a reification of women.[44] With women, including the new generation, restored to their former passivity, the reassertion of male virility (which the women's movement had assailed but not repressed) is complete. Such, in any event, is the message of mainstream cinema.

The 1980s, therefore, is the decade of beautifully constructed images – 'cinema nouvelles-images' – much like the visually exciting dishes of the late 1960s 'nouvelle cuisine'. The age of the surface image is as much the consequence of the death of ideology as it is of the growth over the past thirty years of *'la chose médiatique' par excellence*, the television. Television is a popular cultural production, but it is also political in that it serves as transparence (as an instrument of reflection) for the relevant nation's institutional mythologies. It is the new instrument of myth, replacing cinema as the new form of *écriture* (i.e., of meaning construction). But it is also the new medium of popular culture, displacing cinema from its original position as sole purveyor of the popular and aesthetic. Because it is so readily available, and indeed relatively inexpensive in relation to cinema, television has been better able to fulfil the promise of the cinema. Indeed, more than any other medium, television, with its endless flow of images, has been the prime mover in the dissolution of the great divide between high and low art. Placed at such a disadvantage, cinema has had to adapt its own film-making practices which has meant, in great measure, being a post-aesthetic Abel to an image-conscious Cain.

There is something both paradoxical and sadly ironic about this turn of events. In its early days, French cinema, in order to secure its economic survival by expanding its audiences, called upon renowned composers (Hindemith, Honegger, Saint-Saëns, Satie, for example) to accompany the silent images. This collaboration, along with the *Film d'Art* series, led to the bestowal upon cinema of an aesthetic legitimacy. Almost despite itself, cinema was elevated to the heights of the seventh art. Today, cinema is again obliged to seek economic viability. This time, however, it has had to turn to television – the very medium that threatens its survival – for funding and protection. This appeal has had the converse effect to the one launched in the silent cinema days in that cinema has, by and large, shed its aesthetic aspirations and become increasingly telefilmic, so that for example the much prized *mise-en-scène* of the *Cahiers* group has virtually disappeared.[45] *Subway* has more in common with televisual genres such as pop-videos, advertising clips and designer-violence cop drama series than it does with film genres and diegesis – hence, doubtless, its enormous popularity. Who wouldn't want to watch TV in cinemascope and with Dolby sound?

Although it is easy to put French cinema of the 1980s into the dock and accuse it of covering its screen with images of the already-known that comfort the complacent individualistic viewer of the postmodern age ('I am what I see'), the point has to be made that modernist cinema and classical cinema before it were equally reinforcing of dominant codes and hegemonic modes of living as well as institutional hegemony. Cinema was the first popular art medium of the twentieth century. Soon this century will end and perhaps with it cinema as we know it (i.e., no more celluloid but high-resolution video or virtual montage). Small wonder that historians are already poring over this most conformist of art forms as a visual record of the political culture of this century. There will be new territories to explore in the audiovisual media, but for now it is fitting that this older medium should be made the first arena of historical scrutiny, even if to do so runs the risk of being accused, in turn, of prematurely mausoleumifying it or even sounding its death knell.

5 EMBLEMATIC SHOTS OF THE POSTMODERN ERA OF CINEMA

Civic cinema

The myth of the 'liberated' woman is double-edged: *Les Amants*, Malle, 1958

A-morality and a-socialism as everyday life: *Le Beau Serge*, Chabrol, 1958

Civic cinema continued

Woman undoing her reflection: *Cléo de 5 à 7*, Varda, 1962

1960s postmodern cinema

The death of Hollywood and Gaullian republicanism is nigh: *Le Mépris*, Godard, 1963

1970s authentic cinema

Yves Montand, *the* fetish star in *the* emblematic 'political'
film of the decade: Z, Costa-Gavras, 1969

Fascism as an attraction: *Lacombe, Lucien*, Malle, 1974

1980s postmodern symptomatic (unoppositional) cinema

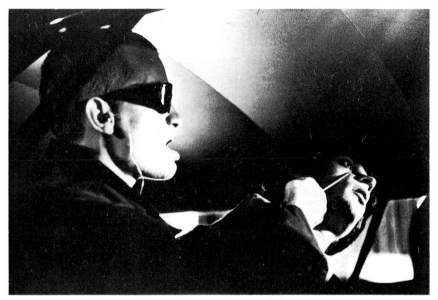

Postmodern designer violence: *Diva*, Beineix, 1980

Postmodern chic: *Subway*, Besson, 1984

In the eyes of the father: *La Puritaine*, Doillon, 1986

Nubility as a desirable commodity: *L'Effrontée*, Miller, 1985

NOTES

1 The distinction is Peter Wollen's (1976, 77–85).

2 The PCF fell from holding 150 seats in the *Assemblée Nationale* in the 1956 general elections to a mere 10 in the 1958 elections. The figures for the PCF make sad reading indeed. In 1956 this party was the most popular of all with 25.6 per cent of the electoral vote. In 1958, that percentage fell to 18.9 per cent, further collapsing to an all-time low of 9.6 per cent in 1986 and remaining quite low at 11.32 per cent in the 1988 general elections (Cole: 1990, 205–11).

3 For further details see Larkin (1988, 302–5) and McMillan (1985, 161–5).

4 For further information see the three excellent accounts of the Fifth Republic in Cole (1990, 1–20), Gaffney (1991, 10–29) and Shields (1991, 69–85).

5 Giscard's background would point to an environment of right-wing thinking. His father's politics in the 1930s saw him associated with extreme right-wing groups (*Action Française, Croix-de-Feu, Parti Social Français*), and during the Occupation his father showed similar tendencies by aligning himself with Pétainism (Larkin: 1988, 337).

6 For more analysis of these issues see Gaffney (1991, 13–29).

7 For more discussion of Mitterrand's and the other candidates' 1988 electoral campaigns see Hayward (1989, 58–80).

8 In his 1981 electoral platform Mitterrand had proposed that immigrants be allowed to vote in local elections, but by 1983 this proposal had been dropped. At the beginning of his first presidency, illegal immigrants were amnestied, regularised and allowed to stay. Subsequently, the pursuit of illegal entrants was resumed and the payment of financial incentives to repatriate (introduced by Giscard) was reintroduced in 1984.

9 For texts on sound see Chion (1982, 1985 and 1988); Rick Altman (ed.) (1980) *Cinema Sounds*, Yale French Studies, no. 60; E.W. Cameron (1980) *Sound and the Cinema*, New York, Redgrave Publishing Company; Stephen Heath and Teresa de Lauretis (eds) (1980) *Technology and Ideology*, New York, Macmillan; and finally, a *Screen* issue (vol. 25, no. 3, 1984) on the soundtrack.

10 For more detail see the *Cahiers du cinéma*'s interview with Jean-Pierre Beauviala (camera designer/inventor and film-maker) in vol. 410, July–August 1988.

11 For an informative overview of the history of French film theory, see *CinémAction* Nos. 47, 1988 and 60, 1990.

12 There were other essayists at the beginning of the twentieth century who were also looking for total structures, such as the Russian formalist Vladimir Propp with his morphological analyses of fairy tales (*Morphologie du conte*), and the Romanian linguist Roman Jakobson with his structural work on poetics and linguistics (*Poetics* and *Essays on General Linguistics*).

13 For a good synopsis of the debate surrounding this theoretical system see Cook (1985, 222–4, 232–6 and on Metz 229–31).

14 The following account is in part a summary of Daniel Serceau's useful article in *CinémAction*, no. 60, 1990, pp. 108–14.

15 Bellour, R. (1975) 'Le Blocage symbolique', *Communications*, no. 23. See Dudley Andrew's (1984, 138–43) critical appreciation of this text.

16 With the apparent final death of Marxism marked by the recent events in the now post-Communist countries, it is interesting to speculate whether feminism will find a new voice in France (as elsewhere).

17 Burch is fiercely dismissive of the New Wave film-makers (especially Chabrol, Malle and Truffaut) in *Film Quarterly*, Winter, 1959. The review journals *Image et Son* and *Jeune cinéma* of the 1960s are highly critical of most of the New Wave production as being out of touch with the political and social arena and issues.

Hennebelle makes these same criticisms in his article in *L'Ecran* (no. 21, January 1974) and perceives part of the problem as the overly bourgeois nature of the industry as a whole.

18 Elsewhere, I have discussed the opinions of one of France's pioneering women film-makers, Alice Guy, on the camera as an enfranchising technology for women: see Hayward (1992).

19 Beurs refers to the Arab/Maghrébin population in France. I have capitalised the other two namings of marginals for reasons of uniformity.

20 For more information on the whole impact of May 1968 on French cinema see Harvey (1980).

21 For full statistics on this point and an informative assessment of the whole of the 1970s French cinema see *Image et son/Ecran*, nos. 355–6, November–December 1980.

22 Exhibition venues included some cinema theatres on the Siritzky circuit. The reader will recall that Siritzky father and son had had their company confiscated during the Occupation because they were Jews. I mention this only because capitalism and liberalism seem to move in strange ways.

23 See *Image et son/Ecran*, no. 355, November 1980, p. 102. Sylvia Kristel starred in this film and was still going strong in *Emmanuelle 4*, made in 1984 by a heavyweight in 1970s porn movies, Francis Leroi, in collaboration with Iris Letans (if this is a female pseudonym or not is unknown to the author). On the question of French porn in the 1970s, see Jeancolas (1979, 243–58).

24 If asked to point to a film about *la chose fascisante/fascinante* that is problematic for its ambiguity, then Michel Mardore's *Le Sauveur* (1971) would be the one I would select. If Lucien Lacombe's misrecognition of the father (which is yet another reading we can impose on that film – he chooses three and directly or indirectly is responsible for their deaths) is a central factor to Malle's film, a more worrying one is at the centre of Mardore's. Fascism is once again represented as an attraction, but this time it has a double signification. An adolescent girl (Nanette) meets an 'angel' – an SS officer black-booted and uniformed (*le sauveur*) – whom she believes to be pure (*le sauveur* mark one) but who turns out to be the minister of death and guilt (*le sauveur* mark two). Already, therefore, Fascism is more 'interesting' as the fetishism with the uniform makes clear (exemplified by the camera work).

25 The three that come to mind are Geneviève Baîlac's *La Famille Hernandez*, 1964, Jacques Davila's convincing *Certaines nouvelles*, 1976 and Alexandre Arcady's rather maudlin *Le Coup de sirocco*, 1978.

26 See *Cahiers du cinéma*, no. 488, October 1991.

27 For an alternative reading on this film see Claire Pajaczkowska (1990).

28 The reader can follow her career in much greater detail in Flitterman-Lewis (1990) and Hayward (1990b and 1992).

29 French citations quoted in *Film français*, no. 1689, September 1977, pp. 20 and 26; the English in *Monthly Film Bulletin*, vol. 54, no. 643, August 1987, p. 231. I could also quote, in this context, Marie-France Pisier's comments about the female point of view in her film *Outremer*: '*dans cette spécificité il y a ma féminité mais cela ne me paraît pas spécifiquement féminin, cela me paraît spécifiquement personnel*' (*Cahiers du cinéma*, no. 434, July/August 1990, p. 30). And see also Françoise Audé (1981) in which she argues against this refusal of a feminist cinema.

30 Quoted in an interview in *Monthly Film Bulletin*, vol. 56, no. 661, February 1989.

31 See Flitterman-Lewis (1990a & b) for an explanation of Dulac's work.

32 In October 1961, for example, 30,000 Algerian workers demonstrated in the streets of Paris against their repressive working conditions and the explicit

racism in them. According to the film-maker who documented the event, Jacques Panijel (*Octobre à Paris*), some 250 were killed or drowned in the *mêlée* with counter-protesters (quoted in Jeancolas: 1979, 160).

33 Jacques Chevalier (1978, 80) coined this felicitous phrase in his very useful analysis of post-1968 films *Image et son*, no. 326, pp. 68–83.

34 Françoise Audé (1975) gives a very insightful analysis on this film and several others belonging to the vein of a politics of refusal.

35 Jeancolas (1979, 219–35), Martin (1984, 82–6) and Prédal (1984, 162–8).

36 See Jeancolas (1979, 229–30), Buache (1990, 20–5), Martin (1984, 82–3) and Comes and Marmin (1985, 55).

37 More evidently in the league of ordinariness and realism in the case of homosexual representation are Claude Miller's *La Meilleure façon de marcher* (1975), Philippe Valois's *Nous étions un seul homme* (1979) and the Serreau film *Pourquoi pas!*.

38 Thus predating by some twenty-five years Peter Greenaway's male dish counterpart in *The Cook, The Thief, His Wife and Her Lover* (1989).

39 François Valet (1991) provides a useful overview of the representation of children in European and Hollywood cinemas.

40 Due to lack of space, comments about the special brands of comedy of Pierre Etaix – touted as the new Max Linder of the 1960s – and Jacques Tati must be limited to just one of anecdotal nature. Neither comedian was particularly successful audience-wise during this decade. The reason for their failure at the box-office cannot be put down to the repetitiousness of their *oeuvre*, since the French show a predilection for more of the same on the comedy front. Etaix's films, in their nostalgia for gentlemanly mores (*Le Soupirant*, 1962) and life in the circus (*Yoyo*, 1964), were too close in their look to silent films on similar subjects to appeal and the anarchy of Tati's anti-materialist film, *Playtime* (1964), was too strong for the generally conservative French taste in comedy, besides which his message had already been made in *Mon oncle*. By the mid-1970s, both gave up making films.

41 Sylvie Dallet (1988) has written a very fulsome and intelligent study on the representation of the French Revolution in the cinema from the silent period to 1988. She carefully links the representation to the socio-political climate of the times and analyses the shifting nature of the meaning of nationalism over the past eighty years.

42 The films are *Blanche et Marie* (Jacques Renard, 1985) in which Sandrine Bonnaire is a Resistance fighter, *De guerre lasse* (Robert Enrico, 1987) in which the star Nathalie Baye is caught between love and political action, *Mon ami le traître* (José Giovanni, 1989) and *Stella* (Laurent Heynemann, 1981) in which the leading female protagonist is in love with a collaborator, and finally *Une affaire de femmes* (Chabrol, 1988) starring Isabelle Huppert as the courageous and well-intentioned abortionist who is sent to the guillotine for her pains.

43 Bill Marshall of Southampton University gave an interesting paper on 'Hegemony and the *film policier* in France in the 1980s' in which he examined the genre in relation to national identity. The venue was the European Popular Cinema conference at Warwick University in 1989.

44 As Brisset (1990, 131) points out, the titles are revealing in and of themselves: *Faut s'les faire ces légionnaires* (Nauroy, 1980), *Les Bidasses aux grandes manoeuvres* (Delpard, 1981), *Les Planqués du régiment* (Caputo, 1983); to Pécas' *quattuor* from 1980 to 1986 must be added Michel Vocoret's *Qu'est-ce qui fait craquer les filles* (1982) and Claude Zidi's number-one hit of 1980 *Les Sous-doués*.

45 In this latter respect, the introduction of telephoto montage (originally a televisual effect) into cinema is largely responsible for the death of the *mise-en-*

scène and long take, two hallmarks of French cinema. This camera lens can zoom backwards and forwards at tremendous speed travelling huge distances in minute parts of a second. The effect is to fragment space completely and render time and motion meaningless.

BIBLIOGRAPHY

Amiel, M. (1979) 'Un glissement vers le cinéma sociologique', *Cinéma 79*, no. 256.

Andrew, D. (1984) *Concepts in Film Theory*, Oxford, Oxford University Press.

Audé, F. (1975) 'Du nouveau dans le cinéma français', *Jeune cinéma*, no. 86.

—— (1977) 'Images de la femme dans le cinéma français de 1958 à 1976' in Barrot, O., Jeancolas, J.-P. and Lefèvre, G. (eds) *Cinéma: Service public*, Créteil 68–76, Paris, François Maspero.

—— (1981) *Ciné-modèles Cinéma d'elles: situation des femmes dans le cinéma français 1956–1979*, Lausanne, L'Age d'Homme.

Aumont, J. (1990) 'The fall of the gods: Jean-Luc Godard's *Le Mépris*', in Hayward, S. and Vincendeau, G. (eds) *French Film: Texts and Contexts*, London, Routledge.

Bonnell, R. (1989) *La vingt-cinquième image, une économie de l'audiovisuel*, Paris, Gallimard.

Brisset, S. (1990) *Le Cinéma des années 80: De 'Diva' au 'Grand bleu'*, Paris, M.A. Editions.

Buache, F. (1990) *Le Cinéma français des années 70*, Renens, 5 Continents, Hatier.

Burch, N. (1959) 'Qu'est-ce que la Nouvelle Vague?' *Film Quarterly*, Winter.

Chion, M. (1982) *La Voix au cinéma*, Paris, Cahiers du Cinéma, Editions de l'Etoile.

—— (1985) *Le Son au cinéma*, Paris, Cahiers du Cinéma, Editions de l'Etoile.

—— (1988) *La Toile trouée (la parole au cinéma)*, Paris, Cahiers du Cinéma, Editions de l'Etoile.

Cole, A. (1990) 'The evolution of the party system' in Cole, A. (ed.) *French Political Parties in Transition*, Aldershot, Dartmouth.

Comes, P. and Marmin, M. (1985) *Le Cinéma français 1960–1985*, Paris, Editions Atlas.

Cook, P. (1985) *The Cinema Book*, London, British Film Institute.

Dallet, S. (1988) *La Révolution française et le cinéma*, Paris, Lherminier, Editions des Quatre Vents.

Flitterman-Lewis, S. (1990a) ' "Poetry of the unconscious"; circuits of desire in two films by Germaine Dulac – *La Souriante Mme Beudet* (1923) and *La Coquille et le clergyman* (1927)', in Hayward, S. and Vincendeau, G. (eds) *French Film: Texts and Contexts*, London, Routledge.

—— (1990b) *To Desire Differently: Feminism and the French Cinema*, Urbana and Chicago, University of Illinois Press.

Gaffney, J. (1990) 'The emergence of a presidential party: the Socialist Party', in Cole, A. (ed.) *French Political Parties in Transition*, Aldershot, Dartmouth.

—— (1991) 'French political culture and Republicanism', in Gaffney, G. and Kolinsky, E. (eds) *Political Culture in France and Germany*, London, Routledge.

Gidal, P. (1989) *Materialist Film*, London, Routledge.

Hanley, D.L., Kerr, A.P. and Waites, N.H. (1988) *Contemporary France: Politics and Society since 1945*, London, Routledge.

Harvey, S. (1980) *May '68 and Film Culture*, London, British Film Institute.

Hayward, S. (1988) 'C'est en filmant qu'on devient filmeron: Agnès Varda, Cinéaste', *ASMCF Review*, no. 33.

—— (1989) 'Television and the French presidential elections 1988', in Gaffney, J.

(ed.) *The French Presidential Elections of 1988: Ideology and Leadership in Contemporary France*, Aldershot, Gower.

—— (1990a) 'French politicians and political communication', in Cole, A. (ed.) *French Political Parties in Transition*, Aldershot, Dartmouth.

—— (1990b) 'Beyond the gaze and into *femme-filmécriture*: Agnès Varda's *Sans toit ni loi*' in Hayward, S. and Vincendeau, G. (eds) *French film: Texts and Contexts*, London, Routledge.

—— (1992) 'A history of French cinema: 1895–1991 – pioneering film-makers (Guy, Dulac, Varda) and their heritage', *Paragraph*, vol. 15, no. 1.

Hebdige, D. (1979) *Subculture: The Meaning of Style*, London, Methuen.

Insdorf, A. (1978) *François Truffaut*, Boston, Twayne G.K. Hall.

Jameson, F. (1983) 'Postmodernism and consumer society, in Foster, H. (ed.) *Postmodern Culture*, London, Pluto Press.

Jeancolas, J.-P. (1974) 'Le Cinéma des Français', *Jeune cinéma*, no. 78.

—— (1975) 'Fonction du témoignage: les années 1939–1945 dans le cinéma de l'après-guerre', *Positif*, no. 170.

—— (1977) *Cinéma 77*, no. 227.

—— (1979) *Le Cinéma des Français: La Ve République 1958–78*, Paris, Stock.

Johnston, C. (1976) 'Women's cinema as counter-cinema', in Nicholls, Bill (ed.) *Movies and Methods*, Berkeley, University of California Press.

King, N. (1990) 'Eye for irony: Eric Rohmer's *Ma nuit chez Maud*', in Hayward, S. and Vincendeau, G. (eds) *French film: Texts and Contexts*, London, Routledge.

Larkin, M. (1988) *France since the Popular Front: Government and People 1936–1986*, Oxford, Clarendon Press.

McMillan, J.F. (1985) *Dreyfus to de Gaulle: Politics and Society in France 1898–1969*, London, Edward Arnold.

Martin, M. (1980) 'Mais qu'est-ce qu'elles veulent?' *Image et Son*, no. 356.

—— (1984) *Le Cinéma français depuis la guerre*, Paris, Edilig.

Mulvey, L. (1981) 'Visual pleasure and narrative cinema', in Bennett, T., Boyd-Bowman, S., Mencir, C. and Woollacott, J. (eds) *Popular Television and Film*, London, British Film Institute and The Open University.

Neale, S. (1985) *Cinema and Technology: Image, Sound and Colour*, London, Macmillan/BFI.

Nicholls, D. (1982) 'From nostalgia to paranoia', *Sight and Sound*, vol. 51, no. 2.

Pajaczkowska, C. (1990) 'Liberté, Egalité, Paternité!' Jean-Luc Godard and Anne-Marie Miéville's *Sauve qui peut (la vie)*', in Hayward, S. and Vincendeau, G. (eds) *French film: Texts and Contexts*, London, Routledge.

Prédal, R. (1984) *Le Cinéma français contemporain*, Paris, Editions du Cerf.

Rigby, B. (1991) *Popular Culture in Modern France*, London, Routledge.

Sadoul, G. (1958) 'Notes on a new generation' *Sight and Sound*, Summer–Autumn.

Sallé, A. (1988) *Les Acteurs français*, Paris, Bordas.

Shields, J. (1991) 'The politics of disaffection: France in the 1980s' in Gaffney, G. and Kolinsky, E. (eds) *Political Culture in France and Germany*, London, Routledge.

Siclier, J. (1961) 'New Wave French cinema', *Sight and Sound*, Summer.

Vallet, F. (1991) *L'Image de l'enfant au cinéma*, Paris, Editions du Cerf.

Varda, A. (1983) Interview in *Cinema Papers*, no. 42.

Vincendeau, G. (1988) 'Vu de Londres: Mais où est donc passée la théorie féministe en France?', *CinémAction*, no. 47.

—— (1991) '1973–91. Lectures féministes', *CinémAction*, no. 60.

Weber, E. (1959) 'An escapist realism', *Film Quarterly*, Winter.

Wollen, P. (1976) 'The two avant-gardes', *Edinburgh '76 Magazine*, Edinburgh Film Festival.

Conclusion

It is difficult to see how a conclusion can usefully function as a coda to this long analysis except by going back to the introductory comments and seeing how, in relation to them, France's cinema has acted as one of the nation's mediators. In the Introduction, the point was made that cinema is a cultural artefact that articulates the nation's myths. Cinema, in this respect, is part of the political culture that enunciates the concept of nation-ness in two contiguous ways. First, as the nation's narrator (one amongst many, to be sure), cinema participates in the process of nation-construction (it helps put it there). Second, as such a discourse it colludes with ideology whose intentionality is to invest a nation with meaning (it helps to keep it there). The reception theory of addressor/addressee within ideology (i.e., that ideology imposes an interpretation of the nation on the subjects and, conversely, the subjects also represent it to themselves – they look at it and see themselves in it) finds an immediate metaphorical representation in the very nature of cinema. Screen and audience are similarly positioned in this narcissistic process. In this instance, the screen becomes the site of the imaginary (of identification) and, subsequently, that of the symbolic (in this case institutional language, the site of myth construction). But this is not all that cinema does, for this would lead to the inference that this site of reflexivity functioned only to fix the meaning of nation-ness. Patently cinema does not do this, any more than does ideology. Just as ideology is historically fluctuating, so too is cinema. Just as a nation's specificity changes according to political, social and economic pressures and mutations, so too does cinema. Thus, as I said in the Preface, the cinema speaks the national and the national speaks the cinema.

In the Introduction, I also made the point that the concept of nation-ness relied heavily on three concepts: validity (or legitimacy), difference (or distinctiveness) and security (or sense of identity). Whilst cinema may function to serve the two-way reflexivity process implicit in ideology, in this latter regard (the triumvirate), the national cinema has revealed that even though France perceives herself as a nation, none the less she has struggled with the implications of nation-ness. This most patently transpires in two areas of cinematic transparence. The first area is one I would describe as being revelatory of an unease that points to a destabilisation of the triumvirate which, in turn, 'threatens' the concept of nation-ness. In this respect, these are represented by moments when cinema is unable to address the political cultural arena either because of external circumstances, or because of a lack of discourses or an inability to mobilise them 'correctly' to facilitate such an address and thereby confront the issues at hand. With regard to the first aspect, there are two such moments of external repression which occurred when France's national cinema was impeded either from being truly national – as during the Occupation period – and/or speaking the national (or leaving a great deal of the national unspoken), as was the case with the lack of transparence on the political arena during the 1950s and early 1960s. As for the other aspect (lack of, or incorrect mobilisation of, discourses), this is most transparent in the three moments in French cinema when an aura of schizophrenia seemed to prevail either because of a desire for denial, as after the two World Wars, or because of a confrontation with split realities, as in the case of the second half of the 1970s. Both sets of moments are revelatory of a sense of a lack of legitimacy and identity on the one hand, and on the other, of a confusion about difference. All three concepts of nation-ness, therefore, are left dangling in the air revealing a lack of confidence in the meaning, or even reality of the notion of nation.

The second area of cinematic transparence, even if it does not necessarily point to confidence in the permanence of the concept of nation, is one which permits destabilising practices, if not to challenge, then at least to address the issue of nation-ness. With regard to this second area, I am thinking of periods in France's cinema history when there is evidence of 'resistance' to the dominant ideology either in the aesthetic or the political cultural arena. Primarily, aesthetic resistance coincides with moments when issues of cinematic practices are very much foregrounded as was the case for the avant-garde cinema of the 1920s and the counter-cinema of the late 1950s. Political resistance coincides with moments when cinema questions institutions as it did most clearly in the late 1960s and through to the late 1970s (its most sustained period) and as it did at an earlier time, albeit with less consistency, in the 1930s. These resistances still reveal a nation that is ill at ease with itself (as represented by the mood of irrationality in the 1930s cinema and the aura of paranoia and schizophrenia in that of the 1970s), but equally they reveal an awareness of and lucidity about issues in need of address. In this respect, at these moments cinema displays the important concept of renewal which is the key to its healthiness. However, as we have seen, this concept is hardly the dominant mode of France's cinema.

This, then, is a first way in which it is possible to say that France does have a national cinema, or that the term national can be inscribed into an overall concept called France's cinema. Another way is to point to the specificities of this nation's cultural artefact that separate it from those of other nations. These come down to three major areas where difference can be established. The first is in production practices, which in France's case means that difference is specified by the artisanal and auteur cinema as well as the specific peripheral cinemas she produces. The second area of distinction is that of filmic modalities which in turn generates the third and last area, modes of address. Filmic modalities point to the dominant generic modes of a nation's cinema, which do not necessarily remain constant or exclusive to it, but which, none the less do reveal (in part) the nation's taste in films. Comedy and *polars* are the overall favourites, but ranking fairly high too is the intimist (psychological) mode of cinema which is not specific to any one genre but more a code and convention peculiar (in the first instance) to France's cinema. In fact, it is precisely in the codes and conventions that difference is established and it is particularly in the discussions around the two dominant genres that I have tried to make clear France's specificity in this area. The iconography of the image as well as that of the *mise-en-scène* are but two pointers to their distinctiveness, as is the case for all other genres (unless they are slavish imitations of other nation's products, which is sometimes the case). The other area, the modes of address – that is, the types of narratives and the traditions of perform-ance – are closely tied up with the concept of codes and conventions. In France's case this has meant, in the first instance, that a very literary tradition has inflected much of her cinematic practice, but correspondingly that that particular proclivity for literary adaptations has also fostered counter-cinematic practices in the form of improvised narratives. In the second instance, stars who have come on to the screen have tended to come from other areas of specular attraction such as the theatre, vaudeville or music-hall. Although, with the Post-New Wave cinema of the last decade or so (1980s and early 1990s), this tradition is becoming somewhat less of a prevalent practice, it remains, for the moment at least, a specificity of France's cinema (and a strong one in terms of the past).

Finally, change is a last essential ingredient to a measuring of the national of a cinema. Change is of course crucial to all national cinemas because of what it says both about its nation's contemporary history and for what it reveals about its longer-term past. Change occurs predomi-nantly, but not exclusively, in two ways: either it is external to the nation and happens through cross-fertilisation, or it is internal and in response to cultural change that can be as much economic as social or political. Cross-fertilisation works at its best when a two-way process is in effect and least well when the influx on the national cinema is so great that the indigenous cinema gets 'colonised'. As we have seen, France's cinema has known all positions in this respect – sometimes to its advantage, at other times to its cost.

The various chapters dealing with the different ages of France's cinema have also traced the internal changes that have impacted upon France's cinema and, conversely, its own impact on the nation's understanding of political cultural change. In this instance (for illustration's sake) I will mention just one aspect of this process of change that I have focused on, that of class and gender representations. If I have dwelt in particular on the working class, the youth class and women, it is because first, those are the representations which are amongst the most dominant in the cinematic discourses, and second, because those changes are revelatory of the nation's perception and construction of its own meaning. Again the image, although changing, is not necessarily on an evaluative scale. If anything, as we have seen, change is circular. At present, on both counts, France's cinema is in the doldrums section of this circular configuration. But if the greatest cliché of all is to be believed, maybe history will repeat itself and cinema will emerge from its rather impoverished and indistinctive mode of pastiche culture and move into a new age that is anything but postmodern. Who knows – perhaps it is already happening.

Select Bibliography

The following is a *selection* of works in book form on French cinema or relevant to the study of French cinema, published in French and in English. Additional material on aspects of cinema can be found at the end of each chapter. For statistics and general updates on the French film industry there are three French journal or broadsheet publications to consult: *Les Cahiers de la Cinémathèque*, *Cinématographie française* and *Le Film français*.

REFERENCE

Bonnell, R. (1989) *La Vingt-cinquième image, une économie de l'audiovisuel*, Paris, Gallimard.

Chirat, Raymond (1975) *Catalogue des films français de long métrage, films sonores de fiction, 1929–1939*, Brussels, Cinémathèque Royale de Belgique. An illustrated edition of the same catalogue was published in 1981 (same publisher).

—— (1981) *Catalogue des films français de long métrage, films de fiction, 1940–1950*, Luxemburg, Imprimerie Saint-Paul.

Chirat, Raymond and Icart, Roger (1984) *Catalogue des films français de long métrage, films de fiction, 1919–1929*, Toulouse, Cinémathèque de Toulouse.

Chirat, Raymond and Romer, Jean-Claude (1984) *Catalogue des films français de fiction de 1e partie 1929–1939*, Bois d'Arcy, Service des Archives du Film, Centre National de la Cinématographie.

Cowie, Peter (yearly since 1964) *The International Film Guide*, London, Tantivy Press.

Franju, Georges (1982) *De Marey à Renoir: trésors de la Cinémathèque Française 1882–1939*, Paris, Avant-Scène Cinéma.

Icart, Roger (n.d.) *Pour Vous, Ciné-Miroir, Cinémonde, 1929–1940, Index 1, films français de long métrage et de fiction*, Toulouse, Documents de la Cinémathèque de Toulouse.

Image et magie du cinéma français: 100 ans de patrimoine (1980), no specified author, Paris, Conservatoire National des Arts et Métiers.

Katz, Ephraïm (1980) *The International Film Encyclopedia*, London, Macmillan.

Lyon, Christopher (ed.) (1984) *The Macmillan Dictionary of Films and Filmmakers, I: Films, II: Filmmakers*, London, Macmillan.

Mitry, Jean (1980–2) *Filmographie universelle*, 26 vols, Bois d'Arcy, Service des Archives du Film.

Passek, Jean-Loup et al. (1986) *Dictionnaire du cinéma*, Paris, Larousse.

Pinel, Vincent (1985) *Filmographie des longs métrages sonores du cinéma français produits et présentés commercialement sur grand écran entre 1930 et 1984 (à*

l'exception des films classés 'X'), Paris, Cinémathèque Française.
Roud, Richard (ed.) (1980) *Cinema: A Critical Dictionary, The Major Filmmakers*, 2 vols, New York, Viking, London, Secker and Warburg.
Sabria, Jean-Claude and Busca, Jean-Pierre (1985) *L'Index du film français – 1944–1984: 40 ans de cinéma en France, Répertoire des films de A à Z*, Paris, Cinéma de France.
Tulard, Jean (1982) *Dictionnaire du cinéma, 'Les Réalisateurs'*, Paris, Laffont.
— (1984) *Dictionnaire du cinéma, 'Acteurs-Producteurs- Scénaristes-Techniciens'*, Paris, Laffont.
Wakeman, John (1987–8) *World Film Directors*, 2 vols, New York, H.W. Wilson.

FILM HISTORY: GENERAL

(with special emphasis on French film history)
Bardèche, Maurice and Brasillach, Robert (1948) *History of the Film*, trans. and ed. by Iris Barry from French 1st edition (1935), London, Allen and Unwin.
— (1954) *Histoire du cinéma (Nouvelle édition définitive en deux volumes)*, Paris, André Martel.
Beylie, Claude and Carcassone, Philippe (1983) *Le Cinéma*, Paris, Bordas.
Le Cinéma (grande histoire illustrée du 7e art) (1982–4), no specified author, 10 vols, Paris, Atlas.
Deslandes, Jacques and Richard, Jacques (1966) *Histoire comparée du cinéma, I: 1826–1896*, Paris, Casterman.
— (1968) *Histoire comparée du cinéma, II: 1896–1906*, Paris, Casterman.
Ford, Charles (1972) *Femmes cinéastes, ou le triomphe de la volonté*, Paris, Denoël.
Jeanne, René and Ford, Charles (1947–62) *Histoire encyclopédique du cinéma*, 5 vols, Paris, Robert Laffont (I) and SEDE (II–V).
Lamartine, Thérèse (1985) *Elles Cinéastes ad-lib 1895–1981*, Montréal, Editions du Remue-Ménage.
Langlois, Henri (1986) *Trois cents ans de cinéma*, Paris, Cahiers du Cinéma and Cinémathèque Française.
Lejeune, Paule (1987) *Le Cinéma des femmes*, Paris, Atlas.
Leprohon, Pierre (1961–3) *Histoire du cinéma*, 2 vols, Paris, Editions du Cerf.
Mitry, Jean (1967–80) *Histoire du cinéma, art et industrie*, 5 vols, Paris, Editions Universitaires.
Moussinac, Léon (1967) *L'Age ingrat du cinéma*, Paris, Editeurs Français Réunis.
Philippe, Claude-Jean (1984) *Le Roman du cinéma, I: 1928–1938*, Paris, Fayard.
— (1986) *Le Roman du cinéma, II: 1938–1945*, Paris, Fayard.
Rhode, Eric (1976) *A History of the Cinema*, New York, Farrar, Straus and Giroux.
Sadoul, Georges (1946–54) *Histoire générale du cinéma*, 5 vols, Paris, Denoël. Reprinted (1973–5) with a few amendments.

FRENCH CINEMA: HISTORY AND CRITICISM

Some books dealing with other national cinemas or other topics have been included under this heading if of sufficient relevance to French cinema.

GENERAL

Agel, Henri (1958) *Miroirs de l'insolite dans le cinéma français*, Paris, Editions du Cerf.
Andrew, Dudley (1978) *André Bazin*, New York, Oxford University Press.

—— (1984) *Film in the Aura of Art*, Princeton, Princeton University Press.
Armes, Roy (1985) *French Cinema*, London, Secker and Warburg.
Arnoux, Alexandre (1946) *Du muet au parlant: mémoires d'un témoin*, Paris, Nouvelle Edition.
Bandy, Mary Lea (ed.) (1983) *Rediscovering French Film*, New York, Museum of Modern Art (contains substantial bibliography).
Bazin, André (ed.) (1984) *La Politique des auteurs*, Paris, Cahiers du Cinéma, Editions de l'Etoile.
Borga, J.-M. and Martinand, B. (1977) *Affiches du cinéma français*, Paris, Delville.
Boulanger, Pierre (1975) *Le Cinéma colonial*, Paris, Seghers.
Braunberger, Pierre (1987) *Cinémamémoire*, Paris, Centre Georges Pompidou, Centre National de la Cinématographie.
Brieu, Christian, Ikor, Laurent and Viguier, Jean-Michel (1985) *Joinville, le cinéma: le temps des studios*, Paris, Ramsay.
Brunius, Jacques-Bernard (1954) *En marge du cinéma français*, Paris, Arcanes.
Buss, Robin (1988) *The French Through Their Films*, London, Batsford.
Cadars, Pierre (1982) *Les Séducteurs du cinéma français (1928–1958)*, Paris, Henri Veyrier.
Chantal, Suzanne (1977) *Le Ciné-monde*, Paris, Grasset.
Chevallier, Jacques (ed.) (1963) *Regards neufs sur le cinéma*, Paris, Editions du Seuil.
Chirat, Raymond and Barrot, Olivier (1983) *Les Excentriques du cinéma français (1929–1958)*, Paris, Henri Veyrier.
—— (1986) *Inoubliables! Visages du cinéma français: 1930–1950*, Paris, Calmann-Lévy.
Comes, Philippe de and Marmin, Michel (1984) *Le Cinéma français: 1930–1960*, Paris, Editions Atlas.
Cottom, J.V. (1983) *Ce monde fou-fou du cinéma français*, Bruxelles, J.M. Collet.
Courtade, Francis (1978) *Les Malédictions du cinéma français*, Paris, Alain Moreau.
Daniel, Joseph (1972) *Guerre et cinéma – Grandes illusions et petits soldats*, Paris, Armand Colin.
Daquin, Louis (1960) *Le Cinéma notre métier*, Paris, Editeurs Français Réunis.
Des Femmes de Musidora (1976) *Paroles . . . elles tournent*, Paris, Des Femmes.
Devarrieux, Claire (1981) *Les Acteurs au travail*, Paris, Hatier.
Diamant-Berger, Henri (1945) *Destin du cinéma français*, Paris, Imprimerie de Montmartre.
Ducout, Françoise (1978) *Les Séductrices du cinéma français, 1936–1956*, Paris, Henri Veyrier.
Frank, Nino (1950) *Petit cinéma sentimental*, Paris, La Nouvelle Edition.
Guérif, François (1981) *Le Cinéma policier français*, Paris, Henri Veyrier.
Guillard, Gilbert (1983) *Le Cinéma français de 1930 à 1981*, Munich, Manz Verlag.
Hammond, Paul (ed.) (1978) *The Shadow and its Shadow: Surrealist Writings on Cinema*, London, British Film Institute.
Harcourt, Peter (1974) *Six European Directors, Essays on the Meaning of Film Style*, Harmondsworth, Middlesex, Penguin Books.
Hillairet, Prosper et al. (1985) *Paris vu par le cinéma d'avant-garde*, Paris, Centre National Georges Pompidou.
Jeanne, René and Ford, Charles (1961) *Le Cinéma et la presse 1895–1960*, Paris, Armand Colin.
—— (1969) *Paris vu par le cinéma*, Paris, Hachette.
Kyrou, Ado (1963) *Le Surréalisme au cinéma*, Paris, Terrain Vague.
Lacassin, Francis (1972) *Pour une contre-histoire du cinéma*, Paris, UGE (10/18).

Lapierre, Marcel (ed.) (1946) *Anthologie du cinéma*, Paris, La Nouvelle Edition.
— (1948) *Les Cent visages du cinéma*, Paris, Grasset.
Lebrun, Dominique (1987) *Paris-Hollywood, les Français dans le cinéma américain*, Paris, Hazan.
Leprohon, Pierre (1954) *50 ans de cinéma français (1895–1945)*, Paris, Editions du Cerf.
Martin, Marcel (1971) *France*, London, Zwemmer, New York, Barnes.
Mazeau, Jacques and Thouart Didier (1983) *Acteurs et chanteurs*, Paris, PAC.
Michalczyk, John (1980) *The French Literary Filmmakers*, Philadelphia, The Art Alliance Press, London, Associated University Presses.
Prédal, René (1972) *La Société française (1914–1945) à travers le cinéma*, Paris, Armand Colin.
— (1980) *80 ans de cinéma: Nice et le 7e art*, Nice, Serre.
Reader, Keith (1981) *Cultures on Celluloid*, London, Quartet.
Richebé, Roger (1977) *Au-delà de l'écran*, Monte-Carlo, Pastorelly.
Roud, Richard (1983) *A Passion for Films, Henri Langlois and the Cinémathèque Française*, London, Secker and Warburg.
Roux, Jean and Thévenet, René (1979) *Industrie et commerce du film en France*, Paris, Editions Scientifiques.
Sadoul, Georges (1953) *French Film*, London, Falcon Press.
— (1979) *Chroniques du cinéma français: 1 1939–1967*, Paris, UGE (10/18).
— (1981) *Le Cinéma français: 1890–1962*, Paris, Flammarion.
Siclier, Jacques (1957) *La Femme dans le cinéma français*, Paris, Editions du Cerf.
Thiher, Allen (1979) *The Cinematic Muse: Critical Studies in the History of French Cinema*, Columbia and London, University of Missouri Press.
Truffaut, François (1975) *Les Films de ma vie*, Paris, Flammarion.
— (1978) *The Films in My Life*, trans. Leonard Mayhew, New York, Simon and Schuster.
Védrès, Nicole (1945) *Images du cinéma français*, Paris, Editions du Chêne.
Virmaux, Alain and Odette (eds) (1975) *Colette: au cinéma*, Paris, Flammarion.
— (1976) *Les Surréalistes et le cinéma*, Paris, Seghers.
— (eds) (1981) *Colette at the Movies*, trans. Sarah W.R. Smith, New York, Ungar.
Weil-Lorac, Roger (1977) *50 ans de cinéma actif*, Paris, Dujarric.
Witta-Montrobert, Jeanne (1980) *La Lanterne magique: mémoires d'une script*, Paris, Calmann-Lévy.

SILENT CINEMA

Abel, Richard (1984) *French Cinema: The First Wave, 1915–1929*, Princeton, Princeton University Press.
Bordwell, David (1980) *French Impressionist Cinema: Film Culture, Film Theory, and Film Style*, New York, Arno.
Coissac, Georges-Michel (1925) *Histoire du cinématographe: de ses origines jusqu'à nos jours*, Paris, Editions du 'Cinéopse'.
Fell, John (1983) *Film Before Griffith*, Berkeley and Los Angeles, University of California Press.
Fescourt, Henri (1959) *La Foi et les montagnes*, Paris, Paul Montel.
Flitterman-Lewis, Sandy (1990) *To Desire Differently: Feminism and the French Cinema*, Urbana and Chicago, University of Chicago Press.
Hugues, Philippe de and Marmin, Michel (1986) *Le Cinéma français: Le Muet*, Paris, Atlas.
Leprohon, Pierre (1982) *Histoire du cinéma muet 1895–1930*, Plan-de-la-Tour,

Editions d'Aujourd'hui (reprint of 1961 edition, Editions du Cerf).
Monaco, Paul (1976) *Cinema and Society: France and Germany During the Twenties*, New York, Elsevier.

THE 1930s

Barrot, Olivier and Jeancolas, Jean-Pierre (1973) *Les Français et leur cinéma, 1930–1939*, Créteil, Maison de la Culture, Losfeld.
Bessy, Maurice (1987) *Histoire du cinéma français: encyclopédie des films 1935–1939*, Paris, Pygmalion.
Beylie, Claude (ed.) (1983) *Cinémagazine 1930*, Paris, Avant-Scène (reprint of original articles).
Chirat, Raymond (1983) *Le Cinéma français des années 30*, Renens, 5 Continents, Hatier.
—— (1987) *Atmosphères: sourires, soupirs et délires du cinéma français des années 30*, Paris, Hatier.
Garçon, François (1984) *De Blum à Pétain: cinéma et société française (1936–44)*, Paris, Editions du Cerf.
Grelier, Robert et al. (eds) (1986) *Mémoires d'en France 1936–1939*, Paris, Aimo.
Guillaume-Grimaud, Geneviève (1986), *Le Cinéma du Front Populaire*, Paris, Lherminier.
Jeancolas, Jean-Pierre (1977) 'Cinéma d'un monde en crise', *La Documentation française*, special dossier.
—— (1983) *15 ans d'années trente, le cinéma des Français, 1929–44*, Paris, Stock.
Lagny, Michèle, Ropars, Marie-Claire and Sorlin, Pierre (1986) *Générique des années trente*, Saint-Denis, Presses Universitaires de Vincennes.
Léglise, Paul (1970) *Histoire de la politique du cinéma français, Tome I: Le Cinéma et la IIIe République*, Paris, Lherminier.
Martin, John W. (1983) *The Golden Age of French Cinema, 1929–39*, Boston, G.K. Hall.
Peyrusse, Claudette (1986) *Le Cinéma méridional 1929–1944*, Toulouse, Eché.
Renaitour, Jean-Michel (1937) *Où va le cinéma français?*, Paris, Baudiniaire.
Strebel, Elizabeth Grottle (1980) *French Social Cinema of the Nineteen-Thirties: A Cinematic Expression of Popular Front Consciousness*, New York, Arno.
Vincendeau, Ginette (1985) 'French Cinema in the 1930s: Social Texts and Contexts of a Popular Entertainment Medium', unpublished Ph.D. thesis, University of East Anglia.
Vincendeau, Ginette and Reader, Keith (1986) *La Vie est à nous, French Cinema of the Popular Front, 1935–1938*, London, British Film Institute.

THE OCCUPATION

Bazin, André (1975) *Le Cinéma de l'Occupation et de la Résistance*, Paris, UGE (10/18).
—— (1981) *French Cinema of the Occupation and Resistance*, trans. Stanley Hochman, New York, Ungar.
Bertin-Maghit, Jean-Pierre (1980) *Le Cinéma français sous Vichy, les films français de 1940 à 1944*, Paris, Ça Cinéma.
—— (1989) *Le Cinéma sous l'Occupation*, Paris, Olivier Orban.
Bessy, Maurice (1986) *Histoire du cinéma français: encyclopédie des films 1940–1950*, Paris, Pygmalion.
Chirat, Raymond (1983) *Le Cinéma français des années de guerre*, Renens, 5 Continents, Hatier.

Ehrlich, Evelyn (1985) *Cinema of Paradox: French Filmmaking under the German Occupation*, New York, Columbia University Press.

Garçon, François (1984) *De Blum à Pétain: cinéma et société française (1936–1944)*, Paris, Editions du Cerf.

Halimi, André (1976) *Chantons sous l'Occupation*, Paris, Olivier Orban.

Jeancolas, Jean-Pierre (1976) 'Cinéma d'un monde en guerre', *La Documentation française*, special dossier.

—— (1983) *15 ans d'années trente, le cinéma des Français, 1929–1944*, Paris, Stock.

Kaplan, Alice Yeager (1986) *Reproductions of Banality (Fascism, Literature, and French Intellectual Life)*, Minneapolis, University of Minnesota Press (contains a long interview with Maurice Bardèche).

Léglise, Paul (1977) *Histoire de la politique du cinéma français, Tome II: Le Cinéma entre deux Républiques (1940–1946)*, Paris, Lherminier.

Peyrusse, Claudette (1986) *Le Cinéma méridional 1929–1944*, Toulouse, Eché.

Rebatet, Lucien (F. Vinneuil) (1941) *Les Tribus du cinéma et du théâtre*, Paris, Nouvelles Editions Françaises.

Régent, Roger (1975) *Cinéma de France, de 'La Fille du puisatier' aux 'Enfants du paradis'*, Paris, Editions d'Aujourd'hui (reprint of 1948 edition).

Siclier, Jacques (1981), *La France de Pétain et son cinéma*, Paris, Veyrier.

FRENCH CINEMA SINCE WORLD WAR II

Agel, Henri et al. (1953) *Sept ans de cinéma français (1945–51)*, Paris, Editions du Cerf.

Armes, Roy (1976) *The Ambiguous Image: Narrative Style in Modern European Cinema*, London, British Film Institute.

Audé, Françoise (1981) *Ciné-modèles, Cinéma d'elles, situations de femmes dans le cinéma français 1956–1979*, Lausanne, L'Age d'Homme.

Barboni, Laurette (1986) *Cinéma d'aujourd'hui: images de cinéma, images de société*, Sèvres, Centre International d'Etudes Pédagogiques de Sèvres.

Barrot, Olivier (1979) *L'Ecran français 1943–1953, histoire d'un journal et d'une époque*, Paris, Les Editeurs Français Réunis.

Bazin, André (1983) *Le Cinéma français de la Libération à la Nouvelle Vague (1945–1958)*, Paris, Cahiers du Cinéma, Editions de l'Etoile.

Bessy, Maurice (1986) *Histoire du cinéma français: encyclopédie des films 1940–1950*, Paris, Pygmalion.

Bonnel, René (1978) *Le Cinéma exploité*, Paris, Editions du Seuil.

Borde, Raymond, Buache, Freddy and Curtelin, Jean (1962) *Nouvelle Vague*, Premier Plan, Lyon, Serdoc.

Bredin, Jean-Denis (1982) *The Bredin Report: On the Future of the French Cinema*, London, British Film Institute.

Buache, Freddy (1987) *Le Cinéma français des années 60*, Paris, Hatier.

Charensol, Georges (1946) *Renaissance du cinéma français*, Paris, Editions du Sagittaire.

Chirat, Raymond (1985) *La IVe République et ses films*, Paris, Hatier.

Clouzot, Claire (1972) *Le Cinéma français depuis la Nouvelle Vague*, Paris, Fernand Nathan.

Collet, Jean (1972) *Le Cinéma en question* (Rozier, Chabrol, Rivette, Truffaut, Demy, Rhomer), Paris, Editions du Cerf.

Degand, Claude (1972) *Le Cinéma, cette industrie*, Paris, Editions Techniques et Economiques.

Douin, Jean-Luc (ed.) (1983) *La Nouvelle Vague 25 ans après*, Paris, Editions du Cerf.

Durgnat, Raymond (1963) *Nouvelle Vague, The First Decade*, Loughton, Essex, Motion Publications.

Ford, Charles (1977) *Histoire du cinéma français contemporain 1945–1977*, Paris, France-Empire.

Goldmann, Annie (1971) *Cinéma et société moderne, le cinéma de 1958 à 1968*, Paris, Anthropos.

Graham, Peter (ed.) (1968) *The New Wave*, London, Secker and Warburg.

Harvey, Sylvia (1978) *May '68 and Film Culture*, London, British Film Institute.

Hennebelle, Guy (1975) *Quinze ans de cinéma mondial, 1960–1975*, Paris, Editions du Cerf.

Hillier, Jim (ed.) (1985) *Cahiers du cinéma 1: the 1950s, Neo-Realism, Hollywood, The New Wave*, London, Routledge and Kegan Paul, British Film Institute (trans. of selection of original *Cahiers du cinéma* articles).

—— (1986) *Cahiers du cinéma 2: 1960–1968*, London, Routledge and Kegan Paul, British Film Institute.

Horton, Andrew S. and Magretta, Joan (eds) (1981) *Modern European Filmmakers and the Art of Adaptation*, New York, Ungar.

Jacob, Gilles (1964) *Le Cinéma moderne*, Lyon, Serdoc.

Jeancolas, Jean-Pierre (1974) *Le Cinéma des Français, 1969–1974, les années Pompidou*, Créteil, Maison de la Culture.

—— (1979) *Le Cinéma des Français – la Ve République, 1958–78*, Paris, Stock.

Leenhardt, Roger (1986) *Chroniques de cinéma*, Paris, Cahiers du Cinéma, Editions de l'Etoile.

Maarek, Philippe J. de (1979) *De mai 68 aux films X: cinéma, politique et société*, Paris, Dujarric.

Martin, Marcel (1984) *Le Cinéma français depuis la guerre*, Paris, Edilig.

Monaco, James (1976) *The New Wave*, New York, Oxford University Press.

Noguez, Dominique (1982) *Trente ans de cinéma expérimental en France (1950–1980)*, ARCEF.

Pivasset, Jean (1971) *Essai sur la signification politique du cinéma*, Paris, Cujas.

Prédal, René (1984) *Le Cinéma français contemporain*, Paris, Editions du Cerf.

Siclier, Jacques (1961) *Nouvelle vague?*, Paris, Editions du Cerf.

—— (1990) *Le Cinéma français 1: de La Bataille du rail à La Chinoise*, Paris, Ramsey.

Société des Réalisateurs de films (1978) *La Règle du jeu: situation du cinéma français: 1968–1978*, Paris, Albatros.

THEORETICAL WORKS

This is a selection of French theoretical works as well as general theoretical works which I consider relevant to French film theory and history, and/or the analysis of French films.

Abel, Richard (1988a) *French Film Theory and Criticism: A History/Anthology, Vol. I, 1907–1929*, New Jersey, Princeton University Press.

—— (1988b) *French Film Theory and Criticism: A History/Anthology, Vol. II, 1929–1939*, New Jersey, Princeton University Press.

Allen, Robert C. and Gomery, Douglas (1985) *Film History, Theory and Practice*, New York, Knopf.

Aumont, Jacques and Leutrat, Jean-Louis (1980) *La Théorie du film*, Paris, Albatros.

Aumont, Jacques et al. (1983) *L'Esthétique du film*, Paris, Fernand Nathan.

Bailbé, Claude, Marie, Michel and Ropars, Marie-Claire (1975) *Muriel*, Paris, Galilée.

Bazin, André (1958–62) *Qu'est-ce que le cinéma?*, 4 vols, Paris, Editions du Cerf.
—— (1967) *What is Cinema?*, 2 vols, trans. Hugh Gray, Berkeley, University of California Press (NB: some French articles are omitted in the English translation).
Bordwell, David (1985) *Narration in the Fiction Film*, London, Methuen.
Bordwell, David and Thompson, Kristin (1986) *Film Art: An Introduction*, 2nd edition, New York, Knopf.
Burch, Noël (1969) *Praxis du cinéma*, Paris, Gallimard.
—— (1973) *Theory of Film Practice*, New York, Praeger.
Chion, Michel (1982) *La Voix au cinéma*, Paris, Cahiers du Cinéma, Editions de l'Etoile.
—— (1985) *Le Son au cinéma*, Paris, Cahiers du Cinéma, Editions de l'Etoile.
—— (1988) *La Toile trouée (la parole au cinéma)*, Paris, Cahiers du Cinéma, Editions de l'Etoile.
Collet, Jean et al. (1977) *Lectures du film*, Paris, Albatros.
Cook, Pam (ed.) (1985) *The Cinema Book*, London, British Film Institute.
Durand, Jacques (1958) *Le Cinéma et son public*, Paris, Sirey.
Dyer, Richard (1979) *Stars*, London, British Film Institute.
Ferro, Marc (1976) *Analyse de films, analyse de sociétés*, Paris, Hachette.
—— (1977) *Cinéma et histoire*, Paris, Denoël-Gonthier.
—— (1984) *Film et histoire*, Paris, Editions de l'Ecole des Hautes Etudes en Sciences Sociales.
Haskell, Molly (1974) *From Reverence to Rape, The Treatment of Women in the Movies*, New York, Rinehart and Winston.
Kaplan, E. Ann (1983) *Women and Film: Both Sides of the Camera*, London, Methuen.
Kay, Karin and Peary, Gerald (1977) *Women and the Cinema: A Critical Anthology*, New York, Dutton.
Kuhn, Annette (1982) *Women's Pictures, Feminism and Cinema*, London, Routledge and Kegan Paul.
Mast, Gerald and Cohen, Marshall (eds) (1979) *Film Theory and Criticism*, New York, Oxford University Press.
Metz, Christian (1968–72) *Essais sur la signification au cinéma*, 2 vols, Paris, Klincksieck.
—— (1971) *Langage et cinéma*, Paris, Larousse.
—— (1974a) *Film Language: A Semiotics of the Cinema*, trans. of *Essais sur la signification au cinéma* by Michael Taylor, New York, Oxford University Press.
—— (1974b) *Language and the Cinema*, trans. of *Langage et cinéma* by Donna Jean Umiker-Sebeck, The Hague, Mouton.
—— (1977) *Le Signifiant imaginaire, psychanalyse et cinéma*, Paris, UGE (10/18).
—— (1982) *The Imaginary Signifier: Psychoanalysis and the Cinema*, trans. Celia Britton, Anhwyl Williams, Ben Brewster and Alfred Guzzetti, Bloomington, Indiana University Press.
Mitry, Jean (1966–8) *Esthétique et psychologie du cinéma, I: Les Structures, II: Les Formes*, Paris, Editions Universitaires.
—— (1987) *La Sémiologie en question*, Paris, Editions du Cerf.
Morin, Edgar (1956) *Le Cinéma ou l'homme imaginaire, essai d'anthropologie sociologique*, Paris, Les Editions de Minuit.
—— (1957) *Les Stars*, Paris, Editions du Seuil.
—— (1960) *The Stars*, trans. R. Howard, New York, Grove Press.
Nichols, Bill (ed.) (1976) *Movies and Methods*, Berkeley, University of California Press.
—— (ed.) (1985) *Movies and Methods*, vol. II, Berkeley, University of California Press.

Ropars-Wuilleumier, Marie-Claire (1970a) *L'Ecran de la mémoire, essai de lecture cinématographique*, Paris, Editions du Seuil.
—— (1970b) *De la littérature au cinéma: genèse d'une écriture*, Paris, Armand Colin.
—— (1981) *Le Texte divisé*, Paris, PUF.
Sarris, Andrew (1973) *The Primal Screen: Essays on Film and Related Subjects*, New York, Simon and Schuster.
Screen Reader 1 (1977) Cinema/Ideology/Politics.
Screen Reader 2 (1981) Cinema and Semiotics.
Short, K.R.M. (ed.) (1981) *Feature Film as History*, Beckenham, Croom Helm.
Simon, Jean-Pierre (1979) *Le Filmique et le comique*, Paris, Albatros.
Sorlin, Pierre (1977) *Sociologie du cinéma, ouverture pour l'histoire de demain*, Paris, Aubier.
—— (1980) *The Film in History (Restaging the Past)*, Oxford, Blackwell.
Turner, Graeme (1986) *National Fictions*, Sydney, Allen Unwin.
Wollen, Peter (1969) *Signs and Meaning in the Cinema*, London, Secker and Warburg.
Zimmer, Christian (1984) *Le Retour de la fiction*, Paris, Editions du Cerf.
—— (1974) *Cinéma et politique*, Paris, Seghers.

Index

V Directors cited in the text